Procedural Politics

Under what conditions, in what ways, and with what effects do actors engage in politics with respect to, rather than merely within, political institutions? Using multiple methods and original data, *Procedural Politics* develops a theory of everyday politics with respect to rules – procedural politics – and applies it to European Union integration and politics. Assuming that actors are influence maximizers, it argues and demonstrates that the jurisdictional ambiguity of issues provides opportunities for procedural politics and that influence differences among institutional alternatives provide the incentives. It also argues and demonstrates that procedural politics occurs by predictable means (most notably, involving procedural coalition formation and strategic issue definition) and exerts predictable effects on policymaking efficiency and outcomes and long-run institutional change. Beyond illuminating previously underappreciated aspects of EU rule governance, these findings generalize to all rule-governed political systems and form the basis of a fuller account of the role of institutions in political life.

Joseph Jupille received his Ph.D. in Political Science from the University of Washington in 2000. He is Assistant Professor of Political Science at Florida International University and Associate Director of the Miami European Union Center. His published work has appeared in, among other places, *Annual Review of Political Science*, *Comparative Political Studies*, and *International Organization*. He has been EU-US Fulbright Fellow and SSRC International Dissertation Fellow. Having been awarded a Jean Monnet Fellowship, he spent the 2003–2004 academic year in the Transatlantic Programme of the Robert Schuman Centre for Advanced Studies at the European University Institute in Fiesole, Italy.

Cambridge Studies in Comparative Politics

General Editor
Margaret Levi   *University of Washington, Seattle*

Assistant General Editor
Stephen Hanson   *University of Washington, Seattle*

Associate Editors
Robert H. Bates   *Harvard University*
Peter Hall   *Harvard University*
Peter Lange   *Duke University*
Helen Milner   *Columbia University*
Frances Rosenbluth   *Yale University*
Susan Stokes   *University of Chicago*
Sidney Tarrow   *Cornell University*

Other Books in the Series

Lisa Baldez, *Why Women Protest*
Stefano Bartolini, *The Political Mobilization of the European Left, 1860–1980: The Class Cleavage*
Mark Beissinger, *Nationalist Mobilization and the Collapse of the Soviet State*
Nancy Bermeo, ed., *Unemployment in the New Europe*
Carles Boix, *Political Parties, Growth, and Equality: Conservative and Social Democratic Economic Strategies in the World Economy*
Carles Boix, *Democracy and Redistribution*
Catherine Boone, *Merchant Capital and the Roots of State Power in Senegal, 1930–1985*
Catherine Boone, *Political Topographies of the African State: Territorial Authority and Institutional Change*
Michael Bratton and Nicolas van de Walle, *Democratic Experiments in Africa: Regime Transitions in Comparative Perspective*
Valerie Bunce, *Leaving Socialism and Leaving the State: The End of Yugoslavia, the Soviet Union, and Czechoslovakia*
Daniele Caramani, *The Nationalization of Politics: The Formation of National Electorates and Party Systems in Europe*

Continued after the Index

Procedural Politics

ISSUES, INFLUENCE, AND INSTITUTIONAL CHOICE IN THE EUROPEAN UNION

JOSEPH JUPILLE
Florida International University

CAMBRIDGE
UNIVERSITY PRESS

CAMBRIDGE UNIVERSITY PRESS
Cambridge, New York, Melbourne, Madrid, Cape Town,
Singapore, São Paulo, Delhi, Mexico City

Cambridge University Press
The Edinburgh Building, Cambridge CB2 8RU, UK

Published in the United States of America by Cambridge University Press, New York

www.cambridge.org
Information on this title: www.cambridge.org/9781107405233

© Joseph Jupille 2004

This publication is in copyright. Subject to statutory exception
and to the provisions of relevant collective licensing agreements,
no reproduction of any part may take place without the written
permission of Cambridge University Press.

First published 2004
First paperback edition 2011

A catalogue record for this publication is available from the British Library

Library of Congress Cataloguing in Publication Data
Jupille, Joseph Henri.
Procedural politics : issues, influence, and institutional choice in the European
Union / Joseph Jupille.
    p.   cm. – (Cambridge studies in comparative politics)
Includes bibliographical references and index.
ISBN 0-521-83253-5
1. European Union countries – Politics and government.   2. European Union.
I. Title.   II. Series.

JN30.J87   2004
341.242′2 – dc22   2003069585

ISBN 978-0-521-83253-3 Hardback
ISBN 978-1-107-40523-3 Paperback

Cambridge University Press has no responsibility for the persistence or
accuracy of URLs for external or third-party internet websites referred to in
this publication, and does not guarantee that any content on such websites is,
or will remain, accurate or appropriate.

To Lisa. *Je t'aime de tout mon cœur.*

Contents

List of Figures		page x
List of Tables		xii
Preface and Acknowledgments		xiii
List of Acronyms Used in the Text		xvii
1	INTRODUCTION: CHOICE, CONSTRAINT, AND EUROPEAN UNION INSTITUTIONS	1
2	THEORIZING PROCEDURAL POLITICS: ISSUES, INFLUENCE, AND INSTITUTIONAL CHOICE	15
3	THE EUROPEAN UNION AS A PROCEDURAL SYSTEM: RULES, PREFERENCES, AND STRATEGIC INTERACTION	42
4	PATTERNS: DETERMINANTS AND EFFECTS OF EU PROCEDURAL POLITICS	82
5	GREENING THE MARKET? PROCEDURAL POLITICS AND EU ENVIRONMENTAL POLICY	127
6	MAD COWS AND ENGLISHMEN: PROCEDURAL POLITICS AND EU AGRICULTURAL POLICY	171
7	CONCLUSION: PROCEDURAL POLITICS AND RULE GOVERNANCE IN THE EUROPEAN UNION AND BEYOND	221
Bibliography		247
Index		271

Figures

1	Approaches to Institutions	page 3
2	Jurisdictional Ambiguity: Overlap and Gaps	21
3	Fusion	29
4	Fission	30
5	Reframing	30
6	Procedures, Dimensionality, and Legislative Outcomes	36
7	Hypothetical Example of Cardinal Preference Ordering	62
8	Simple Procedures	69
9	Cooperation Procedure	71
10	Codecision Procedure	73
11	Institutional Choice Game Tree	74
12	Jurisdictional Fragmentation, 1987–1997	84
13	The Practice of Voting in the Council, 1966–1987	85
14	Three Models of Temporal Variation	86
15	Legal Basis Disputes, 1979–1998	87
16	Legal Basis Disputes and Procedural Politics, 1987–1997	88
17	Winners and Losers at the ECJ, Through Mid-2003	99
18	Sectoral Variation in Procedural Politics	102
19	Jurisdictional Ambiguity and the Probability of Procedural Political Dispute	110
20	Changing Procedural Provisions of EU Treaties, 1957–2003	115
21	Prior Period Disputes and Institutional Change: SEA to TEU	119
22	Issue Overlap: Environment and the Internal Market, 1980–2002	132
23	Dual Legal Basis in Agricultural Legislation, 1969–1995	177

List of Figures

24	Agriculture and Human Health: Issue Overlap, 1980–2002	178
25	Agricultural Legal Basis Cases at the ECJ	184
26	Mad Cow Disease (BSE), 1989–2002	195
27	BSE/Human Health Connection in the UK, 1985–2002	197
28	BSE Regulatory Outcomes with and Without Procedural Politics	216

Tables

1	Rule Preferences and Procedural Coalitions	page 33
2	Summary of Procedural Political Hypotheses	39
3	Votes in the EU Council of Ministers	47
4	Procedural Preference Rankings	62
5	Perfect Bayesian Equilibria for Institutional Selection Game	80
6	Jurisdictional Fragmentation and Legal/Procedural Disputes	89
7	Aggregate Revealed Rules Preferences Among Disputed Cases	92
8	Procedural Preferences: "Proposals" and "Responses"	94
9	Influence Maximization: Predictive Success	96
10	Relogit Estimates of the Determinants of Procedural Political Disputes	108
11	Procedural Politics and Decision-Making Efficiency	113
12	Logit Estimates: SEA-TEU Procedural Change	118
13	Explaining EP Empowerment: SEA to TEU	120
14	Procedural Evolution of EU Environmental Policy	131
15	Issue Framing and Procedural Preferences in EU Environmental Policy	136
16	Predicted Procedural Coalitions in EU Environmental Policy	138
17	Alternatives and Issues in Agricultural Policy	179
18	Predicted Procedural Coalitions in EU Agricultural Policy	183

Preface and Acknowledgments

Rules fascinate me. How can these things that we ourselves devise do what they are supposed to do, which is precisely to prevent us from doing what we might otherwise do (or enable us to do what we otherwise couldn't)? How, in short, can objects of human choice simultaneously serve as sources of human constraint?

These are the fundamental questions addressed in this book. The answers that I give are far from complete, but I think they provide new mileage in helping us to understand what Robert Grafstein (1992) has called the "dual nature of institutions." Indeed, I think Grafstein's lone dichotomy is too simple by at least two factors, and the answers that I give to the questions above operate along three axes: institutional choice and constraint (endogeneity vs. exogeneity), the use of time in institutional explanation (diachronic vs. synchronic), and multiple levels of rules (lower/micro-level/procedural vs. higher/macro-level/constitutional). Two complexes of these factors tend to dominate institutional analysis. One, characterized later as "institutional change," combines an assumption of institutional endogeneity with a focus on constitutions in a diachronic framework. In short, one main approach to institutions is to look at the ways in which humans change constitutions over time. A second complex, later characterized as "institutional effects," combines an assumption of institutional exogeneity with a focus on procedures in a synchronic framework. That is, it focuses on the independent effects of procedures at a given time.

Both approaches are "right," as far as they go, but each could be improved by importing elements of the other. It costs a lot to change constitutions, for example: might they not be viewed best as exogenous constraints? Lower-order procedures are often not uniquely determined but form part of a plural menu of available procedural alternatives: might they not be treated fruitfully as (endogenous) objects of choice? How do at-a-given-time (synchronic) developments influence what happens over time (diachronically)? I seek to contribute to the development of a fuller institutionalism, one that is true, first, to the definitional requirement that institutions be objects of human choice and the practical requirement that they be independent sources of human constraint; second, to the fact that many (most?) institutional arrangements are highly complex and occupy numerous levels of analysis; and third, to the fact that institutions have a past, a present, and a future.

I bring these threads together with an analysis of procedural politics, which I define as everyday politics with respect to rules. My main focus is on the possibilities for everyday institutional choice at a low (procedural) level of analysis. I will state the argument repeatedly in the pages that follow, and so as not to bore the reader too quickly I'll simply say here that I think actors possess much more sophistication about institutions than they are commonly given credit for. That is, I do not think their institution-choosing strategies are limited to over-time changes in higher-order rules. Everyday politics with respect to rules, I believe, is every bit as important as over-time politics over them and everyday politics within them.

I am also, of course, interested in understanding and explaining European Union (EU) integration and politics, in grappling with the nature of this substantively important, empirically unique, but (I think) theoretically informative political system. But here, too, I have a broader and rather more abstract goal: I am quite convinced that the European Union offers unique research opportunities for comparativists and international relations (IR) scholars alike precisely because it is partly international organization and partly hierarchical polity. Stripped of some of the confounding factors that hold nation-states together – history, culture, language, common political traditions, and the like – the EU allows us to isolate the operation of institutions against a relatively noise-free (in the sense of confounding theoretical variables) environment. Unlike the international system, though, the EU is not quite (some might say not at all) an anarchy. The rules here actually mean something. This combination – consequential rules that are allowed, indeed demand, a leading role in conditioning politics – makes the EU a particularly rich laboratory for studying the operation of institutions. As I have argued elsewhere (Jupille and Caporaso 1999; Jupille, Caporaso, and Checkel 2003), study of the EU must draw from a variety of fields and stands uniquely positioned to contribute insights in kind. So I hope and trust that this study of institutions, as applied to the unique polity that is the

Preface and Acknowledgments

European Union, will prove informative across a variety of fields and areas of interest.

If I have drawn liberally or even recklessly from a variety of sources in producing my own account of procedural politics in the European Union, it is because I was consistently allowed, encouraged, and even pushed to think outside and across received boundaries by many people in positions to influence my path. Words could never express how grateful I am to the members of my dissertation committee: Jim Caporaso (chair), Christine Ingebritsen, Bryan Jones, John Keeler, and Margaret Levi. Because I could never do justice to all that they have given me, I will not attempt to enumerate here their gifts to me. Each made countless contributions, and I would like each to know that his or her support has meant the world to me. I have truly been privileged to work with such distinguished scholars, such exemplary individuals, and such dedicated and generous friends. Many other colleagues and friends have given generously of their encouragement and criticism with respect to various aspects of this project. I would like to thank Roni Amit, Dave Andrews, Cliff Carrubba, Jeffrey Chwieroth, Scott Cooper, Keith Dougherty, Debbi Elms, Orfeo Fioretos, Liesbet Hooghe, Cynthia Horne, Dan Kelemen, Amie Kreppel, Gary Marks, Peter May, Matt Moe, Andrew Moravcsik, Neill Nugent, Mary Alice Pickert, Martin Rhodes, Alec Stone Sweet, Helen Wallace, Mike Ward, and John Wilkerson for support, encouragement, and helpful advice on various elements of the manuscript. Apologies to any I may have forgotten. Simon Hix and Mark Pollack read the entire manuscript and provided terrifically challenging criticisms.

I owe further thanks to all of the organizations and individuals who provided financial or logistical support as I moved this project through predissertation, dissertation, write-up, revisions, and beyond. For financial support at various stages of my research and writing I would like to thank the Council for European Studies (CES), the Association to Unite the Democracies, the EU-US Fulbright program, the Social Science Research Council (SSRC), the Institute for the Study of World Politics (ISWP), the University of Washington Graduate School, the European Union Centers (EUC) in Seattle and Miami, and the Florida International University College of Arts and Sciences and Provost's Office. Additional logistical support was provided by the University of Washington, the Instituts d'Études Européennes at the Université Libre de Bruxelles and the Université Catholique de Louvain-la-Neuve, and Florida International University. The Robert Schuman Centre for Advanced Studies in Florence, Italy, provided an inspiring environment within which to undertake the otherwise dull work of copyediting review.

Countless individuals, working within and outside official capacities in the above organizations, provided crucial assistance at various stages of my work. Margaret Nicholson of the Fulbright office in Brussels; Kent Worcester of the SSRC; UW Documents Librarian David Maack; UW Political Science staff Carole Davison-Mulligan, Ann Buscherfeld, Karin Stromberg, Meera Roy, Mark Roskoski, Sharon Redeker, and Cheryl Mehaffey; FIU Political Science secretary Lany Muñoz; and Francesca Parenti at the Schuman Centre provided cheerful and able assistance. Maria Ilcheva of FIU provided research assistance so proficiently that I had trouble keeping up with her. In addition, numerous EU officials gave generously of their time and insights and tolerated my sometimes overzealous pursuit of elusive data. I would like to thank all of my interviewees in Brussels and Luxembourg. From the European Parliament I received extraordinary assistance, most notably from Emilio de Capitani, Wim Hoogsteder, Paulette Bourseau, and a dearly missed friend, the late Chris Piening. Nicole Huckert of the European Commission Secretariat General generously provided the files that became the dataset analyzed in Chapter 4. In all of the EU institutions, officials whose names I do not know provided small kindnesses and services that I cannot repay but that I will never forget.

Cambridge University Press provided excellent support and guidance for this first-time author. I would particularly like to thank series editor Margaret Levi, political science editor Lew Bateman, production editor Janis Bolster, and copy editor Patterson Lamb for their support, encouragement, patience, generosity of time and spirit, and consummate professionalism in shepherding the manuscript (and its author) through the process. They deserve much credit and none of the blame for what you will read in the following pages.

Finally, most important, I would like to acknowledge the love and support of my family. My parents are models of everything that I would hope to be. My sons, Michael, Alexander, and Jackson, have given me untold laughter, optimism, and a love that I never knew possible. Finally, my wife, Lisa, should share equal credit for whatever is worthwhile in this book. Her love, support, smiles, laughter, willingness to listen, intelligence, humor, and unbelievable strength inspire me every day. I dedicate this book to her.

Acronyms Used in the Text

AVC	Assent procedure
AVCU	Assent procedure with Council unanimity
AVF	Facultative consultation procedure
AVFQ	Facultative consultation procedure with Council qualified majority voting
AVFS	Facultative consultation procedure with Council simple majority voting
AVFU	Facultative consultation procedure with Council unanimity
BSE	Bovine spongiform encephalopathy
CAP	Common Agricultural Policy
CJD	Creuzfeldt-Jakob Disease
CNS	Consultation procedure
CNSQ	Consultation procedure with Council qualified majority voting
CNSU	Consultation procedure with Council unanimity
CODQ	Codecision procedure with Council qualified majority voting
CODU	Codecision procedure with Council unanimity
COREPER	Committee of permanent representatives to the EU
EJC	European Court of Justice
EMU	Economic and Monetary Union
EP	European Parliament
EU	European Union
IGC	Intergovernmental conference
IR	International relations
LI	Liberal intergovernmentalism

List of Acronyms Used in the Text

MEP	Member of the European Parliament
MP	Member of parliament
OLS	Ordinary least squares
QMV	Qualified majority voting
SEA	Single European Act
SYNQ	Cooperation procedure
TEU	Treaty on European Union
vCJD	Variant of Creuzfeldt-Jakob Disease

1

Introduction

CHOICE, CONSTRAINT, AND EUROPEAN UNION INSTITUTIONS

> Procedure hasn't simply become more important than substance – it has, through a strange alchemy, become the substance of our deliberations. Who rules House procedures rules the House.
>
> – Robert H. Michel, R-Ill.[1]

This is a book about "procedural politics," the everyday conduct of politics not within, but with respect to, political institutions. The questions it asks are fundamental to political science, and indeed to "institutional" approaches across the social sciences: why, when, how, and with what effects do actors attempt to influence their institutional environment? Why, when, how, and with what effects, by contrast, do rules constrain them? The book develops and tests answers to these questions in the context of EU politics. The results of this inquiry paint a novel picture of EU politics and policymaking, suggesting most importantly (but somewhat paradoxically) that the EU exhibits a more profound degree of rule governance than is usually recognized. But these results generalize far beyond the EU, not only to other international organizations, but also to domestic political systems and, indeed, to all institutionalized political and social systems.

My general argument can be succinctly summarized. I assume that actors seek to ensure the usage of institutions (rules) that maximize their political influence. They are constrained, however, by the strategic nature of institutional choice – the need to interact with others – and by the availability of institutional alternatives. As a result, I argue that incentives (in the form of potential influence gains) and strategic opportunities (in the form of the availability of institutional alternatives) combine to produce procedural

---

[1] Quoted in Oleszek 2001, 11.

politics, everyday politics with respect to rules. Actors play procedural politics through predictable means (most notably, procedural coalition formation and "gaming" the criteria that govern institutional selection) with predictable effects. These effects include, but are not limited to, the rules themselves, the content of public policy and the efficiency with which it is made, and long-run changes in higher-order rules, including the most fundamental rules of all: constitutions. This procedural political cycle reinforces the political primacy of higher-order rules, paradoxically entrenching rather than undermining rule governance.

Subsequent chapters will develop this argument at length. The bulk of this introduction will locate it within the broader institutional literature and relate it to existing work on European Union institutions. The introduction ends with a plan of action for the rest of the book.

Prevailing Approaches

Douglass North has defined institutions as "the rules of the game in a society, or, the humanly devised constraints that shape human interaction" (North 1990, 3). Among its other advantages, this definition embraces what Robert Grafstein (1992) has dubbed the "dual nature" of institutions. On the one hand, institutions represent objects of human creation or choice. They are, as North puts it, "humanly devised." On the other hand, institutions also represent sources of independent effects – they are "constraints that shape." This book gets to the heart of this tension: when are the rules available to strategic actors (as [endogenous] objects of choice), and when, by contrast, are they unavailable (as [exogenous] sources of constraint or independent effects)?

Existing institutional work in political science and on the European Union provides the elements of an answer but not the answer itself. Institutional work differs along many dimensions. One key dimension involves the theoretical place of institutions as either endogenous (explicable in theoretical terms) or exogenous (external to the theory in question) (Jupille and Caporaso 1999; Shvetsova, 2003). A second key dimension involves the level of analysis, with some analysts privileging higher-order institutions (such as constitutions) and others emphasizing lower-order institutions (such as legislative procedures) (Kiser and Ostrom 1982, 208; Ostrom 1990, 1995). These treatments tend to correlate with the explanatory use of time, with those allowing endogeneity and focusing on higher-order rules more likely to take a diachronic (over-time) approach, and those emphasizing

Introduction

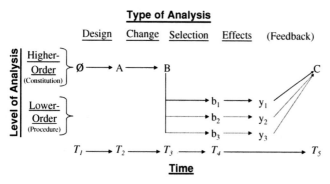

Figure 1 Approaches to Institutions

exogeneity and focusing on lower-level rules more likely to develop synchronic (at-a-given-time) explanations (Knill and Lenschow 2001). Figure 1 identifies four modal types of institutional analysis (design, change, selection, and effects), which offer different mixes of institutional endogeneity and exogeneity, higher-order and lower-order institutions, and diachronic and synchronic explanatory approaches. Decomposing the literature in this way lays bare the raw materials that must be pieced together into a coherent explanation of institutions, including procedural politics, everyday politics *with respect* to rules.

Institutional Design

Theories of institutional design (alternatively, institutional creation) explicitly treat institutions only as dependent variables, that is, as phenomena to be explained with reference to noninstitutional factors such as preferences, power, functional needs, and strategic interactions (Goodin 1996a, 1996b; Koremenos, Lipson, and Snidal 2001). Hence, as shown in Figure 1, they explain over-time movement from an institution-free environment (Ø) to one governed by a new set of higher-order rules (constitution A), at which level design theories tend to operate almost exclusively.[2] One variant views institutions as the by-products of other interactions such as economic exchange (Schotter 1981) or distributional bargaining (Knight 1992). A second, perhaps more common, variant views institutions intentionally, created to serve

---

[2] A possible exception to this might be the crafting of rules in the U.S. Congress, where institutional possibilities are limited only by the preferences, power, and creativity of the relevant institutional creators (the Rules Committee and the substantive committee).

functional or more overtly political goals (Coase 1937/1988; Williamson 1975, 1985; Weingast and Marshall 1988; Horn 1995; Keohane 1984).

The functional design approach has been widely applied in the literature on the EU, the by-product variant less so. Those working in the idiom of "constitutional choice" portray EU member states in an institution-free environment choosing the rules that will best serve their future contracting and political needs (König and Bräuninger 2000; Bräuninger et al. 2001). More influentially, Moravcsik's liberal intergovernmental approach (1991, 1993, 1998) embraces and extends Keohane's (1984) functional theory of international regimes, which explains international institutions as functional responses to international market failures permitting states to capture otherwise unavailable gains from cooperation. Moravcsik's (1998) tripartite explanation of European integration begins with a liberal theory of state preference formation (see Moravcsik 1997), proceeds to model intergovernmental bargaining, and concludes by theorizing institutional choice (design) in the EU.[3] On this last element, he explains institutions as functional responses to the transaction problems that member states face. Institutional design, and in particular the pooling of sovereignty and the delegation of authority to supranational agents, enhances the credibility of commitments by reducing the possibilities for ex post opportunism.

Design approaches are necessary for full institutional analysis. They respond directly to the definitional requirement that institutions be the objects or products of human creation. However, they suffer from problems with respect to each element of the dual nature of institutions. On the "humanly devised" side, they downplay the broader social and historical determinants of institutions (Oberschall and Leifer 1986; Granovetter 1985, 1992; Bromley 1989; Wendt 2001) and the prevalence of collective action problems or multiple efficient equilibria (Krasner 1985, 1991; Garrett 1992; Garrett and Weingast 1993). On the "constraints that shape" side of North's definition, design approaches, which seek to model institutions only as dependent variables, suffer from two problems. First, though design theorists seek fully to endogenize institutions to noninstitutional parameters, they almost invariably end up smuggling rules into the right-hand (independent variable) side of their explanatory equations (Field 1979, 1981, 1984;

---

[3] Of course after the 1950s, the choices that Moravcsik analyzes do not take place against an institutional tabula rasa, and so do not, strictly speaking, represent instances of institutional design. However, Moravcsik largely insulates grand bargaining from the prior operation of EU institutions.

Introduction

Bromley 1989; Scharpf 1999, 165). Second, though they rely quite heavily on anticipated institutional effects to explain institutional design, they often fail explicitly to theorize those effects. To this extent, the connections they draw between design and constraint (effects) resemble assumptions or, at most, inferences, rather than theoretical claims. As Bates puts it, design approaches tend to "confound the analysis of the role of institutions [i.e., anticipated institutional effects] with a theory of their causes" (Bates 1988, 387).

Institutional Change

Theories of institutional change have tended to take seriously the criticisms of the design approach. In particular, while they also work at the level of higher-order rules and portray institutions as endogenous only diachronically, they embrace preexisting higher-order rules as constraints on institutional change. That is, they explain the modification over time of existing institutions or the movement from one set of institutions to another (as from constitution A to constitution B in Figure 1). Existing institutions – sometimes the very institutions that form the objects of choice – themselves constrain institutional innovation. They thus reside on both sides of the explanatory equations offered by theorists of institutional change. These institutional constraints on institutional change derive from numerous sources, including but not limited to institutionally determined risk; uncertainty; discounting, transaction, and other costs; countervailing interest and power; and increasing returns to scale (North 1981; Krasner 1984; Levi 1988; Shepsle 1989; David 1985, 1994; Thelen 1999; Pierson 2000a, 2000b).

Pierson (1996) offers a compelling account of EU institutional change. Pierson's theory explains why formal institutional change following a design logic – that is, with weak prior institutional constraints – is difficult, and why (and in what ways) informal change can and does occur. He argues that although institutions initially reflect their creators' (i.e., EU member states') interests, control "gaps" arise that are difficult (costly) to close. Such gaps result from the partial autonomy of EU institutions, national leaders' restricted time horizons, unanticipated institutional consequences, and exogenous (e.g., electorally induced) shifts in national leaders' preferences. Several factors militate against closure of these gaps, including resistance by (institutionally created) supranational actors, institutional barriers to reform (e.g., supermajority rules for institutional change), and sunk costs and positive feedbacks (see also Marks, Hooghe, and Blank 1996; Pollack 1996, 1997). The rise of difficult-to-close gaps, Pierson concludes, explains both the trajectory of and limitations to EU institutional change (but see Farrell and Héritier 2003).

The institutional change approach, taken generally, exhibits many strengths. It recognizes that institutions are potential objects of choice. Like design approaches, it works at the level of higher-order rules. Unlike them, it theorizes the limits to (constraints on) choice at this level. Most important, among the limits that it identifies are institutions themselves, which can constrain change in any number of ways, as described above. At the same time, though, institutional change approaches suffer from some characteristic weaknesses. They fail to consider the ways in which the lower-order rules established by higher-order institutions might themselves constitute objects of political choice. (In the language of Figure 1, they fail to consider institutional selection.) What is more, they generally fail explicitly to connect lower-order and higher-order rules by theorizing the feedback between the former and the latter. It seems fair to say that they recognize the possibility of such a connection, and that it is consistent with their approach. But to this point this insight remains underdeveloped.

Institutional Effects

Analyses of institutional effects focus on the "constraints that shape" clause of North's definition. They tend to operate at the level of lower-order institutions such as legislative procedures (e.g., procedures b_1, b_2, and b_3 in Figure 1) and tend to work at shorter time scales. Institutions reside only on the right-hand side of effects equations, usually intervening between preferences and power on the one hand and strategies, bargaining, and substantive outcomes on the other, and they are used to explain noninstitutional outcomes (y_1, y_2, y_3) such as power, policies, budgets, and the like. Americanist scholars pioneered and developed the approach (Shepsle 1979, 1986; Denzau and Mackay 1983; Shepsle and Weingast 1984a, 1987; Krehbiel, Shepsle, and Weingast 1987), and while relatively few comparativists have followed suit (Huber 1992, 1996), early efforts by Garrett (1992), Tsebelis (1994), and Steunenberg (1994) spawned dozens of follow-on efforts in the EU literature. EU institutional effects analysts have closely followed the parent literature, taking higher-order rules as given and generating comparative static results of the effects of procedural variation on bargaining dynamics, political power, and policy outcomes.

Introduction

Institutional effects approaches fulfill a critically important role in institutional analysis by theorizing the many and varied ways in which institutions can independently shape political outcomes. They can claim many successes. However, a key omission (failing to consider institutional causes) runs the risk of producing errors of commission. For example, it may be fallacious to infer political power from an effects analysis without considering institutional causes (Krehbiel 1988, 1991; Krehbiel and Rivers 1988; Cox and McCubbins 1993). Similarly, the neglect of institutional choice poorly serves policy analysis. "Far from being exceptional occurrences," Majone writes, "attempts to modify procedural rules and other institutional constraints are so pervasive that no descriptive or prescriptive policy analysis can be complete that does not explicitly take institution-changing behavior into consideration" (Majone 1989, 114). Finally, failure by effects analysts to consider institutional causes unjustifiably – and, given their rationalist foundations, puzzlingly – truncates strategic actors' behavioral repertoires and the range of factors over which they might exercise choice. Effects analyses tend to portray agents as fully sophisticated within institutions but incompletely sophisticated (i.e., naïve or myopic) with respect to them (Krehbiel 1988, 310–311). If institutions produce outcomes in the ways predicted, and if actors prefer the outcomes produced under available institutional alternatives to those produced by rules currently in (or proposed for) use, they face incentives to engage in politics with respect to, and not just within, those rules (Goldberg 1974; Riker 1980; McKelvey and Ordeshook 1984; Moe 1990a, 1990b).

Institutional Selection and Procedural Politics

This book, focusing as it does on everyday politics with respect to rules, relates to existing work in two ways. First, it fills a gap in the literature by explicitly theorizing institutional selection, that is, the synchronic choice of lower-order rules. However, second and perhaps more important, it provides new explanatory leverage on institutional effects, and by explicitly contemplating cross-level, over-time feedback between lower- and higher-order rules, it improves our understanding of institutional change. With respect to the EU, it paints a more coherent and complete picture of the operation of EU institutions than is currently available, moving beyond the stale dichotomy between "everyday politics" (within rules) and "historic grand bargaining" (with respect to rules). In particular, it finds that opportunities for institutional choice present themselves more frequently than previously suspected. At the same time, and somewhat paradoxically, it also bespeaks the EU's transformation from a diplomatic system governed by balance of power principles to a constitutional system governed by the rule of law. Even the most egregious manipulations surrounding lower-order choice tend to reinforce higher-order constraint. More generally, it opens promising new avenues for thinking about the EU in comparative perspective, for thinking about rule governance in the international system, and for thinking about institutions in their "dual nature" and at multiple levels.

Institutional selection involves the choice of a lower-order rule (procedure b_1, b_2, or b_3 from Figure 1, for example) from among a menu of alternatives delineated by the higher order rules (e.g., constitution B). The constitution also usually outlines the process by which procedures will be selected, connecting some antecedent condition to some procedural consequence. Some procedure must be selected if outcomes are to be generated. That selection process can occur more or less automatically (e.g., some condition is met that unproblematically triggers the use of a given procedure), in which case actors are contenting themselves to action *within* rules. Alternatively, the selection process can become politicized, in which case actors find themselves in the realm of everyday politics *with respect to* rules – the realm, that is, of procedural politics.

How does this process unfold? Procedural politics, I have suggested, responds to both incentives and opportunities. On the incentive side I model actors as influence maximizers. That is, I suggest that they seek to ensure the usage of rules that give them the most power in the political/legislative process. This position is controversial, and others are possible. Most generally, there exists little consensus as to whether policy, office, or votes primarily motivate political actors (Müller and Strøm 1999). More narrowly, we can imagine that efficiency, functionality, habit, indifference, or any number of other "motivations" might undergird institutional selection. Happily, the empirical pudding can provide some proof as to which of these potential motivations best explains observed behavior. However controversial, this argument implies that if all rules are politically equivalent – that is, if all provide the same level of political influence – then no incentive to act with respect to them exists. By contrast, as institutional alternatives differ in their influence properties, incentives to engage in procedural politics increase.

Opportunities for procedural politicians to pursue influence are not unlimited, however. In the first instance stands the strategic context. Absent dictatorship, institutional selection is a strategic choice process in which the choice of each actor depends in part upon expectations about the preferences, power, and strategic choices of others. A second, more properly institutional, set of constraints also presents itself. Higher-order rules (constitutions) define the menu of lower-order rules (procedures) and set forth the conditions or criteria for selecting from among them. However, these criteria often correspond with less-than-perfect clarity to the situation in the "real world." Situations can often be "jurisdictionally ambiguous," not determining the use of a single procedure, but potentially inviting the consideration of many. (Ultimately, only one rule can be selected and used.) As this jurisdictional ambiguity increases, procedural alternatives present themselves and procedural political opportunities expand.

In contemplating again the questions posed at the outset – why, when, how, and with what effects do actors attempt to influence their institutional environment? – I have already suggested answers to the first two. Why do actors engage in procedural politics? They do so in pursuit of influence. When do they engage in procedural politics? They do so when incentives and opportunities come together, with influence differences among alternatives defining incentives (gross incentives, in any case), and strategic context and jurisdictional ambiguity defining opportunities.[4] As influence differences among alternatives and jurisdictional ambiguity increase, the likelihood of procedural politics likewise increases. Two questions remain: how do actors play procedural politics, and how does all of this affect important and interesting political outcomes?

Behavior and process will involve the pursuit of influence within strategic and higher-order institutional constraints, but it will also involve attempts to loosen those constraints (equivalently, to create opportunities). Starting with strategic constraints, actors will face incentives to forge coalitions with those sharing their procedural goals. While a straightforward proposition, the theory in Chapter 2 and the empirics in Chapters 5 and 6 suggest and confirm that this often involves the creation of otherwise unexpected partnerships. Procedural politics can make for strange bedfellows.

Strategic, influence-maximizing procedural politicians will also face incentives to loosen the higher-order institutional constraints that they face by "gaming" the constitutional criteria governing institutional selection. This will involve manipulating the degree (or perceptions of the degree) of jurisdictional ambiguity, with those seeking to promote new alternatives increasing it (or reducing it in a favorable direction) and those with the

---

[4] "Opportunities" are properly seen as subsidiary to incentives, but they can be separated for analytical clarity.

opposite preference opposing them. In the case of the EU, the treaty (constitution) forges a link between policy issues and the procedures used to pass laws dealing with them. Different procedures apply in the making of agricultural, environmental, transport, taxation, foreign, and other policies. In this context, "gaming the criteria" means manipulating issue definitions so as to establish the applicability of more favorable rules. Different criteria would produce different games, and while the specific criteria differ from one institutionalized system to another, the procedural political logic should apply equally well to institutional selection in firms, international organizations, European Unions, or nation-states.

Finally, what will be the effects of all of this? First, institutional selection determines which rules will be used in the making of policy, and if the new institutionalism as a whole can agree about one thing, it is that rules influence outcomes. To the extent that institutional selection involves procedural politics, both rules and outcomes will have been affected. Second, however, procedural politics reduces the efficiency of the decision-making process. While Goldberg (1974) and Majone (1989) liken procedural politics to an investment decision, this is arguably investment not in production but in rents. Procedural politics involves expenditures of time and money on influence rather than on the efficient making of good or functional policy.[5] Third, and perhaps most important, procedural politics feeds back into constitutional change. It responds to jurisdictional ambiguities, which represent circumstances with respect to which constitutional contracts are incomplete. It may thus inform contracting parties (in the EU case, member states) about infirmities in their agreements and incite them subsequently to modify higher-order rules.

Plan of the Book

Summarizing, the approach pursued in this book coheres with prevailing approaches to institutions in the European Union and more generally. With design and change approaches, and consistent with North's definition, it treats institutions as at least potentially endogenous. With the effects approach, and also consistent with North's definition, it treats institutions as at least partly exogenous at any given point in time. Thus, like the institutional

---

[5] This may well make sense as a way of creating (even efficiency-reducing) voice opportunities. I offer no normative judgment as to the desirability of these characteristics, only a positive expectation with respect to one of them.

Introduction

change approach, it models institutions as both independent and dependent variables, as predicates and outcomes of politics. But unlike most prevailing work, it explicitly embraces multiple levels of institutional analysis and suggests clear causal chains (including feedbacks) linking higher-order to lower-order institutions. Indeed, if anything it turns on its head the implicit claim that higher-order rules are best seen as endogenous and lower-order rules best treated as exogenous. This fuller picture of the operation of institutions, I suggest, will advance understanding not only of the EU but of rule governed systems more generally.[6]

The remainder of the book develops, tests, and assesses the impact of the theory of procedural politics sketched here. Chapter 2 develops a positive theory of procedural politics, offering a series of testable propositions, tailored to the EU but generalizable to any rule-governed system, about the conditions under which, the ways in which, and the effects with which actors engage in every politics with respect to rules – procedural politics – rather than simply within them. Wherever possible it identifies and operationalizes alternative approaches, though off-the-shelf rivals are not always available. As will be clear, the propositions derive from the full spectrum of social scientific work on institutions, including economics, sociology, legal studies, and all of the traditional subfields of political science.

Chapter 3 fleshes out three premises of the argument – namely, that institutions matter, that actors have preferences over them, and that institutional selection involves strategic interaction among rational influence maximizers – in the EU context. Non-EU specialists should read the chapter for background on the EU's constitutional and legislative system, including brief introductions to the actors and institutions involved. It contains a few mildly technical spatial models, but these and a slightly more technical noncooperative game are placed in an appendix and can be skipped by nonspecialists (results are discussed in the text). It provides the background for the empirical tests undertaken in Chapters 4 through 6.

Chapter 4 provides an aggregate empirical assessment by bringing to bear a broad array of quantitative evidence, both describing variations in procedural politics across issues, actors, and time, and testing specific propositions about the conditions under which procedural politics occurs as well

---

[6] Diermeier and Krehbiel (2003, 132) portray this "Russian doll" approach (i.e., modeling the choice of what they call first-order institutions within parameters set by what they call second-order institutions) as the key strategy for resolving dilemmas associated with the "dual nature" of institutions.

as its effects on legislative efficiency and long-run institutional change. The data exhaustively cover ten years of EU legislative history, from the entry into force of the historic Single European Act (SEA) in 1987 through the end of 1997, and also selectively reach back where indicators are available. The results confirm that procedural politics becomes more likely as the jurisdictional ambiguity of issues increases and as the influence properties of institutional alternatives diverge. Actors consistently promote the use of rules giving them more power over those giving them less. In short, the occurrence of procedural politics varies predictably across issues, actors, and time. In terms of effects, procedural politics significantly reduces policymaking efficiency, roughly doubling the time it takes for laws to pass, and it strongly influences long-run institutional change. These broad patterns invite closer scrutiny, which I undertake in subsequent chapters using a "most different" logic of sectoral comparison.

Chapter 5 brings to bear empirical evidence from the environmental policy sector. Environmental policy is a relatively young but crucially important sector of EU competence. The theory and evidence presented in Chapter 4 identify this sector as uniquely susceptible to procedural politics. Chapter 5 examines procedural politics in the waste management field between 1983 and 1999 and process-traces three rules disputes that were eventually adjudicated by the European Court of Justice (ECJ). These cases span two treaty changes (the Single European Act, entered into force in 1987, and the Maastricht Treaty [Treaty on European Union], entered into force in 1993) and thus offer several opportunities to assess expectations about strategic responses to a changing menu of institutional alternatives. The evidence from these cases strongly confirms overall expectations about the conditions under which, the ways in which, and the effects with which procedural politics occurs. Actors consistently push for rules that increase their power relative to the available alternatives. They consistently join with others sharing their procedural interests, and they attempt strategically to frame issues in ways that abet procedural political strategies (often at the expense of at least short-run substantive preferences). These dynamics generate otherwise-unexpected policy outcomes. Finally, the analysis suggests that procedural politics should have largely disappeared with the advent of a more rationalized relationship between free trade and environmental protection in the 1999 Amsterdam Treaty, which came about partly as a result of feedback processes between lower-order procedural politics and higher-order institutional change.

Introduction

Chapter 6 examines a second, "most different," sector – agricultural policy – to provide a more stringent test of the robustness of the theory. Agricultural policy has traditionally been the most important and well-established sector of EU activity, and both a priori expectations and descriptive evidence from Chapter 4 suggest that it is uniquely resistant to procedural politics. It thus provides a sharp contrast with environmental policy and represents a sector in which procedural politics is least likely to occur. Chapter 6 examines procedural politics in the agricultural sector between 1985 and 1999, and process-traces two disputes judged by the European Court of Justice. The disputes involve the relationship between agriculture and human health, and they show clearly the interaction of policy issues, political influence, and institutional alternatives in the production of procedural politics. The outcome of the first case, Beef Hormones, effectively eliminated jurisdictional ambiguity such that, for almost ten years, there were no serious procedural political disputes in the agricultural sector, despite important fluctuations in issue definitions over the period. The second case, Beef Labeling, demonstrates how a combination of newly available institutional alternatives and fluid issues interact with influence maximization to destabilize prevailing policy networks and generate procedural political disputes. Actors generally push for rules that maximize their influence, although exceptions to this general tendency arise. Careful process tracing of issue framing and coalition formation finds them to be broadly consistent with theoretical expectations. The impact of procedural politics on policy outcomes appears substantial. These findings strongly reinforce results already presented in Chapters 4 and 5. The pairing of environmental and agricultural policy greatly increases confidence in the generalizability of the findings, showing that apparently radically different sectors (old vs. new, horizontal vs. vertical, redistributive vs. regulatory, etc.) operate according to a similar procedural political logic.

The concluding chapter begins by summarizing the arguments and empirical findings. It draws out the implications of the study for several areas of current theoretical controversy in political science. In particular, it illustrates the importance of, and suggests a partial solution to, the choice-constraint paradox in institutional analyses of politics, whereby institutions are defined as objects of human design or choice but are only worth studying insofar as they exert independent effects. It remedies key shortcomings in a variety of work on EU politics, including work emphasizing inherent supranational-national antagonisms, strategic interaction within existing rules, and the putative separation between day-to-day politics (conceived as politics within rules) and "grand institutional bargaining" (conceived as politics over rules). It also confirms the utility of extending theories of procedural choice, issue framing, and agenda setting to a comparative and international context and invites comparisons to a number of political systems in which procedural politics should, in theory, play themselves out. Throughout, the conclusion addresses more concrete issues of rule governance and system transformation in the EU, arguing that, paradoxically, procedural politics illustrates the transformation of the EU from a traditional international organization to a polity increasingly governed by the rule of law.

Conclusion

As it embarks upon its second half-century, the European Union (EU) continues to represent many things to many people. Some view it as a model of successful international cooperation. Others view it as an emerging political form, perhaps one with troubling implications for democratic control. Still others contemplate its role as a partner (or competitor) in world affairs. The European Union may represent all of these things. Yet, from the perspective of this book, the EU represents something far more general, seemingly more mundane but arguably more important: the EU is a system of rules. Indeed, it is a particularly informative set of rules, the intrinsic interest of which is multiplied by its general lessons for the operation of rules in social and political life. We must understand its rules – what they are, how they operate, how they relate to actors' behavior, the outcomes they produce – if we are to understand the EU. And, perhaps somewhat unexpectedly for such a novel political form, to understand the EU is to understand important things about rules in political life.

2

Theorizing Procedural Politics

ISSUES, INFLUENCE, AND INSTITUTIONAL CHOICE

Because it draws its raison d'être from the proposition that institutions matter, institutionalism implies that actors – who presumably care about the outcomes that institutions generate – may face incentives to engage in politics with respect to, rather than simply within, rules. This possibility immediately presents institutional analysts with a dilemma, however, since for rules to be rules, they must not only represent objects of human creation or choice but also sources of human constraint. "A completely flexible [institutional] framework is a contradiction in terms" (Matthews 1986, 914). Clearly, rules are sometimes taken as fixed and given. But when will politics remain within a framework of rules, and when does it take place with respect to that framework? How will such politics unfold, and what will be their effects? This chapter addresses these questions, briefly laying out the conceptual premises of my argument and developing at greater length a theory of the conditions under which, the ways in which, and the effects with which actors engage in procedural politics. Although elaborated with reference to the EU, the theory applies quite generally to institutionalized political and social systems.

Generically, of course, rationalist statements about any behavior reduce to statements about preferences, opportunities, and constraints, or about relative costs and benefits. I do argue in the abstract that procedural politics responds to the opportunities for selecting alternative rules and to the net expected benefits of such institutional selection. The appeal of such statements lies in specifying them operationally and testing them and rival arguments against evidence. In that spirit, I argue more specifically that opportunities arise when issues are jurisdictionally ambiguous, such that any of several available rules might apply. Net expected benefits, for their part, vary as a function of differences in the influence properties of the available alternative procedures, net of the transactions and bargaining costs that attend to procedural politics. Together these incentives and opportunities define the conditions under which procedural politics occurs. I argue further that procedural politics occurs through predictable means (involving procedural coalition formation and strategic issue definition) and exerts predictable effects (on rules choices, on policymaking efficiency and outcomes, and on long-run institutional change). Consideration of the conditions under which, the ways in which, and the effects with which actors engage in politics with respect to rules, rather than simply within them, helps better to explain the nature and operation of the EU's unique emerging polity, as of rule-governed political systems more generally.

After first briefly developing the conceptual premises of the book – which will be further addressed in Chapter 3 – this chapter sets out specific theoretical claims about the conditions under which, the ways in which, and the effects with which procedural politics unfolds. The second section examines the question of conditions, generating a series of testable procedural political and rival hypotheses. The third section turns to procedural political behaviors and processes, offering specific predictions about procedural coalitions and contrasting them with accounts based on pursuit of ideological goals or of the institutionally myopic pursuit of substantive policy. The fourth section offers expectations about procedural political effects, suggesting that inattention to procedural politics prevents thorough understanding of EU rules choices, policymaking efficiency and outcomes, and long-run institutional change. The concluding section summarizes the arguments and sets the stage for the operational application to the EU in Chapter 3 and the empirical work in Chapters 4 through 6.

Conceptual Premises

Three premises underpin the analysis, and here I briefly discuss each of them.

Institutions Matter

That institutions "matter" represents one of the few propositions universally shared by the otherwise very diverse "new institutionalisms" (see generally Cammack 1992; Weaver and Rockman 1993; Koelble 1995; Hall and Taylor 1996; Kato 1996; Lowndes 1996; Immergut 1998; Thelen 1999;

Diermeir and Krehbiel 2003). Institutions might matter in any number of specific ways already identified by existing work. They might facilitate the realization of otherwise unattainable joint or collective gains from exchange by reducing transaction costs; stabilizing expectations; providing low-cost, high-quality information; facilitating monitoring and sanctioning of noncompliance; and so forth (Coase 1937/1988; North and Thomas 1973; Williamson 1975, 1985; Keohane 1984; Milgrom, North, and Weingast 1990; North 1990; Horn 1995). They might mask, facilitate, or safeguard over time the exercise of power (Mearsheimer 1994/95, 1995; Moe 1990a, 222). Abstracting from these specifics, the key point is that institutions matter insofar as they directly or indirectly condition actors' influence and/or important substantive outcomes.

Derived Institutional Preferences

Since institutions matter, actors should have derived preferences over them as a function of their preferences for the "goods" (budgets, policies, level of integration, etc.) that they produce. The qualifier "derived" suggests that actors place no intrinsic value on rules, valuing instead institutionally conditioned outcomes (Krehbiel 1998, 96). The notion of derived institutional preferences depends critically upon actors' beliefs about the causal connections between institutions and outcomes and upon the proposition that they place value on achieving some outcomes over others. Such beliefs and preferences "can transform preferences over policies into preferences over institutions" (Tsebelis 1990, 98).

By extension, as actors' preferences over outcomes diverge, so too will their derived preferences over institutions. Where this is the case, the likelihood of conflicts over institutions increases. "The most important implication of the idea of derived institutional preferences," Bawn argues, "is that there will be disagreement about the choice of institutions whenever there is disagreement about the policies those institutions will produce" (Bawn 1993, 966). "Battles about rules, procedures, institutional arrangements, or legislative organization," Krehbiel concurs, "are in fact battles about public policy and who determines it" (Krehbiel 1991, 1). I remain agnostic about actors' ultimate goals, but I do suggest that whatever they are, influence is a means to them. Accordingly, I assume that actors value influence and derive their preferences for institutions accordingly. I develop and defend this stance in Chapter 3.

Strategic Interaction

In acting on their derived institutional preferences, I suppose that actors are strategic. This suggests, quite simply, that in making her or his own choice, each actor must consider the preferences, power, and anticipated reactions of others in a position to influence the outcome. Collective outcomes result from such jointly made choices. I examine four sets of actors in EU politics: the European Commission, the European Parliament (EP), the European Court of Justice (ECJ), and the EU member states (individually or within the Council of Ministers). A strategic account also directs attention to institutional context (Epstein and Knight 1998). For any given episode of interest, the EU treaty specifies the relevant "rules of the game," including the sequence in which the actors move, the behaviors in which they are allowed to engage, and so forth. Institutions stabilize expectations about what others can and will likely do and permit actors to make informed choices about their own best move in any given situation.

Summary

The foregoing sketches out in rough form the premises underpinning my approach to institutions. It says nothing at all about the conditions under which, the ways in which, or the effects with which procedural politics occurs. It is to precisely those theoretical questions that the chapter now turns.

Conditions: The Determinants of Procedural Politics

Given that institutions matter, that actors have derived preferences over them, and that strategic interaction drives institutional choices, what can be said about the conditions under which everyday politics will take place with respect to rules, rather than within them? In other words, what determines procedural politics?

In general, actors cannot unilaterally (or at least costlessly) select procedures simply as a function of their procedural preferences. Institutional selection, like any other choice and at any level of analysis, is constrained choice. This is true in the first instance because of the need to act strategically. But other factors affect strategic considerations and also independently constrain and condition institutional selection. Here I emphasize two sets of factors – opportunities and incentives, defined respectively as the availability and relative desirability of institutional alternatives – that condition the dependent variable of interest at this stage, namely, the occurrence of procedural politics.

Opportunity: Jurisdictional Ambiguity and the Availability of Alternatives

The first determinant of procedural politics is the availability of institutional alternatives. If only one rule is available, no possibility for institutional selection exists. The availability of multiple institutional alternatives opens up space for choice and for procedural politics. The theoretical task at this point centers on identifying ex ante the conditions under which institutional alternatives will present themselves.

I begin by noting that highly institutionalized systems usually involve multiple levels of (nested) rules, with higher-order rules more costly to change than lower-order ones (North 1990, 47; Goodin 1996a, 23). Kiser and Ostrom identify three primary levels of institutional analysis. The lowest (operational) level deals in rules (e.g., laws) that guide individual action; the intermediate (collective choice) level concerns rules governing the making of those laws (e.g., legislative procedures); and the most overarching (constitutional) level in turn defines and delimits those procedures (Kiser and Ostrom 1982, 208; Ostrom 1990, 1995). I limit my attention to formal EU rules at the constitutional and collective choice levels. Rules at each level – respectively, the EU treaty and day-to-day legislative procedures – constitute the menu of institutional alternatives facing actors at any given point in time.

The treaty level represents one possible locus of institutional choice in the EU, and with few exceptions it represents the only level at which analysts currently theorize EU institutional choice.[1] The European Commission and European Parliament cannot directly engage in institutional choice – design or change – at this level. They do involve themselves in the process by contributing ideas and weighing in politically on the types of treaty changes that they'd like to see, but they are not granted any formal say over the final outcome. The European Court of Justice has no input on formal treaty changes, but, in a sense, its power of constitutional interpretation

---

[1] The *locus classicus* on EU higher-order institutional choice is Moravcsik 1998. Work on the selection of "comitology" procedures, which govern the exercise of the Commission's autonomous (administrative) authority, constitutes an exception (Dogan 1997; Franchino 2000, 2002; Ballman, Epstein, and O'Halloran 2002; Pollack 2003), as does the analytical work by Carrubba and Volden (2001).

gives it some ability to change the meaning of the treaty (Voigt 1999). Most important for my purposes, a simple majority of EU member states can convene a treaty-amending intergovernmental conference (IGC). Should they find working within existing institutions sufficiently onerous or unsatisfactory, member states may attempt to change them in the hopes of obtaining more advantageous streams of future benefits. The anticipated results of such institutional change represent one set of institutional alternatives theoretically available to member states.

However, there is a second set of potential institutional alternatives: the lower-order rules (legislative procedures) established by the treaty, which I will analyze in Chapter 3. The EU treaties contain a great many different procedures for adopting legislation, and this represents a menu of institutional alternatives potentially available for selection. Policymakers cannot just choose a legislative procedure that suits them, however. The EU's constitutional system of "attributed competencies" – whereby EU authority is limited to what the treaty expressly grants – demands that legislation be based on a provision of the treaty or secondary law that specifically enables EU legislative action on the issue in question. The issue at hand, then, determines the "legal basis," of each law, and each legal basis, in turn, determines the legislative procedure to be used. The procedure, as such, is not, in legal theory, directly available as an object of political choice.

The political reality can differ considerably from the legal theory, and in fact the availability of institutional alternatives depends upon the issue in question and its relationship to existing institutional arrangements. Some issues do fall squarely within the purview of a single legal basis and thus wholly determine the legislative procedure. Others, however, are not so clear. Where "jurisdictional ambiguity" (King 1997) exists, the applicability of any given legal basis, and hence procedure, is nonobvious and/or potentially problematic. A jurisdiction, in the sense used here, is a subset of an issue space over which a specific rule (or set of rules) applies to the exclusion of others. Jurisdictional ambiguity, then, refers to the (lack of) correspondence between political issues and the rules used to process them. Where this correspondence is tight – that is, where an issue clearly falls within a single jurisdiction – ambiguity is effectively nonexistent, and no institutional alternatives are available. As the issue-structural correspondence loosens, ambiguity increases and space opens up for consideration of alternative rules for processing the issue at hand.

To assert the importance of jurisdictional ambiguity implies that constitutionally specified jurisdictional arrangements constrain institutional

Theorizing Procedural Politics

selection. This does not require invoking nonrationality, a preference for rule following, or the existence of a coercive arbitrator capable of directly punishing transgressors. Far from it. Instead, for jurisdictions to have "bite" it suffices that some criterion external to the preferences and power of the actors exist for determining "correct" institutional selections and that an arbitrator or arbitration process, capable of raising the expected costs of incorrect choices, exist to adjudicate disputes. The existence of a dispute resolution mechanism, with an arbitrator at the "endgame," makes the decision to manipulate (or not) an inherently strategic one. And the greater the costs of choosing "incorrectly," the greater the constraints on institutional selection. In the next chapter I model a generic game of institutional choice driven in part by such cost parameters: frequently, the possibility of costly action before the ECJ suffices to deter institutional manipulation (politically motivated choice of legally incorrect procedures). Thus the EU, with its Court of Justice, satisfies this condition.

Jurisdictional ambiguity can arise for a number of reasons. Institutional designers may be deliberately vague so as to paper over disagreements or avoid embarrassing the "losers" of a grand institutional bargain. Constructive ambiguity may improve the durability of agreements in the face of changing preferences over time (Gruber 2000). Ambiguity might simply reflect time pressures, political compromises, difficult translations, and poor legal drafting (Pescatore 1987; Curtin 1993; Marks, Hooghe, and Blank 1996). It may reflect the growing complexity of the EU's policy agenda and of treaties incrementally amended to respond to it (Maurer, Wessels, and Mittag 2000, 9). It may reflect the more general inability of boundedly rational institutional designers to produce complete contracts.

Whatever its sources, I highlight two forms that ambiguity can take and illustrate them in Figure 2. In the first, the domains of two or more rules

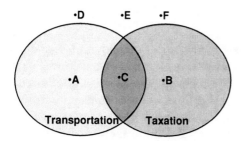

Figure 2 Jurisdictional Ambiguity: Overlap and Gaps

overlap. (This situation may arise when institutional designers encounter and fail fully to separate functionally linked domains.) By way of example, Figure 2 illustrates the relationship between taxation and transportation jurisdictions. Legislative proposals (or laws, or issues, or whatever) A and B each fall within a single jurisdiction, producing no ambiguity and little likelihood of a dispute over the applicable rule. Proposal C, by contrast, which might represent a legislative proposal to create a road toll, inhabits the jurisdictionally ambiguous space falling within both taxation and transportation jurisdictions. Here, ambiguity is high and procedural politics (akin to King's [1997] "turf wars") become increasingly likely. Having anticipated this sort of contingency, the treaty empowers the Court to arbitrate such jurisdictional disputes as may arise.

Second, existing jurisdictions may not exhaustively cover the entire issue space. There may be issues that fall in gaps between or spaces outside existing jurisdictions. This may have been the case at the birth of the jurisdictional arrangements (some issues just weren't considered or included), or it may have resulted only over time – for example, from subsequent changes in the issue space (Talbert, Jones, and Baumgartner 1995, 385–386; King 1997, 17; Baumgartner, Jones, and MacLeod 2000). However such situations come about, issues falling outside existing jurisdictions in the EU represent "gray areas" of Community competence (Teitgen and Megret 1981). In Figure 2, issues D, E, and F fall outside existing jurisdictions, but their ambiguity varies. Issue E exhibits higher jurisdictional ambiguity than does either issue D or issue F.

These reflections generate what I will call the *Ambiguity Hypothesis*. As jurisdictional ambiguity increases, alternatives become available, opportunities to promote the usage of favorable procedures increase, and the likelihood of procedural politics increases, ceteris paribus. Where ambiguity is low, that is, where an issue clearly corresponds to a single existing jurisdiction, little space exists to claim the validity of alternative procedures. Ambiguity makes potential (merely extant) "alternatives" realistically *available* objects of choice.

The availability of institutional alternatives is a necessary precondition to procedural politics, and it varies over actors, issues, and time. Some issues unambiguously dictate use of a single rule; others are jurisdictionally ambiguous, whereby multiple rules might be available. Ambiguity will be high in functionally complex matters, as these will tend to fall into areas of jurisdictional overlap. It will also presumably be high in new areas of public concern, as their precise jurisdictional correspondences have not yet been established through precedent and practice (Majone 1989, 97). These latter fall into jurisdictional gaps. With respect to variations over time, higher-order institutional changes, effected for whatever reason, can both create new alternatives (e.g., new legislative procedures) and rewrite jurisdictional boundaries. Exogenous – or even endogenous (see below) – changes in issues or in issue definitions can have similar effects. As the treaty and as issue definitions change over time, different patterns of availability (opportunity) and, by hypothesis, procedural politics result.

Summarizing this discussion of alternatives, I offer the basic hypothesis that as the availability of procedural alternatives increases, so too does the likelihood of procedural politics. Availability derives not only from the menu of alternatives given in the constitution, but also from their relationship to policy issues. Variations in either or both "issues" and "structure" affect jurisdictional ambiguity and can thus drive procedural politics. Again, an *Ambiguity Hypothesis* results: as the jurisdictional ambiguity of proposed legislation increases, the likelihood of procedural politics also increases, ceteris paribus.

Incentives: The Relative Desirability of Available Alternatives

The existence of procedural alternatives due to jurisdictional ambiguity does not suffice to produce procedural politics, however. Sufficiency depends, in the abstract, on its net expected benefits. This has two components. The first is the opportunity cost of accepting rules as they are, conceived as the influence difference between a proposed procedure and an available alternative. The second determinant is the positive cost (transaction, bargaining, and otherwise) of playing procedural politics. I turn now to consider these factors, which collectively define the incentives for engaging in everyday politics with respect to rules.

Alternatives and Influence. The most straightforward element of this benefit-cost calculation concerns the opportunity cost of accepting (acting within) rules, defined as procedural political benefits forgone and measured as the influence difference for any given actor between proposed procedures and available alternatives. Where alternatives are equal in this respect – in other words, where alternative rules make no difference in terms of an actor's influence over outcomes – this opportunity cost is zero and procedural politics is not incited. Where they are unequal, the actor calculates the difference between the alternatives, and as this difference increases, so too does the probability that he or she will play procedural politics. In all cases, procedural politics, where it occurs, should work in the direction of increased influence and more preferred outcomes. An alternative hypothesis holds that disputes over procedures reflect sincere legal differences about issue-structural correspondence rather than calculations of political advantage (Chayes and Chayes 1993, 188 fn. 43).[2] Here, actors will seek to ensure the usage of one or another rule to maximize not their influence, but legal certainty. Legal appropriateness, rather than political consequences (March and Olsen 1989), would animate procedural choice. This perspective expects no relationship between the influence properties of available alternatives and the existence of procedural politics.

These observations generate an *Influence Maximization Hypothesis*: actors will promote rules affording them more rather than less influence in the legislative process, and as the influence differences among available alternatives increase, the likelihood of procedural politics increases, ceteris paribus. I pit this against a legalistic alternative, which would suggest that actors will promote procedures that maximize legal certainty, with revealed procedural preferences accordingly standing orthogonal to influence differences among the alternatives. This influence maximization hypothesis can capture fine-grained variations in procedural politics over time and across actors and issues. Take any given issue at a single point in time and imagine two institutional alternatives. To the extent that the alternatives vary greatly in the influence they afford at least one actor, the opportunity cost of acting solely within institutions increases, and procedural politics becomes more likely. Where interests are opposed, procedural political disputes will arise. Where alternatives are largely identical, procedural political disputes will not occur (though, as I argue in the next chapter, procedural political calculations may still operate). The influence differences among alternatives, and thus these procedural political dynamics, will vary across issues and time.

Transaction and Bargaining Costs. I state the above propositions in ceteris paribus form because exclusive emphasis on gross procedural political benefits fails to consider its costs (Shepsle and Weingast 1984b, 214).

---

[2] Legal officials in the EU institutions commonly offered this rival hypothesis during interviews in 1997 and 1998–1999. Take, for example, the following dismissal of my hypothesis: "No. We act faithfully and honestly. We may change the legal basis, but only as a function of the substantive modifications to a proposal" (Interview with Council Legal Service official, Brussels, 23 October 1998).

Theorizing Procedural Politics

Some costs stand largely invariant to the strategic context. For example, the choice to call and conduct an intergovernmental conference (IGC), always an option to a simple majority of institutionally unsatisfied member states, will necessarily entail substantial fixed costs. As summits of all EU member states, IGCs entail logistical (travel to and from the conference site), operational (translation, materials, printing new treaties and updating references to them), and other expenses. The choice to engage in procedural politics potentially requires extensive and costly intraorganizational consultations with lawyers, coordination of their activities with other staff and policymakers, interorganizational haggling, and so forth. In short, however permissive the strategic context (and this may vary considerably), procedural politics involves positive costs against which potential benefits must be weighed.

More important, procedural politics is inherently strategic, and where actors' procedural preferences diverge, conflict over appropriate rules may result. This will inherently create bargaining costs that must be weighed against prospective gains. As shown in the next chapter, the magnitude of these expected costs depends upon beliefs about the preferences, power, and behavior of others. If the Commission contemplates procedural politics, what does it expect the Parliament and the member states to do? Will they acquiesce, or will they fight? If they do fight, how far are they willing to go? Will they symbolically dispute the chosen procedure, only ultimately to accept it? Or will they risk (and potentially impose on the Commission) the costs of going to the Court of Justice to challenge the perceived manipulation of EU law? Clearly, their propensity to do so should vary directly with the opportunity cost of (i.e., influence loss associated with) acquiescence. If they do go to the Court, how will it decide? If the Court is unlikely to acquiesce in the Commission's alleged procedural manipulation, the expected utility of procedural politics might actually be negative, an assessment made stronger by the (variable) potential for Court judgments to constitute legal precedents.

Many of these specifications of procedural political costs can be explained in terms of (i.e., reduced to) the jurisdictional ambiguity of issues and the influence differences between institutional alternatives. Bargaining costs will likely rise when, for at least one actor, the alternatives differ greatly. Resistance will likely be more swift and more firm the lower the jurisdictional ambiguity of the issue, and thus the more questionable the manipulation. Some costs, then, are reducible to variations in opportunities and incentives and need not be considered independently of them.

Some cost factors, though, may arise independently of the factors already considered. Intraorganizational factors, such as the number of veto points through which a procedural political dispute must pass or the degree of legal formalism espoused by the in-house legal services, might influence actual or expected procedural political costs, not only for actors within the organization but also for those outside it. For collective actors such as the EU institutions, the most fundamental of these intraorganizational factors would seem to be the preferences of the constituent units (individuals in the Commission, MEPs or political groups [parties] in the EP, and member states in the Council). Presumably, though, these will matter less for the EP and Commission than for the Council. Intraparty cohesion in the EP stands at remarkably high levels (Hix, Noury, and Roland 2003; but see Carrubba et al. 2003), interparty coalitions frequently form (Hix, Kreppel, and Noury 2003; Kreppel and Hix 2003; Kreppel 2000; Kreppel and Tsebelis 1999), and the EP has traditionally been a revisionist institution bent on increasing its power (Corbett, Jacobs, and Shackleton 2000). The Commission, too, can be expected to behave as a classic competence maximizing bureaucracy in this arena (Niskanen 1971; Schneider 2001a) despite the convincingly established importance of partisan and national factors in shaping individual officials' political orientations (Hooghe 1999a, 1999b, 2001, 2002). In short, the EU represents "the only game in town" for these actors, and consequently their constituent parts face strong incentives to push to the background whatever fundamental preference differences they might have, ensuring organizational influence in the first instance and only then (if at all) carving up the attendant political pie (Kreppel 2002a).

The same cannot be said for the member states in the Council. Despite the ever-increasing importance of Europe, they retain some outside options – autonomous action, "creative" implementation, and so forth – should they face politically unfavorable outcomes in the Council. Simply put, member states have less a priori incentive to maximize the Council's power. Preference heterogeneity among member states in the Council should therefore positively influence expected procedural political costs. This factor cuts both ways in terms of predicting procedural politics, however. The Council requires unanimity to challenge a legal basis (procedure). All other things being equal, high preference heterogeneity makes unanimity harder (more costly) to achieve, since consensus will require longer and harder bargaining, more lucrative side payments, more extensive linkage to more important issues, and so forth. This intra-Council perspective, then, generates the testable proposition that as preference heterogeneity among

Theorizing Procedural Politics

Council members increases, so too do the costs (to member states) of procedural politics, which correspondingly becomes less likely. At the same time, however, preference heterogeneity among Council members may incite more adventurous procedural political maneuvers on the part of the Commission and Parliament, which rationally anticipate that the Council will be unable to challenge them. This generates the proposition that Council preference heterogeneity will decrease the costs (to the EP and Commission) of procedural politics, making it more likely. These propositions are testable, both against each other and against a null model positing no relationship between Council preference heterogeneity and procedural politics.

Summary

Summarizing the argument to this point, I have suggested that institutions matter, that actors have derived preferences over them, and that they will interact strategically to ensure the usage of procedures that maximize their political influence. Two factors condition when they will engage in such procedural politics, or everyday politics with respect to rules. First, the opportunity must present itself: some procedural alternatives must be available. This, itself, derives from the particular correspondence between issues and institutions – jurisdictional ambiguity – and opportunity varies with it. Second, the incentives must also present themselves. The benefits of procedural politics in the form of influence gained must more than outweigh its costs, incurred primarily through procedural political bargaining. As institutional alternatives become available, and as they diverge in their influence properties, the likelihood of procedural politics increases.

Having identified and offered testable propositions about the conditions under which procedural politics will play itself out, I proceed to consider the behaviors and processes associated with it, with an ultimate eye toward its effects on important political and institutional outcomes.

The Dynamics of Procedural Politics

The foregoing discussion dealt with the conditions under which procedural politics occurs. Here I turn to consider the ways in which it occurs, to processes and behavior. I emphasize two behavioral correlates of procedural politics – strategic issue definition and procedural coalition formation – that constitute dependent variables at this stage of the argument.

Strategic Issue Definition

Where the issues at hand determine the rules to be used, strategic actors have incentives to offer procedurally motivated definitions of issues in an attempt to "fit" them under favorable rules (Goldberg 1974, 482; Majone 1989, 104; Baumgartner and Jones 1993; King 1997). This tactic can work realistically only where issues are jurisdictionally ambiguous, either because they fall within several overlapping jurisdictions or because they fall outside jurisdictions as actually drawn (refer again to Figure 2). In the EU, the European Court of Justice uses a "center of gravity" criterion to determine which jurisdiction (legal basis), and thus which legislative procedure, applies.[3] While difficult to operationalize, this notion hinges on the proximity of a given issue to one or another jurisdiction.[4] In view of this test, actors will frame issues so as to move (perceptions of) the center of gravity in a favorable direction, thus "resolving" jurisdictional ambiguity in their favor (King 1997, 8). Stated more generally – and this strategy should operate in all systems in which external criteria govern the choice of rules – actors will "game" the criteria to get a favorable procedure. In pursuing this option, each actor considers the preferences, power, and possible reactions of others and explicitly incorporates expectations about eventual Court judgments into the issue definitions that it advances. While persuasion of other actors might be nice, it is ultimately to the Court that this framing behavior is directed. Following in spirit Riker's notion of "heresthetics," which concerns "manipulation of the structure of tastes and alternatives within which decisions are made," (Riker 1984, 55), I identify three forms of strategic issue definition: fusion, fission, and reframing.

"Fusion" joins previously separate legislative proposals so as to tip the center of gravity of the whole toward a favorable procedure, where less than the total number of issues would receive such a rule were they to remain separate. Consider the abstract case illustrated in Figure 3. Suppose that the European Commission had proposed two separate pieces of legislation, labeled A and B, for the Council to consider. A is relatively jurisdictionally unambiguous, and the Council would not object to the procedure to which it would be subject. The Council would seek to ensure the usage of a different

---

[3] For years the ECJ formally rejected the "center of gravity" criterion in favor of one emphasizing the "aim and content" of the measure in question. These criteria are practically indistinguishable, and the Court has since embraced the center of gravity approach.

[4] This criterion closely resembles the "weight of the bill criterion" employed by the U.S. House Parliamentarian in resolving jurisdictional disputes (King 1997, 98).

Theorizing Procedural Politics

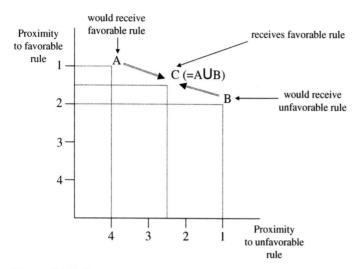

Figure 3 Fusion

rule in the case of B, however, which, as defined, would be processed in procedurally unfavorable circumstances. If the Council fuses A and B into a "new" piece of legislation, C, it could consider the issues raised by both A and B under favorable rules. It thus faces an incentive to do so.

"Fission" rests on similar logic but deals in factoring and separating multidimensional proposals. Here, as in Figure 4, the original proposal, A, is multidimensional but its center of gravity brings it under an unfavorable procedure. In this case, the Council may be able to bring aspects of the proposal under a favorable rule by splitting it into two or more parts. After this "fission" of the original proposal, part of its legislative agenda (proposal C) continues to fall under unfavorable rules, but a separate part, B, can now be processed under favorable rules.

"Issue arithmetic," the addition and subtraction of issues (Sebenius 1983), is a time-honored means of obtaining desired ends, and both fission and fusion will be familiar to students of issue manipulation and agenda setting (Schattschneider 1960; Riker 1983, 1984). A third tactic, "reframing," is also possible. Here, the number of issues remains constant, but actors rhetorically, scientifically, technically, or otherwise redefine those issues so as to move (perceptions of) the center of gravity from an unfavorable toward a favorable procedure. Baumgartner and Jones (1993) develop the general logic and apply it to "venue shopping" in the U.S. Congress (see

Procedural Politics

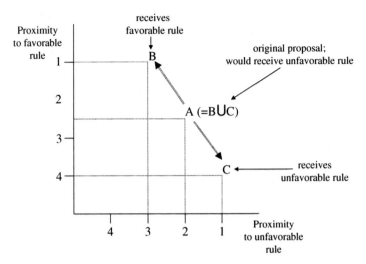

Figure 4 Fission

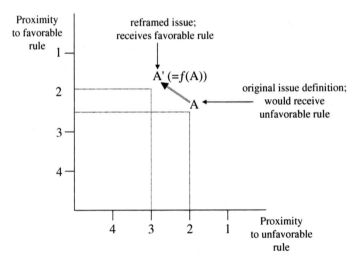

Figure 5 Reframing

also Mattli 2001). Thus, as in Figure 5, a proposal framed as A will receive an unfavorable rule. Through reframing into issue A′, some function of A, however, the proposal now falls within a more favorable jurisdiction.

As King argues, "it is in the details of crafting legislation that the jurisdiction game is at its finest" (King 1997, 8). By hypothesis, all forms

30

of strategic issue definition can occur at all stages of the EU legislative process (Peters 1994). Initial legislative proposals by the European Commission should define issues in procedural political terms, although since no objective baseline for the "real issue" at hand exists, this will be difficult to measure. Where ambiguity exists, the Council and Parliament can be expected, on the margins, to propose substantive amendments consistent with their procedural interests. In particular, since the European Court of Justice tends to look closely at legislative preambles in assessing the "aim and content" (center of gravity) of legislation, amendments to preambular "recitals" are obvious candidates for strategic issue framing (Lord Slynn of Hadley 1993, 16–17). In sum, the Court uses a particular test (the "center of gravity") in determining which procedure should apply, but since objectives can almost always be "spun" in different ways to suit different needs, actors face incentives strategically to frame issues (Emiliou 1994, 499). In an interesting sense, the Court's own test sets the strategic parameters within which, but also with respect to which, others must operate (Stone Sweet, Fligstein, and Sandholtz 2001, 14). As one interviewee put it, "the ECJ has sanctioned this type of behavior to a certain extent because of its 'aim and content' jurisprudence, which tells the institutions precisely what they need to manipulate to pass muster."[5]

These ideas generate a priori expectations about at least some of the substantive positions taken by actors in the EU. Where ambiguity exists actors should systematically promote issue definitions that locate legislative proposals within procedurally favorable jurisdictions. One alternative hypothesis posits sincere pursuit of substantive goals. For example, the European Parliament is generally considered to be the "greenest" (most pro-environment) of the EU institutions.[6] "Sincere" accounts would expect it to promote rules that provide the greatest level of environmental protection, which are those under the "Environment" chapter of the EU treaty. The present account can predict when the EP will behave in this way but can also explain anomalies that arise when the EP offers less environmentally friendly amendments or promotes less "green" rules, such as those found in the "internal market" (free trade) chapter of the treaty. A second alternative hypothesis postulates a relationship between issue definitions and rules that mirrors the one proposed here. Drawn from "garbage can" theories of organizational decision making, it suggests that rather than

---

[5] Interview with Council Legal Service official, Brussels, 23 July 1997.
[6] This proposition is developed in Chapter 5.

issue definitions responding to rules preferences, the reverse obtains: issue definitions determine revealed rules preferences (Cohen, March, and Olsen 1972; Chisholm 1995). Boundedly rational actors will, in this perspective, simply employ the rule that is appropriate to or consistent with their sincere definition of the issue or situation. Summarizing these arguments, I offer a *Framing Hypothesis*, according to which actors will strategically define issues so as to "fit" them under relatively favorable procedures. This line of argument also suggests that some substantive amendments to legislation both follow and are consistent with stated procedural preferences.

Strategic issue definition may not suffice to effect favorable procedural outcomes if other actors have opposed procedural preferences. Those procedurally disadvantaged by one way of framing an issue can be expected to offer competing frames (Baumgartner and Jones 1993, 8, 29). Echoing Bach and Smith (1988, 130), "Parliamentary ingenuity will remain a useful complement to, but a poor substitute for, the ultimate currency of success," which in this case is relative bargaining power or a privileged position in the procedural political decision-making sequence. Phrased more generally, issue framing takes place in a broader political and strategic environment, and other means will usually be called for to promote the usage of favorable procedures.

Procedural Coalition Formation

As a strategic process, procedural politics focuses attention on the preferences, power, and expected behaviors of multiple actors. The straightforward proposition that I offer here, then, is that where actors share procedural interests, they will tend to join forces in the joint promotion of rules they prefer to the available alternatives. Coalitional patterns will vary with the available alternatives and actors' preferences over them.[7]

To illustrate the general logic, consider the stylized example in Table 1 Three institutional alternatives $\{X, Y, Z\}$, exist in the system, any two of which might apply in any given situation. The actors $\{A, B, C\}$ have stable and transitively ordered preferences over those alternatives, with the

---

[7] Of course, collective action problems will sometimes attenuate coalitional tendencies. When a group of actors shares procedural preferences but one commits itself to incurring the expected costs of procedural politics, the others can free ride on the first, gaining the influence benefits without the attendant costs.

Theorizing Procedural Politics

Table 1. *Rule Preferences and Procedural Coalitions*

		Actor		
		A	B	C
	X	1	2	3
Rule	Y	3	1	2
	Z	2	3	1

columns showing each actor's preference rankings. For simplicity, assume no free riding.[8] In a situation in which X and Y are potentially applicable, **B** and **C** will form a procedural coalition in favor of rule Y as against actor **A**, which prefers X. Where X and Z are the alternatives, **A** and **B** will form a pro-rule X coalition against **C**, which prefers rule Z. Finally, where Y and Z are at stake, **A** and **C** would join forces to support rule Z against **B** in support of rule Y.

These expectations suggest themselves as a way of fending off the proposition, implicit in the decades-long debate between neofunctionalist and intergovernmentalist students of the EU, that certain classes of actors stand in more-or-less permanent friend or foe relationships. The putative supranational-national split pits the supranational European Commission, Parliament, and Court on the one side against the intergovernmental Council and member states on the other. I do not deny that such coalitions may form, but by emphasizing substantive and procedural preferences, I offer a theoretical expectation of when they will and will not. Sometimes, this pattern will materialize. At other times, quite opposite patterns can emerge, pitting supranational actors against each other, member states against each other and against the Council, joining member states and supranational actors, and so forth. Ideologies toward or attitudes about supranationalism will, by hypothesis, be irrelevant. The point, quite simply, is that there will be no permanent friends or enemies, only procedural interests. I conclude this discussion by offering a *Procedural Coalition Hypothesis*, stating that coalitions will reflect procedural preferences. A traditional alternative would suggest, by contrast, that coalitions will tend to reflect a supranational-intergovernmental split.

---

[8] In Barry's terminology, assume it is better to be powerful than lucky (Barry 1980).

The Effects of Procedural Politics

To this point, I have developed theoretical expectations about when procedural politics will occur and how it is likely to proceed. Turning now to effects, I argue that in any given case, the approach can explain collective procedural choices as the outcome of a game of procedural politics. Yet this might serve for little if procedural politics (and the rules choices that it determines) did not affect important outcomes. In this section I argue further that procedural politics affects important outcomes in at least three ways. First, and most straightforwardly, procedural politics will decrease the efficiency of EU policymaking, as actors devote resources to fighting over rules rather than crafting legislation. Second, policymaking with procedural politics produces substantive outcomes that differ from those occurring without procedural politics, and accordingly differ from those predicted by prevailing accounts of EU legislative politics. Third, procedural politics "feeds back" into higher-order institutional change by providing information about gaps in the prevailing constitutional contract and by raising the opportunity costs of leaving the treaty unamended. I discuss each in turn.

Policymaking Efficiency

First, procedural politics should decrease policymaking efficiency. Time and resources spent bargaining over rules, rather than only within them, can be characterized as deadweight losses resulting from the incompleteness or imperfections of the EU's fundamental contracts, the treaties. The study of EU decision-making efficiency has recently mushroomed (Golub 1999, 2002; König 2001; Schulz and König 2000), and these studies test for the effects of a staggering number of variables on decision-making efficiency. One of the most unexpected findings (Golub 1999) concerns the relative slowdown in decision-making efficiency following the institutional reforms of 1987 (the Single European Act, SEA) and 1993 (the Treaty on European Union, TEU or Maastricht Treaty). Analysts generally ascribe this to the complication of the legislative procedures, most notably through greater inclusion of the European Parliament. This rather mechanically decreases efficiency (here defined as decision-making speed) by interjecting another actor into the policymaking process. I will seek to test a complementary hypothesis, whereby the slowdown in decision-making efficiency derives from the new endogeneity of rules following these same institutional reforms.[9] According to this *Efficiency Hypothesis*, legislation subject to procedural political disputes will take longer to adopt than legislation not subject to such disputes, ceteris paribus. This expectation is not terribly surprising (indeed, it would be surprising to learn that disputes did not slow things down). But it is important, and allows some assessment of the "costs" of procedural politics to legislative actors, and especially to EU member states.

Policy Outcomes

A second set of effects lies in the procedural political determinants of policy outcomes. Three such influences come to mind. First, procedural politics determines the legislative procedures used, and if the "new institutionalism" has taught us anything, it is that such rules influence outcomes. For example, unanimity rules will tend to make policy change difficult and incremental, producing outcomes close to the status quo ante, or even generating gridlock. Lower agreement thresholds (e.g., various majorities) tend to permit sharper policy departures. The point, quite simply, is that by determining the rule used, procedural politics directly influences the outcome produced.

Second, procedural politics can influence legislative outcomes by making possible new log rolls and package deals. In a related way it may modify the dimensionality of the issue space and generate new outcomes on old dimensions. Consider the situation depicted in Figure 6, for example. The model follows the assumptions and parameters of the models in the next chapter, although here the Commission (which enjoys proposal power) is denoted C and the pivotal member state is denoted M. Suppose that in the absence of procedural political considerations the issue space corresponds to a classic Left-Right dimension, depicted in the top panel. Spatial theory predicts the point Y as the one dimensional outcome. In brief, it represents the point closest to the ideal point of the agenda setter (C) that is acceptable (relative to the status quo) to the pivotal actor in the decision-making body (M).

When procedural politics arises, bargaining occurs over two dimensions. The Commission still proposes the policy closest to its ideal point that the pivotal Council member will accept, but that point now corresponds to

---

[9] The endogeneity was new because, as will be documented in Chapter 4, the dearth of institutional alternatives prior to the SEA suppressed the occurrence of procedural politics; after the SEA, actors began engaging in everyday politics with respect to rules.

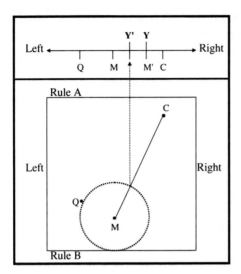

Figure 6 Procedures, Dimensionality, and Legislative Outcomes

Y′ on the Left-Right dimension, even though all other parameters remain constant. The policy difference |Y-Y′| derives exclusively from the addition of a procedural to a substantive political dimension.

Third, procedural politics shapes substantive outcomes to the extent that procedurally motivated issue definitions find expression, via legislative proposals and amendments, in ultimate policy choices. This in turn will vary with the legislative power of the actors promoting alternative issue definitions. The theory predicts systematic variations in the substantive positions of the various actors, as a function of the availability and relative desirability of institutional alternatives. Where the power of those promoting each position is known, substantive outcomes can be more effectively explained.

This claim runs counter to the thrust of most of the burgeoning EU policy analysis literature, which predicts outcomes as a function of power, preferences, and institutionally myopic strategies. Consider again the common claim that the European Parliament favors stringent environmental protection. While remaining agnostic about whether it is fundamentally "green," the present approach can offer predictions about when it will frame issues as if it were, and when it will not do so. The addition of power permits assessment, in a general way, of the differences in outcomes produced by procedural politics. To the extent that the EP is powerful, its procedurally motivated amendments will find expression in policy. Policy may be different because of procedural politics from what it would have been without it.

Institutional Change

Finally, I bridge the existing gap between analyses of constitutional and everyday politics (Wincott 1995; Moravcsik 1995; Sandholtz 1996; Pierson 1996; Rasmussen 2000) by identifying the ways in which procedural politics influences higher-order institutional change – change, that is, in the EU treaties. For Moravcsik, the day-to-day operation of EU institutions does not exert strong feedback effects on subsequent institutional changes. It does so, on the margins, insofar as EU institutions produce material economic effects felt by domestic producer groups, the governments of which then negotiate EU institutional changes in response to their changed demands (see Moravcsik 1998, 490). Preexisting institutions may also matter insofar as they constitute the status quo ante and reversion point to intergovernmental bargaining (Moravcsik 1999b). In general, though, institutional choices, and specifically decisions to pool sovereignty through majority voting in the Council and to delegate it to supranational agents (Commission, Court, and Parliament) reflect a logic of credible commitments, whereby member states seek to cement the bargains that they strike. This is time-specific, and the weight of history should be minimal.

I argue, by contrast, that institutions exhibit much more continuity than might be expected based on the above view. In my account, the connection between everyday politics and long-run institutional change is a direct one. Specifically, I argue that procedural politics *informs* institutional change by identifying gaps in the existing treaty regime and *incites* it by raising the opportunity costs of the constitutional status quo. Procedural politics represents a day-to-day strategic response to, and thus an indicator of, misfit between policy issues and existing institutions. If the EU's institutional architecture represents an intergovernmental contract, issue-structural misfit and the procedural politics that it enables reveal the contract's incompleteness, placing it under strain (Baumgartner and Jones 1993; Baumgartner, Jones, and MacLeod 2000). Procedural politics thus provides information about "gaps" in the existing treaty regime. Member states may predictably respond to such signals by updating their information and negotiating treaty amendments that close those gaps.

As noted above, procedural politics is costly and diverts resources from the efficient pursuit of substantive outcomes that (presumably) originally motivated the creation of EU institutions. These "influence costs" (Milgrom and Roberts 1990) represent deadweight losses to member states. As they rise, so too do the opportunity costs of leaving the EU treaty intact. This is exacerbated to the extent that member states lose procedural political disputes to their supranational agents, thus incurring "agency losses" (Kiewiet and McCubbins 1991, 24–26). Straightforwardly, then, I propose a simple learning and adaptation dynamic whereby procedural political disputes should produce subsequent treaty changes. According to the corresponding *Feedback Hypothesis*, as the frequency of procedural political disputes increases, the likelihood of higher-order institutional change also increases. Corollaries to this emphasize the connections between specific actors' behaviors and specific procedural changes: I expect European Parliament procedural political behavior to correlate with changes in its own future status, and I expect the European Commission to be influential in driving changes to legislative voting rules. These claims distinguish themselves from a null hypothesis closer in spirit to Moravcsik's liberal intergovernmentalism, according to which institutional change responds to variations in member state preferences, bargaining power, and need for credible commitments, and is invariant to day-to-day procedural political disputes.

In sum, attention to procedural politics should improve explanations and understandings of two of the most important sets of outcomes in EU politics, dealing with day-to-day policymaking and "grand bargaining" over the EU's highest-order institutions. It improves the first by problematizing and theorizing the selection of legislative procedures, rather than taking it as given as is currently done. The resulting account redresses the underspecification of existing theories (caused by their failure to consider where rules come from) and their misspecification of the preferences that actors reveal in policymaking and that find expression in legislative outputs. It improves on theories of grand institutional bargaining by showing that higher-order institutional change may not be insulated from the day-to-day operation of EU institutions. Instead, member states respond to procedural politics, in addition to the preferences of domestic producers and their functional institutional needs, in contemplating institutional redesign. Most important, it improves each within an integrated, multiple-level framework that has tended to evade prevailing work. It thus moves beyond policy analysis (comparative politics) approaches and analysis of grand bargaining (international relations) individually, and, inspired by recent historical institutionalist work (Pierson 1996), rigorously theorizes the linkages between them.

Conclusion

In this chapter I have laid out the broad lines of a theory of procedural politics that portrays both higher- and lower-order rules as potential objects of choice and sources of constraint. Departing from basic institutional premises, the overall goal of this chapter has been to think through the conditions under which, the ways in which, and the effects with which procedural politics, defined as everyday politics with respect to rules, occurs. I argue most generally that actors will engage in procedural politics when jurisdictional ambiguity makes available procedures that afford them more influence than the alternatives. When they do decide to target procedures as objects of politics, they interact strategically with others in the system. The ensuing games of procedural politics involve strategic issue definition and procedural coalition formation; they affect rules choices; they influence legislative outcomes; and they inform and incite longer-run and higher-order institutional change. More specific hypotheses are summarized in Table 2.

The approach aims to integrate the disparate insights about institutional choice and constraint at multiple levels of analysis as these are found in the

Table 2. *Summary of Procedural Political Hypotheses*

Ambiguity Hypothesis	As the jurisdictional ambiguity of proposed legislation increases, the likelihood of procedural politics increases.
Influence Maximization Hypothesis	As the influence differences among available alternatives increase, the likelihood of procedural politics increases.
Framing Hypothesis	Actors will strategically define issues so as to "fit" them under relatively favorable procedures.
Procedural Coalition Hypothesis	Coalitions will reflect procedural preferences.
Efficiency Hypothesis	Legislation subject to procedural political disputes will take longer to adopt than legislation not subject to such disputes.
Feedback Hypothesis	As the frequency of procedural political disputes increases, the likelihood of higher-order institutional change also increases.

Note: All hypotheses take ceteris paribus form.

prevailing approaches outlined in the last chapter. It allows for the phenomena that are of interest to each approach – higher-order constraint and/or choice in the case of theories of institutional design and change, lower-order constraint in the case of effects theories – and complements them with an account of institutional selection (synchronic institutional choice). It does so, however, within a common logical framework so that prevailing approaches are coherently reappropriated rather than abandoned or aggregated piecemeal. While thus allowing for and explaining phenomena of prevailing interest, it also seeks to explain "new facts" in the form of institutional selection, procedural political determinants of substantive policy outcomes, and the feedbacks between day-to-day politics and higher-order (and longer-run) institutional change. The resulting account more fully portrays the institutional life cycle linking choice and constraint, at multiple levels of analysis, both at a given time and through the passage of time.

The approach does not try to do everything, however. In particular, its sole emphasis on formal rules leaves unaddressed important issues surrounding informal rules (Farrell and Héritier 2003; Stacey and Rittberger 2003). It posits self-interested, rational actors and offers no leverage on questions of meaning or identity. What is more, it excludes many arguably important players in EU politics – interest groups and subnational authorities, to take two examples – and "reifies" (i.e., treats as unitary) the states and organizations that it does consider. This draws attention away from bureaucratic politics (Peters 1991) and from "multilevel politics" as it is traditionally (geographically) conceived (Marks, Hooghe, 2001). To exclude these issues is not to deny their importance but to make the analysis as tractable as possible. In the end, the evidence will tell whether (or, more likely, to what extent) the approach is a useful guide to understanding politics and policymaking in the European Union, to say nothing of the "nature of the beast" itself and of institutions more generally.

In what follows, I delve more deeply into the substance of procedural politics as it plays itself out in the European Union. Chapter 3 will operationalize, in the EU context, the three premises outlined at the start of this chapter. That is, it will describe the procedural landscape of the European Union and analyze the influence properties of a wide array of EU legislative procedures; specify the preferences of major EU legislative actors over those preferences; and analyze their strategic interaction in playing procedural politics. Chapters 4 through 6 then present a broad array of quantitative and qualitative evidence aimed at testing the expectations derived in this chapter, measuring the extent and impact of procedural politics in the EU,

Theorizing Procedural Politics

and establishing clear causal linkages between hypothesized antecedent and consequent conditions. Chapter 4 works at a broad level of aggregation and is primarily quantitative. This general picture will then be fleshed out in a more detailed way in the case study chapters that follow it, though these, too, are designed to maximize generalizability not only to the universe of EU politics and policymaking, but indeed to the universe of rule-governed political systems.

The European Union as a Procedural System

RULES, PREFERENCES, AND STRATEGIC INTERACTION

William Riker (1980) famously argued that if institutions have effects on things that rational actors care about, then those actors should have preferences over institutions and should be prepared to engage in politics with respect to them. The preceding chapter developed a theory that would extend this insight from the U.S. Congress, where it has been most consistently pursued, to the European Union, where it should be no less true (and should perhaps be more so). It developed the argument that everyday politics with respect to rules – "procedural politics" – responds systematically to the opportunities and incentives facing the actors in any political system. More specifically, procedural politics involves strategic interaction over rules and varies with both the jurisdictional ambiguity of issues and the nature (influence properties) of procedural alternatives. These conditions in place, it occurs by predictable means (strategic issue framing and coalition formation) and with predictable effects (on rules choices, on policymaking efficiency and outcomes, and on long-run institutional change). It represents one aspect of a complete institutional life cycle the totality of which must be accounted for if institutions and their effects are to be properly understood.

This chapter begins the process of systematically applying the argument to the European Union. Specifically, it fleshes out, in the EU context, the three premises underpinning the analysis. The premise that "institutions matter" demands description of the institutional landscape and analysis of the influence and outcome properties of EU legislative procedures, which is undertaken in the first part of this chapter. The premise that "actors have derived preferences over rules" demands an analysis of the procedural preferences of key legislative actors in the EU system, which forms the second part of this chapter. The premise that the promotion of procedural preferences involves strategic interaction demands game-theoretic analysis of EU procedural choice, which is undertaken in the third part of this chapter. The final section lays the groundwork for the empirical tests in Chapters 4 through 6.

"Institutions Matter": EU Legislative Procedures and Their Effects

That institutions "matter" is a truism. Specifying precisely how they matter is a far more important and difficult task, and it is one that logically precedes any rationalist discussion of institutional choice. Here I deploy a series of models aimed at explaining precisely how EU legislative procedures matter. I begin by describing the relevant institutional landscape in the European Union, focusing on the nine legislative procedures (lower-order institutions) most commonly used during the pivotal decade (1987–1997) primarily studied here. I then proceed to analyze their influence and outcome properties on the basis of simple spatial models, which are included in Appendix 3.A, at the end of the chapter.

Constitutional and Legislative System

First, a word of introduction to the European Union constitutional architecture and legislative process: the EU's constitutional system is one of "attributed competencies." This system operates at two levels. At the most general level, the EU treaty delimits the legitimate sphere of EU action and reserves for the constituent member states all powers not explicitly conferred on the EU. At a more specific level, each treaty article empowering action in a given sphere (known as the "legal basis" for such action) specifies the rule (legislative procedure) that will be used in making policy in that area. For example, the legal bases relevant to the making of agricultural, environmental, and taxation policies all employ different legislative procedures, and these differ in the input and influence they afford the main actors and in the outcomes they tend to produce. Every legislative proposal must specify a legal basis and thereby a legislative procedure. While nominally a question of legal certainty, legal basis choices proxy for procedural (lower level institutional) choices, and they are acutely political. Indeed, because it defines the respective powers of the EU and its components on the one hand and the member states on the other, the choice of legal basis has been said to represent "the pivot on which the balance of federalism within the European [Union] turns" (Lenaerts 1992, 28).

The main legislative actors are the European Commission, the European Parliament (EP), and the Council of Ministers. The European Court of Justice, like all high courts, stands formally outside of, but strongly influences, the legislative process (Stone Sweet 2000). The European Commission functions as the EU's executive arm. It enjoys responsibility for proposing legislation and, to some extent, for administering it. The European Parliament, directly elected since 1979, increasingly resembles the lower house of a bicameral legislature (Tsebelis and Money 1997; Tsebelis and Garrett 2000). For many years it enjoyed only nonbinding opinion giving and some delaying power, but it is becoming increasingly powerful (Kreppel 1999, 2002a, 2002b). The Council of Ministers functions roughly as the upper chamber of the EU legislature, though parts of it also fulfill important executive functions. At its apex are different functional configurations of ministers from national governments. Below them stands "COREPER," the committee of permanent representatives (ambassadors) to the EU, who perpetually bargain over EU legislation. Underpinning the system is "the Council machinery," including not only its secretariat but also a complex network of expert committees made up of national and European officials. Overarching it is "the presidency," the system whereby each country leads the Council on a six-month rotating basis. The Council has always enjoyed the power finally to adopt legislation, although increasingly it shares this power (i.e., co-legislates) with the EP.

The precise unfolding of the legislative process depends upon the legislative procedure in use, which itself derives from the legal basis (enabling provision of the EU treaty or secondary law) chosen. Making general statements about this process necessitates trimming away some of the EU's considerable procedural complexity. Accordingly, I will limit my attention to the European Community "pillar" of the three-pillar European Union (EU), and I will focus on just two important dimensions of procedural variation: the role of the European Parliament and the voting rule in the Council. This leads me to focus on only a fraction of the staggering number of possible procedures, but allows me to examine those that have governed the making of the overwhelming majority of EU secondary law. In short, I include all of the main legislative procedures and exclude obscure variants that, in most cases, have never been used, and the arguments developed here generalize within and across pillars and to other procedures and time periods (treaty regimes).[1]

All procedures to be examined, then, share two important elements. First, the European Commission enjoys monopoly proposal power and can withdraw its proposals at any time. It "keeps the gates," enjoying both ex ante and, in effect, ex post vetoes on changes to the status quo.[2] Second, under all procedures, member states may adopt germane amendments to Commission proposals, but they can only do so unanimously. This includes the right to amend the legal basis of the proposal and possibly thereby the legislative procedure in use. Beyond these universal elements, legislative procedures vary along several dimensions, including which actor has the right of legislative initiative, the nature of European Parliament involvement, and the voting rule in the Council. With respect to legislative initiative, I consider only those procedures that involve a Commission proposal, since this has been the case for the huge preponderance of EU legislation adopted since 1958. Parliamentary involvement will be discussed below, in the context of each procedure.

A few general words about Council voting rules: there are three generally used decision thresholds in the Council. When unanimity in the Council is required, each member state wields a veto, but abstentions do not prevent passage (i.e., they are equivalent to a vote in favor). Simple majority, as the name implies, demands only a numerical majority of member states. When the Council votes by "qualified majority," each member state wields a number of votes roughly as a function of its population. Under the twenty-five-member EU (EU25), operative at the time of this writing, 124 votes are distributed among the member states. A "qualified majority" of 88 votes

---

[1] Fuller treatments of procedural complexity are offered in CEC 1995, Annex 8, and European Convention Secretariat, document CONV 216/02, 24 July 2002 (URL *http://register.consilium.eu.int/pdf/en/02/cv00/00216en2.pdf* last consulted 10 July 2003). I follow the methodology of the latter document in focusing on procedures according to variations in EP role and Council voting where the Commission enjoys monopoly proposal power. This focus captures by far the most important and frequently used procedures.

[2] This characterization is controversial. The Council and Parliament can request, but not compel, the Commission to table proposals. The Commission therefore retains ex ante (gatekeeping) control over the agenda. Its effective ex post veto stems from the fact that it can withdraw legislative proposals at any time, even just before the Council votes. This latter interpretation is most controversial with respect to the codecision procedure. Steunenberg (1994), Curtin (1993, 42 n. 102), and others offer interpretations similar to mine, whereas Garrett and Tsebelis (1996, 251–252; Garrett 1995a), Crombez (2001, 121, fn. 10), and others disagree.

passes a law, a "blocking minority" of 37 defeats it. Table 3 charts the evolution of the EU's qualified majority system from 1958. Throughout most of the EU's history, passing legislation under simple majority has been at least as easy as passing it under qualified majority, and, assuming even slightly fluid coalitions, usually easier.[3]

Procedural Landscape

I turn now to a description and assessment of nine EU legislative procedures. Collectively, these procedures have governed the making of almost all binding secondary EU legislation since the founding. I begin with those that are relatively simple (i.e., involve few steps), turning to more complicated rules in the next section. In all cases, I relegate more technical materials to Appendix 3.A following the body of the chapter.

Simple Procedures

Facultative Consultation (AVF).[4] Facultative consultation (in French, *avis facultatif*) is the simplest procedure. In it, the Commission tables a proposal that the Council can amend (by unanimity) and adopt (by one of the three available voting rules: simple majority, qualified majority, or unanimity). The procedure wholly excludes the Parliament unless the Council decides otherwise, though even when the Council so decides the EP is limited to giving nonbinding (advisory) opinions. Three variants correspond to the different voting rules in the Council. The unanimity variant (AVFU) arises most frequently in the Euratom Treaty, although some secondary acts require it for the adoption of subsequent implementing legislation. The qualified majority variant (AVFQ) finds most frequent use in the context of the common commercial policy and customs union, and for this reason constitutes the single most-used procedure. Finally, the rarely used simple majority variant (AVFS) arises when cited treaty provisions do not

---

[3] During most of the history of the EU a quite extreme large-small split has been required to make the two voting rules equivalent in this respect. Absent such stark splits (i.e., given even a small degree of coalitional fluidity), decisions have been more easily adopted under simple majority.

[4] I will generally refer to procedures with a four-letter symbol, the first three of which identify the base procedure (as defined by Parliamentary involvement) and the last of which identifies the voting rule in the Council (simple majority [S], qualified majority [Q], or unanimity [U]).

The European Union as a Procedural System

Table 3. *Votes in the EU Council of Ministers*

Member State	1958–1972 (6)	1973–1980 (9)	1981–1985 (10)	1986–1994 (12)	1995–4/30/2004 (15)	5/1/2004–10/31/2004 (25)	11/1/2004–[a] (25)
Belgium	2	5	5	5	5	5	12
Netherlands	2	5	5	5	5	5	13
Luxembourg	1	2	2	2	2	2	4
France	4	10	10	10	10	10	29
Germany	4	10	10	10	10	10	29
Italy	4	10	10	10	10	10	29
Denmark	—	3	3	3	3	3	7
Ireland	—	3	3	3	3	3	7
United Kingdom	—	10	10	10	10	10	29
Greece	—	—	5	5	5	5	12
Portugal	—	—	—	5	5	5	12
Spain	—	—	—	8	8	8	27
Austria	—	—	—	—	4	4	10
Finland	—	—	—	—	3	3	7
Sweden	—	—	—	—	4	4	10
Poland	—	—	—	—	—	8	27
Czech Republic	—	—	—	—	—	5	12
Hungary	—	—	—	—	—	5	12
Slovakia	—	—	—	—	—	3	7
Lithuania	—	—	—	—	—	3	7
Latvia	—	—	—	—	—	3	4
Slovenia	—	—	—	—	—	3	4
Estonia	—	—	—	—	—	3	4
Cyprus	—	—	—	—	—	2	4
Malta	—	—	—	—	—	2	3
TOTAL VOTES	17	58	63	76	87	124	321
Qualified Majority	12	41	45	54	62[b]	88	232
(as % total votes)	70.6%	70.7%	71.4%	71.1%	71.3%	71.0%	72.3%
Blocking Minority	6	18	19	23	26	37	90
(as % total votes)	35.3%	31.0%	30.2%	30.3%	29.9%	29.8%	28.0%

[a] The Draft Constitution of June 2003 would maintain this distribution until 1 November 2009.
[b] Plus majority of member states, subject to additional verification of 62% of EU population.

specify a voting rule in the Council.[5] It has been used for vocational training measures and legislation pertaining to statistics.

Consultation (CNS). The consultation procedure closely resembles *avis facultatif*: "the Commission proposes and the Council disposes." It differs in that under consultation, the Council cannot adopt legislation until it has received the (nonbinding) opinion of the European Parliament.[6] The EP has skillfully parlayed this obligation into a modicum of influence under the procedure, which it exercises by sending legislation back to committee (failing to issue its opinion), thereby threatening an impatient Commission and Council with delay (Nicoll 1988; Baziadoly 1992). Varela also identifies nonnegligible EP power under the procedure to the extent that it allows the EP to acquire and transmit information at low cost (Varela 2000). In practice, however, the Council can, and often does, ignore the EP's opinion under the consultation procedure. In any case, since neither time nor information figure into the spatial models that I develop in Appendix 3.A, my analysis ignores these potential elements of EP influence.

The consultation procedure enjoys a long pedigree. Its qualified majority variant (CNSQ) has long governed agricultural policymaking (making it a very well used procedure) and has been used for transport and other policy areas. Its unanimity variant (CNSU) has found use, among others, in the areas of indirect taxation, approximation of national laws, and social security legislation as well as for adoption of measures not specifically provided for in the treaty (article 308). There is no simple majority variant. Whatever the voting rule, I ignore the Parliament and model CNS (as AVF) procedures as two-stage games in which the Commission proposes and the Council disposes (amends and/or adopts).

Assent (AVC). Consider now the assent procedure (in French, *avis conforme*). The 1987 Single European Act (SEA) established this procedure for association agreements with third countries and the admission of new member states to the EU. Subsequent treaty revisions have extended it to, among other areas, citizenship provisions, aspects of the cohesion funds, the establishment of a uniform electoral procedure for the EP, and certain international agreements. In this procedure, the Commission proposes, the

---

[5] Article 205 (ex article 148) of the treaty establishes that the Council "shall act by a majority of its members" unless otherwise provided for.

[6] The Court of Justice clarified this obligation in the famous "Isoglucose" judgments of 1980. See Case 138/79, *Roquette Frères v. Council* [1980] ECR 333 and Case 139/79, *Maizena v. Council* [1980] ECR 393. Kirchner and Williams (1983) provide a clear assessment.

Council decides by unanimity[7] (thus, AVCU), and the European Parliament can reject or accept (assent to) the act by voting "up or down," that is, with no right of amendment. Assent is thus a three-stage game: the Commission proposes, the Council decides, and the EP assents (or fails to assent).

In considering all of these simple procedures, the spatial models derived in Appendix 3.A, at the end of this chapter, support three conclusions. First, with unanimity in the Council, the Commission and all member states must prefer change in the same direction away from the status quo if legislation is to be proposed and enacted. Under the assent (AVCU) procedure, the Parliament must also be on that side of the status quo. Under majority procedures, by contrast, the Commission and some fraction of Council members can overcome resistance by as many as half of the total number of member states. Majority voting can make some member states absolutely worse than they would have been under the status quo ante. Second, the Parliament cannot formally affect policies under any of these procedures except when it prefers the status quo to any otherwise achievable outcome under the AVCU procedure, in which case it can veto legislation and uphold the status quo. Under any other simple procedure, the EP can be made absolutely worse off. Third, the range of winning proposals (and the extent of Commission agenda-setting power) relates inversely to the number of players whose agreement is needed to change the status quo. Under unanimity, all member states must agree to a change, and the ideal point of the most reluctant Council member limits the range of feasible outcomes. Under QMV, a usually larger fraction of member states must agree to any change in the status quo, and the ideal point of a more centrist state establishes the range of feasible outcomes. Simple majority voting in the Council generally amplifies these effects.

Complex Procedures

Cooperation. The 1987 Single European Act (SEA) introduced the cooperation procedure (SYNQ, from the Greek for cooperation) into several articles of the treaty, dealing with the internal market, worker health and safety, and the free movement of labor and services. Maastricht removed it from some of these areas but extended it to various aspects of transport, Economic and Monetary Union (EMU), social policy (such as the European

---

[7] Maastricht article 106(5) did create a QMV variant of the assent procedure, but it has never been used.

Social Fund and professional training), research, environmental policy, and development cooperation. It also introduced a modified version of cooperation in the so-called social protocol, which until 1997 excluded the United Kingdom. The Amsterdam Treaty effectively eliminated the cooperation procedure in favor of codecision, and there and in the Nice Treaty it remains in force for only a few provisions on Economic and Monetary Union (EMU).

The cooperation procedure has generated a decade of controversial and productive theorizing and empirical analysis (see Bieber 1992; Corbett 1989; Corbett and Schmuck 1992; Crombez 1996; Earnshaw and Judge 1997; Fitzmaurice 1988; Kreppel 1999; Lodge 1987; Moser 1996, 1997a; Tsebelis 1994, 1996; Tsebelis and Kalandrakis 1999; König and Pöter 2001). Following Steunenberg, I model the cooperation procedure as a potentially six-stage complete information game. The first three steps resemble the QMV consultation procedure: (1) the Commission proposes, (2) Parliament considers the legislation and gives its opinion, with the Commission possibly amending its proposal, and (3) the Council amends and/or adopts a policy, which in this procedure is called its "common position." The Parliament (4) then considers the common position in its second reading. It faces three options. If it accepts the common position, it returns the legislation to the Council, which adopts the act. If it rejects the common position, the Council can unanimously override this "rejection;" if the Council fails to do so, the measure lapses. If the EP offers amendments to the common position, the Commission (5) decides whether or not to accept them. Those that it accepts can be adopted by QMV in the Council (6) or rejected by unanimity. Those EP amendments that the Commission does not accept can be unanimously taken up by the Council and included in the final legislation.

The literature, and the analysis in the Appendix (at the end of the chapter) derived from it, suggests that the cooperation procedure afforded the Parliament potentially meaningful influence in the legislative process. Unlike other QMV procedures, the EP could sometimes prevent a situation in which it was made worse off by changes to the status quo. More constructively, the EP could sometimes obtain its own most preferred policy. The Commission would, over many preference configurations, anticipate EP preferences and modify its proposals accordingly. Overall, then, when compared to other QMV procedures, cooperation produced "a shift in power in favor of the European Parliament. Parliament may limit, at least in some cases, the agenda-setting power of the Commission," which "to some extent reduces the influence of the Commission on the final outcome" (Steunenberg 1994, 654).

Codecision. The codecision procedure, also much analyzed, came about with the 1993 Maastricht Treaty. The 1999 Amsterdam Treaty simplified and extended it, and the 2003 Nice Treaty extended this simplified version (known as "codecision II") yet again. I focus my attention on the Maastricht procedure, now known as codecision I, because it operated during the period analyzed empirically in Chapters 4 through 6.[8] Codecision with QMV in the Council (CODQ) replaced the cooperation procedure for internal market and free movement provisions. Maastricht applied it for the first time to certain areas of vocational training, public health, consumer protection, trans-European networks, and environmental action programs. Both the Amsterdam and Nice Treaties substantially extended the range of the procedure, such that it is very widely applicable, almost the general rule for substantial legislation. Some articles, for example dealing with culture and the multi-annual research program, establish a variant (CODU) in which the Council must act by unanimity throughout the procedure.

The QMV codecision procedure resembles cooperation in its early stages: Commission proposal, EP opinion, modified Commission proposal, Council common position, and EP second reading. (I will not address CODU here, but the reader can simply substitute unanimity for Council QMV throughout the procedure.) Again, the EP faces three options at second reading: to approve, amend, or reject the common position. If it approves the common position, a qualified majority of the Council can then pass it into law. If Parliament amends the common position, and the Commission and a qualified majority of the Council approve of those amendments, the common position so amended becomes law. Amendments that the Commission does not approve require unanimity for adoption in the Council. If achieved, the measure (common position plus EP amendments) passes. If the Council fails to adopt even a single EP amendment, or if the EP exercises its third option and rejects the common position, a conciliation committee is convened.

In conciliation, the Commission plays a mediating role while an equal number of representatives of the Parliament and Council bargain bilaterally

---

[8] Steunenberg (1997, 1998), Steunenberg and Dimitrova (1999), and Hix (1999a) analyze the 1996–1997 debate over reforming codecision. Crombez (2000, 2001), Hix (1999a), and Tsebelis and Garrett (2000, 2001) have analyzed the resulting "codecision II" procedure in the Amsterdam Treaty. Dashwood (2001), Tsebelis and Yataganas (2002) and Moberg (2002) analyze decision-making provisions of the Nice Treaty. See also Tsebelis 2002.

Procedural Politics

in search of a compromise. Conciliation might take one of two paths. If a qualified majority of the Council delegation and a simple majority of the EP delegation approve a joint text, it returns to both houses for consideration. If a qualified majority of the Council and an absolute majority of the EP approve the joint text, it becomes law. If both bodies do not approve the joint text, the measure dies. If, by contrast, conciliation fails and no joint text is approved, a third reading commences and proposal power reverts to the Council. It can propose its earlier common position plus any EP amendments to the Parliament, which can either veto the proposal by an absolute majority (the bill thereby lapsing) or fail to veto it, in which case this last Council proposal becomes law. This third reading was suppressed at Amsterdam, with the resulting "codecision II" procedure both much simpler and much more favorable to the Parliament than its Maastricht predecessor had been.

How did codecision I affect power and outcomes? All analysts seem to agree that the Commission enjoys less influence under codecision (I or II) than it did under cooperation. Most important, provisions for conciliation deprive the Commission of most of its agenda power, since the EP and Council can make modifications without Commission approval.[9] A consensus also exists that absent other changes, the EP's absolute veto under codecision would increase its power relative to cooperation (Crombez 1997a; Scully 1997a, 1997b; Moser 1997b; Tsebelis 1997). Some have argued, however, that the EP was worse off under codecision I than it had been under cooperation, because it traded its meaningful conditional agenda-setting power under cooperation for an unwieldy veto under codecision (Garrett 1995a; Garrett and Tsebelis 1996, 2001; Tsebelis 1997; Tsebelis and Garrett 2000). Most others (cited above; see also Varela 1999) have strongly disputed this contention.

Two related disagreements, both of which concern bargaining in the Council, seem to drive this dispute. First, Tsebelis and Garrett grant the QMV pivot greater power in intra-Council bargaining than do Moser, Scully, and others, and the former place greater emphasis on unanimously achievable alternatives to Commission proposals than do the latter.[10] The

---

[9] The debate continues, however, as to whether the Commission can still withdraw its proposals at this stage. If the situation ever arises, the Court will likely be called on to make this determination.

[10] In particular, Tsebelis and Garrett model intra-Council bargaining as a two-stage game in which amendments are offered in the first stage and voted unanimously against the status quo in the second. I believe that the Commission proposal remains "on the table" while

second point of disagreement, since Amsterdam a purely academic question, revolves around the Council's rights under the vaguely drafted (and now deleted) article 189b(6) of the Maastricht Treaty. While all agree that the Council made a "take-it-or-leave-it" offer to the Parliament when conciliation failed, they disagree on what this offer could look like. Some interpret Council discretion under this article expansively and suggest that a qualified majority of the Council could offer any of an infinite number of proposals to the EP (Tsebelis 1997; Garrett and Tsebelis 1998). Others read the article more restrictively, and suggest that the Council could only re-offer its earlier common position (which would have been influenced by EP/Commission agenda power earlier in the game) or offer the common position plus at least some whole EP amendments. Under the latter interpretation, adopted here, the EP could never do worse under codecision than under cooperation, and it could sometimes do better (Moser 1997b).[11]

Summary

Rather than summarizing all nine of the procedures considered, I offer a few general points. The models provide a specific way of determining how and to what extent institutions matter, offering particular leverage on actors' relative power and the spatial location of legislative outcomes. This is a particular way of analyzing institutions that is not entirely innocent in terms of the questions that it can address and the answers to them it can provide. I focus on formal properties of institutions, essentially ignoring informal institutional dynamics (Farrell and Héritier 2003; Stacey and Rittberger 2003). Further, even from the set of formal institutional properties, I select only those that are directly relevant to influence and outcomes and that form part of the core focus of the existing literature. Specifically, I focus on the roles of the European Commission, European Parliament, and Council of Ministers, ignoring generally secondary players such as the Economic

---

member states are considering amendments and is voted last against the status quo. In this latter game, using the standard preference configurations (Commission and at least one member state to the right of the QMV pivot's indifference point to the status quo), at least one member state (call it M_r, as in Appendix 3.A) would reject all proposed amendments in favor of the Commission proposal, which a qualified majority could accept in a paired contest against the status quo.

[11] Empirical tests by Kreppel (1999, 2002b) and Tsebelis *et al.* (2002) confirm this analytic conclusion.

and Social Committee or Committee of the Regions, and I treat all actors as rational and unitary rather than unpacking their full internal complexity. These limitations reflect a conscious choice to privilege parsimony over descriptive accuracy.

Procedural Preferences

This section uses the foregoing analysis of institutional effects to construct procedural preference rankings for each legislative actor in the EU. The assumption that actors seek to maximize their influence in the policymaking process and prefer procedures giving them more influence to those giving them less drives this exercise.

Before starting, this influence maximization assumption bears some discussion. Any actor's motivations can be of potentially infinite complexity. Political party specialists identify three widely used assumptions about actor motivations, whereby actors pursue either policy (public policy outcomes), office (power or influence), or votes (responsiveness to constituents or to mandate). The best treatment of this question (Müller and Strøm 1999) concludes that actor motivations are generally so complex that any single-stranded assumption will represent a simplification. For the sake of simplicity and clarity, I assume that actors are motivated by the pursuit of political power (influence). There are several reasons for this choice. First, it is the most general assumption, partly subsuming policy-seeking behavior (since influence can be used to affect outcomes) and applying to all actors regardless of the existence or strength of an electoral connection with voters. Second, formal power varies primarily by procedure, while both policy- and vote-seeking motivations will vary on a case-by-case basis (e.g., at the level of individual bills and laws). Third, this assumption is the most overtly political, and thus disciplinarily distinct: "were we assigning key variables among the social sciences," Robert Goodin has argued, "the key variable within political science would be 'power'" (Goodin 1996a, 15). Fourth and finally, one measure of the worth of any assumption is its ability to generate testable hypotheses that perform well empirically (Friedman 1953). The wisdom of this choice, in short, will be proven in the empirical pudding.

That said, the influence maximization assumption is not without its problems. Three difficulties, all having to do with possible tensions between substantive preferences and preferences for influence, stand out. First, substantive preferences may generate indifference to institutional alternatives, where the latter produce similar policy outcomes.[12] Second, more strongly, in any given case an actor's substantive preferences can, at least in the short run, cut against maximizing its abstract "influence" as conceived here. For example, while in the abstract – that is, over a large number of cases and preference configurations – the Commission may benefit from majority rules, in a specific case its ideal point may lie close to the status quo, rendering unanimity more attractive. Finally, in some real-world cases, actors' procedural preferences may be unrelated to their own influence. If it is better to be lucky than powerful (Barry 1980) – that is, if actors can achieve their goals regardless of their own direct influence, perhaps by relying on the influence of others who share their preferences – then they will not systematically prefer rules giving them more influence to rules giving them less.

Given these limitations, the influence maximization assumption will generate some incorrect predictions. Yet, rather than try to modify my own expectations to render them safe from empirical disconfirmation, I take the opposite approach. I retain a clear assumption of influence maximization and derive falsifiable empirical expectations from it. I try to capture fundamental motivations in the empirical analysis. The assumption and the propositions derived from it may very well prove wrong. But it seems preferable to see a clear prediction falsified than a fuzzy prediction "confirmed."

Auxiliary Assumptions

Because the spatial models generate similar predictions about power and outcomes across many procedures and preference configurations, I deploy several interconnected auxiliary assumptions to generate strict procedural preference orderings – that is, orderings in which actors never find themselves indifferent as between two alternatives. With some variation, these assumptions reasonably approximate the reality of EU politics and policymaking.

1. *Participation*. Holding influence constant, the Parliament prefers to participate more rather than less in the legislative process.

---

[12] That is, there are likely to be many situations wherein different procedures produce outcomes that are sufficiently similar that actors would not have strong procedural preferences based on outcome-differences alone.

Since 1979, European citizens have directly elected their members of the European Parliament (MEPs). The EP thus sees itself as the embodiment of public participation in EU affairs and the guarantor of the EU's popular legitimacy (such as it is). The participation assumption intends to capture this element of the EP's utility function: it should intrinsically value participation, even absent discernible impact on substantive outcomes.[13] More pragmatically, the assumption is both intuitive and useful. It permits differentiation between the *avis facultatif* procedures, in which the EP is not even asked for an opinion, and the consultation procedures, in which it is. This is particularly important since, in formal terms, the EP cannot affect equilibrium outcomes (i.e., it is powerless) under either procedure. With different roles in the Community system and different sources of legitimation, neither the Commission nor the Council necessarily shares this intrinsic desire to participate in the policymaking process.

2. *Indirect influence.* Holding their own influence and participation constant, the Parliament and Council prefer procedures favoring the Commission to procedures favoring each other.

While both the Council and Parliament enjoy important (if imperfect) leverage over the Commission, they lack it vis-à-vis each other. All other things being equal, they prefer to empower the agent that they can control (the Commission) rather than the co-principal that they cannot (i.e., each other). The European Commission exists and serves with the indulgence of the member states, which thereby gain an important source of control over it. As the agent of the member states, the Commission must, within some range of discretion, attend to the preferences of its principals (Crombez 1997b; Hug 1997, 2003; Franchino 2000, 2002; Pollack 1997, 2003). The Commission also serves at the pleasure of the Parliament, which in 1999 effectively wielded its long-standing power to censure the Commission (see generally Wright 1998). "The Commission," according to a leading legal text, "is accountable to the Parliament for its part in decisionmaking by the Council.... Thus the Parliament has an important instrument at its disposal in order to influence such decision-making, to the extent to which the Commission's role therein is substantial" (Kapteyn and VerLoren van Themaat 1998, 440). Neither Parliament nor Council can control each

---

[13] Although this differs from the argument made by Varela (2000), it captures his essential insight, which is that information transmission is fundamentally important to a would-be representative legislature.

other, however. The EP directly serves EU citizens and cannot accurately be seen as the agent of the member states (Pollack 1997). National ministers in the Council also serve citizens (albeit indirectly in the EU context) as elected members of their national parliaments and, from there, appointed members of national governments. The EP can exert no real control over them.

3. *Economy.* Without prejudice to the indirect influence assumption, and holding their own influence and participation constant, actors prefer the most direct route to achieving desired outcomes. Subject to the above conditions, they thus prefer procedures that involve the fewest steps and the least influence for others.

This represents the most heroic of the three auxiliary assumptions. All other things being equal, actors prefer the most direct and least costly route to the outcomes they desire. Additional legislative steps are not preferred except to the extent that they increase influence. This, in turn, implies that actors do not intrinsically value deliberation and that they seek to make policy rather than block it or take positions. Despite these imperfections, the economy assumption again bears fruit in permitting specification of strict preference rankings whereas the unadulterated influence maximization assumption does not. It works especially well for the European Commission, one of the "primary institutional interests" of which "is to have its proposals adopted, and as rapidly as possible" (Golub 1997, 16–17). Here, as before, it seems preferable to generate a risky proposition and subject it to the possibility of falsification than to derive fuzzy propositions capable of accommodating any observation.

In conjunction with the models, then, these auxiliary assumptions permit derivation of strict procedural preference rankings for each actor. After summarizing how each procedure affects each actor, I specify these rankings below. I then develop, in part four of the chapter, an abstract game of institutional choice in which procedural preferences play a crucial role.

Preference Rankings

European Commission. The simple- and qualified-majority (QMV) facultative consultation (AVF) procedures (AVFS and AVFQ) represent the best and second-best procedures from the Commission's point of view because under them it enjoys broad agenda-setting power without having to worry about, or risk delay by, the Parliament. QMV consultation (CNSQ) follows quite closely, inviting minor EP involvement and retaining all of the Commission's agenda powers. The cooperation procedure (SYNQ) limits its agenda power somewhat and introduces additional legislative stages, so it is somewhat less desirable than the simpler QMV procedures. QMV codecision (CODQ) represents the least desirable of the QMV procedures because it limits Commission agenda power even further and uneconomically complicates the legislative process. Unanimity procedures consistently afford the Commission less influence. Of these, AVFU is the most economical, followed closely by CNSU. Assent (AVCU) introduces the possibility of a Parliamentary veto, which further truncates the range of feasible proposals. Unanimous codecision (CODU) is the worst procedure for the Commission, doubly reducing the range of feasible proposals and increasing the number of steps between Commission proposal and legislative outcome.

European Parliament. QMV codecision (CODQ) affords the EP the most influence and is thus, by assumption, its most preferred procedure. The Parliament always does at least as well under this as under any other procedure, with the added protection of an airtight veto over undesirable changes to the status quo. Empirical work on EP success under codecision supports this analytical conclusion (Tsebelis et al. 2002; Kreppel 1999, 2002b). Assessing the relative desirability of the cooperation procedure (SYNQ) and unanimous codecision (CODU) poses problems. While SYNQ increases the range of outcomes that the EP can effect, CODU grants it an absolute veto. If, over a large number of cases in a large number of policy areas, member state preferences are normally distributed, it will enjoy the extended range of influence far more than the circumscribed chance of wielding a veto. This applies a fortiori to the extent that the EP has "progressive" preferences (i.e., usually seeks substantial movement away from the status quo), which is the reasonable operative assumption in most of the literature (Garrett 1995a).[14] These considerations militate in favor of broader influence and conditional veto (SYNQ) over narrower influence and firmer veto (CODU). The assent procedure (AVCU) resembles CODU but allows extremely circumscribed EP participation. Moving down the list, the EP should favor QMV consultation (CNSQ) to unanimous consultation

[14] See, however, Bednar, Ferejohn, and Garrett (1996), who speculate that a more representative EP (i.e., one with preferences closer to those of its constituents) would cease to exhibit such strongly pro-integration preferences.

(CNSU). Both allow it minimally to participate but the former affords it greater indirect influence via the expanded agenda power of the European Commission. Simple majority, qualified majority, and unanimous facultative consultation (AVFS, AVFQ, and AVFU) round out the EP's rankings, differentiated only by the indirect influence assumption.

Council. Deriving preference rankings for the Council poses considerable problems because it is composed of numerous member states with potentially divergent preferences. Of the three main legislative actors (Parliament, Commission, and Council), it makes the least sense to talk about the institutional interests of the Council as such. As a general matter, and working at the level of the individual member states – rather than the Council as a whole, the notion of derived institutional preferences suggests that reluctant member states (i.e., those whose ideal points lie close to the status quo) should favor unanimity procedures and median or revisionist states should favor QMV. This suggests that procedural preferences need to be analyzed on a case-by-case basis for each member state. Political economists offer fruitful ways of tackling this problem (Garrett 1992; Lange 1993; Sprinz and Vaahtoranta 1994; Moravcsik 1997, 1998). For current purposes, however, they prove unwieldy. For any moderately large number of cases, proposal- or sector-specific member state–level preference data will generally be lacking.

What, then, can we expect the Council to prefer? Soft generalizations and one analytical condition are of assistance in cutting into this question. The soft generalizations boil down to the following: the Council prefers, wherever it can, to act by unanimity. Rational choice theorists have dealt at length with the general conditions under which political actors may seek to form such "oversized coalitions" (including, in the extreme, "coalitions of the whole") (Weingast 1979; Shepsle and Weingast 1981; Carrubba and Volden 2001). In the EU case, member states exhibit extreme reluctance to "minoritize" (i.e., outvote) their fellows. This may be the result of a "consensus culture" (Golub 1997). It might result from the fact that Council interactions are infinitely iterated, or that member states have differing preference intensities over linked issues, and tit-for-tat or reciprocity strategies may be in effect. In short, member states realize that in the course of Council interactions over myriad issues, they may find themselves potentially outvoted in the future or on linked issues, and so they avoid outvoting reluctant partners in the hope of receiving reciprocal deference in related interactions.[15] While this fails to explain the many cases in which member states do outvote each other (even on tremendously sensitive issues) it does suggest a general tendency derived independently of the evidence adduced in the chapters that follow. And, as data on Council decision making become available, this generalization becomes less soft and better established (Mattila and Lane 2001).

It also makes sense on analytical grounds to suspect that whatever its own or its members' "true" preferences, when procedural political disputes occur the Council will tend to *reveal* a preference for unanimity over QMV procedures. This insight derives from the constitutionally determined sequence and structure of EU decision making, and in particular the respective roles of the Commission (which proposes) and the Council (which decides). Suppose that the Commission, which enjoys monopoly proposal power, proposes a majority voting procedure, as the models suggest that it should seek to do. When member state preferences are even moderately heterogeneous, such that at least one member state lies sufficiently far from the most reluctant member state,[16] the Council cannot effect a change of voting rule. Knowing that a change to unanimity would lead to outcomes further away from its ideal point, the right-most member would not support it. However, if member state preferences are homogeneous, or if issues are linked, they may be able to obtain the unanimity necessary to change the procedure proposed by the Commission. Intuitively, when disputes occur, the Council will face a majority voting proposal. Council changes must be unanimously agreeable and presumably will tend in the direction of unanimity procedures. Whatever its true preferences, then, when rules disputes occur the Council will generally reveal a preference for unanimity over QMV procedures.[17]

---

[15] When asked why a member state interested in moving away from the status quo would agree to a change in legal basis such that unanimity would be required, a Council Legal Service official replied, "On any particular file, there is unequal interest.... There is a sense that one needs to help a member state with difficulty, so that when the time comes, they can call in the favor. If they have no particular axe to grind, they don't mind. They simply say, 'I'll be flexible on this point, but when the time comes, I'll want reciprocity'" (Interview, Brussels, 2 March 1999).

[16] Formally, where at least one M_i (say, M_r) exists such that, for a QMV outcome X, $M_r - M_u(Q) > M_r - X$.

[17] I expect that some readers will find this conclusion objectionable in light of the progressive expansion of QMV at the expense of unanimity procedures in successive treaty modifications. I would simply suggest that "constitutional choice" (higher-order institutional creation/change) differs in important ways from the selection of procedures to govern specific,

The European Union as a Procedural System

With the above in mind, the Council should reveal a preference first for unanimous facultative consultation (AVFU), which protects individual member states, limits strategic manipulation by the Commission through its agenda power, and economizes on interactions with the Parliament. Unanimous consultation (CNSU) follows closely. Given its limitation of supranational agenda powers, relative simplicity, and the stringent conditions for a successful EP veto, assent (AVCU) ranks third. Unanimous codecision (CODU) complicates matters but is otherwise quite favorable to the Council. In terms of majority procedures, the failure to weight various objectives (influence, indirect influence, participation, and economy) creates some ambiguities where these are in conflict. In deciding between QMV facultative consultation (AVFQ), QMV consultation (CNSQ), cooperation (SYNQ), and QMV codecision (CODQ), I emphasize that equilibrium outcomes are often similar across the four procedures. What differentiates them is the transfer of power and participation from the Commission, which the Council can indirectly influence, to the Parliament, which it cannot. Simple majority facultative consultation (AVFS), I conclude, so (relatively) deprives the Council and its members of influence that it must rank last.

Summary

The point of the foregoing is to generate clear empirical expectations about procedural preferences in the EU. Table 4 summarizes the procedural preference rankings generated in this section. These rankings will be used in three ways. First, they permit predictions about different actors' procedural choices in any given situation as a function of the available alternatives. I simply predict that given a choice, the actor will express a preference for the procedure with the lower rank number. Second, and directly related, the rankings permit predictions about procedural political coalitions. Both of these empirical predictions will be falsifiable. Third, I will also use the rankings and rank differences as measures of the opportunity cost of engaging in politics within rules as opposed to playing procedural politics. As discussed in the last chapter, this can be expected substantially to shape patterns of institutional choice and constraint.

short-run interactions, not least in the degree of information that actors possess about the consequences of their institutional choices, their preferences over those consequences, and so forth. As a result, it is not necessarily inconsistent to observe actors simultaneously preferring QMV in the aggregate future and unanimity in the specific present.

Procedural Politics

Table 4. *Procedural Preference Rankings*

Procedure	CEC	EP	CM
AVCU	8	4	3
AVFQ	2	8	5
AVFS	1	7	9
AVFU	6	9	1
CNSQ	3	5	6
CNSU	7	6	2
CODQ	5	1	8
CODU	9	3	4
SYNQ	4	2	7

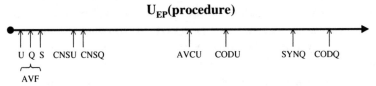

Figure 7 Hypothetical Example of Cardinal Preference Ordering

These preference rankings exhibit some characteristic weaknesses. Most important, the ordinal scale only very roughly captures the "true" differences, in influence or utility terms, between the alternatives. Consider the EP, for example, in conjunction with the stylized presentation in Figure 7. Each procedure holds a certain amount of utility for the EP – denoted U_{EP} (procedure) – which by definition increases as one moves from less- to more-preferred procedures. The cardinal distances between consecutively ranked alternatives need not be equal, however. For example, the EP may just barely prefer any of the facultative consultation (AVF) procedures to the other by virtue of the indirect influence assumption. But the utility increase in moving from QMV consultation (CNSQ) to assent (AVCU) may be much more substantial. Needless to say, I have no cardinal measure of preferences over procedural alternatives. I simply raise the issue to sensitize the reader to the very rough nature of the rank measures.

Strategic Interaction: A Game of Procedural Politics

To this point I have put some EU-specific flesh on the bones of the premises that "institutions matter" and that actors have derived institutional preferences. It remains to flesh out a third premise, according to which EU procedural choice is strategic choice, and systematically to bring together the strands of this analysis into a coherent and testable account of procedural politics. Given that rules matter and that actors have derived preferences over them, how can actors be expected to interact jointly in the selection of rules that will subsequently govern their legislative behavior? What factors do they consider when choosing to choose rules or be constrained by them? How do their preferences over alternatives, their perceptions of others' preferences and behaviors, and the sequence in which they act affect this interaction? This section suggests that EU rules choices can be modeled as procedural political games, in which the nature (i.e., effects) and availability of institutional alternatives, actors' preferences over them, the nature of policy issues, and the structure of procedural decision making all play a role.

A Simplified Model of Procedural Politics

These issues can be explored by asking the following question: why do actors sometimes propose or accept politically unfavorable rules in the European Union when politically more favorable alternatives exist? This represents a core puzzle not only of this book but indeed of rationalist institutional analysis more generally. I argue that rules choice reflects strategic interaction centering on three features: actors' preferences for available institutional alternatives, their beliefs about the preferences and strategies of other actors (especially the dispute resolver, the court), and the decision making sequence. I develop a simple noncooperative model of rules choice with incomplete information that confirms the importance of these three factors and explains the puzzle adduced above. In short, the model suggests that under certain conditions – where influence gains are available and issues are jurisdictionally ambiguous – it pays (in expected utility terms) to initiate procedural political disputes. Where favorable conditions are absent, procedural politics may still operate, but no disputes are apparent, and proposing or agreeing to operate within even politically unfavorable rules represents the rational choice.

Consider the following abstract example, in which two players – the Commission and the Council of Ministers – interact strategically in choosing one from among two possible rules (Left and Right). (I exclude the European Parliament for simplicity, but the logic of the game would remain unaffected if it were included.) The Court of Justice, while not participating in rules choices at the legislative stage, stands ready to strike down rules choices should this prove necessary (i.e., should they represent political manipulation of rules in contravention of "good law"). Assume that the Commission prefers rule Left and that the Council prefers rule Right. Assume further that the Court is constrained by the dictates of "good law," and that under certain circumstances the issue-structural correspondence is such that Left is the legally correct choice, while under other circumstances good law dictates that it choose Right. The Commission and Council have only uncertain beliefs about the true issue-structural correspondence and hence about which rule the Court would eventually uphold were it asked to adjudicate a dispute.

In this hypothetical example, rules choices follow a standard sequence in which the Commission proposes a rule, the Council decides on it, and the Commission can challenge if it is overturned at the decision stage. The Council's decision to overturn the Commission's proposal imposes a cost on both parties.[18] Since the losers of Court cases pay both their own and the winners' costs, losing Court cases is quite costly, and winning them imposes no additional costs or benefits.[19] In what follows, I show how procedural political processes and outcomes result from strategic interaction between these two actors. In the second appendix to this chapter (Appendix 3.B) I develop a formal model of this single-shot, noncooperative game of incomplete information. Here I strip away the technicalities and show that the nature of institutional alternatives (and actors' preferences over them), their expectations about others' preferences and behavior – and especially, those of the Court, which will be influenced by the nature of the issue at hand – and the structure of decision making all influence the ways in which actors will play procedural politics, as well as the visibility of those efforts. The model suggests that in many circumstances, it is rational to be constrained by rules, in the sense of proposing or agreeing to work within relatively

---

[18] For the Council, overturning Commission proposals requires unanimity, and side payments may be required to buy off reluctant member states (Martin 1993, 127–129). Being overturned is also costly for the Commission, as it may lose credibility, the claim to impartiality, member state trust, or other valuables.

[19] I assume that there is no precedent value in Court decisions. If there were, this might substantially increase the benefits of winning and the costs of losing. On the general lack of precedent value of ECJ jurisprudence see Conant 1998, 60–64. McCown (2001) suggests that precedent does operate in precisely this area. While allowing for precedent value might prove an interesting extension, it would complicate the analysis considerably, and so I do not pursue that option here.

The European Union as a Procedural System

unfavorable ones, but in other situations overt procedural politics, in the form of engaging in procedural political disputes, constitutes the rational choice.

In what follows, I walk through several scenarios corresponding to one or more of the five equilibria derived in the appendix. Consider, first and most simply, a situation in which both the Commission and the Council believe that the issue in question most appropriately falls under rule Left, such that the Court would uphold Left and reject Right, at a cost to the defender of the latter. This is a favorable circumstance for the Commission, which prefers rule Left, and unfavorable for the Council, which prefers Right. Given these beliefs of each actor, which are also known to the other, the Commission would be foolish to propose an unfavorable rule (Right), all the more so since the Court would not even uphold that choice. The Council, for its part, would be foolish to play procedural politics if the Commission proposed Left, despite the fact that left is undesirable to it. In equilibrium, this game plays itself out shortly and sweetly: the Commission proposes Left, and the Council accepts it. The casual observer might assume that actors were acting naively within rules, taking them for granted. It is also possible, however, and I would suggest more likely, that both actors are engaging in procedural political calculations. No fight occurs, however, and actors appear to engage in politics solely within, and not with respect to, rules. The same dynamics operate when both Commission and Council believe that the Court will uphold Right. In that case, the Commission would appear to propose a rule unfavorable to itself, which the Council would accept. Again, no fight would be apparent.

The above logic more or less holds for four of the five equilibria that I calculate in the appendix, though in other cases actors update their beliefs upon observing the moves of others. That is, under most belief-strategy combinations, no fight over rules is predicted. In one equilibrium, however, the parties do find themselves brought before the court at the end of the procedural political game. Not surprisingly, in that game actors have divergent beliefs about which is the legally correct rule, and hence about what the Court would choose if called to adjudicate a dispute. The Commission believes that the Court would uphold its preferred rule, Left, and so stands prepared both to propose Left at the beginning of the game and to challenge any eventual Council overturn of that proposal. The Council, for its part, holds the opposite belief: it thinks that the Court would uphold its

Procedural Politics

overturn, and so it is prepared to undertake it.[20] True enough, the Council incurs overturn costs, perhaps having to buy off reluctant member states. But the benefits in the form of influence gained (through use of the more preferred rule) more than outweigh those costs.

In this circumstance, not surprisingly, the Commission proposes its preferred rule, Left; the Council overturns that proposal; and the Commission takes the case to court. Without knowing the true legal state of the issue (i.e., whether it more appropriately fits under Left or Right), we cannot say who will win this court case. But it is clear that rather than simply selecting a rule and getting on with the business of politics acting within it, actors are transparently operating with respect to the rules. What is more, in this scenario they incur the costs not only of overturning or being overturned, but also, for one party, of losing the Court case.

Summary

What does this simple game tell us about procedural politics, everyday politics with respect to rules? Three points stand out. First, strategic interaction with respect to rules may not be visible to the naked eye and may be observationally equivalent to institutional myopia, or to sophistication merely within but not with respect to rules. What may appear to be noncalculated rule-following behavior may, instead, reflect participants' negative assessments of either the opportunity to win a potential court case or the incentive to try. For that reason, the empirical examination in subsequent chapters will often focus on observable cases of procedural politics (disputes between actors), even though procedural politics is postulated to operate even when no dispute is apparent. Second, the game provides a set of tools for addressing a core empirical puzzle motivating this book: why do actors sometimes accept or even propose undesirable rules when more desirable alternatives exist? They do so either because they have nothing to gain or because they think that it will result in costly failure.

Third, and more interesting, the model suggests specific factors that will explain variations in episodes of choice, constraint, and institutional disputes over time and across actors and issues. Two sets of parameters from the model stand out, and they relate directly to the materials discussed in the last chapter and to the empirical materials that will follow. The first

---

[20] In connecting these results to the theory in the last chapter and the empirics in the next three, I will be implying that jurisdictional ambiguity generates divergent priors.

is the nature of available institutional alternatives and actors' preferences over them. When actors are indifferent as between the alternatives, not surprisingly, no rules disputes occur. As assessments of the alternatives diverge, conflict becomes more likely. The second is the nature of the issues and, more particularly, the legality of different procedural choices given the issues at hand. When actors believe that "good politics" (pushing for a favorable procedure) also represents "good law" (such that the Court will uphold them), they will pursue a procedural political strategy. When they suspect that the Court will overturn them (at cost), they will not be so incited. And crucially, when issues are truly ambiguous in terms of the rules appropriate to addressing them – related in the game to divergent beliefs about the types of issues being considered – procedural political disputes become more likely. Indeed, among the five equilibria to the game, the one that played out as a visible procedural political conflict involved such divergent beliefs. These variables – the nature of and preferences over institutional alternatives, and (beliefs about) the relationship of policy issues to existing institutional arrangements – correspond directly to incentives and opportunities as defined in the last chapter and will continue to reappear throughout the rest of the book. They drive procedural politics.

Conclusion

As noted in Chapter 2, statements about rational institutional choice rely on three premises. First, institutions matter in the sense of affecting outcomes. Second, actors have preferences over those outcomes, and hence derived preferences over those institutions. Third, in nondictatorial settings, institutions find application as a result of strategic interaction among the relevant institutional choosers. This chapter has addressed the institutions, actors, and strategic interactions underpinning procedural politics in the specific context of the EU. It began by analyzing precisely how procedures matter in EU policymaking. Combining these results with a series of plausible auxiliary assumptions allowed statements about which procedures actors should prefer. The chapter then proceeded to consider a game of procedural politics in which the nature of available rules (in terms especially of their correspondence with substantive issues), actors' preferences over those rules, and actors' beliefs about others' motivations and behaviors jointly determine procedural political processes and outcomes.

The rules of the game, in short, seem both to respond to and to condition strategic behavior. Armed with the theoretical propositions from Chapter 2

Procedural Politics

and the EU-specific analyses of this chapter, I turn in Chapters 4 through 6 to my empirical examination. Chapter 4 tests expectations about the conditions under which, the ways in which, and the effects with which procedural politics occurs, with special attention to aggregate variation across issues, actors, and time. Chapters 5 and 6 delve more deeply into specific sectors of EU policymaking. The collective results will illuminate not only procedural politics within the EU, nor even only aspects of the EU itself, but more general features of governance in rule-governed political systems.

Appendix 3.A: Analyzing EU Legislative Procedures

EU legislative procedures can be enormously complex, and the development of a set of fairly simple tools can aid greatly in explaining and understanding them. Happily, following efforts by Tsebelis (1994), Garrett (1992), Steunenberg (1994), and others, a vast literature has grown up around EU legislative procedures that permits fairly precise statements about their influence and outcome properties. This appendix appropriates these models to present purposes, in order to understand the influence properties of rules and thereby to generate expectations about actors' procedural preferences. As in the body of the chapter, I consider relatively simple procedures first, then move on to discuss more complex variations.

Modeling Simple Procedures

I model these procedures in Figure 8 using the following assumptions and parameters.[21] I assume a one-dimensional choice space, including a status quo (Q) that precedes legislative activity and is the default outcome in the absence of agreement. Actors have Euclidean preferences over the space, meaning that they have an ideal point (most-preferred policy outcome) and that their utility declines in the distance from that ideal point in either direction.[22] They enjoy complete and perfect information about the rules of the game, the location of the status quo, and others' ideal points and utility functions, and they behave strategically within these one-shot games. I

---

[21] See generally Krehbiel (1988) and Strom (1990). I replicate many features of the models developed by Bernard Steunenberg (1994).

[22] I assume, without loss of generality, that this decline is symmetrical, that is, the same on either side of the ideal point.

The European Union as a Procedural System

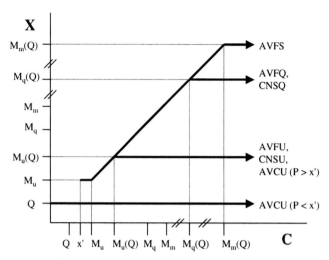

Figure 8 Simple Procedures

portray the Commission (C) and Parliament (P) as unitary actors, although since both are voting bodies their positions will reflect the ideal points of their pivotal (usually median) members.[23] I disaggregate the Council into member states, one of which is most reluctant and is pivotal under unanimity (M_u) and at least one of which is pivotal under qualified majority voting (M_q). I also include the median member state (M_m), which I assume to lie to the right of the QMV pivot, and the member state most interested in policy change (M_r). For simplicity, and without loss of generality, I assume that member states have equal voting weights. I denote player i's point of indifference to the status quo as $i(Q)$, and I also include a point x' such that $x'(Q)$ (not illustrated) lies barely to the left of the most reluctant Council member, M_u. Actors reason via backward induction in arriving at their own best strategy. Finally, all of these parameters remain constant during the legislative process.

The bold line in the figure maps equilibrium outcomes, X, for different locations of the Commission's ideal point, C. Consider first the procedures that require unanimity in the Council. Here, the ideal point of the most reluctant member state, M_u – also known as the unanimity pivot – delimits the range of possible outcomes. For any proposal that the Commission

[23] Tsebelis (1995) considers this issue for the European Parliament and finds that relaxing this assumption exerts few analytical effects.

would make, the Council can only adopt proposals in the M_u to $M_u(Q)$ range.[24] Member states can amend at least to M_u any proposal to the left of that point. The unanimity pivot will veto anything to the right of this range, since points in that range leave it absolutely worse off than it would be under the status quo, which it can enforce with its veto. If the Commission lies to the left of x', it makes no proposal because it prefers the status quo to anything that the Council will adopt. When the Commission lies between x' and M_u, it can propose M_u and this will be the outcome, because member states unanimously prefer that point to the status quo, but cannot agree unanimously to amend it. If the Commission prefers policies in the M_u to $M_u(Q)$ range, it can propose and obtain its ideal point. While the most reluctant Council member prefers to move to the left, at least one member state prefers to move to the right. As they cannot achieve the unanimity required to amend the proposal, but since they all prefer it to the status quo, they adopt it unanimously. If the Commission lies to the right of the unanimity pivot's status quo indifference point, its best proposal is $M_u(Q)$, which the Council unanimously adopts.

The assent procedure nuances these conclusions only slightly. In particular, if the Parliament lies at or to the left of x' (i.e., if $P \leq x'$), it will veto the legislation because it prefers the status quo to anything that the Council can adopt. With complete information, the Commission knows this and makes no proposal. In such a situation, the Parliament can enforce the status quo against the wishes of the Commission and the Council.

Analysis of the QMV procedures (AVFQ, CNSQ) follows the same logic. Here, the pivotal Council member – the QMV pivot – is M_q. If the Commission holds conservative preferences in the sense of lying close to the status quo, QMV changes nothing. Until the Commission's ideal point reaches $M_u(Q)$, the outcomes of QMV and unanimity variants remain identical. As before, it will not open the gates until its ideal point reaches x'. When it

[24] To be precise, the Council can unanimously adopt anything between Q and $M_u(Q)$. But until its ideal point reaches x', the Commission will not open the gates, because member states can amend any proposal to the left of M_u at least to M_u, and perhaps farther to the right, which by the definition of x' would leave the Commission worse off than the status quo. Once it passes x' the Commission may open the gates, but any outcome to the left of M_u is, from the member states' perspectives, Pareto-inferior at least to M_u, and possibly to other feasible points as well. Practically speaking, then, M_u to $M_u(Q)$ is the relevant range for the Council.

The European Union as a Procedural System

lies within the M_u to $M_u(Q)$ range, it can still propose and obtain its ideal point. This dynamic, whereby the Commission proposes and obtains its ideal point, now extends across a potentially broad spectrum, to $M_q(Q)$, the point at which the QMV pivot is indifferent relative to the status quo. Potential proposals to the right of that point will fail, however, for they make the QMV pivot worse off than it would be under the status quo. With complete information, the Commission does not table such losing proposals. Thus, $M_q(Q)$ bounds achievable legislative outcomes under these QMV procedures.

Complex Procedures

Cooperation Procedure. I model the cooperation procedure in Figure 9. In many situations, the equilibrium outcome under cooperation remains unaffected by the EP and resembles that of the other QMV procedures (see also Tsebelis and Garrett 1996, 354–355). Consider an EP ideal point (P) to the right of the pivotal member of the Council, which means that $P(Q)$ lies to the right of $M_q(Q)$. As in the diagram, outcomes map Commission preferences precisely as they did in the QMV procedures examined in Figure 8. Any amendments the EP might offer can gain neither (a) Commission acceptance and QMV passage nor (b) unanimity passage against the Commission proposal.

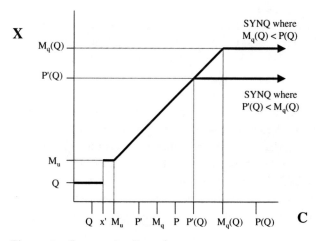

Figure 9 Cooperation Procedure

However, the EP can usually affect outcomes when it lies to the left of the Commission and the Council pivot. All of these situations reflect the intuition that the threat of an EP rejection may sometimes limit the range of proposals that a rational Commission can offer. Most generally, as in the lower line in Figure 9, the Parliament's indifference point to the status quo, here $P'(Q)$, can generally replace $M_q(Q)$ as the limiting outcome if the EP lies to the left of the Commission and the pivotal member of the Council. In other situations (not illustrated), if the EP is reluctant ($P \leq x'$) and the Council is split over the direction of changes in the status quo (at least $M_u < Q$) the threat of an EP rejection can enforce the status quo, which it could not do under any of the QMV procedures dealt with so far. While there are exceptions if the Commission and Parliament are relatively close to the status quo, the EP can influence outcomes under a considerable number of preference configurations.

Codecision Procedure. To simplify, I will follow Steunenberg (1997, 213–217) and analyze a stylized version of codecision for a specific preference configuration. Steunenberg begins with an exogenously determined common position, x, and analyzes codecision as a four-stage game.[25] In the first stage, Parliament offers a joint text to the conciliation committee. The Council considers the proposal in the second stage. If a qualified majority agrees, the proposal becomes law. If it does not agree, it offers the common position to the Parliament. In the third and fourth stages the EP and a qualified majority of the Council, respectively, accept or reject the common position. Assume that the Commission seeks a relatively small change to the status quo and that its ideal point lies outside of the unanimity win-set (Q to $M_u(Q)$) but to the left of the QMV pivot in the Council (M_q). Assume further that the EP prefers substantial changes to the status quo. The top panel of Figure 10 includes the Commission. This preference configuration generates a common position, x, which is equivalent to the outcome under other QMV procedures and is illustrated in the lower line.

The lower line shows that with this preference configuration under codecision, the EP and a qualified majority in the Council can attain a different outcome under CODQ than was possible under the SYNQ procedure. The logic is straightforward. The EP must offer a proposal that, from the perspective of a qualified majority in the Council, is at least as good as or

[25] See Steunenberg 1997, 213–215 for a discussion of this simplification.

The European Union as a Procedural System

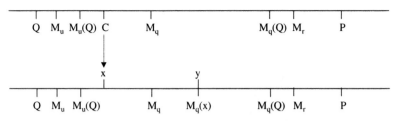

Figure 10 Codecision Procedure

better than point x. Because M_q remains the Council pivot, anything between x and the Council pivot's point of indifference to x – that is, $M_q(x)$ – constitutes a feasible outcome. The EP thus makes the proposal that is closest to its ideal point and that a qualified majority in the Council prefers to x. In short, the best proposal the EP can offer is precisely at $M_q(x)$, which becomes the outcome (y) of the codecision procedure. Not surprisingly, CODU (not illustrated) would greatly restrict the range of feasible outcomes and, with this preference configuration, would make the most reluctant member state's indifference point to the status quo ($M_u(Q)$) the locus of Council and EP bargaining.

Summary

The body of the chapter provides summary assessments of these nine legislative procedures.

Appendix 3.B: An Incomplete Information Game of EU Procedural Choice

I model rules choice as a single-shot, four-player game involving a nonstrategic player Nature (**N**), the European Commission (**C**), the Council of Ministers (**M**), and a nonstrategic European Court of Justice (**J**). For simplicity, I omit the European Parliament, though the logic of the game would remain the same were it to be included. These actors interact over the applicability of one of two rules, Left (*L*) and Right (*R*). In the game, **N** moves first by choosing a policy issue that should legally be adopted using rule *L* with probability α and using rule *R* with probability $(1-\alpha)$. Uncertain about whether a Type *L* or a Type *R* issue is involved, **C** at the second (*proposal*) stage proposes a rule, *L* or *R*. At the third (*decision*)

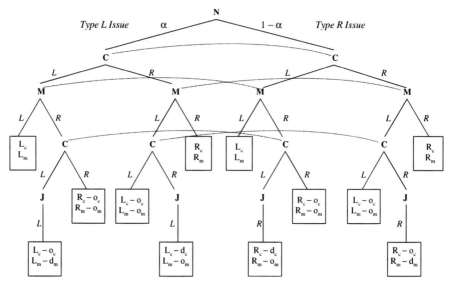

Figure 11 Institutional Choice Game Tree

stage, **M** is also uncertain about the true issue. It can either accept the proposed rule, in which case the game ends, or overturn it. If **M** overturns **C**'s proposed rule, the game proceeds to a fourth (*challenge*) stage, in which a still-uncertain **C** chooses to accept the overturn or challenge it before the Court. **J**, which is not uncertain (it knows which rule should legally apply), moves last, at the *judgment* stage. It nonstrategically chooses L for $\alpha \geq .5$ and R for $\alpha < .5$. Its decision cannot be appealed (i.e., the game ends after **J**'s move). Figure 11 provides the extensive-form representation of the game.

The terminal nodes of the game are boxed, with payoffs for **C** listed first and those for **M** below them. I use the following notation for the various payoffs and beliefs:

- L_i = Left outcome payoff to player i
- R_i = Right outcome payoff to player i
- o_i = cost to player i of an overturned proposal
- d_i = cost to player i of being defeated in Court
- α_i = player i's probability assessment of the issue type (the Commission will be denoted cp in the proposal stage and cc in the challenge stage).

The European Union as a Procedural System

Assume that Court defeats are more costly than overturns, that is, that $o_i < d_i$ for all i. Assume further the following utility functions:

- $U_c(L_c) > U_c(L_c - o_c) > U_c(L_c - d_c) > U_c(R_c) > U_c(R_c - o_c) > U_c(R_c - d_c)$
- $U_m(R_m) > U_m(R_m - o_m) > U_m(R_m - d_m) > U_m(L_m) > U_m(L_m - o_m) > U_m(L_m - d_m)$.

In what follows, I solve the game using the perfect Bayesian equilibrium (PBE) solution concept. Accordingly, all players follow a belief-consistent best-response strategy. Proceeding by backward induction, I assess each player's best response given its own beliefs about issue type (α_i), others' beliefs about issue type ($\alpha_{j \neq i}$), and others' moves in the game.

Challenge Stage

At the challenge stage, **C** calculates its best responses to all possible contingencies, given its beliefs about the type of issue that is involved.

First, if it observes L, **C** assesses its moves as follows:

$EU_{L|L}$
$= \alpha_{cc} {}^*(L_c - o_c)$
$\quad + (1 - \alpha_{cc}) {}^*(L_c - o_c)$
$= L_c - o_c$

$EU_{R|L}$
$= \alpha_{cc} {}^*(L_c - d_c) + (1 - \alpha_{cc}) {}^*(R_c - o_c)$
$= \alpha_{cc} L_c - \alpha_{cc} d_c + R_c - o_c - \alpha_{cc} R_c + \alpha_{cc} o_c$
$= \alpha_{cc} {}^*(L_c - d_c - R_c + o_c) + R_c - o_c.$

Setting these two terms equal to find **C**'s point of indifference yields

$L_c - o_c = \alpha_{cc} {}^*(L_c - d_c - R_c + o_c) + R_c - o_c.$

Solving for α_{cc} yields

$\alpha_{cc} = (L_c - R_c)/(L_c - d_c - R_c + o_c).$

For all allowable values of α_{cc} (i.e., for $0 \leq \alpha_{cc} \leq 1$), then, **C** has a dominant strategy to play $(L|L)$ at the challenge stage, since $EU_L > EU_R$ at zero, one, and all points in between.

Second, if **C** observes R, **C** calculates as follows:

$EU_{L|R}$
$= \alpha_{cc} {}^*(L_c - o_c)$
$\quad + (1 - \alpha_{cc}) {}^*(R_c - d_c)$
$= \alpha_{cc} {}^*(L_c - o_c - R_c + d_c)$
$\quad + R_c - d_c$

$EU_{R|R}$
$= \alpha_{cc} {}^*(R_c - o_c) + (1 - \alpha_{cc}) {}^*(R_c - o_c)$
$= R_c - o_c.$

Setting these two terms equal to each other yields

$$\alpha_{cc}{}^{*}(L_c - o_c - R_c + d_c) + R_c - d_c = R_c - o_c.$$

Solving for α_{cc}, we find that **C** is indifferent between L and R at

$$\alpha_{cc} = (d_c - o_c)/(L_c - o_c - R_c + d_c).$$

For values of α_{cc} greater than (or, by assumption, equal to) this, $L|R$ yields greater expected utility, and for values less than this, $R|R$ is superior (this is obtained simply by plugging in values of α_{cc} and solving for the expected utility of each move). As a result, any PBE must contain either

$$(L|L, L|R): \alpha_{cc} \geq (d_c - o_c)/(L_c - o_c - R_c + d_c)$$

or

$$(L|L, R|R): \alpha_{cc} < (d_c - o_c)/(L_c - o_c - R_c + d_c)$$

in the challenge stage portion of **C**'s strategy.

Decision Stage

Moving back to **M**'s calculus at the decision stage, we must distinguish two situations corresponding to different values of α_{cc} at **C**'s challenge stage.

First, consider the scenario in which

$$\alpha_{cc} \geq (d_c - o_c)/(L_c - o_c - R_c + d_c).$$

If **M** observes L, then it calculates the expected utility of its alternatives as follows:

$$\begin{aligned} EU_{L|L} &= \alpha_m{}^{*}(L_m) \\ &\quad + (1 - \alpha_m)^{*}(L_m) \\ &= L_m \end{aligned}$$

$$\begin{aligned} EU_{R|L} &= \alpha_m{}^{*}(L_m - d_m) + (1 - \alpha_m)^{*}(R_m - o_m) \\ &= \alpha_m L_m - \alpha_m d_m + R_m - o_m - \alpha_m R_m + \alpha_m o_m \\ &= \alpha_m{}^{*}(L_m - d_m - R_m + o_m) + R_m - o_m. \end{aligned}$$

Setting these two terms equal to find **M**'s point of indifference yields

$$\alpha_m = (L_m - R_m + o_m)/(L_m - d_m - R_m + o_m).$$

For values of α_m greater than this, $L|L$ yields greater expected utility, and for α_m less than (or, by assumption, equal to) this, $R|L$ is superior.

If **M** observes R, it is simply shown that it has a dominant strategy to play $(R|R)$, since $EU_L = L_m - o_m$ and $EU_R = R_m$ for all α_m and $U_m(L_m - o_m) < U_m(R_m)$.

As a result, any PBE must contain either

$$(L|L, R|R): \alpha_m > (L_m - R_m + o_m)/(L_m - d_m - R_m + o_m)$$

or

$$(R|L, R|R): \alpha_m \leq (L_m - R_m + o_m)/(L_m - d_m - R_m + o_m)$$

for

$$\alpha_{cc} \geq (d_c - o_c)/(L_c - o_c - R_c + d_c).$$

Second, consider the scenario in which

$$\alpha_{cc} < (d_c - o_c)/(L_c - o_c - R_c + d_c).$$

If **M** observes L, then it calculates the expected utility of its alternatives as follows:

$$\begin{aligned} EU_{L|L} &= \alpha_m{}^*(L_m) \\ &\quad + (1 - \alpha_m){}^*(L_m) \\ &= L_m \end{aligned} \qquad \begin{aligned} EU_{R|L} &= \alpha_m{}^*(R_m - o_m) + (1 - \alpha_m){}^*(R_m - o_m) \\ &= R_m - o_m. \end{aligned}$$

Since $U_m(L_m) < U_m(R_m - o_m)$, $R|L$ always yields higher expected utility. Similarly, if **M** observes R, it calculates the expected utility of its alternatives as

$$\begin{aligned} EU_{L|R} &= \alpha_m{}^*(L_m - o_m) \\ &\quad + (1 - \alpha_m){}^*(L_m - o_m) \\ &= L_m - o_m \end{aligned} \qquad \begin{aligned} EU_{R|R} &= \alpha_m{}^*(R_m) + (1 - \alpha_m){}^*(R_m) \\ &= R_m. \end{aligned}$$

Since $U_m(L_m - o_m) < U_m(R_m)$, $R|R$ always yields higher expected utility.

Since R always represents **M**'s best response given **C**'s (challenge stage) belief-strategy combination, $(R|L, R|R)$ for all α_m forms part of any PBE where

$$\alpha_{cc} < (d_c - o_c)/(L_c - o_c - R_c + d_c).$$

Proposal Stage

Moving finally to **C**'s move at the proposal stage, we must now distinguish four situations representing different optimal belief-strategy combinations at other stages of the game.

First, consider the case in which

$$\alpha_{cc} < (d_c - o_c)/(L_c - o_c - R_c + d_c)$$

and

$$\alpha_m \leq (L_m - R_m + o_m)/(L_m - R_m - d_m + o_m).$$

Here,

$$EU_L = \alpha_{cp}{}^*(R_c - o_c) + (1 - \alpha_{cp})^*(R_c - o_c) = R_c - o_c$$

$$EU_R = \alpha_{cp}{}^*(R_c) + (1 - \alpha_{cp})^*(R_c) = R_c.$$

Because $U_c(R_c - o_c) < U_c(R_c)$, **C** has a dominant strategy to propose R.

Second, where

$$\alpha_{cc} < (d_c - o_c)/(L_c - o_c - R_c + d_c)$$

and

$$\alpha_m > (L_m - R_m + o_m)/(L_m - d_m - R_m + o_m),$$

C's expected utility from L is equal to L_c and $EU_R = R_c$. Since $U_c(L_c) > U_c(R_c)$, under this belief and strategy combination **C** has a dominant strategy to propose L.

Third, consider the situation in which

$$\alpha_{cc} \geq (d_c - o_c)/(L_c - o_c - R_c + d_c)$$

and

$$\alpha_m > (L_m - R_m + o_m)/(L_m - d_m - R_m + o_m).$$

Here, **C** calculates as follows:

$$EU_L = \alpha_{cp}{}^*(L_c) + (1 - \alpha_{cp})^*(L_c) = L$$

$$EU_R = \alpha_{cp}{}^*(R_c) + (1 - \alpha_{cp})^*(R_c) = R_c.$$

Since $U_c(L_c) > U_c(R_c)$, **C** has a dominant strategy to propose L in these circumstances.

Fourth, consider the situation in which

$$\alpha_{cc} \geq (d_c - o_c)/(L_c - o_c - R_c + d_c)$$

and

$$\alpha_m \leq (L_m - R_m + o_m)/(L_m - d_m - R_m + o_m).$$

Here,

$$\begin{aligned}
EU_L &= \alpha_{cp}{}^*(L_c - o_c) \\
&\quad + (1 - \alpha_{cp})^*(R_c - d_c) \\
&= \alpha_{cp}{}^*(L_c - o_c - R_c + d_c) + R_c - d_c
\end{aligned}$$

$$\begin{aligned}
EU_R &= \alpha_{cp}{}^*(R_c) + (1 - \alpha_{cp})^*(R_c) \\
&= R_c.
\end{aligned}$$

Setting these two terms equal, we find **C**'s point of indifference at proposal stage as $\alpha_{cp} = d_c/(L_c - o_c - R_c + d_c)$. For values of α_{cp} greater than this, L is the best proposal, and for values less than this, R is superior.

To summarize, any PBE must contain one of the following for **C** at the proposal stage: R where

$$\alpha_{cc} < (d_c - o_c)/(L_c - o_c - R_c + d_c)$$

and

$$\alpha_m \leq (L_m - R_m + o_m)/(L_m - d_m - R_m + o_m);$$

or L where

$$\alpha_{cc} < (d_c - o_c)/(L_c - o_c - R_c + d_c)$$

and

$$\alpha_m > (L_m - R_m + o_m)/(L_m - d_m - R_m + o_m);$$

or L where

$$\alpha_{cc} \geq (d_c - o_c)/(L_c - o_c - R_c + d_c)$$

and

$$\alpha_m > (L_m - R_m + o_m)/(L_m - d_m - R_m + o_m);$$

Table 5. *Perfect Bayesian Equilibria for Institutional Selection Game*

	Beliefs			Strategies	
	α_{cc}	α_m	α_{cp}	C	M
1	$\geq (L_c - R_c)/(L_c - R_c - d_c - o_c)$	$> (L_m - R_m + o_m)/(L_m - R_m - d_m + o_m)$	all	$L; L\|L, L\|R$	$L\|L, R\|R$
2	$\geq (L_c - R_c)/(L_c - R_c - d_c - o_c)$	$\leq (L_m - R_m + o_m)/(L_m - R_m - d_m + o_m)$	$\geq d_c/(L_c - R_c - o_c + d_c)$	$L; L\|L, L\|R$	$R\|L, R\|R$
3	$\geq (L_c - R_c)/(L_c - R_c - d_c - o_c)$	$\leq (L_m - R_m + o_m)/(L_m - R_m - d_m + o_m)$	$< d_c/(L_c - R_c - o_c + d_c)$	$R; L\|L, L\|R$	$R\|L, R\|R$
4	$< (L_c - R_c)/(L_c - R_c - d_c - o_c)$	$> (L_m - R_m + o_m)/(L_m - R_m - d_m + o_m)$	all	$L; L\|L, R\|R$	$L\|L, R\|R$
5	$< (L_c - R_c)/(L_c - R_c - d_c - o_c)$	$\leq (L_m - R_m + o_m)/(L_m - R_m - d_m + o_m)$	all	$R; L\|L, R\|R$	$R\|L, R\|R$

or

$$L: \alpha_{cp} \geq d_c/(L_c - o_c - R_c + d_c)$$

where

$$\alpha_{cc} \geq (d_c - o_c)/(L_c - o_c - R_c + d_c)$$

and

$$\alpha_m \leq (L_m - R_m + o_m)/(L_m - d_m - R_m + o_m);$$

or

$$R: \alpha_{cp} < d_c/(L_c - o_c - R_c + d_c)$$

where

$$\alpha_{cc} \geq (d_c - o_c)/(L_c - o_c - R_c + d_c)$$

and

$$\alpha_m \leq (L_m - R_m + o_m)/(L_m - d_m - R_m + o_m).$$

Combining all of these best-response belief and strategy combinations yields five PBEs, given in Table 5 with only some rearrangement of the order of the parameters to facilitate substantive interpretation.

I describe the dynamics and outcomes of each in the text.

5

DETERMINANTS AND EFFECTS OF EU PROCEDURAL POLITICS

This chapter begins the empirical assessment of procedural politics in the European Union. Because this topic has never been treated systematically, one of the goals of this chapter is to paint a picture of the general incidence of procedural politics, including the extent to which it occurs; the time periods, actors, and issues involved; and its effects on important outcomes. The focus throughout will be on the directly observable manifestation of procedural politics, in the form of procedural political disputes (disagreements by two or more actors over which procedure should be used in adopting legislation). Beyond the descriptive task, I seek to test specific theoretical predictions from Chapter 2, based in part upon the analysis and operationalizations developed in the last chapter. Accordingly, this chapter begins with a descriptive examination of variations in procedural politics across time, actors, and issues. These descriptive statistics will provide first-cut assessment of some of the theoretical expectations developed in Chapter 2. Next, I test the general argument about the conditions under which procedural politics is said to occur, namely, as a function of opportunity (the availability of procedural alternatives through jurisdictional ambiguity) and incentives (influence differences among alternative procedures). These tests focus exclusively on the 1987–1997 period, for which an original dataset has been constructed. Armed with these positive results, I then consider some specific effects of procedural politics, showing them to be theoretically consistent and important both in everyday politics and in terms of the long-run evolution of EU institutions. The chapter concludes with a summary of the aggregate results, laying the base for the sectoral analysis that will follow in Chapters 5 and 6.

Patterns

Procedural Politics Across Time, Actors, and Issues

This section works systematically through descriptive statistics dealing with variations in procedural politics across time, actors, and issues. These empirical materials not only describe a set of phenomena with which few are familiar but also aid in assessment of alternative theoretical explanations of procedural politics. I begin by assessing over-time variation in procedural political disputes, move to consider variation across actors (including an assessment of actors' motivations), and conclude this section with a look at cross-sectoral variation.

Variations over Time

Before documenting over-time variation in disputes, a prior question arises: what should we expect this history to resemble? From a "legalistic" perspective little should have changed from the early days of the European Community (EC) to the present-day European Union. Disputes over the applicability of different rules reflect sincere legal disagreements and resolve themselves with an eye toward legal certainty rather than political gain. Disputes might ebb and flow year-on-year, but they should not reveal any underlying trend or even qualitative punctuations.

A second view connects a structural characteristic of the EU's policy environment, the complexity of its policy agenda, to institutional fluidity and hence to legal or procedural disputes. U.S. Congress scholars have argued that growing policy complexity generates increased attention to the rules needed to manage it (Bach and Smith 1988), and that entropic tendencies doom attempts to align institutions more closely to policy issues (Baumgartner, Jones, and MacLeod 2000). In contemplating this line of argument, we need to attend to how best to measure policy complexity. Golub (1999) measures it in the EU context as the number of EU competencies (areas of policy authority), showing that complexity has increased. I validate this assessment with a measure of complexity emphasizing jurisdictional fragmentation, which captures the (annual) average number of Commission administrative units involved in the drafting of legislation, based on a random sample of 240 pieces of legislation adopted during the 1987–1997 period. As shown in Figure 12, policy complexity as measured this way has indeed increased during the time period in question, from an average of just over 3 drafting units in 1987 to 5.5 in 1997. In short, the

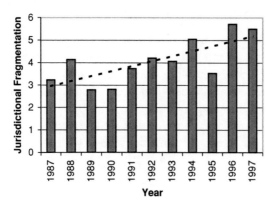

Figure 12 Jurisdictional Fragmentation, 1987–1997

antecedent conditions are propitious for the policy complexity model, and the approach anticipates a growing frequency of procedural politics over time.

The view of over-time change offered in this book is not entirely inconsistent with the policy complexity model but offers a more agentic than structural causal logic. I would argue that actors rationally adapt to their changing policy and institutional environment. Institutional changes, put simply, shape the menu of procedural alternatives available for selection, simultaneously resolving old ambiguities (presumably!) and creating new ones. In short, institutional change restructures both opportunities and incentives. On this view, actors both anticipate and respond to institutional change by engaging in procedural politics more during the periods immediately preceding and following the entry into force of treaties than during the middle of each treaty regime. A year or more often passes between the signing of treaties and their entry into force, during which time actors rationally anticipate future procedural politics and jockey for position. The fighting continues during the early part of each treaty regime, but through learning and the strategic foreclosure of options (e.g., via Court judgments), it slows until the next bout of anticipatory adaptation.

To assess this proposition, it helps to locate the relevant institutional changes. Three stand out. The first is located in the early-to-mid 1980s, when the "Luxembourg Compromise" began to erode. The Luxembourg Compromise had, from the mid-1960s, eliminated any meaningful procedural political incentives because it ensured that all legislation would be

Patterns

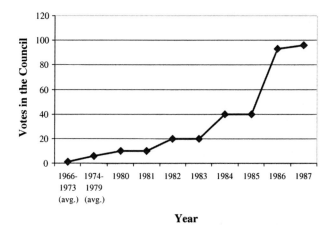

Figure 13 The Practice of Voting in the Council, 1966–1987. *Sources*: De Ruyt 1989, 116 (for pre-1980 and 1980–1984; see also Kranz [1982] and Dewost [1980]); Dashwood 1989, 79 (for 1980); Dewost 1987, 168 (1982, 1984, 1985); Wessels 1991, 146 (1986–1989). Figures prior to 1985 constitute extremely rough estimates.

adopted by consensus.[1] A secular increase in the use of majority voting began to appear as early as 1980 (Dewost 1980), and in 1982 member states hastened the demise of the Luxembourg Compromise when they rebuffed a United Kingdom attempt to invoke it (*Common Market Law Review* 1982; *European Law Review* 1982; Teasdale 1993, 571). After that point, EU member states increasingly returned to the letter and spirit of the treaty, demonstrating growing willingness to adopt legislation by majority voting where the treaty provided for it. The very rough data in Figure 13 confirm the narrative.

The move to majority voting made available "new" institutional alternatives, drawing a sharp contrast between treaty provisions allowing for majority voting and those continuing to require unanimity. This provided possible incentives for procedural politics. For the time period that I will examine, the formal treaty changes brought about by the 1987 Single European Act (signed in 1986) and the 1993 Maastricht Treaty (signed in 1992) furnish the second and third punctuations around which I expect the frequency of disputes to vary. The same would presumably hold for the 1999 Amsterdam Treaty and the 2003 Nice Treaty.

---

[1] The Luxembourg Compromise had established that single member states could prevent passage of legislation, even when the treaty called for majority voting, by invoking their "vital national interests." See *Bull. EC* 3/1966, 9, for the text of the compromise.

Procedural Politics

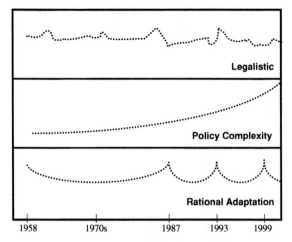

Figure 14 Three Models of Temporal Variation

Figure 14 graphically summarizes the three sets of expectations about over-time variation expressed in the "legalistic," "policy complexity," and "rational adaptation" models.

What does the evidence say? Figure 15 summarizes the occurrence of legal basis disputes from 1979 to 1998 using the only three data sources for which complete time series are available.[2] It includes evidence from internal documents on opinions written by the European Commission's legal service, from archival research at the EP's Legal Affairs Committee, and from publicly available reports of cases brought before the European Court of Justice. These data definitely understate, perhaps considerably, the real number of disputes. However, they have the advantage of being consistent and complete throughout the period, making it possible systematically to consider over-time variation. Controlling for the amount of legislation adopted does not materially affect these trends or conclusions.

The legalistic model fails on visual inspection. It would predict just as many disputes prior to the mid-1980s as after it, a pattern that clearly does not find support in the evidence. Clearly, something happened after about 1984 that produced previously unseen frequencies of intra- and

---

[2] The time series extends back to 1958 for the Commission and the Court, but EP records were available only since the advent of direct elections in 1979. Prior to 1979 the Commission legal services wrote two legal basis opinions (one in 1972, one in 1977), and the ECJ heard no legal basis cases.

Patterns

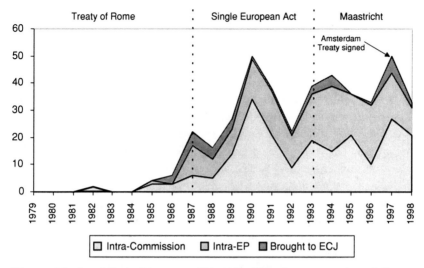

Figure 15 Legal Basis Disputes, 1979–1998. The three categories of dispute ("intra-Commission," "intra-EP," and "brought to ECJ") refer to the source of the evidence. Commission documents were the most vague, and referred only to legal basis questions arising within that institution. EP documents often contained more detail, but I aggregated them for purposes of presentation into disputes that arose within the EP. The final category includes legal basis disputes that gave rise to a case before the European Court of Justice.

interinstitutional disputes about the legal basis of EU legislation.[3] This manifested itself earliest in the European Commission, the legal services of which began addressing a steady flow of legal basis questions in 1985. Similarly, the first three cases to come before the ECJ were all lodged in 1986. For the EP, the big change occurred with the advent of the Single European Act in 1987.

The policy complexity model cannot be rejected at this stage, for it indeed may be able to account for the growth in disputes after the mid-1980s. More definitive assessment must await additional data. The rational adaptation model fits the data reasonably well, though here too the evidence could be more convincing. The mid-1980s growth of disputes responds to the

---

[3] Legal basis disputes are not always procedural political. Sometimes a fight over legal basis does not equate to a disagreement about procedure, since different legal bases can use the same procedure. But in all of the Court cases ($N = 35$) and in 181 of the 182 cases involving the EP's Legal Affairs Committee, these legal basis disputes were also procedural political. Data from the Commission gave no procedural details. Overall data from the 1987–1997 period show that just under half of all legal basis disputes have procedural implications (and, I would submit, motivations).

informal institutional change attendant on the demise of the Luxembourg Compromise. Increases prior to the entry into force of each treaty (recall that the Maastricht Treaty entered into force only in November 1993, so most of that year's data predate the Maastricht regime) could be said to reflect anticipatory adaptation. The uptick in 1997 could reflect anticipation of the entry into force of the Amsterdam Treaty, signed in that year but not entered into force until 1999. Ups and downs during each regime fit more roughly. Proceeding conservatively, it makes sense not to reject either the policy complexity or rational adaptation models at this stage. Summarizing, it is only since the mid-1980s that procedural politics has played itself out in the European Union. In order further to scrutinize the period that forms the core of this study, 1987–1997, and to bring different data to bear on the models of temporal variation, Figure 16 reports trends in legal basis disputes and in procedural politics from 1987 through 1997 using a slightly different dataset.

The graph again identifies the treaties in force during the period: the Single European Act (SEA) from 1 July 1987, and the Maastricht Treaty (Treaty on European Union) from 1 November 1993. It charts trends over

Figure 16 Legal Basis Disputes and Procedural Politics, 1987–1997. Data exclude figures for the Commission reported in Figure 15 and include data from the Council. Reliable data on the Council date only to 1987 and so were excluded from the longer time series, whereas Commission data contain little information on specific legislative acts in question and so were not comparable with the other data used in the shorter time series.

Patterns

the period in pure legal basis disputes (i.e., those not involving a change in procedure) and procedural disputes (those legal basis disputes that do involve a change of procedure). As noted, the legalistic model already fails on the longer time series, and additional evidence to be presented will refute it even more convincingly. The relatively high proportion of pure legal basis disputes, that is, changes of legal basis not involving a change of procedure, might be taken to indicate that legalism holds sway, such that procedural politics operates less forcefully than expected. This conclusion would misrepresent the claims being advanced here. It is not being claimed that actors will never adjust legislative provisions such as the legal basis in the pursuit of legal certainty. Instead, I am simply claiming that when such a change does involve a change of legislative procedure, actors will tend to favor the legal basis (and procedure) giving them more influence to the one giving them less. This says nothing at all about the relative frequency of legal basis disputes not involving a change of procedure.

The policy complexity model would expect an over-time trend toward more frequent disputes, and this finds support in the longer time series. It finds little support in the 1987–1997 data, but the smaller numbers involved make this judgment less certain. Bivariate correlations, reported in Table 6, do not permit rejection of the null hypothesis that this structural characteristic – policy complexity, measured as jurisdictional fragmentation – bears no relationship to the frequency of either legalistic or procedural political disputes. The coefficients, while positive, cannot confidently

Table 6. *Jurisdictional Fragmentation and Legal/Procedural Disputes*

		Jurisdictional Fragmentation	Legalistic Disputes as % of All Acts	Procedural Political Disputes as % of All Acts
Jurisdictional Fragmentation	Pearson correlation	1.000	.048	.389
	Sig. (1-tailed)	—	.444	.118
	N	11	11	11
Legalistic Disputes as % of All Acts	Pearson correlation	.048	1.000	.374
	Sig. (1-tailed)	.444	—	.129
	N	11	11	11
Procedural Political Disputes as % of All Acts	Pearson correlation	.389	.374	1.000
	Sig. (1-tailed)	.118	.129	—
	N	11	11	11

be distinguished from chance, and so the null hypothesis cannot be rejected.

The shorter time series provides slightly clearer support for the rational adaptation model. Around each critical juncture (treaty change), disputes rise, then decline, and then rise again with the approach of the next treaty. While the number of data points remains too small definitely to say, it is also possible that the shorter duration of the Maastricht uptick represents a learning process relative to the Single Act. The Single Act truly did represent a new situation for EU actors, and disputes increased fairly steadily for several years before dropping to lower levels. Maastricht witnessed a shorter period of procedural political ferment.

In sum, this descriptive examination of trends in legal basis and procedural political disputes over time offers some support for the arguments advanced in Chapter 2, while other approaches based on a legalistic approach to institutions or focusing on the structural context of EU policymaking perform less well. Procedural politics, it would seem, responds systematically to institutional change. This is not unexpected: institutional change involves modification of higher-order institutions, which alters the menu from which lower-order institutions (procedures) are selected. When combined with the foundational results adduced in the next main section, however, these results provide solid support for the theory and show it capable of capturing over-time variation in addition to aggregate trends.

The Actors in Procedural Politics

For all of this, it remains possible that procedural politics does not happen for the posited reasons. This book emphasizes rational actors pursuing political influence, which can be termed the influence maximization hypothesis (corresponding to an assumption of the same name). This hypothesis finds support in the relogit equation estimated in the next part of this chapter, which shows that the more unfavorable a proposed procedure is for either the Council or the Parliament, the more likely is a procedural political dispute. The timing of the major qualitative change in the longitudinal data also seems supportive of this hypothesis. It was only from the mid-1980s, with the move to greater majority voting in the Council, that available alternatives actually differed in the influence they afforded different actors. The Commission began paying more attention to the legal basis of legislation that it proposed around that time. The EP waited until 1987 to begin procedural politicking in earnest, which is consistent with the idea

Patterns

that only after the SEA created the cooperation procedure did the EP face a real incentive to try to weigh in on the procedures that would govern the policymaking process.

And yet, it is possible that these aggregate findings disguise other causes, or imply a causal relationship where only a spurious one exists. In particular, as discussed in Chapter 2, there is a serious, if largely unarticulated, rival to this view.[4] I encountered it often in the course of several dozen interviews with lawyers operating in the various EU legal services. According to this view, actors may indeed find themselves in disagreement over the legal basis of EU legislation, but this results from sincere legal disagreements rather than procedural political calculations. If this view were correct, then we would expect to see no relationship between the influence properties of alternative legislative procedures and actors' revealed preferences for those rules. Indeed, since lawyers from all three EU legislative organizations (the Council, Parliament, and Commission) undergo the same legal training, if politics were not involved we would expect to see no systematic differences across the three organizations in terms of the rules proposed and accepted. My own expectation, by contrast, suggests that actors should consistently promote the use of rules that maximize their influence in the political process.

The question I ask in contemplating the actors in procedural politics, then, is a simple one: when disputes over rules occur, do actors indeed promote the usage of rules that maximize their influence? Answering it requires moving beyond the simple presence or absence of a procedural dispute. It requires the additional step of coding each actor's revealed procedural preferences and comparing them to the revealed preferences of others. I present a first cut of evidence in Table 7, which draws from the universe of disputed cases to tally the number of times each actor revealed a preference for each of the nine legislative procedures.

Even at this highly aggregated level, the data provide some confirmation of the influence maximization hypothesis. Each actor shows some striking proclivities that differentiate it from the others. The EP, for example, seeks far more frequently than do others to use the assent procedure (AVCU), which gives it a veto over changes to the status quo. EP advocacy of the co-operation procedure (SYNQ) is equally striking, and it alone advocated use of the unanimous codecision procedure (CODU), which is something like

---

[4] That Cullen and Charlesworth (1999) felt moved to publish an article in a leading EU law journal refuting the legalistic hypothesis provides some confirmation of its existence.

Table 7. *Aggregate Revealed Rules Preferences Among Disputed Cases*

Procedure	Parliament		Commission		Council	
	N	%	N	%	N	%
AVCU	9	4.27	3	1.35	1	0.45
AVFQ	14	6.64	37	16.67	20	9.01
AVFS	8	3.79	18	8.11	19	8.56
AVFU	7	3.32	9	4.05	6	2.70
CNSQ	74	35.07	83	37.39	64	28.83
CNSU	27	12.80	24	10.81	81	36.49
CODQ	12	5.69	13	5.86	4	1.80
CODU	3	1.42	0	0.00	0	0.00
SYNQ	57	27.01	35	15.77	27	12.16
TOTALS	211	100	222	100	222	100

a complicated version of assent. The Commission, for its part, appears especially favorable to the QMV facultative consultation procedure (AVFQ), which allows it to bypass the EP but protects its agenda power. Indeed, the Commission seems to favor all of the facultative consultation procedures, suggesting that its own procedural preferences often lead it to freeze its putative supranational ally, the Parliament, out of the legislative process. The Council advocates the unanimous consultation procedure (CNSU) at an extraordinarily high rate. It strongly resists the QMV codecision procedure (CODQ), but it rather puzzlingly demonstrates high support for use of what I consider its least preferred procedure, the simple majority facultative consultation procedure (AVFS).

These aggregate figures, which lend partial support to my theoretical expectations, are characterized as "first cut" because they fail to control for a variety of factors, not the least available procedural alternatives. Recall that the treaty establishes a correspondence between policy issues and legislative procedures. Some issues present no real alternatives, some present only relatively undesirable alternatives, and some issues make available many procedures with a range of influence properties. It thus makes sense, as a second cut, to consider which alternatives are actually available, and this suggests disaggregating the data from the population of disputes to closer scrutiny at a lower level of analysis. Unfortunately, no ready-made indicator of available alternatives exists, and as a next-best solution I let the actors themselves identify the available procedures. That is, I look at specific combinations of proposals to use a given procedure and responses to those

Patterns

proposals, on the assumption that actors will tend to propose procedures that, in their assessment, stand some nonzero chance of being appropriate to the situation.

Table 8 tabulates "responses" by the European Parliament and Council of Ministers to the procedural "proposals" made by the Commission and by each other.[5] For each respondent, I array the procedures from least to most favorable as these were determined in Chapter 3. The table allows easy visual determination of a number of important observations. First, along the diagonal (bordered cells), the responder agreed to the proposed procedure. Observations falling in those cells are theoretically neutral. Second, observations falling off the diagonal are theoretically informative. Moving along the row to the right of the diagonal (in the unshaded region) tabulates the number of times the responder revealed a preference for a more desirable procedure – that is, one affording it more influence – than that which had been proposed. These observations are consistent with the influence maximization hypothesis. Tallies in any given cell to the left of the diagonal (in the shaded region) indicate that the responder revealed a preference for a procedure giving it less influence. These observations undermine the influence maximization hypothesis. Finally, while this has to be approached cautiously, the distance off the diagonal gives some sense of the "strength" of the procedural political demand: the farther an observation falls from the diagonal, the higher the stakes are in the procedural political dispute.

The table reports two additional statistics, labeled "acceptance" and "demand." Acceptance, as the name suggests, indicates the proportion of proposals to use a given procedure that went undisputed.[6] Demand simply relates the number of times a responder sought to use a given procedure (reading down the columns) to the number of proposals to use that procedure to which it responded. Both of these figures, while rough, are intended to facilitate comparison across procedures for any given actor and across actors for any given procedure.

---

[5] The use of the terms "proposal" and "response" is slightly inaccurate because in some cases the "proposer" (e.g., the Council) expresses its preference after the "responder" (e.g., the Parliament). The point is simply to compare the two actors' revealed procedural preferences on a case-by-case basis.

[6] For the EP, this actually represents the proportion of acceptance among all of its responses to proposals to use a given rule, and not to all proposals. The EP does not always enjoy the right to reveal a procedural preference, and so to calculate acceptance as a fraction of all proposals without factoring in responses would underestimate acceptance of the *avis facultatif* procedures, to which it cannot always respond.

Table 8. *Procedural Preferences: "Proposals" and "Responses"*

Commission Proposal	N	AVFU	AVFQ	AVFS	CNSU	CNSQ	AVCU	CODU	SYNQ	CODQ	Acceptance
					EP Plenary "Response" (N = 211)						
AVFU	8	6			1						86%
AVFQ	37		14		7	8	1		1		45%
AVFS	18			8	2			1	3	1	53%
CNSU	24				16		1	2	5		67%
CNSQ	84				1	67	4		10	1	81%
AVCU	3						3				100%
CODU	0							0			n/a
SYNQ	35								35		100%
CODQ	13								3	10	77%
TOTAL	222	6	14	8	27	75	9	3	57	12	76%
DEMAND		86%	45%	53%	113%	90%	300%	n/a	163%	92%	

Council "Proposal"	N	AVFU	AVFQ	AVFS	CNSU	CNSQ	AVCU	CODU	SYNQ	CODQ	Acceptance
					EP Plenary "Response" (N = 211)						
AVFU	6	4									100%
AVFQ	20		1		1	4	9		1		6%
AVFS	19		1	6	1	2		1	3	1	40%
CNSU	81	2	8	1	21	27	1	2	16	2	26%
CNSQ	64		4		1	37	7		11	4	58%
AVCU	1						1				100%
CODU	0							0			n/a
SYNQ	27								26	1	96%
CODQ	4									4	100%
TOTAL	222	6	14	8	27	75	9	3	57	12	66%
DEMAND		150%	88%	53%	34%	117%	900%	n/a	211%	300%	

Commission Proposal	N	AVFS	CODQ	SYNQ	CNSQ	AVFQ	CODU	AVCU	CNSU	AVFU	Acceptance
					Council Response (N = 222)						
AVFS	18	13				2			3		72%
CODQ	13		4	3	3				3		31%
SYNQ	35			24	1				10		69%
CNSQ	84	2			44	9			28	1	52%
AVFQ	37	4			12	5		1	14	1	14%
CODU	0						0				n/a
AVCU	3				3			0			0%
CNSU	24				1	3			20		83%
AVFU	8					1			3	4	50%
TOTAL	222	19	4	27	64	20	0	1	81	6	46%
DEMAND		106%	31%	77%	76%	54%	n/a	33%	338%	75%	

EP Plenary "Proposal"	N	AVFS	CODQ	SYNQ	CNSQ	AVFQ	CODU	AVCU	CNSU	AVFU	Acceptance
					Council Response (N = 222)						
AVFS	8	6				1			1		75%
CODQ	12	1	4	1	4				2		33%
SYNQ	57	3		26	11	1			16		46%
CNSQ	75	2			37	9			27		49%
AVFQ	14	1			4	1			8		7%
CODU	3	1					0		2		0%
AVCU	9				7			1	1		11%
CNSU	27	1			1	4			21		78%
AVFU	6								2	4	67%
TOTAL	211	15	4	27	64	16	0	1	80	4	41%
DEMAND		188%	33%	47%	85%	114%	0%	11%	296%	67%	

Note: Includes data from only the 222 procedural disputes. It thus provides information about how actors behave *when disputes occur*.

Patterns

Several caveats in interpreting the data should be noted. First, many of the cells involve very small numbers and as a result percentages give only a very rough guide to actual procedural preferences. Second, both the acceptance and demand figures can reflect what sorts of alternatives are realistically available to a proposed procedure, but in a large-N setting it is impossible even to guess at which procedures might have stood as realistic alternatives to those proposed. Thus, high acceptance, for example, might reflect a dearth of alternatives as much as, or instead of, a preference for a given procedure.

With those cautions in mind, the data do prove suggestive. Cell-by-cell assessment would prove tedious and largely repetitive, and so I limit myself to a few general observations. First, the overwhelming preponderance of cases falls within the range that is either neutral or consistent with the influence maximization hypothesis. Second, the EP and especially the Council reveal distinct clusters of procedural political preferences. The EP, with the puzzling exception of the unanimous variant, rejects the facultative consultation procedures at a relatively high rate, and it also tends not to accept the unanimous consultation procedure. It tends to accept and demand the assent (AVCU), cooperation (SYNQ), and QMV codecision (CODQ) procedures at much higher rates. (EP acceptance of codecision procedures "proposed" by the Commission is artificially low in these figures. In all three cases in which the EP "rejected" a Commission proposal to use the codecision procedure, the Council had already changed the procedure to cooperation, presenting the EP with a virtual fait accompli.) The Council evinces a very strong preference for the unanimous consultation procedure (CNSU), as well as a rather puzzling attachment to the procedure that, on my analysis, gives it the least influence – the simple majority facultative consultation procedure (AVFS).[7]

Interpreted in this way, these data provide solid overall support for the influence maximization hypothesis. True, there are many intervening factors (such as the actual availability of alternatives) that lessen the ability to make solid inferences about procedural preferences. However, as noted, the table can also be interpreted more generally, and at that level the influence

---

[7] One possible explanation would focus on the nature of the issues dealt with under the procedure. The AVFS procedure tends to be used very rarely, and generally with respect to exceptionally arcane and usually highly technical issues (e.g., statistics legislation). It could well be that member states just don't care which procedure is used in adopting laws in these areas. Later I find that, indeed, procedural political disputes become more likely the more important is the legislation in question.

Table 9. *Influence Maximization: Predictive Success*

Respondent: Proposer	Correct	Incorrect	Neutral	N	Correctly Predicted (%)
EP:CC	48	4	159	211	92.3
EP:CM	94	17	100	211	84.7
CM:EP	84	27	100	211	75.7
CM:CC	79	29	114	222	73.1
CC:EP	44	8	159	211	84.6
CC:CM	78	30	114	222	72.2
ALL CASES	427	115	746	1288	78.8

maximization hypothesis receives solid support. Recall that the shaded part of the table represents a region of disconfirmation of my argument, the boxed cells are theoretically neutral, and the nonshaded part represents a region of confirmation of the influence maximization hypothesis. Examining these various regions suggests that actors do, indeed, prefer procedures giving them more influence to those giving them less.

Predictive success varies from actor to actor, however, as shown in the summary figures in Table 9. The table reports the correct, incorrect, and neutral predictions for the Parliament (EP) and Council (CM) from Table 8, and includes additional data on the European Commission (CC), all from the perspective of the "responder's" preference ranking, and all drawn from a dataset of 222 procedural political disputes, representing the known universe during the 1987–1997 period.

On this analysis, the European Parliament most aggressively seeks to maximize its own influence, and where it involves itself in a procedural political dispute the analysis correctly predicts over 87 percent of the positions that it takes. Interestingly, the Parliament also seems rather more aggressive with respect to the Commission than with respect to the Council, and this even though it agrees far more frequently with Commission proposals than with the Council. While decisive evidence to this effect is lacking, I would nonetheless suggest that procedural political calculations, rather than supranational affinities, can accommodate both of these observations, while a naive perspective emphasizing the putative supranational-intergovernmental split cannot.[8] Instead of the latter, I find that narrow

---

[8] It is worth noting here that the procedural preference rankings of the EP and the Commission derived theoretically in Chapter 3 are not statistically significantly correlated with each other ($R = -.317$, $p = .406$).

institutional interests – procedural preferences – drive procedural political behavior. Sometimes procedural politics drives the Commission and Parliament together (as against the Council); sometimes it drives them apart (and perhaps to cooperation with the Council). Overall, predictive success (defined as successful predictions as a percentage of all non-neutral observations) stands lower for the Commission (76.6%) and the Council (74.4%) than for the EP. Given the absence of controls (as for example, the proposal-response sequence), which can allow in anomalous results (e.g., the EP's "rejection" of codecision in three cases), the overall predictive success of almost 79 percent provides extremely solid support for the influence maximization hypothesis.

As a last point on variation in procedural politics across actors, consider the set of procedural political disputes that have come before the European Court of Justice and been decided through mid-2003 (see Appendix 4.A).[9] The cases hold particular interest for two reasons. First, the preferences that actors reveal in their dealings with the Court arguably represent costly, and to that extent credible and informative, signals, rather than cheap talk. That is, they should, more than other cases, reflect actors' true preferences, those in which they are willing to invest. Second, they offer an opportunity to address directly the revealed procedural preferences of the ECJ. Judicial decisions are central to the strategic logic of procedural politics, and indeed they (and beliefs about them) substantially drive the action in the game model developed in Chapter 3. However, since the Court is relatively unconcerned with what the models in Chapter 3 capture – legislative influence – I have not deduced preference rankings for it. I will thus proceed inductively in examining the Court's revealed procedural preferences.

Rather than working through all of the evidence dealing with the legislative actors, much of which will resemble the preceding, I briefly summarize it before turning to the Court. Evidence from Court cases strongly confirms the procedural political expectation that actors promote rules that increase their influence in the political process. Using the rankings from Chapter 3, the models correctly predict 100 percent of the interventions by both the European Commission and the European Parliament. They perform less well in predicting Council positions (65%). In general, an obvious

---

[9] Seven cases involve legislation adopted pre-SEA and thus are not included in the data already reported. The remaining twenty-seven cases concern twenty-five acts already included above.

pattern appears. The member states and the Council tend to promote the use of unanimity (favoring majority voting in only 51% of the cases). The supranational actors, and especially the Commission, tend to favor the use of majority voting procedures. The Commission does so in every case but one, and in that case no majority voting alternative was available. Thus, the evidence strongly supports the influence maximization hypothesis and strongly disconfirms a legalistic alternative.

Turning now to the European Court of Justice, the evidence yields some surprises. Without getting into the details of the theoretical debate about the ECJ, two strands stand out. The first portrays the ECJ as a strategic agent that is sensitive to negative reactions from its member state principals but that exploits control gaps to the extent feasible (Garrett and Weingast 1993; Garrett 1995b; Garrett, Kelemen, and Schulz 1998). The second portrays the ECJ as effectively unconstrained, free to pursue its sincere (probably pro-supranational) preferences (Rasmussen 1986; Burley and Mattli 1993; Mattli and Slaughter 1995, 1998). The evidence from these cases, which have collectively been referred to as "the pivot on which the balance of federalism in the EU turns" (Lenaerts 1992), strongly supports the view of the Court as unconstrained by member state responses. However, it also undermines the rival to this view by demonstrating just how problematic is the notion of "supranational."

Empirically, the ECJ strongly favors the European Commission, appears generally indifferent to the EP, and strongly disfavors member states and the Council of Ministers. Following the methods of (and keeping in mind the caveats about) the foregoing analysis, I coded the alternatives in each case with the ranking assigned to each procedure for each actor. I then simply calculated the rank difference between the ECJ's choice and the alternative procedure from the perspective of each actor. On average the ECJ issues rulings that improve Commission influence by 2.5 rank steps, leave EP influence basically unchanged, and reduce Council influence by 2.6 rank steps.

More informatively, the ECJ finds in favor of the Commission far more frequently than it rules against it, the opposite applies for the Council, and the EP presents a mixed profile in this respect. In making this claim I go beyond whether a given actor was a plaintiff or a defendant in a specific case, and whether it won or lost. I include cases in which the actor itself was not involved, because the Court's choice from among procedural alternatives shapes its influence nonetheless. I illustrate these tendencies in

Patterns

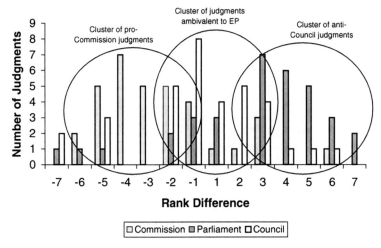

Figure 17 Winners and Losers at the ECJ, Through Mid-2003

Figure 17, which shows the distribution of ECJ judgments across rank differences for each actor.

A negative rank difference reflects a procedural political improvement relative to the alternative. The Commission wins far more than it loses and it wins more than any other actor, as indicated by the cluster of cases (labeled "pro-Commission") in the negative rank difference region, to the left. The Council, by contrast, tends to lose: judgments primarily result in worse procedural outcomes, as suggested by the cluster of cases (labeled "anti-Council") to the right of the figure. The EP holds a middle ground in this respect, losing only slightly more than it wins, the ECJ thereby appearing ambivalent toward the EP.

In sum, the aggregate evidence concerning variations in procedural politics across actors consistently supports the arguments advanced in Chapter 2. Actors seek to ensure the usage of procedures that maximize their influence in the political process. The theory does not perfectly predict these variations in procedural preferences across actors, facing special difficulties with the Council, but it clearly outperforms expectations based on no difference among actors or based on alleged supranational-versus-intergovernmental affinities. Indeed, with respect to the latter, it undermines the very category of supranational. It succeeds in explaining when supranational alliances will form, but it also succeeds in explaining when they do not. In that sense, it accounts for variations also accounted for by prevailing views, all while explaining additional facts, and all of this within a spare framework emphasizing only opportunities and incentives (influence maximization).

Variations by Issue Area

To this point, I have assessed variations in procedural politics over time and across different actors, finding consistently strong support for the arguments developed in Chapter 2. I have also suggested that procedural politics should vary systematically across issues. The next part of this chapter undertakes a statistical assessment of this proposition at the level of individual laws. For now, though, the focus is on the more aggregated level of policy sectors.

What should we expect to see in terms of cross-sectoral variation in procedural politics? With the approach developed in Chapter 2, procedural politics is expected to occur in sectors characterized by jurisdictional ambiguity, such that multiple procedures with different influence properties might apply. But how can we know, in general, where a sector will come down in this respect? Lawyers and policy analysts frequently distinguish "horizontal" sectors, governing issues that cut across a wide range of public policy concerns, and "vertical" sectors that stand as distinct and autonomous policy areas. Kapteyn and VerLoren van Themaat (1998), for example, classify agriculture and fisheries, transport, energy, and industrial policy/research and technology as vertical sectors, and environment, consumer protection, public health, culture, education, tourism, sport, youth and senior citizens, and similar policies as "horizontal and flanking" policies. Their distinction corresponds fairly well to what I would expect in terms of highly jurisdictionally ambiguous sectors (subject to high levels of procedural politics) versus jurisdictionally clearer sectors that should, by hypothesis, be more resistant to procedural politics.

As in other instances in this book, no off-the-shelf theoretical alternative presents itself. Policy networks analysis probably comes closest. It would be inclined to ascribe procedural politics, everyday politics with respect to rules, to variations in three factors: relative sectoral insularity, relative stability of sectoral policy community membership, and resource dependencies among community members (Peterson 1995). Insular sectors populated by a stable group of highly interdependent members, which shade toward the ideal type of a "policy community," should be relatively immune to procedural political disputes. Highly diffuse or penetrated issue areas with fluid groups of participants and ever-shifting patterns of resource exchange, which shade toward the opposite ideal type of an "issue network," should be far more susceptible to such disputes. This set of expectations generates empirical predictions identical to my own: agriculture, a classic policy community, should be immune to procedural politics, as should other stable sectors. Environmental policy, youth, culture, and related areas should all prove more susceptible to procedural politics.

Here, then, it would seem that the two approaches are observationally equivalent. The first step in teasing all of this out, of course, lies in establishing whether the common predictions of the two approaches are correct, or whether, by contrast, something else is doing the explanatory work. Unfortunately, sectoral identification poses some significant problems. First, no "objective" sectoral identification exists in a world in which procedural politics operates. Actors are expected strategically to frame proposals from their initial conception, and placing them in one or another category is an obvious tool in support of a policy of strategic issue definition. Second, even were this not the case, much legislation simply defies easy categorization, and different indicators classify the same acts differently. Consider the following example. A proposal comes out of the Commission's Directorate-General VI (Agriculture), with input from three other Directorates-General (Employment, Internal Market, and Consumer Policy). It is subject-classified as "approximation of laws, foodstuffs, fruit and vegetables, plant health legislation, environment." It receives three separate classification codes (03502000, 03605100, 03605400), four subject headings (Agriculture, Environment, Consumer Protection, Health), and no fewer than six descriptors ("foodstuff; foodstuffs legislation; fruit; meat product; pesticide residue; vegetable"). It proceeds to the EP's Committee on the Environment, Public Health, and Consumer Protection and is amended by the Commission's Environment Directorate before being adopted by the Agriculture Council.[10] Now comes the question: what is "the issue" or "the sector" involved? The answer, of course, is that there isn't one. Different indicators are likely to produce somewhat different results.

[10] This describes Council Directive 97/41/EC of 25 June 1997 amending Directives 76/895/EEC, 86/362/EEC, 86/363/EEC and 90/642/EEC relating to the fixing of maximum levels for pesticide residues in and on, respectively, fruit and vegetables, cereals, foodstuffs of animal origin, and certain products of plant origin, including fruit and vegetables, OJ L 184, 12 July 1997, 33–49.

Faced with this difficulty, I simply use EP parliamentary committees to indicate the subject matter of EU legislation. This has the overriding advantage of ease and availability. It has the serious disadvantage that large swaths (approximately 50 percent) of EU legislation fail to pass through the Parliament at all and thus will not be identified by this method. My point, here, however, is simply to get a sense of the cross-sectoral variations in procedural politics and to assess whether they correspond to opportunities and incentives in the hypothesized way.

I begin with a baseline (null) model of no sectoral effects by calculating the percentage of EP standing committee reports adopted by each committee during the 1987–1997 period. If sectors did not vary in terms of procedural politics, we would expect the committee share of procedural political disputes to equal the share of reports written. I then calculate a procedural political differential (actual procedural political disputes minus baseline expectation), with positive numbers indicating high susceptibility to procedural politics and negative numbers indicating low susceptibility. Figure 18 presents the results of these calculations.

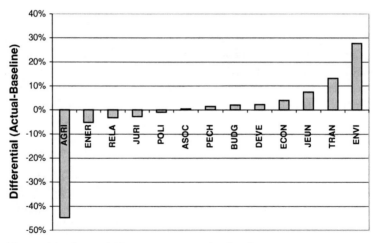

Figure 18 Sectoral Variation in Procedural Politics. *Key*: AGRI = Agriculture; ENER = Energy; RELA = External Relations; JURI = Legal Affairs; POLI = Political Affairs; ASOC = Social Affairs; PECH = Fisheries; BUDG = Budget; DEVE = Development and Cooperation; ECON = Economic and Monetary Affairs; JEUN = Youth and Culture; TRAN = Transport; ENVI = Environment, Public Health, and Consumer Protection.

Patterns

The results correspond as well to the expectations of procedural politics as to those of policy networks analysis. With the glaring exception of the transportation sector (TRAN), the sectors with the highest differentials (most susceptible to procedural politics) are "horizontal" in nature: social affairs, youth policies, and environmental policy. The two sectors with the lowest differentials (and thus least susceptible to procedural politics) are classic "vertical" sectors, agriculture and energy. The low and high extremes also represent opposite ends of the policy networks continuum, with the agricultural policy community expected to be characterized by procedural stability and the environmental policy issue network by procedural fluidity.

The main exception, transportation policy, bears mentioning for the light it sheds on procedural politics. Following the entry into force of the Single European Act (SEA) in mid-1987, the EP's Committee on Transport was one of the first aggressively to seize on the sense of possibilities for increased EP influence under the new internal market rules, which would use the cooperation procedure. However, its efforts flew in the face of EU law and were doomed to failure. Transport had very few SEA dossiers (reporting on only 2.4% of all legislation that underwent a legal basis change as a result of the new treaty), but it nonetheless joined the Environment committee (which had almost 37% of the total number of dossiers changed by the SEA) as the number one demander of legal basis changes within the EP.[11] In a curt note from April 1989, the EP's Legal Affairs Committee pointed out that it had never supported a single Transport Committee request to change the legal basis of an act, and it lectured Transport on the vertical nature of its sector and the availability of specific, sectoral rules.[12] Among the top eight procedural political EP committees, only the ultra-vertical Energy committee and the external relations committee fared worse in convincing the plenary to embrace their procedural political maneuvers. The very fact of this failure confirms the determinants of sectoral variation: transport, along with agriculture and others, is a vertical sector the rules of which are both clear and exclusive. As a general matter, jurisdictional ambiguity is low if not nonexistent, and procedural politics is correspondingly difficult to play.

---

[11] For the committee distribution of SEA dossiers, see EP Doc. A2-2/87, 26 March 1987.

[12] Note from Dietmar Nickel to M. Barzanti, EP Legal Affairs Committee dossier 33/89, 18 April 1989.

Summary

To summarize the foregoing, systematic variation across time, actors, and issues broadly confirms the arguments advanced in Chapter 2 about the conditions under which procedural politics – more precisely, in this empirical context, procedural political conflict – occurs. The rise of contemporary procedural political disputes in the mid-1980s conforms closely to the theoretical logic, which emphasizes the existence of procedural alternatives that differ in their influence properties. This timing confirms the hypothesis advanced in Chapter 2 whereby influence differences among alternatives were postulated to increase the likelihood of disputes. Furthermore, when alternatives are demonstrably available, actors consistently (at an overall rate of around 80%) reject rules that give them less influence in favor of those that give them more. The influence maximization hypothesis thus finds clear confirmation as against its rival. Systematic cross-sectoral variation strongly supports the ambiguity hypothesis, whereby jurisdictional ambiguity is an important predicate of procedural politics. "Horizontal" sectors, jurisdictionally ambiguous by their very nature, produce a far greater proportion of disputes than one would expect based on their overall contribution to EU legislative output. Vertical sectors contribute far less than expected, and indeed less overall.

Finally, addressing an issue to which I will attend more over the course of the next two chapters, a broad array of evidence suggests that actors join forces for procedural political rather than ideological reasons. This supports the procedural coalition hypothesis as against a traditional alternative positing fixed supranational-intergovernmental coalitions in the EU. The Commission has shown itself perfectly willing to abandon the EP's aspirations for more influence when this furthered its own procedural political aims. What is more, evidence from ECJ cases suggests that the very notion of "pro-supranational" rules rests on shaky ground: rules that favor one supranational actor (e.g., the Commission) may not favor another (e.g., the Parliament). The Court shows itself to be quite activist in promoting majority voting in the Council and quite inattentive to the revealed preferences and costly signals of the member states. One observer summarized the Court's stance as follows: "any enrichment, every improvement, in Community competence is treated favorably, whatever the legal form and the methods followed.... The Court shows itself to be favorable to every advance. By contrast, strict treaty rules... become an impenetrable rampart whenever opposition to any sort of reversal of integration is involved" (Blumann 1988, 512).

The Determinants of Procedural Politics

These initial results, based on descriptive statistics about the occurrence of procedural politics across time, actors, and issues, give confidence that the arguments advanced in Chapter 2 help to explain the conditions under which (and to a lesser extent, the ways in which) procedural politics occurs. It is in the nature of these data, however, that separate parts of the picture are treated separately, with few controls possible. These limitations make it desirable to test theoretical expectations in a multivariate setting, where the marginal impact of each factor can be assessed, controlling for the impact of other important factors. I turn now to such a multivariate assessment.

Data and Research Design

To the end of testing my own and alternative hypotheses, I compiled a dataset of procedural political disputes, instances in which one or several actors (EP committees, EP plenary, member states, or the Council) disputed a procedure proposed by another.[13] Using databases obtained from the European Commission and European Parliament, archival research in Brussels and Luxembourg, documentary and interview evidence from all three legislative institutions plus the European Court of Justice, records from selected national parliaments and executives, and exhaustive searches of other primary and secondary sources, I discovered 222 such cases. Because disputed legislation represented such a small fraction of the total (4.7%), random sampling proved inefficient, and I instead pursued a choice-based sampling strategy, coding the relevant measures for all of the disputes and for twice as many nondisputes (N = 444) randomly sampled from the rest of the population.

With the dependent variable thus coded dichotomously (dispute, no dispute), I proceeded to measure the independent variables central to my own

---

[13] It bears mentioning again that procedural politics is expected to operate even when no dispute occurs. Because no actor discernibly disputes a procedure does not mean that this actor did not behave strategically. It simply means that procedural politics could not easily be detected.

argument as well as a series of control measures. I coded jurisdictional ambiguity, the key hypothesized determinant of procedural political opportunity, as the total number of Commission units (e.g., Directorates-General) involved in the drafting of legislation. The Commission's Secretariat-General assigns legislative dossiers to those administrative units that can reasonably claim an interest in the subject matter. Thus, the greater the number of policy domains involved, the greater the number of referrals and the higher the measure. These data derive from the Commission's Prelex database.[14] The ambiguity hypothesis suggests that the greater the ambiguity (here measured as just noted), the greater the opportunity, and thus the more likely procedural political dispute becomes. I therefore expect this coefficient to be positively signed.

On the incentives side, I use the procedural preference rankings derived in Chapter 3 as measures of the relative desirability (actually, undesirability) for each actor of proposed procedures. For the Council, I thus coded Commission proposals in terms of Council procedural preference rankings. For the EP, I similarly coded rules proposed by the Commission and by the Council.[15] A lower number indicates a more desirable procedure, a higher number a less desirable one. Thus, as this measure increases, the less desirable is the proposed procedure, the greater is the incentive to oppose it, and, by the influence maximization hypothesis, the more likely procedural political dispute becomes. Here again I expect a positive sign.

I further sought to control for factors that might influence procedural political opportunities and incentives. In terms of opportunities, I generated a measure of Council preference heterogeneity along a substantive (Left-Right) dimension. On one interpretation, a more heterogeneous Council will have greater difficulty mustering the unanimity required to change a proposed procedure, making disputes less likely. On another, supranational actors will strategically exploit disagreement by fighting more vigorously any rules proposed by the Council. Following the general approach outlined by Kim and Fording (2001), I calculate individual government scores as the portfolio weighted average position of government parties. As a proxy for

---

[14] Available online at *http://europa.eu.int/prelex/apcnet.cfm?CL=en*, last consulted 7 July 2003.
[15] Presumably, all actors respond to rules "proposed" by all others. For the EP I could include both Commission and Council "proposals." I could not build a similar composite measure for the Council (including Commission and EP "proposals") because the EP does not always have an opportunity to express a procedural preference. Thus, any composite measure for the Council including rules proposed by the EP (which only appear in some of the cases) would be unreliable.

substantive (policy) preferences I compute daily scores on the Left-Right dimension (Laver and Hunt 1992) using party data from the Manifestos Data Set produced by the Manifestos Research Group (MRG) (Budge et al. 2001). I then follow König (2001) by calculating Council heterogeneity measures as the maximum distance between any two member states. A statistically significant positive coefficient would confirm the "unanimity constraint" interpretation, a significant and negative one the "strategic exploitation" interpretation.

I also introduced controls for other incentives beyond influence maximization. Presumably, for example, procedural politics might be more likely with respect to important legislation, since it is possible that preferences for influence derive from preferences over policy outcomes, with the latter being more intense for important legislation. Following Golub (1999), I include a dummy variable to account for the legislative instrument being used. Directives, on this analysis, are used for more salient and controversial legislation than are (usually technical) Regulations or (usually hortatory) Decisions. The more important the legislation, one might expect, the greater the incentive to pursue a procedural political strategy. Since I code this variable as Directive = 1, I expect a positive sign on this coefficient. In the same spirit, I control for "integration incentives" (the desire to advance EU integration) by introducing a measure of average member state favorability toward the EU. I did so by calculating government scores (using the Kim and Fording procedure) from Ray's (1999) expert survey data on party positions on the EU.[16]

Estimation and Results

In terms of the statistical model to estimate, the logistic regression suggested by the dichotomous dependent variable would produce biased estimates due to the sampling frame that I use. Accordingly, I estimated a "rare events logit" (relogit) model (Tomz, King, and Zeng 1999) using weighted correction to address the overrepresentation of disputes in the sample, thus eliminating bias introduced by selection on the dependent variable (King and Zeng 2001a, 2001b). Table 10 presents results of the relogit estimation of the determinants of procedural political disputes on 664 cases (two were excluded for missing values).

---

[16] I use Ray's data here since debate exists as to whether the MRG data on this question actually measure salience rather than position (cf. Laver and Garry 2000; Budge 2001).

Table 10. *Relogit Estimates of the Determinants of Procedural Political Disputes*

	Coefficient (Robust S.E.)
Opportunities	
Jurisdictional Ambiguity	0.172***
	(0.032)
Council Left-Right Disagreement	−0.020
	(0.037)
Incentives	
(Policy) Important Legislation	0.528*
	(0.247)
(Institutional) Anti-EP Procedure	0.226***
	(0.022)
(Institutional) Anti-Council Procedure	0.175*
	(0.069)
(Ideological) Pro-Integration Council	−2.79**
	(0.853)
Constant	11.45*
	(5.04)
Likelihood ratio $\chi^2 = 215.36$	
$p > \chi^2 = .000$	
Pseudo-$R^2 = .26$	
N = 664	

Note: Relogit does not generate summary statistics, and the figures reported correspond to an uncorrected logit model in which all coefficients allow for identical substantive interpretations.
* $p < .05$, ** $p < .01$, *** $p < .001$

The results provide strong support for my central arguments. The overall model allows for better predictions of the log-odds of disputes than would be possible without inclusion of these explanatory variables. Both jurisdictional ambiguity and institutional incentives increase the log-odds of procedural political dispute, even when controls are introduced for preference constraints and for noninstitutional incentives such as the importance of legislation and the desire to promote European integration. The results thus confirm the ambiguity and influence maximization hypotheses. Other factors also matter: the log-odds of a dispute do increase for important legislation (Directives), and ideological support among member states for the EU does decrease those odds. Only the effects of the substantive preference constraint are indistinguishable from chance ($P > |z| = 0.59$), though this might have to do as much with the roughness of the instrument (a general Left-Right measure) as with the absence of any real effect. There are no important time effects: analysis with a time-period dummy for the Maastricht regime shows that variable to be insignificant, with all other variables remaining unaffected.

On the basis of these results, it is clear that opportunities and incentives condition procedural politics. How much impact do they have? Probability models such as logistic regression suffer from the key drawback that estimated coefficients defy easy substantive interpretation, and taken by themselves make it hard to articulate the substantive impact of the statistical relationships (Liao 1994; Long 1997). Fortunately, simple transformations of the results enable a clearer assessment of such impact. Thus, as an aid to substantive interpretation, I transformed the logit coefficients into the probability of a dispute using the following general formula for models with k independent variables (Liao 1994, 12; King and Zeng 2001a):

$$\Pr(Y = 1) = 1/(1 + e^{-(\alpha + X1\beta1 + X2\beta2 + \cdots + Xk\beta k)}).$$

This enables estimation of the marginal impact on the probability of a dispute of changes in a given independent variable, controlling for the values of the others or setting them at interesting levels.

Figure 19 simulates the effects of jurisdictional ambiguity on the probability of procedural political dispute under a variety of scenarios. As the statistical results already suggested, jurisdictional ambiguity increases the probability of a dispute. With all other values at their sample means, movement from the lowest level of jurisdictional ambiguity to the mean level (4.4) increases the probability of a dispute by roughly two-thirds, though the absolute probability remains low (less than four percent in the simulation). Because jurisdictional ambiguity is strongly right-skewed, much higher values appear quite rarely, but for exceptionally ambiguous measures the probability of a dispute exceeds 75 percent, even with all other factors held at their sample means.

The figure also illustrates the combined effects of jurisdictional ambiguity (opportunity) and institutional alternatives (incentives) in the production of procedural politics. With average ambiguity, disputes are only one-third as likely when the procedure most favorable to the EP (QMV codecision) is used as under average conditions. Using the most pro-Council procedure reduces the probability by half. Most striking, unfavorable procedures greatly increase the probability of procedural politics. Again, the Council

Procedural Politics

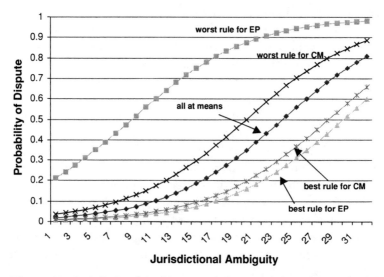

Figure 19 Jurisdictional Ambiguity and the Probability of Procedural Political Dispute

appears far less sensitive in this regard. With the worst rule for the Council and everything else at its sample mean, the probability of a dispute stands at just over 5 percent. Substitute "Parliament" for "Council" and the result is eye-opening: with average ambiguity, a dispute is almost ten times more likely when the EP faces its most unfavorable procedure as when it faces an average procedure, and the absolute risk races to above one-quarter very quickly. Indeed, all other things being average, legislation using the most unfavorable rule to the EP (the unanimous facultative consultation procedure) faces about a one-third chance of forming the object of a procedural political dispute, and at higher levels of ambiguity disputes become highly probable when the EP faces a strongly unfavorable rule.

Summary

The preceding description represents the core statistical result of the chapter: procedural politics responds to opportunities and incentives, with the former conceived as jurisdictional ambiguity and the latter including not only the "usual suspects" – the importance of legislation, attitudes toward European integration – but also influence maximization. These results suggest that the relative observed rarity of procedural politics in the European Union (affecting less than 5 percent of the laws adopted between 1987 and

1997, by my measures) derives from the constraints imposed by higher-order institutions (the treaty), both in the form of jurisdictional clarity and (more likely) in a frequent dearth of attractive procedural alternatives. It does not seem to reduce to the alleged propensity to follow rules, to take them for granted, or to pursue appropriate behavior simply within them, as more sociologically inclined theorists would tend to suggest. It does not seem to reduce to sincere technical attempts to make good law, or honestly to make sense of bad law, as legal scholars might have it and many interviewees insisted. Instead, actors are engaging in procedural politics under predictable conditions, and these are the conditions developed in Chapter 2.

In what ways and with what effects do actors engage in procedural politics? Direct and extensive treatment of the ways will have to await the smaller-N environment of Chapters 5 and 6. The question of effects will also be examined there, but it can be considered in the aggregate here.

Procedural Political Effects

To establish that procedural politics occurs under predictable conditions – when opportunities and incentives align – and for predictable reasons – to maximize influence – is all well and good. However, knowing this does not establish that procedural politics is important to understanding the EU, its political and policymaking processes outcomes, and its long-run development, less still broader issues concerning the nature of institutions. Procedural politics may only matter on its own terms, or in the slightly broader sense of producing the rules that govern everyday politics. I reject this view. Chapter 2 suggested that procedural politics should exert predictable and important effects on things that matter in the EU, most notably on the rules used in making policy, on policymaking efficiency and outcomes, and on constitutional change. The study of specific procedural choices and policy outcomes proves very difficult in a large-N setting, and I address myself to them in the smaller-N setting of Chapters 5 and 6. Here, I limit myself to brief consideration of two of the most important sets of postulated effects of procedural politics, on decision-making efficiency and on (long-run and higher-order) institutional change.

Decision-Making Efficiency

Presumably, member states created the European Union at least in part to get things done – that is, to make policy. It also makes some sense to think that in general and all other things being equal, they would wish to do so as efficiently or inexpensively as possible. Scholars have recently addressed themselves to the question of EU decision-making efficiency (Golub 1999, 2002; Schulz and König 2000), establishing several of its determinants as well as an empirical picture of variation over time and across issues. Not surprisingly, however, they neglect procedural politics. And yet, fighting over rules takes time and represents the diversion of resources toward the pursuit of influence rather than to the making of policy. On the one hand, then, the analysis that follows offers a corrective to prevailing work on decision-making efficiency. Beyond that, it gives a rough measure of the "costs" of procedural politics and of its important but previously unrecognized impact on the EU.

I specify an ordinary least squares (OLS) regression model of EU decision-making lag, taking the days between Commission proposal and Council adoption as the dependent variable. The model includes several variables that have figured prominently in analyses of decision-making speed, and some of which are found in the above relogit estimation of the determinants of procedural politics. The independent variable of primary theoretical interest here is procedural political dispute. I regress decision-making speed on it while controlling for Council substantive preference heterogeneity and heterogeneity with respect to the EU, average Council support for the European Union, the importance (form) of legislation, policymaking complexity, and the level of EP involvement. The preference measures are identical to those used above. With respect to form of legislation, it makes sense to think that Directives should take longer to adopt because they are more important and usually more controversial than other instruments. For policymaking complexity I use the jurisdictional ambiguity measure used above, and similarly I code EP involvement using the procedural preference rankings from Chapter 3. According to the prevailing literature, all coefficients should be positive with the exception of average member state support for the EU. I expect procedural political dispute to relate positively to decision-making lag (i.e., to slow decision making down).

I ran these tests on a dataset of 237 randomly sampled pieces of legislation adopted between 1987 and 1997.[17] Table 11 presents the results.

---

[17] The use of a random sample permits generalization to the universe of EU legislation *adopted* during this period. Consideration of only adopted acts simplified the analysis considerably, since it obviated the "right-censoring" problem inherent in samples that include legislation proposed but not yet adopted. However, the simplification comes at a cost, insofar as the results are not directly comparable to other work in this area, which focuses on legislative proposals both adopted and unadopted.

Patterns

Table 11. *Procedural Politics and Decision-Making Efficiency*

Dependent Variable: Adoption Lag	Coefficient (S.E.)
(Constant)	2339.368*
	(968.998)
Council Left-Right Divergence	8.362
	(5.623)
Council EU Divergence	−26.252
	(55.059)
Council Average EU Support	−440.982**
	(148.235)
Directive	376.369***
	(55.718)
Jurisdictional Ambiguity	14.146**
	(5.095)
EP Involvement	10.329***
	(2.803)
Procedural Political Dispute	215.737*
	(83.691)
N = 237	
Adj. R^2 = .31	

*** $p < .001$, ** $p < .01$, * $p < .05$

The results are generally consistent with existing claims about the determinants of EU decision-making speed, although some exceptions arise. On the confirmatory side, member government support for the EU decreases decision-making time, and Directives, policymaking complexity (jurisdictional ambiguity), and EP involvement all increase it. Somewhat surprisingly, preference heterogeneity in the Council cannot reliably be said to affect decision-making speed, although in the case of Left-Right divergence at least this may have as much to do with the rough nature of the measure as with the absence of a real relationship. Crucially, for present purposes, procedural politics substantially influences decision-making efficiency. Controlling for most of the factors identified in the literature (member state preferences, instrument and policy complexity, and EP involvement), procedural political disputes increase decision times by almost 216 days on average. With legislation enduring, on average, 175 days between proposal and adoption, the effect of a procedural political dispute is to more than double average decision times.

These results suggest two things. First, speculatively, it is at least possible that some of the decision-making slowdown of the post–Single European Act (SEA) period, detected by Golub and attributed by him to growing parliamentary involvement, may be due to the post-SEA explosion in procedural politics. The absence of pre-SEA data precludes making this inference directly, but it stands as a possibility worth exploring in future studies of EU decision-making efficiency. Second, procedural politics is tremendously costly. While measures of the amount of money spent preparing, preempting, and/or litigating procedural politics simply do not exist and are impossible to estimate, we can use decision-making delays as a proxy for monetary costs and conclude that procedural politics involves substantial deadweight losses to member states. That being the case, member states face incentives to eliminate the ambiguities and influence differences that give rise to procedural politics. That is, procedural politics generates incentives to change the EU treaties, to close the gaps, and to avoid future decision-making delays resulting from everyday politics with respect to, rather than within, rules.

Institutional Change

Following from this, then, it makes sense to look at one of the most important sets of postulated procedural political effects, the feedback from everyday (and lower-order) rules fights (procedural politics) to long run (higher-order) institutional change. In particular, I focus on the way that the procedural menu changes over time in response to legal basis and procedural political disputes. To simplify the analysis and to link it as tightly as possible with existing work on EU institutional choice, the focus will be on both the pooling of national sovereignty in the form of majority voting in the Council of Ministers and the delegation of national sovereignty in the form of empowerment of the European Parliament.

Figure 20 traces the evolution of majority voting rules in the Council (as a percentage of all treaty articles empowering it to adopt legislation, left-hand axis) and a simple "power score" for the European Parliament.[18] From the Rome Treaty (with its three transition periods), through the Single

---

[18] The EP "power score" assigns points to each procedure (AVF = 1, CNS = 2, AVC = 3, SYN = 4, COD = 5), multiplies this number by the frequency with which the procedure appears in the treaty, and divides that product by the total number of provisions specifying the EP's legislative role. It is intended simply to facilitate over-time comparison of the consecutive treaties.

Patterns

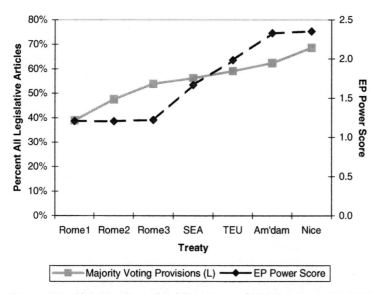

Figure 20 Changing Procedural Provisions of EU Treaties, 1957–2003. *Source*: Based on the author's calculations, but inspired by and broadly consistent with data compiled by Andreas Maurer (2001; Maurer, Wessels, and Mittag 2000).

European Act (SEA), the Treaty on European Union (TEU, or Maastricht Treaty), and on through the Amsterdam and Nice Treaties, Council majoritarianism has steadily increased. At the same time, successive treaty modifications have consistently and substantially empowered the European Parliament.

These two basic facts are among the most important in the history of European integration, indicating to an important extent the transformation of EU governance from a mode characteristic of international relations to one more characteristic of authoritative polities, and yet until recently few studies tried systematically to explain them (McCown 2003; Rittberger 2003). As noted in Chapter 2, the main explanation of EU institutional change, liberal intergovernmentalism, focuses on member state preferences (especially sector-specific preferences) for integration and argues that institutional choices (i.e., decisions to pool or delegate sovereignty) reflect a logic of credible commitments, whereby member states seek to cement the bargains that they strike. A second interpretation might focus on institutional inertia, on the weight of the past (which can take the specific form of path dependency, but can take other forms, as well), which can go under the general heading of historical institutionalism. A third argument, the one advanced here, is a hybrid. I argue that everyday politics (specifically, procedural politics) both informs and incites longer-run institutional change. I expect that legal basis and procedural political disputes under a given treaty will influence procedural changes undertaken in the subsequent round of treaty revisions, with disputes involving the EP particularly influential for changes in its future status, and disputes involving the Commission influential with respect to legislative voting rules.

Aggregate testing of these claims poses some significant methodological obstacles, which may be why it has not yet been attempted. These obstacles, and my relatively limited explanatory goals – does procedural politics feed back into long-run institutional change? – dictate that I proceed incrementally, keeping limitations and uncovered terrain firmly in mind. In particular, I will limit myself to explaining procedural changes in the Maastricht Treaty potentially wrought by procedural politics during the prior period, governed by the Single European Act. For each first-pillar treaty article providing for the adoption of legislation, I coded two specifications of the dependent variable of procedural change. A first is dichotomous – did the procedure change, in terms of EP role and/or Council voting rule, relative to the procedure in place under the previous treaty? The second specification is simply one of the narrower categories (EP role), measured as rank differences between the prior and the subsequent treaties.[19] Thus, I am asking whether procedural change occurred, and to what extent it had certain specific properties associated with the role of the European Parliament.[20]

On the independent variable side, I focus on a number of factors. For every legal basis providing for the adoption of legislation, I coded the number of times the Parliament and Commission invoked that legal basis where either a pure legal basis or a procedural political dispute took place. I included only disputes that occurred between the July 1987 entry into force

---

[19] I used the ordinal scale for the EP role as above, in Figure 20. The rank difference measures subtract the later from the earlier period. Larger numbers, then, will reflect moves in the direction of EP empowerment.

[20] Testing similar expectations about changes in voting rule proved impossible, since they were extremely rare: 3 of 103 articles from the SEA to Maastricht, 8 of 155 from Maastricht to Amsterdam. It turns out that most of the gains in majority voting come about through the creation of new articles and provisions rather than through the modification of existing ones.

of the SEA and the December 1991 intergovernmental agreement on the later treaty.[21] On this basis, and using information generated from Celex on the number of acts adopted, I calculated a "dispute differential" capturing the difference between each treaty article's fraction of all disputes (of that type for that actor) and each treaty article's share of all legal bases for legislation adopted during the period. The greater this dispute differential, the greater the susceptibility of the article to disputes.[22]

To control for Moravcsik's argument about credibility, I gave appropriate treaty articles a credibility score based on Franchino's (2002) study of credibility versus efficiency as drivers of member state executive delegation (in secondary legislation) to the European Commission. These measures have the key advantages that they are cross-sectoral and so can presumably be used to help explain variation across legal bases, and that they are independent of the treaties themselves but get at the issue of credibility problems inherent in different issue areas. They have a number of limitations, too. The nineteen sectors that Franchino examines map onto only about forty treaty articles, which limits the number of cases that can be included in the statistical analysis. Perhaps more important, some of these scores are based on very few legislative provisions, sometimes only one (as in the case of company law, which corresponds to post-Amsterdam article 52 of the treaty). This, in particular, demands caution in interpreting the analysis that follows. No member state preference measures were included, simply for lack of cross-national cross-sectoral data. Future extensions to the Amsterdam Treaty, though, may be able to employ preference measures derived from Hug and König's (2002) exemplary study of the Amsterdam intergovernmental conference. They code the number of member states preferring a supranational solution in 79 different issues arising at the Amsterdam intergovernmental conference (IGC). For the Maastricht changes, such preference measures are unavailable.

---

[21] There is usually a delay of a year or two between agreement on a treaty and its entry into force. To include cases occurring after agreement but before entry into force made little sense as the hypothesized effects (incorporation into treaty change) could never materialize, the new treaty having already been agreed.

[22] This technique effectively normalizes the number of disputes for the number of legislative acts involved. Raw counts, for example, would grossly overemphasize agricultural legislation. By using the differential, we can see how many disputes occurred compared to what one might naturally expect based on the fraction of legislation based on the article in question.

Table 12. *Logit Estimates: SEA-TEU Procedural Change*

Dependent Variable: SEA-TEU Procedural Change	Coefficient (S.E.)
Dispute Differential	79.514*
	(37.295)
Credibility Score	2.065
	(1.353)
(Constant)	−2.859**
	(1.039)
Likelihood ratio $\chi^2 = 8.55$	
$p > \chi^2 = .0139$	
pseudo-$R^2 = .185$	
N = 42	

* $p < .05$, ** $p < .01$

The analysis begins by testing for the effects of legal basis/procedural political disputes and credibility problems on procedural change (coded dichotomously: change = 1, no change = 0). With all variables specified as above, the results are presented in Table 12.

The coefficients of both dispute differentials and credibility are positive, as expected, but credibility fails to achieve statistical significance, and thus we cannot reject the null hypothesis that it stands unrelated to procedural change. Disputes, by contract, are positive and statistically significant at the .05 level. We can reject the null hypothesis of no relationship here and infer that as disputes during the prior treaty regime with respect to a given legal basis increase, the likelihood of a procedural change to that legal basis (treaty article) also increases. The model chi-square statistic is also significant at the .05 level, allowing us to conclude that these variables do help in explaining procedural change. Perhaps more important (Menard 1995, 17), the model successfully predicts almost 79 percent of outcomes during this period.

How substantively important are these effects of prior-period disputes on subsequent treaty changes? As earlier, here I assess substantive impact by transforming the logit output into statements about the impact of changes in the value of independent variables of interest on the probability that the event of interest (here, procedural change) will occur. Figure 21 illustrates the effects of changes in the dispute differential

Patterns

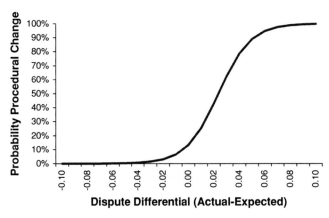

Figure 21 Prior Period Disputes and Institutional Change: SEA to TEU

on the probability of procedural change, holding credibility at its mean value.

The simulated effect of disputes (actually, dispute differentials) on the probability of procedural change, holding credibility problems at their mean, is strong. Where differentials are negative – that is, where treaty articles account for a greater share of legislation adopted than of legal basis or procedural political disputes – procedural change is an extremely low probability event, given an average level of credibility problems. When the differential reaches around –2 percent, the probability begins to increase rapidly, and at a differential of around +5 percent, procedural change becomes a near-certainty. Procedural politics during the SEA period influenced long-run institutional change, and this influence appears to have been substantial.

What of the more specific set of changes made to the role played by the European Parliament in the EU legislative process? Clearly the most significant change from the Single Act to the Maastricht Treaty was the creation of the new codecision procedure in the latter treaty, giving the EP both the conditional agenda-setting power it had been enjoying under the Single Act and an airtight veto over changes to the status quo. To what extent did this change and the others in the EP's role reflect a response to procedural politics, especially procedural politics played by the Parliament itself, in the earlier period?

To answer this question, I specified a linear regression model with the rank-difference change to EP role as the dependent variable, and three independent variables: credibility problems in the issue area in question,

Table 13. *Explaining EP Empowerment: SEA to TEU*

Dependent Variable: EP Role Change (Rank Difference)	Coefficient (S.E.)
(Constant)	0.0741
	(0.16)
Dispute Differential: Commission	−1.587
	(2.532)
Dispute Differential: EP	4.236*
	(2.145)
Credibility Score	0.496*
	(0.261)
N = 42	
Adj. R^2 = .112	

* $p < .10$

European Parliament legal basis and procedural political disputes, and European Commission legal basis and procedural political disputes. Moravcsik's liberal intergovernmentalism expects the first to show a positive sign and to attain statistical significance, while probably expecting no statistical significance for the other two variables. My own approach, by contrast, suggests that even controlling for credibility problems, EP disputes will matter for changes to the EP's role, whereas Commission disputes, aimed as they are at maximizing the Commission's own influence, will be irrelevant. Table 13 presents the results of this analysis.

These results give some comfort to both intergovernmentalism and the approach developed here, indeed perhaps suggesting complementarities that future research might exploit. As expected, disputes involving the European Commission do not seem to matter as determinants of change in the EP's legislative role. Both credibility and EP disputes show expected signs and are statistically significant, albeit only at the .10 level (p = .056 and p = .055, respectively). Overall variance explained, with R^2 = .11, remains quite low. Thus, while the results presented here are strongly consistent with theoretical expectations developed in Chapter 2, it seems clear that additional work, including additional variables and extending to additional time periods, will be called for.

This subsection has pursued the goal of assessing the feedback hypothesis from Chapter 2, whereby everyday politics with respect to rules (procedural politics) inform and incite subsequent changes to the menu of procedural alternatives as defined in the EU constitution (treaty). The logic of that claim was straightforward: procedural politics exploits, and to that extent identifies, gaps in the member states' intergovernmental contract, informing them of which areas pose jurisdictional problems. At the same time, procedural politics imposes costs on member states in the form of legislative delays, and so incites institutional change. Thus, I expected a positive empirical relationship between procedural politics on the one hand and subsequent treaty changes on the other. The best-articulated explanation of EU institutional change, liberal intergovernmentalism, strongly downplays any relationship, if not denying it altogether.

The results strongly confirm that procedural politics influences long-run change. Whether one conceives of change generally (i.e., as either involving the EP's role or the Council voting rule) and dichotomously (change/no change), or whether one operationalizes change more narrowly (EP role rank difference between earlier and later treaties), procedural politics and legal basis disputes influence long-run change, even when one controls for the logic of credible commitments. These effects are theoretically consistent, and in the case of basic change they appear quite strong. In short, feedback effects between the everyday operation of EU institutions and their long-run change appear to operate. Whether and to what extent this involves information and incentives remains unclear and must form the object of future research in this area.

The above results seem largely inconsistent with an intergovernmental account attributing relatively little causal weight to everyday politics as a determinant of long-run institutional change. In particular, it would appear quite difficult to assimilate the demonstrated effects to an account in which member states foresee and control the effects of their institutional choices. The credibility measures perform well enough, however, that there would seem to be good cause to consider procedural politically induced treaty change as complementary with a sufficiently modified intergovernmentalist account, one more firmly grounded in notions of incomplete contracting and learning. On this account, EU institutional change would be seen to respond not only to contemporary member state preferences, bargaining power, and contracting needs, but also to the weight of past institutions. Procedural politics informs and incites institutional change; under these conditions member states presumably learn institutional lessons and incrementally, rather than fundamentally, change rules and procedures.

Summary

More will be done in the upcoming chapters to assess the effects of procedural politics on important outcomes in the European Union. The point of this section has been to test expectations about some of the most important hypothesized effects of procedural politics against aggregate data. The results suggest that procedural politics decisively affects what the EU does (how efficiently it operates) and, indeed, what it is (its basic institutional architecture). Procedural politics may indeed represent "the pivot on which the balance of federalism in the EU turns" (Lenaerts 1992), and in time this major conceptual issue will be addressed. But for the time it suffices to suggest that understandings of what the EU is and does will suffer to the extent that they ignore procedural politics, and benefit to the extent that they consider it.

Conclusion

This chapter has accomplished several tasks. It began by descriptively examining over-time, cross-actor, and cross-issue variations in procedural politics, finding them consistent with the approach developed in Chapter 2, especially insofar as the conditions driving procedural politics are concerned. Statistical results from the second part of the chapter confirm the theory even more strongly: procedural politics responds to opportunities and incentives, with opportunities opened up by jurisdictional ambiguity and incentives prominently including the desire for political influence. Procedural politics thus occurs for predictable reasons and under predictable conditions. The third part of the chapter showed that procedural politics exerts predictable and important effects. It reduces decision-making efficiency, and the delays that it creates can be thought of as the influence costs of procedural politics. It also shapes long-run institutional change, consistent with the expectation that procedural politics in any given period should inform and incite constitutional adaptations undertaken to govern subsequent periods.

And yet, much remains undone. First, in terms of the theory developed in Chapter 2, little time has been given to scrutinizing theoretical expectations about the ways in which actors play the procedural political game, and more remains to be done with respect to procedural political effects. What more can the theory tell us about processes and outcomes that we didn't already know and that we need to know if we are to understand EU politics and policymaking, not to mention institutions more generally? Second, it

Patterns

makes sense to move beyond the aggregate statistical relations primarily examined in this chapter in order to delve more deeply into the causes generating them. True, observed patterns seem to conform to the expectations of the theory, which ascribes to them a particular set of causal forces. Yet, are these causes indeed at work, or are others responsible? Third, even once these things – the processes at work, the outcomes in the balance, and the reasons driving all of it – are established, it will be necessary to assess more systematically what all of this means for understanding the European Union itself and the nature of rule governance within and outside it. To foreshadow, I will suggest that procedural politics bespeaks a more profound degree of rule governance than prevailing approaches would lead us to expect. Fights over lower-order rules take place within, and to that extent reinforce, higher-order rules, and this is a ubiquitous feature of institutionalized systems. I will develop this insight at greater length in Chapter 7.

In the meantime, in what follows I pursue these remaining tasks in bringing additional evidence to bear on the determinants, operation, and effects of procedural politics in the EU. This will, to some extent, involve a change of gears, as I delve more deeply into procedural politics but focus on fewer cases. This need not limit the generalizability of the subsequent analysis. Adequate case selection can enable both deep scrutiny and broad relevance. In choosing cases, I find motivation in the apparent ability of "policy networks" analysis to explain procedural politics, or at least cross-sectoral variation in it. The challenge posed by this alternative literature, as by the specific alternatives identified in Chapter 2 and the ubiquitous intergovernmental and neofunctionalist contenders, dictates that further testing and assessment of the theory of procedural politics be undertaken on the basis of a careful research design aimed at isolating discriminating predictions and systematically subjecting them to a wide variety of evidence and insight. With this in mind, Chapters 5 and 6 pursue a logic of sectoral analysis (Conant 1999) that involves both intra- and intersectoral comparisons. This will entail examination of the two sectors identified above as sitting at the extremes of susceptibility to procedural politics, environmental and agricultural policy.

The within-sector examination will proceed on the basis of a most similar system comparative case study design, wherein cases are selected that resemble each other as closely as possible on all relevant attributes – and especially in the factors adduced by alternative explanations – but that differ on critical independent variables identified by the theory of procedural politics developed in Chapter 2. I introduce the sector-specific logic at the beginning of each relevant chapter. Across sectors, I employ a most different systems design. This takes as its starting point that procedural political variables operate across the full spectrum of EU politics and policymaking, and that network attributes should not influence the incidence of procedural politics. Departing from this assumption of homogeneity, I examine cases drawn from allegedly different sectors and assess the relationship between procedural political variables. "If the subgroups of the population derived from different systems do not differ with respect to the dependent variable," Przeworski and Teune (1970, 35) write, "the differences among these systems are not important in explaining this variable. If the relationship between an independent and the dependent variable is the same within the subgroups of the population, then again the systemic differences need not be taken into consideration." This design, then, permits both generalization of my own approach and effective elimination of the policy networks alternative. Structured in this way, the analysis demonstrates that nominally and empirically very different sectors, agricultural and environmental policy, operate according to an identical procedural political causal logic. As an added benefit, considering these two very different yet uniquely important sectors provides both broad and deep empirical coverage, increasing confidence in the robustness of the argument. The overall picture that results, then, will prove an empirically richer and more compelling one.

Patterns

Appendix 4.A. *Procedural Political Cases Before the European Court of Justice*

Case No.	Case Name	Plaintiff Procedure	Defendant Procedure	ECJ Procedure	ECR Reference
45/86	Commission v. Council (Generalized Trade Preferences)	AVFQ	CNSU	AVFQ	[1987] ECR 1493
68/86	UK v. Council (Hormones)	CNSU	CNSQ	CNSQ	[1988] ECR 0855
131/86	UK v. Council (Battery Hens)	CNSU	CNSQ	CNSQ	[1988] ECR 0905
51/87	Commission v. Council (Generalized Tariff Preferences)	AVFQ	CNSU	AVFQ	[1988] ECR 5545
131/87	Commission v. Council (Animal Glands and Organs)	AVFQ	CNSU	AVFQ	[1988] ECR 5459
165/87	Commission v. Council (Harmonized Commodity Descriptions)	AVFQ	CNSU	AVFQ	[1989] ECR 0259
242/87	Commission v. Council (Erasmus)	AVFS	CNSU	CNSU	[1989] ECR 1425
275/87	Commission v. Council (Temporary Admission of Containers)	CNSU	AVFS	AVFS	[1989] ECR 1615
C-11/88	Commission v. Council (Undesirable Substances and Animal Nutrition)	CNSQ	CNSU	CNSQ	[1989] ECR 3743
56/88	UK v. Council (Vocational Training)	CNSQ	CNSU	CNSQ	[1989] ECR 3799
C-62/88	Greece v. Council (Chernobyl)	CNSQ	AVFQ	AVFQ	[1990] ECR I-1527
C-70/88	Parliament v. Council (Chernobyl)	SYNQ	CNSU	SYNQ	[1991] ECR I-2867
C-51/89j	UK and Others v. Council (COMETT II)	CNSU	AVFS	AVFS	[1991] ECR I-2757
C-300/89	Commission v. Council (Titanium Dioxide)	SYNQ	CNSQ	CNSQ	[1991] ECR I-4529
C-295/90	Parliament v. Council (Students' Rights)	SYNQ	CNSU	SYNQ	[1992] ECR I-4193
C-155/91	Commission v. Council (Waste Framework Directive)	SYNQ	CNSU	CNSU	[1993] ECR I-0939
C-350/92	Spain v. Council (Certificate for Medicinal Products)	CODQ	SYNQ	SYNQ	[1994] ECR I-2587

(continued)

Appendix 4.A *(continued)*

Case No.	Case Name	Plaintiff Procedure	Defendant Procedure	ECJ Procedure	ECR Reference
C-187/93	Parliament v. Council (Waste Shipment Regulation)	CNSU	CODQ	CODQ	[1995] ECR I-1985
C-360/93	Parliament v. Council (EU-US Public Procurement)	CODQ	AVFS	AVFS	[1995] ECR I-3723
C-426/93	Germany v. Council (Business Registers for Statistical Purposes)	CODQ	AVFQ	CODQ	[1996] ECR I-1195
C-84/94	UK v. Council (Working Time Directive)	SYNQ	CNSU	SYNQ	[1996] ECR I-1689
C-233/94	Germany v. Parliament & Council (Deposit-Gurantee Schemes)	CNSU	SYNQ	SYNQ	[1996] ECR I-5755
C-268/94	Portugal v. Council (India Cooperation Agreement)	CNSU	CNSQ	CNSQ	[1996] ECR I-6177
C-271/94	Parliament v. Council (EDICOM)	CNSU	CODQ	CODQ	[1997] ECR I-2405
C-22/96	Parliament v. Council (IDA)	SYNQ	CNSU	SYNQ	[1998] ECR I-3231
C-42/97	Parliament v. Council (Linguistic Diversity)	CODU	CNSU	CNSU	[1999] ECR I-0869
C-164/97j	Parliament v. Council (Forests)	SYNQ	CNSQ	SYNQ	[1999] ECR I-1139
C-189/97	Parliament v. Council (Mauritania)	AVCU	CNSQ	CNSQ	[1999] ECR I-4741
C-209/97	Commission v. Council (SID, Mutual Administrative Assistance)	CODQ	CNSU	CNSU	[1999] ECR I-8067
C-269/97	Commission v. Council (Beef Labeling and Registration)	CODQ	CNSQ	CNSQ	[2000] ECR I-2257 (FR)
C-36/98	Spain v. Council (Danube Convention)	CNSU	CNSQ	CNSQ	[2001] ECR I-00779
C-377/98	Netherlands v. Parliament & Council (Biotech Patenting)	CNSU	CODQ	CODQ	[2001] ECR I-0000 (nyr)
C-93/00	Parliament v. Council (Beef Labeling II)	CODQ	AVFQ	CODQ	[2001] ECR I-0000 (nyr)
C-281/01	Commission v. Council (Energy Star Agreement)	AVFQ	CNSQ	AVFQ	[2002] ECR I-0000 (nyr)

5

Greening the Market?

PROCEDURAL POLITICS AND EU ENVIRONMENTAL POLICY

The data presented in the previous chapter confirm the key argument of this book: actors engage in everyday politics with respect to rules whenever opportunities and incentives align. They play procedural politics, that is, to the extent that jurisdictional ambiguity makes institutional alternatives available and to the extent that those alternatives differ in the influence they afford the EU Parliament, Commission, Council, or member states. Procedural politics varies systematically and in a theoretically consistent way over time and across actors and issues. It exerts strong and theoretically expected effects on policymaking efficiency and long-run institutional change.

The data in Chapter 4, drawn as they are from a dataset of some forty-seven hundred pieces of EU law, are necessarily general, and the tests used suffice to establish associations but may lack the depth to support the causality underlying them. Do procedural political disputes occur for the reasons identified by the theory? When they do occur, what behavioral dynamics characterize them? How do procedural political disputes affect policy and institutional processes and outcomes in concrete cases? How and to what extent do these processes and outcomes differ from those normally posited by students of EU politics and policymaking, to say nothing of institutions more generally?

This chapter and the next empirically address these important issues using logics of both intra- and intersectoral comparison. This chapter examines procedural politics in EU environmental policymaking. It begins by summarizing the procedural development of EU environmental policy. The second part adapts general hypotheses about strategic issue framing and procedural coalition formation to this sector, and then specifies the design and case selection requirements for testing them empirically. The third part traces procedural political processes and outcomes in three cases of

EU environmental policymaking. The fourth part summarizes the findings and lays the groundwork for the application to agricultural policymaking in Chapter 6. The analysis increases my confidence in the causal nature of the observed relationships between institutional alternatives and procedural politics, outperforms alternative explanations of legal basis disputes and amendment and coalitional behavior, and demonstrates the important substantive impact of procedural politics on EU policy and institutions.

Legislative Procedures and EU Environmental Policy

A Procedural History of EU Environmental Policy

The birth and development of EU environmental policy represents a fascinating story from any number of perspectives (see generally McCormick 2001). Here I limit myself to telling the procedural side of the story, tracing the evolution of rules used to make EU environmental policy through four phases from the birth of the Common Market in 1958 to the Nice Treaty in 2003. The evidence shows clearly that institutional change has been the order of the day, and this frequent change provides numerous opportunities to assess political responses to a changing menu of procedural alternatives.

The Treaty of Rome: 1958–1987. A first phase in the procedural development of EU environmental policy stretches from the entry into force of the Rome Treaty in 1958 until the entry into force of the Single European Act (SEA) in 1987. As the original treaty made no mention of environmental protection, during this period the Council based its legislation on articles 100 (now article 94, dealing with harmonization of national provisions for the purpose of promoting the common market) and 235 (now article 308, and akin to an "implied powers" clause). Scholars and policymakers extensively debated the legal appropriateness of this situation (see EP 1970, 1972; CEC 1971a, 1971b; Carpentier 1972; Touscoz 1973; Burhenne and Schoenbaum 1973; Gerard 1975; Grabitz and Sasse 1977; Steiger 1977; von Moltke 1977; Close 1978; House of Lords 1978; House of Commons 1984; Rehbinder and Stewart 1985; Usher 1985, 1988). However, in 1980 the European Court of Justice (ECJ) upheld this practice. It established that EU environmental measures based on common market provisions were valid to the extent that divergent national environmental regulations inherently distorted competitive conditions, and it was the EU's job to eliminate these distortions (Case 91/79, *Commission v. Italy* [1980]

ECR 1099; Case 92/79, *Commission v. Italy* [1980] ECR 1115). Both legal bases effectively available during this time employed the same unanimous consultation procedure, in which the Commission proposes legislation, the EP gives a nonbinding opinion, and the Council amends or/and adopts legislation by unanimity.

The Single European Act (SEA): 1987–1993. The modification of the Rome Treaty by the Single European Act (SEA) in 1987 dramatically changed this state of affairs (Krämer 1987; Vandermeersch 1987). The SEA introduced into the treaty a new environment title (comprising articles 130R-T) that called for use of the unanimous consultation procedure unless member states unanimously decided to proceed by way of qualified majority vote. Article 130T also afforded member states tremendous "post-decisional" autonomy, authorizing them to enact "more stringent protective measures" compatible with other treaty provisions (especially free trade) even after the EU had legislated.

A second new addition to the treaty, article 100A (post-Amsterdam article 95), dealt primarily with legislation to complete the internal market, and it used the cooperation procedure (see Chapter 3). Further, at the insistence of green member states it included a provision whereby EU environmental harmonization measures had to take as a base a high level of protection (article 100A(3)) and allow member states outvoted by the new majority voting provisions to continue to apply existing high-standard national legislation (article 100A(4)).[1] In short, Germany and Denmark feared that QMV would be used to adopt "dumbed-down" environmental standards, and they insisted on this provision to protect their own high standards. As under article 130T, these latter measures had to be compatible with the treaty's other requirements (i.e., they could not discriminate or disproportionately restrict trade). Unlike article 130T, however, article 100A(4) derogations could not be enacted *after* EU harmonization measures, and they were subject to review by the European Commission (Flynn 1987; Langeheine 1989, 353–358; Kapteyn and Verloren van Themaat 1998, 781–783). Article 100A(4) thus presented stricter constraints on national freedom of action than did article 130T. All of these procedural differences made the environmental provisions rather more attractive for member states than internal

---

[1] "Denmark Wins Assurances from EEC Partners That National Laws Will Not Be Compromised," *International Environment Reporter*, 12 February 1986, 29; Jacqué 1986; Gulmann 1987.

market rules in the enactment of environmental legislation under the SEA regime. Indeed, precisely the desire to circumvent article 100A in the making of environmental policy motivated insertion of the environment title into the treaty.

The Maastricht Treaty: 1993–1999. The Treaty on European Union (TEU), better known as the Maastricht Treaty, governed the third phase of EU environmental policy (Wilkinson 1992; Freestone and Ryland 1994). Maastricht brought about several critical procedural changes to EU environmental policymaking. The environment chapter now generally employed the cooperation procedure (article 130S(1)). Article 130S(2) made exceptions for provisions of a fiscal nature, town and country planning, land use, the management of water resources, and measures significantly affecting a member state's choice of energy sources and the structure of its energy supply, which would all operate under the unanimous consultation procedure.[2] Finally, article 130S(3) established that environmental action programs would be adopted under the QMV codecision procedure. Thus, within the environment chapter alone, three different legislative procedures became available after Maastricht. The codecision procedure now governed internal market measures (via the amended article 100A), ensuring that internal market and environmental sectors remained procedurally distinct but generating new patterns of alternatives and preferences over them.

The Amsterdam and Nice Treaties: 1999–. The Amsterdam Treaty, which entered into force in 1999 and which renumbered every article of the treaties,[3] generally "ratcheted" environmental procedures up to the same level as those used in the internal market. Both areas would henceforth generally be governed by Amsterdam's "new and improved" version of the QMV codecision procedure, known as "codecision II." The various

---

[2] This article has never been used in a Commission proposal or for final legislation. Southern member states have often called for its use within the Council, but despite occasional support from the Council Legal Service they have never managed to convince the other member states. Interviews with Council Legal Service officials, Brussels, 2 March 1999, 15 March 1999, 18 March 1999. In early 2001 the ECJ rejected Spain's attempt to challenge the nonuse of article 130S(2) (Case C-36/98, *Spain v. Council*, judgment of 30 January 2001, [2001] ECR-0000).

[3] I have chosen to refer primarily to the original numberings since the study's empirical coverage is limited mostly to the pre-Amsterdam period. Where appropriate, I refer to the post-Amsterdam numbering.

Table 14. *Procedural Evolution of EU Environmental Policy*

	1958–1987 Rome	1987–1993 SEA	1993–1999 TEU	1999– Amsterdam/Nice
Principal Legal Basis				
Internal Market	Article 100	Article 100A	Article 100A	Article 95
Environment	Article 235	Article 130S	Article 130S(1)	Article 175
Principal Legislative Procedure				
Internal Market	CNSU	SYNQ	CODQ	Codecision II
Environment	CNSU	CNSU	SYNQ	Codecision II
"High Level of Protection" (Environmental Guarantee) Applies to				
Internal Market	No provision	Proposals	Proposals	Measures
Environment	No provision	Measures	Measures	Measures
Protected National Provisions				
Internal Market	No provision	Existing	Existing	New and existing
Environment	No provision	New or existing	New or existing	New and existing

Source: Derived from Krämer 1998, 110.

derogations under the environment title remained, and these were clarified but not substantively changed in the Nice Treaty, entered into force in 2003. These derogations aside, the internal market (article 95) and environmental policy (article 175) now stand procedurally identical.

Summary and Assessment. Table 14 summarizes the procedural development of EU environmental policy. For each treaty regime it identifies the main legislative procedure, the target of the "environmental guarantee" if any,[4] and the degree of post-decisional autonomy enjoyed by member states under both internal market and environmental legal bases.

Focusing especially on the legislative procedures in use in this sector, it becomes clear that institutional change has been the order of the day for EU environmental policy. Procedural diversity remained operative until Amsterdam, though the precise institutional alternatives, and thus predicted patterns of procedural politics, varied from period to period. I exploit this treaty-to-treaty variation in designing the empirical analysis later in this chapter.

---

[4] The "environmental guarantee" is a treaty-given assurance that certain acts will pursue a "high level" of environmental protection.

Jurisdictional Ambiguity

While necessary, such procedural diversity does not suffice to produce procedural political disputes. Some measure of jurisdictional ambiguity is also necessary. Importantly, environmental policy exhibits jurisdictional ambiguity in spades. It represents a "very complex and almost by definition multidimensional" policy sector (Tsebelis and Kalandrakis 1999, 126). This results both from the nature of the issues involved and from the way that the treaty addresses them.

Considering the issues, environmental protection naturally constitutes a "horizontal" issue area. It cuts across "vertical" domains such as transport and agriculture and overlaps with other horizontal provisions such as those governing the internal market. Figure 22 illustrates the overlap between environmental and internal market considerations in EU legislation. On average during the 1980–2002 period, about one-fifth of EU environmental legislation invokes classic "internal market" language such as "harmonisation," "approximation," or "common market." When compared with other sectors such as agriculture, this figure is quite high, and so, by implication, is jurisdictional ambiguity. However, relative to other sectors

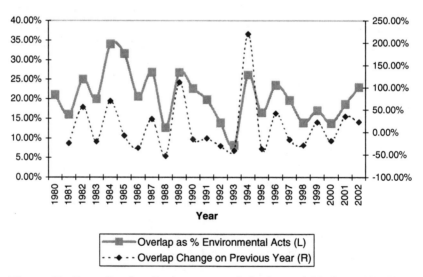

Figure 22 Issue Overlap: Environment and the Internal Market, 1980–2002. *Source*: Constructed from Celex database, last consulted 7 July 2003. Denominator = all measures under Celex classification heading 15.10 (environment); Numerator = text or title keyword "harmonisation" or "approximation" or "common market."

the year-on-year change is relatively low (coefficient of variation = .305, compared to 1.22 for agriculture), and the over-time trend is basically flat. In plain English, jurisdictional ambiguity resulting from the overlap of environmental policy and free trade (internal or common market) stands high but remains relatively stable throughout the period under study.

Three characteristics of EU legal drafting amplify the innate jurisdictional ambiguity of environmental policy. First, the treaty often employs vague or excessively general language, such that the fine distinctions needed to trigger different rules are difficult to make in practice. For example, what precise threshold determines whether a matter is "*primarily*" of a fiscal nature" or "*significantly* affects" the choice of energy supply, as would be required to trigger one of the post-Maastricht article 130S(2) procedural derogations (Freestone and Ryland 1994, 160; Lenaerts 1994, 874–875)?

Second, the EU treaty makes occasional use of "integration provisions" requiring that concerns from one issue be integrated into legislation in other areas. Environmental policy represents one such integrative issue. The treaty requires that environmental protection be "integrated into the definition and implementation" of other Community policies (article 6 [ex article 130R(3)]). These include but are not limited to agriculture, transport, regional policy, competition, state aids, transport, social policy, and research policy (Krämer 1991, 154–155, 167–168; Barents 1993, 98). Article 95(3) (ex article 100A(3)) further reinforces the environment-internal market link by alluding to harmonization measures intended to protect the environment. Such cross-jurisdictional integration "troubles the demarcation of the scope of application of the respective provisions" (Somsen 1992, 140). It creates jurisdictional ambiguity.

Third, and related, the treaty consistently uses so-called *renvois* (roughly, "interfaces") linking certain treaty articles to others. This "most vicious form of legal drafting" (Pescatore 1987, 16) opens up the possibility that either treaty article (or both) might apply in any given case, making it difficult to identify where the domain of one stops and another begins.

In sum, environmental policy offers many opportunities to test expectations derived from the theory of procedural politics. The menu of institutional alternatives has changed with successive treaty revisions, providing actors with varying incentives to fight about legislative rules. Jurisdictional ambiguity is consistently high, affording actors the opportunity to fight. The data in Chapter 4 have already shown that, indeed, procedural politics arises frequently in this fertile soil. Assessing the causality behind these patterns, as well as systematically assessing expectations about procedural political means and effects, will require operationalization of theoretical expectations to this sector and the development of a research design appropriate to these tasks.

Theory, Methods, and Case Selection

Hypotheses

In Chapter 2 I derived several testable propositions about procedural political determinants and processes. Here I operationalize these expectations in the environment sector, specifying substantive expectations of the theory of procedural politics and alternatives to it.

According to the influence maximization hypothesis, with an increase in influence differences among available institutional alternatives, which form a key procedural political incentive, there is an increase in the likelihood of procedural politics. In the environmental sector, this hypothesis predicts no disputes prior to the Single European Act (SEA), as the conceivable legal bases were identical in the influence that they afforded the various actors. In assessing this proposition I will here, as elsewhere, seek to discern whether the actors express a preference for the rule giving them more influence (as determined by the models), and whether this preference seems to exert causal impact. Observations along these lines would further validate the models in Chapter 3 as well as the theoretical claims underpinning them, all the while disconfirming a "legalistic" alternative hypothesis. Different observations would mean that the models are flawed, the theory is disconfirmed, or both.

Turning to strategic issue definition, which defied the aggregate analysis of Chapter 4, the framing hypothesis suggests that actors will strategically frame issues so as to "fit" them within procedurally favorable jurisdictions (legal bases). Given the procedural preferences adduced in Chapter 3 and the procedural history of EU environmental policy outlined above, this proposition suggests a clear evolution of issue definitions for each actor over time. Prior to the 1987 entry into force of the SEA, the theory of procedural politics offers no specific predictions. It will not differ from the "procedurally sincere" alternative explanation, because one of the necessary conditions for procedural politics, the availability of institutional alternatives, was simply lacking during this period. Following the entry into force of the SEA, I expect the Commission and Parliament to frame jurisdictionally ambiguous measures as internal market measures, which entail the relatively favorable cooperation procedure, whereas I expect the Council to employ an environmental issue definition (using the unanimous consultation procedure). Under the Maastricht regime, which is where the empirical analysis ends, I expect the EP and Council to retain their respective issue frames (internal market and environment), whereas I expect the Commission to switch from internal market to environment. The Commission's behavior, then, offers the critical test of this proposition in this sector.

An alternative hypothesis suggests that actors will frame policies in ways consistent with their sincere substantive preferences, regardless of the treaty regime in force. I derive a priori expectations about actors' sincere preferences by examining the secondary literature on EU environmental policy. With respect to the EP, analysts have made strong claims to the effect that the EP is the "greenest" of the EU institutions (see generally Arp 1992; Collins 1995; Hannequart 1979; Judge 1993; Judge and Earnshaw 1994; Judge, Earnshaw, and Cowan 1994; Tsebelis and Kalandrakis 1999, 127). From a sincere perspective, then, the EP should define issues as environmental and should propose amendments supportive of that issue definition.

With respect to the European Commission, equally strong claims have been made about its neoliberal (i.e., free trade) orientation (Buchwitz 1998; Scharpf 2000). The claim has most notably been made when the issue involves free movement of goods and unfettered competition on the one hand as against environmental protection on the other (Greenpeace International 1991; Hildyard 1993).[5] From this perspective, then, the Commission should uniformly promote free trade as against environmental protection throughout the period under study.

With respect to the Council of Ministers, finally, member states are often classified as either environmental "leaders" or "laggards" (Sbragia 1996). Prior to the SEA, member states are expected to evince no distinctively procedural preference. After the SEA and throughout the rest of the period, though, environmental rules offered something to both groups and all member states are expected to have preferred them to the internal market alternative. "Laggards" took comfort in the SEA unanimity voting requirement, and Maastricht compensated their loss of veto power with provisions permitting derogations from measures that would prove unduly

---

[5] The pre-SEA period may constitute an exception insofar as the Commission was struggling for "turf" à la King (1997), such that it could be represented as a competence maximizer. (The EU lacked explicit competence in environmental policy until the SEA.) In that circumstance, it should evince a preference for environmental protection throughout the period, as this represented a "growth area" for Community competence. This, too, is testable.

Table 15. *Issue Framing and Procedural Preferences in EU Environmental Policy*

Actor	Hypothesis	Pre-Single Act –1987	Single Act 1987–1993	Maastricht 1993–1999
Commission	Sincere	Internal market	Internal market	Internal market
	Procedural politics	Internal market	Internal market	Environment
Parliament	Sincere	Environment	Environment	Environment
	Procedural politics	Environment	Internal market	Internal market
Council	Sincere	Sincere	Unchanged	Unchanged
	Procedural politics	Sincere	Environment	Environment

Note: The cells predict both the procedural preference and the predicted issue frame.

burdensome (article 130S(5)). For environmental "leaders," article 130T always contained generous provisions allowing member states to adopt national environmental measures more stringent than the Community norm. Thus, both types of states would prefer environmental rules under both sincere and procedural political perspectives.[6]

Table 15 summarizes these expectations about issue framing and procedural preferences in the environmental sector. Each row offers predictions from each perspective (sincere and procedural political) about over-time changes in an actor's framing of issues. For the Commission, then, the sincere perspective suggests that an internal market issue frame should hold sway unabated throughout the period. The procedural political approach remains largely agnostic in the pre-SEA period, but it clearly predicts that under SEA rules the Commission will prefer internal market rules. Equally important, it predicts a Commission "flip flop" with the arrival of the Maastricht treaty, such that it switches from favoring internal market to favoring environmental rules. For the Parliament, the sincere approach posits an environmental frame pre-SEA, about which procedural politics remains agnostic. Should this frame remain unchanged throughout the period, the sincere perspective will have been confirmed and the procedural politics approach disconfirmed. Should the EP reverse its field following entry into

[6] The only exception to this might be a situation in which green member states seek to force laggards to adopt higher standards, in which case, pre-SEA at least, the QMV of article 100A would be preferable.

force of the SEA, then the sincere approach will have been disconfirmed and procedural politics supported. I also expect it to maintain the internal market issue frame through the Maastricht regime. The Council affords the least opportunity to test competing explanations directly. Competitive testing will be possible only if it frames issues as "internal market" pre-SEA and subsequently changes its position post-SEA. Such a shift would confirm procedural politics and disconfirm the sincere model.

With respect to the timing of substantive amendments, Chapter 2 suggested that at least some substantive modifications will both follow and support expressed rules preferences. A legalistic rival suggests that issue definitions precede rather than follow rules choices. Here I will simply scrutinize the sequence of substantive modifications and expressions of rules preferences. Recall that, from the legalistic point of view, rules choices should follow (reflect) the aim and content of legislative acts. From the procedural political point of view, by contrast, rules choices should *precede* at least some substantive modifications, with some of the latter being undertaken in support of procedural political efforts. As a corollary, substantive modifications are expected to be consistent with expressed rules preferences. Operationally, then, substantive modifications that both follow and support expressed rules preferences will support procedural political expectations and disconfirm legalistic expectations.

Turning now to coalitions, operational versions of the procedural coalition hypothesis and alternatives to it flow directly from the combination of procedural preferences and the development of the environmental sector. Here, the prevailing wisdom predicts supranational-intergovernmental coalitions throughout the period in question. Procedural politics offers no distinct leverage on coalition formation pre-SEA, as there was no procedural variation among the alternative legal bases. During the SEA period, I predict a procedural coalition of the Commission and Parliament as against the Council. This is testable against a null hypothesis of random coalition formation but is not directly testable against the traditional rival, because during this period the two hypotheses are observationally equivalent. However, the process-tracing method can be leveraged for making causal inferences by seeking out evidence for or against each set of posited causes of coalitional behavior. Available institutional alternatives during the Maastricht Treaty regime, by contrast, permit a direct test of the two propositions. The prevailing wisdom predicts a continuation of the same supranational-intergovernmental split anticipated for the SEA period. Procedural politics, by contrast, predicts a new coalitional pattern, pitting

Table 16. *Predicted Procedural Coalitions in EU Environmental Policy*

Hypothesis	Pre-Single Act –1987	Single Act 1987–1993	Maastricht 1993–1999
Procedural politics	Substantive coalitions	Commission and Parliament v. Council	Parliament v. Commission and Council
Prevailing wisdom	Commission and Parliament v. Council	Commission and Parliament v. Council	Commission and Parliament v. Council

the EP against the Commission and Council. Table 16 summarizes these expectations.

Research Design and Case Selection

To test these hypotheses and more generally to explore the causal nature of observed relationships, I trace processes in a series of three cases (pieces of legislation) in the environmental sector. I develop a quasi-experiment using a "most similar systems" comparative case study design, with treaty change representing the experimental "treatment." Specifically, I consider treaty changes that modify the procedural landscape (i.e., that change the procedure used by at least one of the available legal bases) as natural experiments and empirically assess predictions about behavior and outcomes before and after the treatment. In selecting cases, I use the most-similar systems design logic advanced, among others, by Przeworski and Teune (1970) and Lijphart (1975). I thus select cases that are as similar as possible on all attributes except those of direct theoretical interest, which in this sector, given the relative constancy of jurisdictional ambiguity (opportunity), tend to be the nature of available institutional alternatives (incentives). The constancy of confounding factors eliminates them as explanations of variations in outcomes.

This logic leads me to focus on a single but centrally important sector of EU legislative activity (waste management) and select a series of cases that collectively, and in some cases individually, span different procedural (treaty) regimes. The waste sector was among the earliest targets of EU environmental policy and has long represented one of that policy area's central pillars. The three cases that I examine – the Titanium Dioxide Directive, the Waste Framework Directive, and the Waste Shipment Regulation – are the cornerstones of this waste management regime. From a research design perspective, they present similar legal, political, and public policy profiles. Each involves the same set of nominal issue definitions, internal market or environmental policy. Each deals substantively with the perceived trade-off between free trade and environmental protection. All form a part of the EU's waste management regime. And, as illustrated earlier in Figure 22, the overlap between the two issues fluctuates relatively little year to year and reveals no real over-time trend, which allows me to concentrate on changes in the menu of institutional alternatives against a background of consistently high jurisdictional ambiguity.

These similarities permit some measure of control for variation in confounding factors such as changing actor preferences and exogenous changes in issue definitions. The cases vary primarily in the procedural alternatives available at the time of initial proposal, during the legislative process, and at the time of adoption. Thus, I select cases on one of the main independent variables of interest, namely, the nature of procedural alternatives. The European Court of Justice plays a transparently central role across the series of cases, which helps cement the connection between these empirical materials and the game model developed in Chapter 3. Individually and collectively, then, the cases provide numerous opportunities to assess the theoretical expectations developed in Chapter 2 and operationalized above.

Waste Management and Procedural Politics

The following cases trace procedural political behavior and outcomes as these respond to changes in the menu of institutional alternatives. At issue in each of the cases is the selection of either internal market rules governing the conditions of competition and trade in the EU or environmental protection rules less directly concerned with free trade and competitive distortions. The narrative begins with the issue of titanium dioxide waste, followed by general waste management and concluding with waste shipments.

Titanium Dioxide

Titanium dioxide is a whitening pigment used primarily in paints. Its production generates substantial toxic effluent, including iron and acid waste. The EU's efforts to regulate waste from this industry date to its first environmental action program of 1973, with legislation first adopted in

1978.[7] As expected, that original legislation raised no procedural political issues, as the available legal bases (articles 100 and 235) employed the same legislative procedure (unanimous consultation, CNSU). A second piece of legislation came about in 1989[8] and was the object of an intense procedural political dispute that I will examine in detail.

Legislative History. In 1983 the European Commission first tabled the legislative proposal that would become the Titanium Dioxide Directive. It did so on the basis of articles 100 (post-Amsterdam article 94) and 235 (post-Amsterdam article 308).[9] This choice of legal basis was procedurally irrelevant, since both articles employed the unanimous consultation procedure (CNSU), wherein the Commission proposes, Parliament gives a nonbinding opinion, and the Council decides by unanimity. The Commission identified the main aim of the proposed Directive as "the prevention and progressive reduction, with a view to its elimination, of pollution caused by waste from the titanium dioxide industry."[10] Early in the legislative process, the Commission insisted that "the aspect of improving conditions of competition should not be given too much prominence, since *protection of the environment should remain the main aim of the proposed Directive.*"[11] Prior to the SEA, then, the Commission clearly framed the proposal as primarily aimed at environmental protection.

Member state officials took a different view. In a working draft from 1983, they agreed to wording for article 1 according to which the Directive "lays down ... procedures for harmonizing the programs for the reduction and eventual elimination of pollution from existing establishments and is *intended to improve the conditions of competition in the titanium dioxide industry.*"[12] In the pre-SEA period, member states unambiguously held competitive considerations to be the most important aspects of the legislation.

At dozens of subsequent meetings between 1983 and 1985, these positions remained unchanged.[13] The Commission maintained that the

---

[7] Directive 78/176, OJ L 54, 25 February 1978, 19–24.
[8] Directive 89/428, OJ L 201, 14 July 1989, 56.
[9] COM(83) 189 final, 14 April 1983.
[10] Explanatory Memorandum to COM(83) 189 final, para. 9.3, p. 32.
[11] Council Doc. 8261/83 ENV 119, 20 July 1983, 5, emphasis added.
[12] Council Doc. 9514/83 ENV 145, 10 October 1983, emphasis added.
[13] See the following Council Docs.: 10277/83, 10331/83, 10455/83 + cor 1, 10864/83, 4484/84, 6120/84, 6209/84, 6228/84, 7733/84, 7774/84, 8124/84, 8596/84, 8736/84, 9241/84, 9648/84, 10476/84, 10843/84, 4974/85, 5127/85, 5151/85, 5451/85, 6976/85, 7461/85, 7432/85, 9964/85, and 10400/85.

measure aimed primarily at environmental protection, the Council that it dealt primarily with competitive conditions in the industry in question. The EP, for its part, seemed slightly to favor an environmental interpretation of the aim and content of the measure. In its 1984 Resolution approving the proposed Directive, it first mentioned environmental considerations, and then the need for harmonization, "not least in order to avoid distortions of competition."[14]

Enter the SEA and its accompanying procedural changes (discussed above). In early 1987 the Commission drew up a list of pending legislative proposals for which the entry into force of the SEA would entail a change of legal basis and/or of legislative procedure. The titanium dioxide proposal figured on that list, with a new proposed legal basis of article 100A (internal market, post-Amsterdam article 95) entailing the cooperation procedure.[15] In light of the procedural change wrought by the SEA, then, the Commission attempted to fit the proposal under internal market, as opposed to environmental rules. The European Parliament approved the change in legal basis later that year.[16] Both the Commission and EP had changed their positions, switching from a pro-environment to a pro-market legal basis (and from the unanimous consultation procedure to the cooperation procedure). Given their pre-SEA positions and the preferences ascribed to them in Chapter 3, this is precisely what the approach outlined in Chapter 2 would predict.

National officials questioned the proposed change of legal basis (and legislative procedure) from their first post-SEA reexamination of the proposal in September 1987. A number of delegations now argued that the proposal dealt primarily with environment and should use the environmental policymaking procedure – unanimous consultation – that decidedly favored them.[17] This represented a clear reversal of these members' previous issue frame. At subsequent meetings, the Commission defended its choice, emphasizing that the proposed Directive "was designed to stop the present serious distortions of competition" in the sector in question, and as such "contributed to the internal market and came within the scope of article 100A."[18] At this stage of the deliberations, five member states (Denmark, Greece,

---

[14] OJ C 127, 14 May 1984, 34.
[15] COM(87) 393, 7 August 1987, Annex I, 21.
[16] EP Doc. A2-2/87, 26 March 1987.
[17] Council Doc. 8632/87 ENV 158, 29 September 1987, 2.
[18] Council Doc. 4363/88 ENV 13, 4 February 1988, 25; see also Council Doc. 4233/88 ENV 7, 21 January 1988, 2.

Spain, France, and the UK) firmly opposed the Commission's choice of legal basis, two (Belgium and Germany) expressed muted sympathy for it, and most were undecided. Italy insisted that should the Commission's choice be upheld, it must not constitute a precedent for future legislation, and in subsequent meetings Greece joined it in this position.[19]

In March 1988, the Commission produced a memo justifying its choice of legal basis. It noted that the proposed legislation derived from article 9(3) of the original (1978) Directive, which called on the Commission to propose extensions aimed at "the harmonization of [national programs] in regard to the reduction and eventual elimination of pollution and the improvement of the conditions of competition" in the industry. The Commission proceeded to argue that the proposed Directive pursued both internal market and environmental objectives, and that the legal basis should reflect "the center of gravity or the main objective" of the proposal, which it identified as removing distortions to industrial competition caused by differing national regulations.[20] Environmental protection, the Commission now explicitly claimed, was only an accessory or secondary goal of the proposed legislation.

At meetings from March through October of 1988, member state representatives exchanged views on the proper legal basis several times, with momentum gradually building for article 130S and its legislative procedure, unanimous consultation.[21] After these lengthy discussions, the Council agreed on 24 November 1988 to change the legal basis proposed by the Commission. In reaction to this unanimous decision, the Commission entered a statement into the Council minutes objecting to the change, reasserting its position that article 100A was more appropriate and reserving for itself "the right to make use of all legal means available under the Treaty to redress the situation."[22]

---

[19] Council Doc. 4707/88 ENV 25, 24 February 1988, 10; Council Doc. 4991/88 ENV 41, 10 March 1988, 9–10.

[20] SEC(88) 304, Note of the Services of the Commission: The legal basis of the proposal for a Council Directive on the reduction of pollution caused by waste from the titanium dioxide industry, 2 March 1988.

[21] Council Doc. 5022/88 ENV 45, 9 March 1988; Council Doc. 6017/88 ENV 75, 6 May 1988; Council Doc. 6279/88 ENV 85, 18 May 1988; Council Doc. 6605/88 ENV 98, 2 June 1988; Council Doc. 6865/88 ENV 108, 8 June 1988; Council Doc. 7462/88 ENV 122, 7 July 1988; Council Doc. 7932/88 ENV 133, 1 August 1988; Council Doc. 8717/88 ENV 164, 18 October 1988; Council Doc. 8766/88 ENV 166, 24 October 1988; Council Doc. 8950/88 ENV 172, 4 November 1988.

[22] Council Doc. 10211/88 ENV 217, 12 December 1988, Annex II, 20.

One month later, the Commission adopted a modified proposal for a Directive that explicitly reframed the issue as internal market rather than environmental protection. It justified this effort in two ways. First, it claimed that new evidence attested to "big, and widening, differences in the conditions of competition in the titanium dioxide industry," in which national regulation increased costs by between 10 percent and 20 percent.[23] Second, it claimed that though it had changed the legal basis of the proposal following the entry into force of the SEA, it had never adapted the text to reflect this change. As a result, the Commission proposed several textual amendments to the proposal that make it a masterwork of strategic issue definition. At every turn, it reinforced the internal market credentials of the proposed Directive and downplayed its origins as an environmental protection measure. After a first recital referring to the original 1978 Directive, the second referred both to harmonization and competitive conditions, the third to price distortions caused by national regulations, the fifth to competitive conditions (again), the sixth to harmonization (again), and the seventh and eighth to the internal market. Among general statements motivating the act, only the fourth and half of the sixth even mentioned environmental protection, and both did so using language drawn verbatim from article 100A (internal market) rather than 130R (environment). These textual modifications transparently attempted to bring the proposed legislation under the purview of the internal market.[24]

Because the change of legal basis entailed a "substantial modification" of the text, the Council was bound under ECJ jurisprudence to reconsult the Parliament on this aspect of the legislation. It did so on the same day that the Commission submitted its amended proposal. The Parliament's Legal Affairs Committee, asked by the EP's Environment Committee to consider the legal basis of the proposal, came down squarely in favor of article 100A, which would give the EP potentially important influence under the cooperation procedure.[25]

The EP Environment Committee Report embraced the same position. While granting that national legislation on titanium dioxide was adopted for

---

[23] COM(88) 849 final, 26 January 1989, 2, referring to an earlier cost study presented in SEC(84) 250.
[24] Several sources informed this analysis. See letter from Beate Weber, president of the EP Environment Committee, to Lady Elles, president of the EP Legal Affairs Committee, 22 February 1989; House of Commons, 16th Report from the Select Committee on European Legislation, Session 1988/89, HC 15–xvii, p. ix.
[25] EP Committee on Legal Affairs and Citizens' Rights document 153/88, 16 March 1989.

Procedural Politics

environmental reasons, it suggested that Community-level harmonization was, of necessity, driven by the need to eliminate competitive distortions. It did proceed to argue in favor of a "high level of environmental protection," but did so using the language of article 100A(3) rather than the environment chapter of the treaty.[26] The Environment Committee report took the same approach to textual modification as did the Commission's first amended proposal. It proposed several new recitals to the legislation. The first emphasized the cost disparities arising from divergent national legislation, the third flatly stated that "the principal object of the present Directive is... the elimination of the distortions of competition" in the industry, and the fourth posited that "the object of the present Directive and the approximation of programs is the establishment and correct functioning of the internal market."[27] In parliamentary debate the rapporteur urged the Parliament to join the Commission in a possible Court case to decide the matter.[28]

On 25 May 1989 the EP plenary supported the Commission and rejected the Council's choice of legal basis.[29] The Commission, seemingly bolstered by this support, made a last-ditch effort at persuading the Council of its position by adopting a second amended proposal,[30] but it failed to rally any support. On 9 June 1989 the Council unanimously adopted the act on the basis of article 130S (with Belgium and Italy abstaining on this part of the decision). The Commission again threatened in a statement in the minutes "to exploit the legal means available" for redressing this perceived abuse of legislative procedure.[31] Interestingly, and ultimately quite importantly, Council lawyers urged the Council to engage in a bit of substantive modification of the text – known in all three institutions as "massaging" or *habillement* ("dressing up") – in order to support the legal basis change. But the Council itself never made these changes, so both the title and the first article of the Directive continued to refer explicitly to harmonization, a catchword for the internal market. A Council lawyer contends that

> the Council of Ministers was its own worst enemy in [the Titanium Dioxide] case.... The Council did change the legal basis, after a great deal of discussion, to 130S, but it did not amend Article 1. *This was clearly a harmonization measure.* We

[26] EP Doc. A2-90/89, 20 April 1989, 12.
[27] EP Doc. A2-90/89, 20 April 1989, 7–8.
[28] *EP Debates* no. 2-378, 23 May 1989, 80.
[29] OJ C 158, 26 June 1989, 248.
[30] COM(89) 292 final, 8 June 1989.
[31] Council Doc. 7183/89 ENV 112, 12 June 1989.

pointed out [to national civil servants] that they should re-draft Article 1. But they wouldn't change it because their ministers had already agreed to it as it was, and they did not want to involve their ministers again.[32]

Thus, the Council never engaged in the final bit of post hoc textual modification that the Court's legal basis test demands and the theory of procedural politics predicts. The law went into the books legally based on environmental provisions of the treaty, but using internal market language.

Titanium Dioxide Before the Court. The aggrieved institutions immediately prepared a court case to challenge the measure. In September the Commission formally lodged its complaint before the Court, which on 21 February 1990 granted leave to the EP to intervene in support of the Commission.[33] After an initial hearing, the ECJ's Advocate General – a jurist who writes an advisory legal opinion for the Court to consider – argued that the Court should uphold the Commission's claim in favor of article 100A.

On 11 June 1991, the European Court of Justice followed the Advocate General and set forth its historic (for some, infamous) judgment in the Titanium Dioxide case (Case C-300/89, *Commission v. Council* [1991] ECR I-2867). The Court began by establishing that the Directive simultaneously and indissociably pursued two objectives, namely environmental protection and protection of competitive conditions in the single market. As such, the Court suggested, no single legal basis could be discerned using the center of gravity criterion. Under normal circumstances, its jurisprudence called for the cumulation of legal bases, with the most "demanding" of multiple procedures being used. However, the Court held that articles 130S and 100A could not be cumulated in this way, as the procedural result would be a hypothetical cooperation procedure with unanimity in the Council. Since the cooperation procedure depended for its distinctiveness on the ability of the EP to alter voting requirements in the Council, the use of unanimity throughout the procedure would "denature" it and deprive the EP of the influence that the framers of the treaty intended it to have.

Faced with this difficulty, the Court adduced several factors militating in favor of article 100A (internal market, cooperation procedure) as against

---

[32] Interview with Council Legal Service official, Brussels, 2 March 1999.
[33] For details of the EP's internal deliberations see Dietmar Nickel, Note for the attention of Dr. Robert Ramsay, Head of the President's Private Office re: Titanium Dioxide, 19 June 1989.

article 130S (environment, unanimous consultation procedure). Among these were the need maximally to involve the EP in EU decision making (reflecting a "fundamental democratic principle"), the "integration provision" in article 130R(2) (according to which environmental protection needed to be considered in the making of policy in other areas), and the availability of article 100A by virtue of the wording of its paragraph 3, which mentioned environmental harmonization. In short, the ECJ decided in favor of the Commission and Parliament (and the cooperation procedure) and against the Council (and unanimous consultation), ordering the Council to pay court costs and annulling the Directive.

Reaction to the judgment came swiftly (Barents 1993; Barnard 1992; Bradley 1992; Crosby 1991; de Sadeleer 1991; Robinson 1992; Somsen 1993). The EP relished an important victory and vowed to institutionalize the ad hoc procedural political coalition it had formed with the Commission in the case.[34] Council officials cited the important long-term and general consequences of the judgment, characterizing it as a reversal of the Court's already well-established jurisprudence whereby the choice of legal basis must reflect "objective factors which are amenable to judicial review," notably the aim and content of the legislation (see inter alia Case 45/86, *Commission v. Council* [1987] ECR 1493, point 11).[35] Council lawyers suggested that procedural political considerations (especially concerning the role of the EP) were *precisely* what the Court used in finding against the Council, and they expressed resentment at this seemingly sudden and apparently political jurisprudential shift.[36]

Whatever the other impact of the judgment, it did not stop additional procedural political disputes in the area of waste management from arising. It differed so markedly from the Court's earlier legal basis jurisprudence that it raised as many questions as it answered. Indeed, on the very day that the Court issued its Titanium Dioxide judgment, it received a new complaint involving nearly identical issues. The new case involved the 1991 Waste Framework Directive, the legislative cornerstone of the EU's waste management edifice.

---

[34] Ezio Perillo, Note à l'attention de M. VINCI – Objet: Arrêt du 11 juin 1991, dioxyde de titane, 13 June 1991.
[35] Council Doc. 7468/91 JUR 72 ENV 222, 11 July 1991, 9.
[36] "On a mal ressenti ce jugement" (Interview with Council Legal Service official, Brussels, 15 July 1997); interview with Council Legal Service official, Brussels, 2 March 1999.

Greening the Market?

Waste Framework Directive

Waste management has long figured centrally in EU environmental policy. The first environmental action program of 1973 first articulated the need for such a regime, and it eventually gave rise to a general Directive on waste in 1975.[37] (The original Titanium Dioxide Directive resulted from this effort as well.) As with Titanium Dioxide, and as predicted by the theory, the original waste Directive raised no procedural political issues. The Council replaced that original Directive with a new one, the so-called Waste Framework Directive, in March 1991.[38] This Directive gave rise to two and a half years of intense substantive and procedural political debate. In what follows I again trace the history of the legislation, all of which occurred under the SEA treaty regime, with an eye toward the behavioral dynamics and substantive outcomes associated with procedural politics in the EU.

Legislative History. The initial proposal for a directive amending the 1975 waste Directive dates to August 1988.[39] The Commission based the proposal on article 100A (internal market, now article 95), which used the relatively favorable cooperation procedure rather than the unfavorable unanimous consultation procedure found in the environment chapter at the time. The explanatory memorandum to the proposal perfunctorily defended the choice of legal basis, claiming that divergent national waste management legislation "can distort the conditions of competition and thereby directly affect the establishment and functioning of the internal market." Textually, the Commission clearly framed the proposal in internal market terms. The first recital,[40] in particular, provided a textbook justification of article 100A, emphasizing disparities in national regulations and the competitive distortions to which they gave rise. The Commission explicitly mentioned environmental protection nowhere in the preamble to the proposed legislation.

---

[37] Directive 75/442 of 15 July 1975 on waste, OJ L 194, 25 July 1975, 39ff.
[38] Directive 91/156/EEC of 18 March 1991 amending Directive 75/442/EEC on waste, OJ L 78, 26 March 1991, 32–37.
[39] COM(88) 391 final, Proposal for a Council Directive amending Directive 75/442/EEC on waste, 5 August 1988.
[40] "Recitals" are (allegedly pro forma) statements of motivation or justification for legislation. They usually begin with the phrase "Whereas" and collectively form the preamble to legislation.

The Parliament's Environment Committee responded favorably to the proposal. Substantively, it sought to strengthen its environmental aspects by extending the regulatory framework beyond disposal to include the prevention, recycling, and re-use of waste.[41] It made no mention of the legal basis at this time, implying full support for the Commission's choice.

The Council machinery first examined the proposal in January 1989. Numerous delegations immediately expressed doubts about 100A and a preference for article 130S. By the summer of 1989 eight member states firmly opposed the Commission's choice of legal basis.[42] One member state, Belgium, supported it.[43] Beyond mere opposition to the Commission's choice, elements of strategic manipulation began to appear. In particular, France and Germany suggested splitting the Directive into two pieces, the bulk of which would use article 130S and the unanimous consultation procedure, and the smaller part of which, dealing with recyclable waste, would use the less-preferred article 100A and the cooperation procedure.[44] Furthermore, Germany and Denmark both insisted that they attached priority to the disposal of waste at its source – that is to say, to limiting the waste trade in Europe – a goal they alleged to be incompatible with article 100A.[45]

Environmental ministers discussed the issue at length in early September 1989.[46] Asked to defend its choice of legal basis, the Commission advanced

---

[41] EP Doc. A2-74/89, 7 April 1989; OJ C 158, 26 June 1989, 232–237.

[42] See Council Doc. 4478/89 ENV 14, 8 February 1989, 3; House of Common Select Committee on European Legislation, Session 1987/88, 38th Report, HC 43–xxxviii, pp. vii–xi; Council Doc. 5892/89 ENV 59, 11 April 1989, 3; Council Doc. 6731/89 ENV 90, 13 June 1989, 3.

[43] This might be explained in two ways. First, Belgium is arguably the most federalist of the EU member states and it frequently supports the use of *communautaire* legal bases. (Note that this would cut against my theoretical expectations.) Second, as a small country with little waste disposal capacity, Belgium depends on waste management services in neighboring member states. The Directive threatened to implement the so-called principle of self-sufficiency, whereby each member state would be responsible for its own waste, and so Belgium sought to protect the principle of free movement of wastes, arguably better done under article 100A than 130S. Later I argue that the latter, procedural political, explanation better accounts for Belgium's position. The statistical evidence from Chapter 4 – and more narrowly, clear evidence from the third case discussed in this chapter (below) – cut decisively against the ideational explanation and in favor of the procedural political.

[44] Council Doc. 7895/89 ENV 133, 17 July 1989, 5.

[45] Council Doc. 8189/89 ENV 142, 1 August 1989, 3–4; see also "Environment: Ministers Set to Discuss Environment Agency, Waste, Tropical Forests, and Biotechnology at September 19 Council," *European Report* no. 1520, 6 September 1989, pp. iv/1–2.

[46] "Environment Council: Positive Results Concerning Genetically-Modified Organisms, The European Environmental Agency, and Risk Prevention; Major Debate on Waste," *Agence Europe* no. 5094, 21 September 1989, 8.

three arguments. First, waste processing was a growing sector of industrial activity and services. It was economically important and should be part of the harmonized internal market. Second, different national rules on waste management distorted competition in this industry. Third, recyclable waste (called "secondary raw materials" in the industry) was a "good" and should be subject to the EU's free movement provisions.[47]

The Commission subsequently took up ten amendments offered by the EP and incorporated them into a modified legislative proposal. These amendments sought to promote waste prevention, clean technologies, and recycling, and they enhanced supervision by national authorities.[48] Textually, the modified proposal added a second recital that touched on environmental protection, but did so in the language of article 100A (internal market), referring to the need to "achieve a high level of environmental protection" (taken almost verbatim from article 100A(3)). I surmise that the Commission was responding to Parliament's pro-environment substantive preferences but was careful not to do so in a way that would facilitate a reframing away from its (and the EP's) preferred legislative procedure (the cooperation procedure), which applied to the internal market area.

In April 1990 the Irish Presidency circulated a new draft proposal based on article 130S.[49] Subsequent meetings through June found all but two member states more or less firmly supportive of this position, with Belgium still in favor of 100A and France now inclined that way.[50] The Commission maintained its earlier arguments, now responding to green member states' fears of a regulatory "race to the bottom" by reminding them that the "environmental guarantee" in article 100A(3) would ensure that its choice of legal basis would not come at the expense of the environment.[51] Despite this argument, in early June the Council adopted a "common orientation" unanimously changing the legal basis of the proposed Directive to article 130S. As with Titanium Dioxide, the Commission

---

[47] Council Doc. 8410/89 ENV 152, 8 September 1989, 3–4; Council Doc. 8843/89 ENV 174, 12 October 1989, 3.
[48] COM(89) 560 final, 20 November 1989.
[49] Council Doc. 5714/90 ENV 80, 11 April 1990; compare with Council Doc. 5238/90 ENV 45, 22 March 1990 from the Council Working Party's 2 March 1990 meeting.
[50] Council Doc. 6217/90 ENV 99, 10 May 1990, 3; Council Doc. 6597/90 ENV 113, 22 May 1990, 5; Council Doc. 6776/90 ENV 129, 31 May 1990, 6; Commission Doc. SI(90) 414, 1 June 1990.
[51] Commission internal memo, "For the Attention of Commissioner Ripa di Meana: Environment Council 7/8 June 1990: General Briefing," 6 June 1990.

"reserve[d] the right to exploit all the legal means available at the appropriate moment."⁵²

Shortly after this meeting, work began on a new text of the Directive. Member states deleted preambular provisions using internal market language and replaced them with environmental catchphrases. A new fifth recital emphasized that "any disparity between member states' laws on waste disposal and recovery can affect the quality of the environment, and interfere with the functioning of the internal market."⁵³ These changes addressed themselves directly to the ECJ, which of necessity examines both the language used and the order in which words appear in determining the aim and content of legislation.⁵⁴ More substantially, member states modified the definitions set out in the Directive's first article. They removed all reference to waste transport, an element upon which the Commission had relied in attempting to justify the use of article 100A.⁵⁵ All of this, I submit, represents a clear attempt to downplay the internal market credentials of the measure and to reframe it in environmental terms. These textual manipulations form part of a concerted procedural political strategy.

The Council's "substantial modification" of the text obligated it to reconsult the EP. Reporting on the legal basis change in November 1990, the EP Environment Committee vehemently disputed the appropriateness of article 130S. While sarcastically applauding the Council's apparent interest in environmental protection, it held that the substance of the Directive as it stood did not correspond to its nominally pure intentions. The Committee identified three Council tactics used to bolster its change of legal basis: the preambular changes noted above, the removal of transport from article 1, and the promotion of national self-sufficiency in waste management rather than Community policy. The report asked the Council to reinsert the Commission's recitals invoking competitive distortions, and went on to recommend that the EP support any eventual Commission legal action and bring action itself if the Commission did not.⁵⁶

---

⁵² Council Doc. 7026/90 ENV 139, 13 June 1990, 1.
⁵³ Council Doc. 7461/90 ENV 150, 28 June 1990, 3.
⁵⁴ Interview with European Court of Justice Legal Secretary, Luxembourg, 22 July 1997; other interviewees ridicule this practice as "naïve" (Interview with European Parliament Legal Affairs Committee staff lawyer, Brussels, 9 July 1997).
⁵⁵ Compare the text of article 1 in the Commission proposals (where transport does appear), in Council Doc. 6776/90 ENV 129 (where it remains), and Council Doc. 7461/90 ENV 150 (where it no longer appears).
⁵⁶ EP Doc. A3-0307/90, Report of the Committee of the Environment, Public Health and Consumer Protection on the legal basis of the proposal from the Commission to the Council

Greening the Market?

At the EP's plenary session of February 1991, MEP Ken Collins expressed outrage at the change in legal basis, and most especially about the re-consultation by the Council only on that and not on the new substance of the bill. "We are quite prepared to go to court on this.... they can go ahead and [adopt the measure on 130S] and, if they do so, we will take them to Court. Either we do that or the Commission does that or the Commission withdraws its proposals."[57] He went on to assert the institutional importance of the issue: "We cannot ever allow the Council to start off on one track and then at the last moment suddenly change the legal base like this without properly consulting Parliament." Most interesting, procedural political considerations appear to trump (short run) substantive preferences. The EP Legal Affairs Committee, in a letter annexed to the Environment Committee report, had already asked the Commission to withdraw the proposal should the Council persist with article 130S. MEP Collins, in his speech, reiterates this request three times in the space of a few minutes. The EP had a clear substantive interest in the legislation and was indeed quite favorable even to the substantive provisions (such as national self-sufficiency) that the Council adopted. But it preferred to revert to the status quo ante of outdated and manifestly inadequate legislation rather than have its prerogatives ignored in the adoption of desirable legislation.[58]

The Council received and ignored the EP's opinion, agreeing in principle to the Directive on the basis of article 130S.[59] The Commission, at this time, entered a new statement into the minutes aimed directly at cementing a coalition with the Parliament. After reasserting the propriety of article 100A and threatening to take legal action, it opined that "the change in legal basis calls into question the prerogatives of the European Parliament since it deprives it of the possibilities provided for in the cooperation procedure."[60] As with Titanium Dioxide, the lines of cleavage were clearly drawn, and on 18 March 1991, the Council adopted the Waste Framework Directive on the basis of article 130S, using the unanimous consultation (CNSU) procedure.

---

for a directive amending Directive 75/442/EEC on waste, 16 November 1990, explanatory statement, p. 6.

[57] *EP Debates* no. 3-401, 22 February 1991, 339.

[58] This may be consistent with a longer-run maximization, and ample evidence exists to suggest that where institutional interests are concerned, the EP behaves in precisely this way (Hix 2002).

[59] *Bull. EC* 12-1990, point 1.3.149, p. 67.

[60] Council Doc. 5072/91 ENV 80, 12 March 1991, 3.

Waste Framework Directive Before the Court. In contemplating Court action, EP lawyers made much of the then-recent conclusions of the Court's Advocate General in the Titanium Dioxide case, which augured well for the case at hand.[61] The Court's 11 June 1991 judgment in the Titanium Dioxide case set the stage for a renewed battle. "Flush with the results obtained" in that case (de Sadeleer 1993c, 606), the Commission brought an annulment action against the Council's legal basis choice for the Waste Framework Directive. It did so, not coincidentally, on the *very day* that the Titanium Dioxide judgment was handed down.[62] Discussing a closely related case involving hazardous waste, an MEP suggested that "There is every indication now that the Commission and the European Parliament have already won their case. Hardly two weeks ago in fact the EC Court of Justice gave what might be called a judgment of principle on the titanium dioxide directive, which in essence has to do with the same set of problems as the directive we are discussing."[63] With this mind-set, Parliament decided in September 1991 to join the Commission in order to defend its institutional interests independently and to establish Titanium Dioxide more firmly as operative law.[64] The Council again served as the defendant in this new case.

In its 17 March 1993 judgment in the Waste Framework case (Case C-155/91, *Commission v. Council* [1993] ECR I-939], the European Court of Justice effectively reversed itself. Following the opinion of its Advocate General, it found in favor of article 130S (the Council's position) as against article 100A (favored by the Commission and the Parliament). Unlike the judgment in Titanium Dioxide, the judgment here was direct and narrow. It contented itself with an analysis of the aim and content of the measure, both of which, it found, leaned primarily in favor of environmental protection (article 130S) rather than article 100A. The Court allowed that the Directive would affect the internal market, but found these effects to be ancillary. Following earlier jurisprudence (Case C-70/88, *Parliament v. Council* [1991] ECR I-4529, paragraph 17), it held that mere incidental effects on market conditions do not justify recourse to article 100A. By this

---

[61] European Parliament Legal Affairs Committee staff memo, "Nota para el ponente Lord Inglewood sobre la Directiva del Consejo por la que se modifica la Directiva 75/442/EEC relativa a los residuos," 15 May 1991, 4–5.
[62] OJ C 189, 20 July 1991, 12–13; the Commission lays out its case in Doc. JUR(91) 03094 IP, 11 June 1991.
[63] *EP Debates* no. 3-407, 8 July 1991, 27.
[64] Letter from Graf Stauffenberg, Chairman of EP Legal Affairs Committee, to EP President Enrique Baron Crespo, 19 September 1991.

reasoning, the Court concluded that the Waste Framework Directive was an environmental measure properly based on article 130S.

Like Titanium Dioxide, the Waste Framework judgment generated substantial reaction (de Sadeleer 1993a, 1993b; Krämer 1993, 295; Somsen 1993). Many interpreted it as a capitulation to EU member states. More creatively, it might be thought to be a clever sop thrown to them in full knowledge of the impending entry into force of the Maastricht Treaty, which would mean that a pro-Commission procedure (cooperation) would be used for making future waste management policy. (Recall from Chapter 4 that the ECJ overwhelmingly favors the Commission in procedural political disputes that come before it.) Whatever the case may be, and whatever the other advantages or disadvantages of the judgment, one problem seemed clear. It failed to eliminate the substantial jurisdictional ambiguity in the waste management sector. One judgment in this line of case law (Titanium Dioxide) held in favor of article 100A, one (the Waste Framework Directive) in favor of article 130S. Legal uncertainty continued to reign in this sector, offering scant guidance for legislation still under discussion (Geradin 1993a, 425–427; Somsen 1993, 128; von Wilmowsky 1993, 564). Among such legislation was a proposed Regulation on Waste Shipments, to the consideration of which I now turn.

Waste Shipments Regulation

Cross-border trade in industrial waste had plagued the EU, to great public dismay, at least since the early 1980s (Jupille 1996). An initial Directive, adopted in 1984, established a limited regulatory regime.[65] As with the previous two cases, and as predicted by the theory, the pre-SEA Directive witnessed no procedural political dispute. With the imminent arrival of the "1992" single market deadline and in light of international developments in the regulation of the waste trade, the European Commission in October 1990 proposed a Regulation on waste shipments intended to ensure safe transport of waste.[66] The legislation that resulted, the Waste

---

[65] Council Directive 84/631/EEC of 6 December 1984 on the supervision and control within the European Community of the transfrontier shipment of hazardous waste, OJ L 326, 13 December 1984.
[66] COM(90) 415; "Commission Plan Would Control Movement of Waste Inside, Outside Member States," *International Environment Reporter*, 26 September 1990, 381; "Plan for Major Extension of EEC Rules on Waste Shipments Launched," *ENDS Report* no. 190 (November 1990): 37–38, 40.

Shipments Regulation,[67] was the third major waste management law to undergo a procedural political challenge before the European Court of Justice. Although not perfect from a research design perspective, because its legislative history does not fully straddle the entry into force of a new treaty regime, the case permits assessment of changing procedural political patterns associated with the 1991 agreement on and anticipated entry into force of the Maastricht Treaty.

Legislative History. The Commission, in early drafts of the proposal, confidently asserted that "a double legal basis ineluctably imposes itself."[68] Insofar as the measure dealt with harmonization of national provisions in order to secure the internal market, it required article 100A (internal market, cooperation procedure). Because it also dealt with the external waste trade, it would have to use article 113 (commercial policy, AVFQ procedure). Following the usual rule of thumb, the cumulation of these two legal bases required use of the more onerous procedure, in this case cooperation. Recall that given the nature of the issue and the corresponding institutional alternatives – with article 130S (environment, unanimous consultation procedure) as the other alternative – the cooperation procedure was the best the Commission could expect to do.

The first examination of the measure by the Council machinery again produced strong opposition to the legal basis proposed by the Commission. While "several delegations" expressed general doubts, Germany, Greece, and the Netherlands already firmly pronounced themselves in favor of the environmental legal basis, article 130S, as of January 1991.[69] By the second examination, Germany and the UK were already inquiring as to the possibility of enacting stricter measures than those proposed by the Commission,[70] a procedural interest that cuts against article 100A and in favor of article 130S.

The EP's first report on the proposal came down strongly in favor of article 100A: "Surely the free movement of goods cannot apply to certain goods only and not to others. Waste definitely comes under the heading of

---

[67] Council Regulation (EEC) No 259/93 of 1 February 1993 on the supervision and control of shipments of waste within, into and out of the European Community, OJ L 30, 6 February 1993, 1–28.
[68] COM(90) 415, draft of 4 September 1990, 5.
[69] Council Doc. 4373/91 ENV 30, 29 January 1991, 2.
[70] Council Doc. 4572/91 ENV 40, 11 February 1991, 3.

Greening the Market?

goods."[71] The EP did propose numerous substantive amendments to the legislation, most notably seeking to limit extra-EU exports of hazardous waste to less-developed countries.[72] The Commission took up some of these amendments in a revised proposal, still based on articles 100A and 113, prepared for the March 1992 meeting of the Environment Council.[73]

Meetings during the spring and summer revealed a Council largely in agreement that the legal basis of the proposed Regulation should be article 130S rather than article 100A. Belgium alone held out, claiming to favor the Commission's internal market legal basis (100A).[74] By mid-1992 the Commission began sounding a more legalistic note, arguing that "the question of the choice of legal basis is related to the content of the Regulation."[75] "Concerned," for its part, "that what happened to the [Waste Framework Directive] might occur again," the EP's Environment Committee tabled in early October 1992 a motion that would call for the use of article 100A (with 113) rather than article 130S.[76]

---

[71] EP Doc A3-0301/91/B, Report of the Committee on the Environment, Public Health and Consumer Protection on the Commission proposal for a Council Regulation on the supervision and control of shipments of waste within, into and out of the European Community [Rapporteur: Karl-Heinz Florenz], 6 November 1991, 41; *EP Debates* no. 3-411, 19 November 1991, 61.

[72] OJ C 326, 16 December 1991, 130–148; "Parliament Seeks Stricter Requirements For Ecological Labeling, Waste Movements," *International Environment Reporter*, 20 November 1991, 616; "Action on Waste Export Measure Delayed by Commission, Parliament Disagreement," *International Environment Reporter*, 15 January 1992, 3–4; "Waste: Commission Sticks to Its Guns on Transfers," *European Environment* no. 1751, 11 March 1992, iv/5; "Waste: European Parliament Waves Through Report on Transfers," *European Report* no. 1752, 14 March 1992, iv/17; Legislative Resolution (Cooperation procedure: first reading) embodying the opinion of the European Parliament on the Commission Proposal to the Council for a regulation on the supervision and control of shipments of waste within, into, and out of the European Community, OJ C 94, 13 April 1992, 276.

[73] COM(92) 121 final, amended proposal for a Council Regulation (EEC) on the supervision and control of shipments of waste within, into, and out of the European Community, 23 March 1992.

[74] "Environment Council: EEC Hold-Up on Movement of Waste," *European Report* no. 1755, 25 March 1992, iv/16–17; "EC: Conclusion of Environment Council," *Agence Europe*, 25 March 1992; Council Doc. 6519/92, 19 May 1992; Council Doc. 6359/1/92 REV 1, 19 May 1992, 2; Commission Doc. SI(92) 395, 22 May 1992; Council Doc. 6359/1/92 REV 1 COR 2, 26 May 1992; Council Doc. 6890/92, 3 June 1992. Coverage as late as October 1992 reports a Belgian position in favor of article 100A (*European Report* no. 1804, 17 October 1992, iv/11).

[75] Commission Doc. SI(92) 395, 22 May 1992, 9.

[76] "European Parliament Committee Tables Resolution on Waste," *European Report* no. 1803, 14 October 1992, iv/1.

The EP's fears proved well founded, as a political breakthrough on the two-year-old proposal occurred at the Council meeting of 20 October 1992. This agreement, generally regarded as "historic" because it allegedly established the primacy of environmental over free trade considerations, yielded a procedural political and substantive logroll that satisfied all member states. As it happens, Belgium's interest in article 100A had more to do with its desire to be able to ship its waste to other Community countries than with its purported ideological support for federal European solutions. As a small country, Belgium (along with Luxembourg) lacked the facilities necessary to treat all of its own waste. As such, it demanded the right to continue sending waste to Germany, France, and other EU neighbors for treatment.[77] As discussed at the end of this chapter, the documentary record provides unequivocal evidence that Belgium leveraged the unanimity requirement for changing the legal basis to gain substantive concessions from the majority of member states. Thus, the Regulation, while generally restrictive of waste shipments, made exception for waste produced in small states such as Belgium and Luxembourg, which larger neighbors with adequate disposal facilities found themselves obligated to accept.

With respect to the change in legal basis, the position of the European Commission holds particular interest. Following the 20 October meeting, Environment Commissioner Karel van Miert stated that "the unanimous decision of the Council to base the Regulation on article 130S of the EC treaty is a one-off decision motivated by special circumstances that do not affect the Commission's continuing position on other issues referred to the Court of Justice nor the European Parliament's prerogatives. Moreover, the Commission continues to believe that the provisions in the Regulation concerning shipments to or from non-EC countries require the addition of article 113."[78] Compared to the two cases already examined, here the

---

[77] Elie Le Du, *Les Echos*, 9 April 1992, 22; "Environment Council: Ministers Bogged Down over Waste," *European Report* no. 1772, 28 May 1992, iv/20; "Ministers Fail to Reach Unified Position on Waste Shipments Prior to Earth Summit," *International Environment Reporter*, 3 June 1992, 348; "French Decree and French-German Decisions," *European Report* no. 1791, 2 September 1992, iv/10–11; "Nation Copes with Mounting Trash in Wake of French Ban on Imports," *International Environment Reporter*, 23 September 1992, 598–599; Bronwen Maddox, "EC Toxic Waste Accord Is Near," *Financial Times*, 20 October 1992, 3; "Ministers Reach Political Agreement on Waste Transfers," *European Report* no. 1805, 21 October 1992, iv/10–11; Philippe Lemaitre, "L'importation de déchets ménagers pourra être interdite au sein de la CEE," *Le Monde*, 22 October 1992, 19.

[78] "Full Details on Waste Shipment Regulation," *European Report* no. 1806, 24 October 1992, iv/19.

Greening the Market?

Commission acquiesced meekly to the Council's change of legal basis, failing to threaten Court action and expressing positive indignation only with respect to the abandonment of article 113, and not of article 100A.[79] The Commission's acquiescence proved decisive and, given prevailing expectations about its neoliberal preferences, strongly counterintuitive. It had, quite simply, "reverse[d] a longstanding proclivity to use article 100A as the basis of environmental provisions which affect the trade in goods" (Skroback 1994, 106).

The EP applauded the environmental victory but lamented the procedural defeat. It grilled the Council President about the slight, but was told that to push the procedural issue would be to risk the substantive outcome. A journalist noted the tension in the EP's position: "Article 130S, which is geared to environmental measures, is more in line with the Parliament's political approach to the dossiers in question, but article 100A, which is for measures needed to create the single market, entitles [it] to [a] second reading" under the cooperation procedure.[80] The EP's Environment Committee adopted a second report on the Regulation. Substantively, it sought to reinsert stringent protective measures such as Community controls on domestic waste movements and a ban on all waste shipments to developing countries. Procedurally, it disputed the legal basis chosen and reasserted the appropriateness of articles 100A and 113.[81] EP plenary debate saw repeated procedural political discourses and ample anticipation of the Maastricht Treaty, which would afford the EP meaningful influence even under article 130S when it upgraded that article to the cooperation procedure.[82] The full EP adopted the report in late January 1993.[83]

---

[79] Commission document SI(1992) 0781/1, 21 October 1992. See also statements by Commissioner Paleokrassas, *EP Debates* no. 3-426, 18 January 1993, 27. The Commission's desire for article 113 assimilates easily to procedural political logic. Article 113 (post-Amsterdam article 133) is the legal basis for Community commercial policy, and, importantly, its use implies "exclusive Community competence" over the matters covered rather than shared competence with member states or exclusive national competence. In external relations, the Commission exhibits a general preference for article 113 (post-Amsterdam article 133) over all other articles. Thus, its position on the legal basis here is consistent with the broader notion that legal bases are desired only for their broader procedural political effects.

[80] Brian Love, "EP Spells Trouble for Council on Waste and Eco-Audits," *Reuter Textline Western Europe*, 4 December 1992.

[81] EP Doc. A3-0004/93, 8 January 1993; "Shetland Oil Spill and Waste Shipments Under MEPs' Scrutiny," *European Report* no. 1826, 13 January 1993.

[82] *EP Debates* no. 3-426, 18 January 1993, 24–27.

[83] OJ C 42, 15 February 1993, 82–84; "Waste Shipments: Move Towards Legal Action in EC Court of Justice," *Europe Environment* no. 402, 19 January 1993; "Parliament Approves

EP officials immediately began planning a legal attack on the Regulation that would shortly be adopted by the Council. The EP felt bolstered by two pieces of still-operative ECJ jurisprudence. First, the Titanium Dioxide judgment – which would not be "reversed" by the Waste Framework Directive judgement for some six months – strongly suggested that the EP would find a supporter in the Court (Robinson 1992, 116).[84] Second, a July 1992 judgment in the "Walloon Waste" case (Case C-2/90, *Commission v. Belgium* [1992] ECR I-4431) had firmly established that waste was a good, subject in principle to the EU's internal market regime. This suggested that waste shipments should be regulated under article 100A (Hancher and Sevenster 1992, 364; von Wilmowsky 1993, 563).[85] In light of all of this, the EP Legal Affairs Committee "unanimously decided that, on the day after the Council approves the regulation on the legal base which it intends . . . we shall take the matter to the Court because we are convinced we are right."[86]

Despite the support adduced by the EP, the Court's jurisprudence to that point had alternated between support for internal market and environmental provisions in a rather incoherent way. According to one analyst, "Conflicting precedents preclude even a mere guess at the treaty article on which the proposed regulation on waste shipments has to be based" (von Wilmowsky 1993, 562). I have already discussed ongoing confusion after the Titanium Dioxide and Waste Framework Directive cases. Much the same could be said of the Walloon Waste judgment, "the full implications [of which were] difficult to fathom."[87]

In light of this ambiguity, and despite EP threats, the Council definitively adopted the Waste Shipment Regulation on 1 February 1993 (for analyses see Roselsky 1993; Skroback 1994; Sommer 1994). Textually, the Council appeared to have learned from its earlier mistakes: it deleted all reference

---

Amended Proposal on Waste Shipments, Reiterates Threat," *International Environment Reporter*, 27 January 1993, 38.

[84] European Parliament, Legal Affairs Committee, "Note à l'attention du membre chargé des questions de base juridique, M. Carlos Perreau de Pinninck Domenech," dossier 99/92, 15 January 1993; see also statement by MEP Bowe at the 18 January 1993 plenary, suggesting that *Titanium Dioxide* decisively militates in favor of article 100A (*EP Debates* no. 3-426, 26).

[85] EP Legal Service Doc. SJ-127/92, "L'arrêt de la Cour de justice du 9 juillet 1992 dans l'affaire C-2/90 et la base juridique de deux actes législatifs – demande d'une note d'évaluation de la commission de l'environnement," 18 November 1992.

[86] *EP Debates* no. 3-426, 26.

[87] "Waste and EC Principles of Free Movement of Goods," *ENDS Report* no. 210, July 1992, 38.

to the internal market in the legislative preamble. Observers noted that this would support the Council's preferred article 130S: "in order to determine the objective of the measure, the Court will particularly look at the statements of purpose – and all references to the completion of the internal market or the distortion of competition have disappeared from the text" (Schmidt 1995, 198; see also de Sadeleer 1994, 95). In every other respect the text reproduced verbatim the October 1992 political agreement.

Waste Shipments Before the Court. On the unanimous recommendation of the Environment Committee, the EP lodged its annulment action before the Court in April 1993.[88] Anticipating the Council's defense, the EP argued that despite appearances to the contrary, the aim of the Regulation was not per se to limit waste movements but rather to define and regulate permissible shipments. When pushed at the oral hearing, it went further, suggesting that article 100A could be used for any measure regulating free movement (including, in extremis, eliminating it), and not just for measures aimed at facilitating free movement. The Council, not surprisingly, argued forcefully that the aim and content of the measure pled in favor of environmental protection and article 130S. The Commission remained conspicuously absent, having chosen not to intervene on the side of the Parliament, as Parliament had done for it in the two earlier cases.

The Court's Advocate General, consistent with prevailing practice, closely scrutinized the legislative preamble, finding that "the objectives set out in the preamble relate exclusively to environmental protection and the protection of health" (para. 9). He flatly contradicted the EP in finding that article 100A requires measures that promote, rather than restrict, the free movement of goods (para. 43; see also Bos 1991; de Sadeleer 1994, 115). More specifically, he held that "the aim of the Regulation is not to define those characteristics of waste which will enable waste to circulate freely within the internal market; rather, it is to provide a harmonized set of procedures whereby movements of waste can be prevented and controlled in accordance with national law" (para. 44). On this reasoning, article 130S represented the correct legal basis.

In its judgment of 28 June 1994, the Court again sided with the Council (Case C-187/93, *Parliament v. Council* [1994] ECR I-2857). In effect,

---

[88] Letter from Ken Collins to Egon Klepsch, number 01218, of 2 March 1993; see also "Waste Shipment Regulation Could End Up in the Dock," *European Report* no. 1839, 27 February 1993, iv/20-21; OJ C 147, 27 May 1993, 10.

it found that the circumstances of the Waste Framework Directive case applied by analogy. Quite simply, the primary aim of the Regulation was environmental protection, and the mere fact that the measure would have effects on the internal market did not suffice to bring it under the ambit of article 100A. As a result, the Council had acted properly in basing the measure on article 130S of the treaty. Observers suggested that this reaffirmation of the Waste Framework judgment dispelled any lingering doubts about the legal basis for waste management legislation (de Sadeleer 1994, 114; London and Llamas 1995, 41–43).

Theoretical Assessment

I have intensively examined the legislative and procedural political history of three pieces of European Union legislation dealing with waste management. I selected the cases to control, to the extent possible, for the nature of the issues at hand and for variations in confounding factors such as actors' preferences. The cases offer the added benefit of representing consecutive steps in the ECJ's legal basis jurisprudence in the area of environmental policy. I now assess this evidence in light of the theoretical expectations developed in Chapter 2 and operationalized in Chapter 3 and above. How do the theory of procedural politics and alternatives to it fare in explaining the conditions under which, the ways in which, and the effects with which actors engage in everyday politics with respect to rules?

Conditions

Partly by virtue of case selection, which controls for variations in jurisdictional ambiguity, the nature of available institutional alternatives drives procedural politics in this set of cases. In particular, consecutive treaty modifications by the Single European Act and the Maastricht Treaty changed the influence properties of the available alternatives. Those institutional changes thus represent natural experiments and provide opportunities to assess theoretical expectations about the conditions under which procedural politics occurs.

Actors' revealed procedural preferences consistently confirm expectations generated by the models in Chapter 3. Prior to the SEA, no actor mentioned the legal basis, precisely because all were indifferent to the procedurally identical alternatives. Under the SEA regime, the EP, as predicted, favored the internal market rule (cooperation procedure) to the environment rule (unanimous consultation), as did the European Commission. The Council revealed the opposite preference for these alternatives. Crucially, all three of these positions represented switches relative to the issue frames advanced prior to the SEA, when procedural political incentives were nonexistent. During the run-up to the Maastricht Treaty, the EP continued to favor internal market rules, which would soon use the codecision procedure, to environmental rules, which would soon employ the cooperation procedure. The Council, predicted to reveal the opposite preference, did so. Crucially, the evidence also confirms a Commission "switch" from the internal market (cooperation during the SEA and codecision under Maastricht) to the environment (unanimous consultation during the SEA, cooperation thereafter), which is a key prediction that differentiates procedural politics from its rivals.

The bulk of the evidence, then, supports the influence maximization hypothesis, according to which actors promote the usage of rules that maximize their influence (as defined by the models in Chapter 3) in the political process. I searched for but found scant evidence – one claim by France in one document, which disappeared thereafter – contradicting this expectation. Putative ideological attitudes toward European integration or supranationalism played no discernible role. What is more, the cases clearly confirm this relationship as causal rather than spurious: actors play procedural politics precisely for the reasons identified by the theory. That is, they behave as rational influence maximizers, attentive not only to incentives but also to opportunities and strategic and institutional constraints.

Means

In theory, two forms of strategic behavior should accompany procedural politics. First, actors should engage in strategic issue definition so as to "fit" issues under favorable rules. At least some substantive positions should both follow and be consistent with procedural preferences. Second, actors should incline toward procedural, rather than ideological or narrowly substantive, coalition formation. At the beginning of the chapter I specified procedural political and alternative expectations with respect to each of these behaviors. Which finds support in the evidence?

Strategic Issue Definition. The cases reveal a single attempt at procedurally motivated "fission" of legislative proposals, and no attempts at fusion. In terms of the third variant of strategic issue definition identified in

Procedural Politics

Chapter 2, reframing, the cases show it to be ubiquitous. Details in terms of the direction (for expectations, refer back to Table 15) and timing of framing behavior strongly support the procedural politics view and strongly disconfirm the sincere view.

The Titanium Dioxide case offers clear evidence of strategic reframing. In a crucial (because discriminating) test, the Commission, Parliament, and Council all reversed their previous claims about the principal aim and content of the Directive following the entry into force of the Single European Act. Throughout the legislative process all actors tabled strategic textual modifications aimed at reinforcing their preferred legal basis. The Commission did so rather egregiously, especially in its first amended proposal. The Parliament and Council demonstrated similar, if only slightly more subtle, proclivities, although the Council's failure to "massage" the title and first article of the text to remove references to harmonization was said to contribute significantly to its ultimate Court defeat.[89] Finally, if we consider the positions taken prior to the SEA as baselines of "sincere" preferences, the case offers clear evidence in favor of the procedural political view as against the alternative. That is, amendments followed a procedural political rather than a sincere substantive logic.

The Waste Framework Directive case similarly confirms procedural political expectations about strategic issue definition. The Parliament's behavior is most instructive in this regard, for it permits the clearest competing test of alternative framing hypotheses. Under the traditional view, the EP should promote strong environmental protection. Under the procedural political view, it may continue to promote the substantive goal, but it should offer amendments tending to frame the issue as economic rather than environmental. The evidence clearly favors the procedural political view. The EP did indeed call for greater environmental protection and tabled amendments to this effect, all the while claiming the applicability of internal market rules. What is more, the evidence suggests that procedural preferences can actually override substantive preferences, at least in the short run. By asking the Commission to withdraw the proposed Directive, the EP effectively favored institutional interests over environmental protection. The same might be said to apply for the other actors as well.

---

[89] In addition to the interview cited in the case study above, Macrory (1991, 15) contends, "Clearly, the explicit reference in the... Directive to the harmonization of pollution reduction programs for the industry, both in its title and the first article, was a powerful factor" in the Court's decision.

Writing before the judgment in the Waste Framework case, two analysts characterized the procedural political dispute as a "high stakes gamble," going on to note that if the Directive

> were to be quashed by the Court of Justice, the carefully drafted new legal edifice of [EU] waste management would come crumbling down and may prove very hard to reconstitute, as sad experience with the titanium dioxide directive demonstrates. Both the Commission, by pursuing its hard-line internal market stance, and the Council, by ignoring the Court's titanium dioxide ruling, are playing with fire. The environment may well be the ultimate loser in this power struggle. (Wheeler and Pallemaerts 1992, 176)

All actors, it would seem, had an interest in moving away from the substantive status quo ante. But on this interpretation, all were willing to risk at least short-term substantive losses in the pursuit of procedural political gains.

The Waste Shipment Regulation bespeaks a similar tension between short-run substantive and longer-run procedural political interests. The European Parliament, for example, clearly had a sincere substantive preference for stringent controls on intra-Community waste shipments. But it insisted on legislating under internal market rules, better suited to liberalizing than to restricting or even eliminating the movement of "goods." It tried to frame a near-total ban on waste shipments as a specification of the limits on the free movement of goods, and thus as a free trade measure. Implausible on its face, this stance demonstrates the legal gymnastics in which actors are willing to engage in the pursuit of procedural political advantage. It did much the same with respect to international waste shipments, for which dissenting voices criticized it from within.[90] All of this clearly confirms the framing hypothesis and undermines "sincere" alternatives to it.

Consider now different expectations about the timing of substantive changes and expressions of rules preferences. From the procedural political perspective, at least some substantive modification (i.e., reframing) will follow, rather than precede, rules choice, and it will serve to reinforce procedurally preferable rules. From the sincere or "legally correct" perspective, rules choices follow exclusively from the substance of the text. Titanium Dioxide offers clear evidence in favor of this proposition at every stage, most notably in the Commission's amended proposals. In the Waste Framework case, similarly, important substantive changes – in particular to the preamble

---

[90] *EP Debates* no. 3-426, 20 January 1993, 156.

of the legislation but also in this case to critically important definitions in article 1 – followed rather than preceded expressions of preference for one as opposed to another legal basis. I want to be careful not to overstate the case here. The legislative history of the Framework Directive suggests that most member states sincerely sought to limit, as much as possible, cross-border waste shipments. But the timing proves crucial, and it supports the procedural political view as against the legalistic rival.

The only apparently disconfirming piece of evidence – the Commission's "legally correct" stance on the legal basis voiced in early 1992 during Waste Shipment Regulation negotiations – makes sense once we consider its procedural incentives, discussed below. I contend, and indirect evidence supports the notion, that the Commission anticipated the entry into force of the Maastricht Treaty, and that its apparently "legally correct" position was actually taken with its post-Maastricht procedural political interests firmly in mind.

Before proceeding, it makes sense to consider alternative explanations. Consider the change from the pre-SEA period to the SEA regime. Did preferences change? Possibly. Jacques Delors took over the Commission presidency in 1985 and staked his leadership on the Single Market program, which might have led him to favor the internal market over environmental interpretations of a whole host of measures. The second direct elections in June of 1984 of the European Parliament occurred between its pre-SEA resolution and its post-SEA switch in favor of the internal market interpretation. A handful of national governments changed composition. It is possible that each of these events might have produced sincere changes in issue definitions consistent with the observed pattern. It is not clear, however, why such changes would work in favor of the internal market for the Commission and the Parliament, but in favor of the environment for the ten member states involved, many of which saw no change in political leadership. At a minimum, the sincere perspective must be further specified before it can compete with the parsimony of the procedural politics model.

Coalition Formation. Turning now to the hypotheses on coalition formation, recall from Table 16 that, during the SEA period, procedural political and prevailing approaches are observationally equivalent. That the coalitions observed in both the Titanium Dioxide and Waste Framework cases reflect a supranational-intergovernmental split therefore supports both perspectives. However, process tracing lends credence to the procedural political over the traditional view. No observed behavior, no

Greening the Market?

document, no interview, nor any other evidence that I have uncovered suggests the importance of ideology – supranational or intergovernmental – in coalition formation. When the Commission enjoined the Parliament to intervene on its behalf in the Waste Framework legal case, it framed its appeal in institutional-procedural rather than ideological – that is, pro-supranational – terms. It appealed to the EP's narrow institutional interests. And, in the same vein, MEPs identified friends and foes in terms of the institutional interests of the Parliament rather than the defense or promotion of integration or supranationalism.

Importantly, the arrival of the Maastricht Treaty in the early 1990s provides a discriminating test of the two perspectives. While the traditional view predicts a coalitional pattern identical to that under the SEA,[91] procedural politics predicts a defection by the Commission from the side of the Parliament to the side of the Council. Although subtle, precisely this occurred in the case of the Waste Shipment Regulation. Following the December 1991 signing of the Maastricht treaty the Commission abandoned its erstwhile ally. Throughout the 1992 negotiations on the Waste Shipment Regulation the Commission paid lip service to, but failed to defend, EP prerogatives. Its failure to initiate annulment proceedings (as in the two SEA-era cases), and more clearly still its failure even to intervene before the Court in support of the Parliament, all attest to its change in position. This failure is unusual and potentially puzzling. By the terms of article 211 (ex article 155), the Commission is supposed to serve as the so-called guardian of the treaties. Indeed, of the universe of thirty-four legal basis cases judged by the ECJ between 1987 and the first half of 2003, Waste Shipments is one of only five in which the Commission did not involve itself. True, it did not intervene in support of the Council. But that would have been flagrant, given the recency and previous depth of its support for article 100A. Given the otherwise close similarity to the two earlier cases, I believe that this difference can be ascribed to Commission preferences over the available institutional alternatives, and thus to procedural politics.

---

[91] I could also identify a second rival prediction according to which substantive preferences determine coalitional patterns. In the case of the Waste Shipment Regulation, this would predict a coalition of those inclined to limit waste movements (the EP and most member states) against those more favorable to such shipments (the Commission and perhaps Belgium and Luxembourg). This pattern clearly fails to materialize in favor of the coalitions predicted by the theory of procedural politics.

Effects

All of the above might be for naught if procedural politics and the strategic maneuvers to which it gives rise did not influence important substantive outcomes in the European Union. I will not consider policymaking efficiency here, though it seems apparent that procedural politics slowed the legislative process in these cases considerably. Given the difficulty of establishing the counterfactuals and the clarity and strength of the overall findings, I will rest my case on decision-making inefficiencies with the statistical results from Chapter 4. Instead, I will focus on policymaking and treaty changes. To what extent did procedural politics impinge upon the substance of EU environmental policy and upon subsequent amendments to the Treaty of Rome?

Policy Outcomes. In Chapter 3 I identified three pathways by which procedural politics might affect policy outcomes. The first pathway operated directly: procedural politics determines rules, and rules can affect outcomes. This pathway did not appear to generate EU legislative change in the cases at hand. The Council adopted legislation on the basis of unanimity rules to which member states had unanimously agreed, as against Commission proposals. In short, the unanimity rule could not autonomously – that is, independently of member states' preferences, power, and bargaining – shape outcomes because it was wholly endogenous to those same factors.

However, evidence from the readoption of the Titanium Dioxide judgment after the ECJ's annulment does suggest that the first pathway enabled the adoption of *national* environmental laws that would have been illegal in the absence of procedural politics. Recall from Table 14 that during this time period, environmental treaty provisions differed from internal market provisions in that they allowed the maintenance and enactment of new national environmental measures, even where the EU had already legislated. Following adoption of the original Titanium Dioxide Directive on the basis of article 130S (environment), the Netherlands and Germany availed themselves of this facility, which they would have lacked had the Commission's proposed legal basis been retained. Then, when it came time to readopt the measure on the basis of article 100A as required by the Court's judgments, their existing national measures could still be, and indeed were, protected.[92]

---

[92] Commission document SI(92) 172, 13 March 1992; Commission document SI(92) 193/1, 20 March 1992; Commission document SI(92) 194, 25 March 1992; and especially Commission document SI(92) 395, 22 May 1992.

Greening the Market?

In short, procedural politics substantially changed the regulatory landscape in these two countries.

The second pathway by which procedural politics could influence policy outcomes was less direct. Procedural politics increases the dimensionality of the bargaining space, creating issue linkages that can be exploited to produce substantive outcomes that otherwise would not have occurred. Outlying member states may extract substantive concessions in exchange for their support of the majority's procedural political position. (The majority requires this support because the legal basis can only be changed by unanimity.) This precise logic played itself out in the case of the Waste Shipment Regulation. Although unprecedented in the extent to which it subjugated free trade to environmental protection, the Regulation made a critical and otherwise puzzling exception for hazardous waste shipments from small countries such as Belgium to large countries such as France. I argue that other member states had a more intense preference on the procedural dimension, and Belgium – which has always been the most Commission-friendly member state, but which, lacking indigenous management capacity, also desperately needed to be able to export waste to its neighbors – had a more intense preference on the substantive dimension. In a classic logroll, Belgium abandoned the Commission in favor of the Council's procedural position and in return won the small country substantive exception.[93] Establishing the counterfactual poses tremendous difficulties, but I maintain that straightforward institutional effects analysis (i.e., with institutions remaining exogenous), Schelling-style bargaining theory, and other approaches fail to explain this outcome, while procedural politics succeeds.[94]

Third, procedural politics might influence policy outcomes through the incorporation of procedural-politically motivated amendments into final legislation. The three pieces of legislation that I have examined bear the distinctive markings of disputed legislation, although establishment of a

---

[93] The documentary record clearly confirms this interpretation. Commission officials reported in early October that "the Belgian delegation intimated that if it obtained satisfaction [on more lax provisions] it could support the other delegations wishing to change the legal basis" (Commission document SI(1992) 0716/1, 2 October 1992 [author's translation]). After the deal was done, officials confirmed that "unanimous Council agreement on the legal basis was obtained by way of a concession to Belgium" involving simplifying the procedures for shipping "green" (nondangerous) waste (Commission document SI(1992) 0781/1, 21 October 1992 [author's translation]).

[94] See Jupille 1996 for an exhaustive examination of this case.

baseline is difficult and, in the absence of full-text electronic resources,[95] the exercise defies easy quantification. In general, the Council enjoys a last mover advantage here, and substantive alterations usually reflect its preferences. However, each actor attempted to influence the Court's assessment of primary aim and content by "massaging" the legislative preambles at every opportunity. Especially after the Council's defeat in the Titanium Dioxide case, then, these legislative preambles clearly reflect its procedural political preoccupations. Furthermore, the Council eliminated any definition of "transport" from the Waste Framework Directive in order, the EP contended, to deflect claims that it should have been based on internal market rules. Affecting one of the four key definitions proposed by the Commission, this represented a substantial change.

Institutional Change. Finally, to what extent, if any, has procedural politics in the environmental sector generated constitutional change? Kelemen (1995) has argued that the Maastricht Treaty's procedural revisions of the internal market and environmental chapters represented a "state response" to the "supranational activism" of the Commission, Parliament, and Court in the Titanium Dioxide case. On this argument, the SEA's procedural landscape incited the Parliament and Commission to collude in favor of article 100A (SYNQ procedure) as against article 130S (CNSU procedure), despite the fact that member states manifestly intended to retain the CNSU procedure for most environmental policymaking. By upgrading article 100A to the CODQ procedure and article 130S(1) to the SYNQ procedure in the TEU, Kelemen argues, member states effectively split the Commission-Parliament coalition, the former now joining the member states in preferring article 130S to article 100A.

This account has tremendous appeal and, as it happens, the Maastricht procedural change had precisely this effect, as evidenced by the Waste Shipment Regulation. Yet, the causal claim does not withstand close scrutiny. First, intuitively, it seems a rather drastic step for member states to switch all internal market measures to the CODQ procedure solely in response to a single unfavorable Court judgment in the environmental sector. Second, empirically, I have uncovered no evidence in support of this

---

[95] Final legislation and some preparatory documents are available electronically and could be easily content-analyzed, but for the period under study the number of documents is very small and unevenly distributed across institutions (more easily accessed for the Commission, not at all accessible for the Council, with the EP in a middle position).

Greening the Market?

claim and interviewees in the EU institutions greeted it with considerable skepticism.[96]

A connection does arguably exist, however, between day-to-day procedural politicking and subsequent treaty changes. Consider the following question: why did member states upgrade the environment chapter from unanimous consultation (CNSU) to cooperation (SYNQ) at Maastricht, and from cooperation (SYNQ) to QMV codecision (CODQ) at Amsterdam? It may be the case that they did so to respond to Parliamentary demands or Parliamentary practice. This may represent willing accommodation, whereby the EP simply convinced them of the legitimacy of its demands for more power in this area.[97] Alternatively, it may represent forced accommodation, whereby the EP could credibly threaten to continue invoking high "influence costs" (Milgrom and Roberts 1990) on member states, which respond by acceding to its demands.[98] While I find the latter explanation both more consistent with the logic of my approach and more compelling, the evidence remains too scanty to draw any definitive conclusions.

Conclusion

In conclusion, the cases at hand generally strongly support procedural political expectations, and procedural politics consistently outperforms alternative approaches in explaining the evidence. Actors expressed rules preferences consistent with those deduced using the models in Chapter 3. They framed policies and formed coalitions in precisely the ways predicted by the theory of procedural politics. The evidence suggests that the relationship was causal rather than merely spurious. Actors consistently took the positions, offered the amendments, and formed the coalitions that they did *because of* procedural political considerations. This behavior had an impact on legislative outcomes and may have contributed to subsequent

---

[96] Interview with Council Legal Service official, 2 March 1999.
[97] Consider, by way of analogy, the Maastricht modification of article 230 (ex article 173) to enable the Parliament to bring annulment proceedings before the Court alleging breach of prerogative. According to Dubinsky (1994, 316 fn 86, 344 fn 183), this modification directly resulted from the EP's arguments in the "post-Chernobyl" case, which dealt with the legal basis of EU legislation regulating the importation of radiation-contaminated foodstuffs (Case C-70/88, *Parliament v. Council* [1990] ECR I-2041). See also McCown 2003.
[98] Hix (2002) and Steunenberg and Dimitrova (1999) both make a similar claim with respect to the creation of the "codecision II" procedure at Amsterdam.

amendments to the EU's constitutional architecture. Existing approaches capture few of these dynamics because they view institutions as fixed and given in the short run and as potential objects of choice only in the longer run. Procedural politics furnishes the necessary tools.

To what extent, though, can the environmental experience be generalized? It is an empirical outlier, highly susceptible to procedural politics by the nature of the issues and institutional alternatives involved. Can the same inferences be drawn for other sectors of EU activity? Fuller assessment of the theoretical predictions and confident generalization to all of EU politics (and beyond) require exposure to a broader array of evidence. Chapter 6 brings such evidence to bear through an examination of procedural politics in the agricultural sector.

6

Mad Cows and Englishmen

PROCEDURAL POLITICS AND EU AGRICULTURAL POLICY

Procedural politics, the conduct of everyday politics with respect to rules, occurs under predictable conditions, by predictable means, and with predictable effects. It occurs when incentives, conceived as possible gains in influence, and opportunities, conceived as the creation of new institutional alternatives because of jurisdictional ambiguity, align. It characteristically involves procedural coalition formation and strategic issue framing, and it influences rules choices, policymaking efficiency and outcomes, and constitutional change. The previous chapter examined these issues in the context of European Union environmental politics and policymaking, showing that procedural politics outperforms alternative explanations of environmental positions taken, issue frames advanced, coalitions formed, and outcomes generated. When rules are at least partly endogenous to the day-to-day political process, accounts of politics with respect to them must augment and in some cases substitute for accounts of politics within them if we seek to understand legislative behavior, policymaking outcomes and efficiency, and institutional change.

The present chapter extends the empirical examination to a second sector: agricultural policymaking. This sector, when coupled with environmental policy, offers many interesting methodological opportunities. Agriculture is often viewed as the antithesis of the environmental sector in terms of history, issues, operative institutions, and legislative dynamics. Where environmental policy is a "new" area of EU competence, part of the treaties only since the mid-1980s, agriculture enjoys the longest pedigree of any EU policy with the possible exception of the customs union. Environment also represents a "new" (i.e., postmaterial) issue, while agriculture is a classic "old" (i.e., redistributive) one. While environment remains an area of "mixed competence," characterized by an intermingling of national and

European responsibilities, agriculture is the quintessential "Community" policy, where European law has replaced and now preempts national measures. Finally, and critically, while a loose "issue network" with fluid memberships, few resource interdependencies, and constantly evolving rules characterizes environmental policy, agriculture represents a textbook "policy community," with well-established members, high resource interdependencies among them, and a stable institutional environment. This last difference, especially, sharply distinguishes the two sectors in terms of the expectations generated by existing theories of EU politics and policymaking.

Agriculture might be characterized as the "least likely" sector for procedural politics. Indeed, the data in Chapter 4 confirm that the sector has been largely immune from procedural political conflict. Yet this immunity is best explained in procedural political terms, which captures not only intersectoral differences (as policy networks analysis does), but also over-time differences within sectors (which policy networks analysis does not). Added value in explaining rules, issue frames, coalitional behavior, and legislative and institutional outcomes in this sector, furthermore, would bespeak a high degree of adaptability and generalizability of the basic arguments.

Part one of the chapter traces the procedural history of the agricultural sector. Part two then operationalizes, in this sector, the general procedural political hypotheses set forth in Chapter 2. It also suggests the design and case selection logics necessary to test them empirically. Part three then traces procedural politics in two cases of agricultural policymaking. Part four assesses, in light of the evidence, predictions about the conditions under which, the means by which, and the effects with which procedural politics occurs. The evidence broadly supports the theory. It suggests that institutional and policy analysis ignores everyday institutional endogeneity at its peril, and that the approach developed in this book more powerfully explains rules choices, policy dynamics and outcomes, and (higher-order) institutional change than do alternatives to it.

Legislative Procedures and EU Agricultural Policy

By any number of measures, agriculture holds pride of place as the most important EU policy. It constitutes about 25 percent of Community legislation and a similar fraction of ECJ case law (Kapteyn and VerLoren van Themaat 1998, 1166). For years it accounted for some two-thirds of the EU budget, although this has since dropped to under 50 percent (Hix 1999b, 246). In many ways it represents a quintessentially European policy, exhibiting both the promise and pathologies of EU politics and policymaking. Always a politically important area, it was subject to extensive integration from the early days of the Common Market. I begin by assessing the procedural lay of the land in this key sector.

A Procedural History of EU Agricultural Policy

Compared to the environmental sector, the procedural history of EU agricultural policy is a straightforward one. The 1958 Treaty of Rome devoted its second title (articles 38–47) to agriculture. Article 39 set out the objectives of the Common Agricultural Policy (CAP), emphasizing the maintenance and development of the socially important agricultural sector. It placed a decidedly secondary emphasis on consumer interests with a long-neglected goal of reasonable prices. Procedurally, articles 43(2)(3) and 43(3) empowered the Council to adopt agricultural legislation under the consultation procedure – that is, on the basis of a Commission proposal after consulting the Parliament – by unanimity during the first two phases of the transition period (1958–1966) and by qualified majority voting (QMV) thereafter. Renumbered with the Amsterdam Treaty, article 37 (ex article 43), continues to provide the legal basis for the vast majority of original EU agricultural legislation. It has never been procedurally modified during the many bouts of treaty revision and remains, as of this writing, one of the last and most important holdouts for the traditional consultation procedure. Thus, while agriculture initially represented one of the most *communautaire* sectors from a procedural perspective (because it called for qualified majority voting), it has appeared increasingly anachronistic in its limitation of the role of the European Parliament (Kapteyn and VerLoren van Themaat 1998, 1141).

In terms of informal procedural characteristics, for years member states rarely voted in the Council of Ministers, despite treaty provisions authorizing them to do so.[1] This was especially true after the 1966 Luxembourg Compromise, by the terms of which member states could effectively veto important legislation when vital national interests were at stake.[2] Beginning in the early 1980s, however, the consensus principle began to change. In a "crucial turning point," in 1982 a majority of member states rebuffed the

---

[1] Staff and budgetary matters constituted exceptions to this general rule (Nicoll 1984, 37).
[2] *Bull. EC* 3/1966, 9.

UK's attempt to veto the 1982 price package as a way to gain leverage over the related issue of its general budgetary contribution. Characterizing the attempt as an abuse of the Compromise, they outvoted the UK and adopted the package (*Common Market Law Review* 1982; *European Law Review* 1982; Teasdale 1993, 571). This broke the mystique surrounding the Luxembourg Compromise, although member states did periodically invoke it after that point (Vasey 1988).[3] Voting, as shown clearly in Chapter 4, began to occur more frequently, and as a practical matter, the QMV consultation (CNSQ) procedure used in agriculture began to take on true meaning.

While agriculture has remained untouched at successive bouts of treaty revision, other treaty provisions potentially relating to this sector have undergone substantial change. Provisions for completing the internal market moved from the unanimous consultation procedure (article 100) to the cooperation procedure (article 100A, post-Amsterdam article 95) after the 1987 entry into force of the Single European Act (SEA), and from there to codecision with Maastricht and thereafter. Environmental policy entered the treaty under the unanimous consultation procedure (article 130S) in 1987, employed the cooperation procedure from 1993 to 1999, and has used the Amsterdam codecision procedure since then. Different aspects of regional and social policy can use any of a number of legislative procedures that differ from article 43's QMV consultation. Most important, the 1993 Maastricht Treaty enacted provisions on consumer protection and human health, the latter of which was subject to an "integration provision" (in article 129(1)(3)) identical to the one found in the environmental sector, whereby these issues need to be considered in the making of policies in all other areas. Further complicating matters, the Maastricht provision also contained a *renvoi* (interface) to article 100A, suggesting the applicability of that article's legislative procedure (QMV codecision).

In sum, while procedural constancy has reigned in the agriculture treaty articles, procedural diversity has marked other, potentially related, areas.

Jurisdictional Ambiguity

While necessary, such procedural diversity does not suffice to produce procedural politics. Some measure of jurisdictional ambiguity is also necessary. While ambiguity is much lower in agriculture than in environmental

---

[3] See also "Veto-mania," *Economist*, 18 February 1995, 48–49.

policy, and despite agriculture's status as a classic "vertical" policy sector, in practice it touches on a wide range of public policy issues. It serves as an important instrument of EU social policy and relates intimately to the EU's other redistributive policies (regional, structural, and cohesion funds). It connects organically to EU environmental policy through the relationship of farming to the land and the natural environment. It touches on issues such as food safety; consumer protection; human, plant, and animal health; and so on. It involves the harmonization of divergent national measures, a tool also used in the making of the EU's more general market in goods.

I will focus on the intersection between agriculture on the one hand and human health and policy harmonization on the other hand. With respect to these areas, jurisdictional ambiguity has existed from very early on (see, e.g., Ventura 1967, 70). As Barents has noted, "As a more or less clear description of what constitutes the common agricultural policy is absent, the relation between articles 43 and other treaty provisions is opaque," which can easily lead to procedural political dispute (Barents 1988, 3). Since many of these overlapping and related areas use different legislative procedures, after about the early 1980s agriculture satisfied – with variations across issues and over time – the hypothesized preconditions for procedural politics.

Historically, and focusing on the "structure" side of the issue–structural correspondence equation, legislation simultaneously involving agriculture and veterinary, phytosanitary, or human health questions posed the greatest problems. From 1958 until the mid-1980s these problems reduced to a debate between the Commission and the Council over article 43 (QMV consultation procedure, preferred by the Commission) and article 100 (unanimous consultation, preferred by the Council). In June 1964, member states came to a modus vivendi (with each other, but not with the Commission) in which they agreed in practice to use article 100 for measures touching on veterinary, phytosanitary, and human health matters.[4] Recall that this decision was taken in anticipation of the changeover to majority voting in 1966. While the changeover never occurred (because of the Luxembourg Compromise), the agreement held. For the following twenty-plus years, the Commission would base its proposals in these areas on article 43, whereupon the Council would change the legal basis to article 100. Indeed, from 1964 until 1994 the Commission only five times proposed a

---

[4] Advocate General Mischo gives this history in his Opinion in the Battery Hens litigation (Case 131/86, *United Kingdom v. Council* [1988] ECR 905, paras. 9–10).

joint legal basis of articles 100 and 43, while the Council adopted 155 acts on this dual legal basis. However, this was not really procedural political, involving rather the form of legislation than the way in which it would be adopted.[5]

The Court was finally called upon to adjudicate the long-running dispute only in 1986, after agreement on the SEA and the growth in majority voting gave the legal basis distinction fuller (procedural) importance. In its twinned judgments in the *Hormones* and *Battery Hens* cases,[6] the first of which I will examine in detail below, the ECJ set forth an uncharacteristically clear test for determining the applicability of article 43 (agriculture) as against other treaty provisions, most notably article 100. It held that any measure dealing with a product listed in Annex II of the Rome Treaty that contributed to the CAP objectives laid out in article 39 must be based on article 43 of the treaty and thus use the CNSQ legislative procedure. The Court read the CAP objectives expansively to include matters pertaining to veterinary, phytosanitary, and human health,[7] and it posited an indissoluble link between the CAP and policy harmonization such that recourse to article 100 would be unnecessary (Barents 1993, 97–98). In short, "all measures which relate [in any way] to the realization of the free movement of agricultural products contribute by their nature to [the CAP objectives in article 39], and as such constitute a matter falling...under article 43" (Kapteyn and VerLoren van Themaat 1998, 1132). In a series of related cases brought around the same time, the Court amplified and extended this precedent; but it was so consistent in its support of the basic principle that by around 1989, the matter became "settled" case law (Blumann 1996, 55–56, 63–66; Case 131/87, *Commission v. Council* [1989] ECR 3743; Case

---

[5] Article 37 (ex article 43) allows for the adoption of Regulations, which are directly applicable in national law, while article 94 (ex article 100) only allows for Directives. Requiring national implementation, Directives afford member states greater post-decisional autonomy, and member states thus prefer them. The Commission has the opposite preference (interview with Commission DG VI official, Brussels, 6 April 1999). While procedural political in inspiration, this is a separate question from that of the legislative procedure, though it might make for an interesting extension of the procedural political logic developed in this book.

[6] Case 68/86, *United Kingdom v. Council* (Hormones) [1988] ECR 855; Case 131/86, *United Kingdom v. Council* (Battery Hens) [1988] ECR 905.

[7] "Efforts to achieve objectives of the common agricultural policy...cannot disregard requirements relating to the public interest such as the protection of consumers or the protection of the health and life of humans and animals, requirements which the Community institutions must take into account in exercising their powers" (Case 68/86, para. 12).

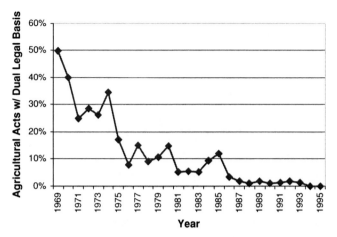

Figure 23 Dual Legal Basis in Agricultural Legislation, 1969–1995. Calculates the ratio of acts based on both articles 43 and 100 to acts adopted on the basis of inter alia article 43. *Source*: Celex, author's calculations.

C-11/88, *Commission v. Council* [1989] ECR 3799; Case C-331/88, *Fedesa* [1990] ECR I-4203.).[8]

Beyond all the "legalese," a clear bottom line appears: by about early 1989, the ECJ had effectively wrung the jurisdictional ambiguity from the area of agricultural policy, at least insofar as the interpretation of available structures was concerned. Any measure dealing in any way with an Annex II product and pursuing broadly defined CAP objectives was to be based on article 43. Figure 23 reports the fraction of agricultural acts (those based inter alia on article 37 [ex article 43] of the treaty) jointly based on treaty articles dealing with the common/internal market (articles 94 or 95 [ex articles 100 or 100A]) and confirms the reduction of structural ambiguity in this sector. This might be the end of the story, as article 37 (ex article 43) has not yet been the object of a procedural modification during treaty revisions. However, the combination of procedural diversity in related areas (adduced

---

[8] The issue has come up again more recently, and the Court has reasserted and even amplified this jurisprudence. See, for example, Case C-180/96R, *United Kingdom v. Commission* [1996] ECR I-3903, para. 63, in which the Court asserts "the paramount importance to be accorded to the protection of health" in agricultural measures based on article 43. It reaffirmed this in its full judgment, Case C-180/96, *United Kingdom v. Commission* [1998] ECR I-2265, para. 120.

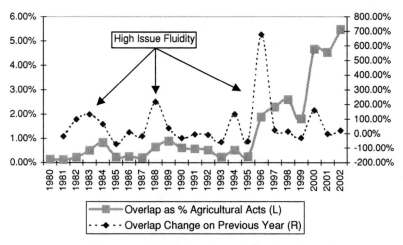

Figure 24 Agriculture and Human Health: Issue Overlap, 1980–2002. *Source*: Constructed from Celex database, last consulted 7 July 2003. Denominator = all measures under Celex classification heading 03 (agriculture); Numerator = text or title keyword "human health." A validity check using Nexis-Lexis coverage between 1985 and 1998 (normalized per Woolley 2000) generates similar results.

above) and exogenously changing issues led to a return of ambiguity during the 1990s.

Turning to the issues side of the equation, agriculture has become increasingly penetrated by a broad range of what might be termed "postmaterial" issues. This chapter focuses on the intersection of agriculture and human health. Figure 24 illustrates the changing overlap between these two issues over two decades. Two observations are pertinent here. First, agriculture exhibits relatively and absolutely low jurisdictional ambiguity, tending to hover below one percent overlap for most of the period examined. Second, though, as illustrated by the dotted line, the issue overlap in the agricultural sector is more volatile than in other sectors such as environmental policy (coefficient of variation = 1.22). The spikes in issue overlap, in particular, represent periods of relatively high issue fluidity. This produces jurisdictional ambiguity, suggesting that those periods, all other things (and especially the menu of alternatives) being equal, should be more susceptible to procedural politics.

Table 17 combines the nature and availability of institutional alternatives to generate over-time predictions about the probability of procedural political disputes in this area. It identifies the available sectors as well as

Table 17. *Alternatives and Issues in Agricultural Policy*

Period	Available Sector(s)	Article[a]	Procedure	Overlap	Predicted Probability of Dispute
1980–81	Common Market	100	CNSU	Low	Low
	Agriculture	43	CNSU[b]		
1982–85	Common Market	100	CNSU	High	High
	Agriculture	43	CNSQ		
1986–87	Common Market	100	CNSU	Low	Low
	Agriculture	43	CNSQ		
1988–93	Agriculture	43	CNSQ	High	Low
1994–95	Agriculture	43	CNSQ	Low	Low
	Human health	129	CODQ		
1996–97	Agriculture	43	CNSQ	High	High
	Human health	129	CODQ		

[a] Given in pre-Amsterdam article numberings, since all examined periods predate the 1999 entry into force of the Amsterdam Treaty.
[b] By virtue of the Luxembourg Compromise.

their corresponding legal bases and legislative procedures, defines overlap as the percentage of all acts invoking both sectors, and roughly estimates the probability of a dispute as the interaction of these factors. The various combinations permit nuanced causal claims about the factors behind the (in)frequency of procedural politics. At times, structural alternatives are lacking. At other times, issues overlap little. In theory, it is only as these two conditions come together that procedural politics becomes likely.

The earliest period (1980–1981) doubly militates against procedural politics insofar as no real alternatives exist and issues overlap very little. The second period (1982–1985) meets both conditions for procedural politics. The move to majority voting procedurally differentiated common market rules (including human health) from agricultural rules, and issue overlap nearly quadrupled before dropping back to earlier levels. The third period (1986–1987) meets the institutional diversity criterion for procedural political disputes but exhibits little jurisdictional ambiguity. Incentives for procedural politics existed, but opportunity did not. The fourth period (1988–1993) holds considerable interest because while issue overlap was considerable, no structural alternatives appeared (by virtue of the Court's decisive judgments in favor of the agricultural legal basis). Following entry into force of the Maastricht treaty, alternatives became available, but issues overlapped little during the fifth period. Finally, the 1996–1997 period again meets both necessary conditions for procedural political disputes.

Theory, Methods, and Case Selection

Hypotheses

Chapter 2 generated several testable propositions about procedural political conditions, processes, and outcomes. Here I operationalize these expectations in the agricultural sector, specifying substantive expectations of the theory of procedural politics and alternatives to it.

According to the ambiguity hypothesis, increases in jurisdictional ambiguity raise the probability of procedural politics, ceteris paribus. The data in Chapter 4 work best in assessing this hypothesis across issues and at the level of individual laws. Here I will focus on the implications of this hypothesis for variation over time in a single sector. Operational predictions flow directly from the last column of Table 17. Two comparisons will bear the greatest interest in assessing the determinants of disputes. The first involves the mid-1980s and the period around 1990; issues were fluid in both these periods, but institutional alternatives existed during only one of them. I expect procedural politics to have occurred more frequently in the period when both conditions held (i.e., the mid-1980s) than in the period when one condition was not present (ca. 1990). The second involves the 1994–1995 and 1996–1997 periods; both of these offer institutional alternatives, but only the latter is characterized by overlapping issues. With identical procedural alternatives, I expect disputes in the later period but not the earlier one as a direct result of differences in issue overlap.

According to the influence maximization hypothesis, as the influence differences among available institutional alternatives increase, so too does the likelihood of procedural political dispute. In the agricultural sector, then, I predict relatively few serious disputes prior to the early-1980s growth in majority voting, at which time the formal procedural differences between articles 43 (QMV consultation) and 100 (unanimous consultation) became material. Different actors should respond to this set of alternatives differently, however. Most clearly, the Commission will have a strong interest in article 43 as against article 100, while the EP has an almost negligible interest. As illustrated in a stylized way in Chapter 3, the EP is almost indifferent as between these two procedures. It should slightly, but only very slightly, prefer QMV consultation, and only by virtue of the "indirect influence" assumption. After early 1989, no alternatives exist and so disputes should effectively dry up. After 1993, the emergence of an alternative to the agricultural legal basis – with the addition of human health articles by the Maastricht Treaty – should create a new series of disputes in which the EP especially has a strong interest in treaty articles other than article 43 (post-Amsterdam article 37), since many of them use the pro-EP codecision procedure.

As earlier, in considering the agricultural sector I treat the procedural preference rankings in Chapter 3 as testable propositions and assess whether actors in fact express rules preferences consistent with the models. Behavior consistent with expectations will both validate the models and confirm the procedural political view of legal basis choice, all while disconfirming a legalistic view. Behavior inconsistent with procedural politics would suggest flaws in the models, the theory that they operationalize, or both.

The framing hypothesis, drawn from the theory of procedural politics, suggests that actors will strategically frame issues so as to "fit" them within procedurally favorable jurisdictions (legal bases). Given the procedural preferences adduced in Chapter 3, considering only the agricultural and human health alternatives, and given the procedural history of EU agricultural policy outlined above, the framing hypothesis suggests the following evolution of issue frames for each actor over time. From the early 1980s, the Commission should deploy an agricultural issue frame and the Council should frame measures as primarily involving human health.[9] After approximately 1988 and until 1993, the theory of procedural politics offers no specific predictions. One of the necessary conditions for procedural politics, the availability of alternatives, is simply lacking during this period. Following the entry into force of the Maastricht Treaty, I expect the Parliament to frame jurisdictionally ambiguous measures as involving human health or consumer protection (thereby invoking use of the codecision procedure), whereas I expect the Council and the Commission to maintain an agricultural issue definition (using QMV consultation).

---

[9] This may be considerably tempered early in the period, as the ECJ did not set forth its legal basis test inciting strategic issue framing until early 1987 and did not reaffirm the test until early 1988.

An alternative view suggests that actors will frame policies in ways consistent with their sincere substantive preferences, regardless of the treaty regime in force. Unlike the environmental sector, the agricultural literature offers no clear a priori assessments of sincere preferences. I will thus rely on several tools to assess this hypothesis. Substantive positions that cut against procedural preferences work to confirm this alternative view and disconfirm procedural political expectations. Substantive consistency over time in the face of variations in procedural political incentives and opportunities will cut in the same direction. Consistency across contexts, finally, may also help to assess substantive sincerity as against procedural political sophistication.

With respect to the timing of substantive changes and rules disputes, I will follow the same protocol as in Chapter 5. That is, I will simply scrutinize the sequence of substantive modifications and expressions of rules preferences. Substantive modifications that both follow expressions of rules preferences and cut in a procedurally favorable direction will tend to confirm procedural political expectations as against the legalistic perspective. Substantive modifications that tend to move the center of gravity of legislation away from politically favorable procedures will disconfirm the framing hypothesis and implicate the influence maximization hypothesis as well.

Turning now to procedural coalition formation, an operational version of the procedural coalition hypothesis flows directly from the combination of procedural preferences and the development of the agricultural sector. Here, the prevailing wisdom predicts supranational-intergovernmental coalitions throughout the period in question. The procedural approach predicts the same pattern from the early- to mid-1980s through the Court's judgments of 1988. That is, it expects the Commission and Parliament to join forces against the Council. Two caveats bear mentioning, however. First, the Parliament's interest in procedural matters should be slight during this period, inasmuch as neither of the available alternatives affords it much influence. Second, to the extent that the predicted pattern does appear, I will search for evidence of ideological support for supranationalism (which would support the approach that rivals my own) as well as for evidence of procedural coalition formation, thus reducing the problem of observational equivalence among rival approaches. That is, I will move beyond observed correlations and will seek to identify the motivations underlying (that is, the causes of) observed coalitional behavior, at which level rival approaches do make divergent predictions. For the SEA period, similarly, I expect no distinctly procedural coalition formation, but consistent with the underpinnings of my approach I will suggest that substantive

Table 18. *Predicted Procedural Coalitions in EU Agricultural Policy*

Hypothesis	Pre-Single Act –1987	Single Act 1987–1993	Maastricht 1993–1999
Procedural politics	Commission and Parliament v. Council	Substantive coalitions	Parliament v. Commission and Council
Prevailing wisdom	Commission and Parliament v. Council	Commission and Parliament v. Council	Commission and Parliament v. Council

preferences, rather than ideologies with respect to integration, will drive coalition formation.

The post-1993 period, by contrast, discriminates between the two approaches. I predict that the Parliament will face off against both the Commission and the Council. The alternative approach continues to predict a supranational-intergovernmental split. Observed coalitional patterns constitute the primary evidence. However, here again I will seek to uncover the causes of observed behavior, considering evidence both for and against procedural politics and rival approaches. I summarize these expectations in Table 18.

Research Design and Case Selection

To assess procedural political expectations about issue framing, coalition formation, and legislative outcomes in the agricultural sector, I first illustrate some general patterns in procedural political disputes in this sector. I then again turn to the process-tracing method, to assess not only the conformity of observations with predictions but also the underlying causes driving those observations. Accordingly, I examine two cases to verify the causal nature of the empirical relationship and to assess procedural political dynamics and outcomes in the agricultural sector. The first involves the 1985 Hormones Directive, which was proposed and adopted during the first period identified in Table 17. The second case involves EU legislative activity following the "mad cow" crisis in the mid–1990s, which resulted in a Regulation on beef identification and labeling. Individually, each case presents a unique profile involving different combinations of institutional alternatives (incentives) and jurisdictional ambiguity (opportunities). As a pair, the cases examine in depth the two periods predicted in Table 17 to experience procedural political conflict. However, the narrative also touches on both earlier

Agriculture, Human Health, and Procedural Politics

General Trends in the Agricultural Sector

To begin, let's place the cases in the broader context of legal basis litigation in the agricultural sector. Recall the predictions from Table 17, whereby two periods should be most susceptible to procedural political disputes. How well do these predictions stand up to the evidence? Figure 25 confirms that indeed the availability of procedurally divergent institutional alternatives generates predictable patterns of disputes. The series of cases involving legislation adopted between 1985 and 1987 dried up following the Court's judgments in the Battery Hens and Hormones cases. Indeed, the last case in that series, Case C-11/88, was lodged at the Court on 13 January 1988, barely five weeks prior to those judgments. After these judgments, no case involving article 43 arose until 1997, despite high levels of issue overlap at points during this period. This pattern is consistent with my expectation that jurisdictional ambiguity and divergent alternatives combine to govern procedural politics. More fundamentally, it supports the strategic perspective taken up in the game model in Chapter 3, wherein actors' expectations about Court judgments influence the extent to which they will engage in everyday politics with respect to rules.

Having thus located the cases in their broader context, I turn now to examine in depth two procedural political disputes in this area.

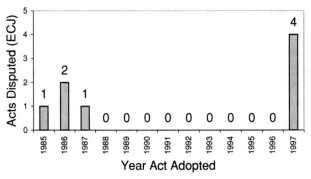

Figure 25 Agricultural Legal Basis Cases at the ECJ

Beef Hormones

Legislative History. The modernization and intensification of agricultural production has greatly expanded the use of advanced techniques, including the application of sophisticated pesticides, fertilizers, and genetic engineering in plant production and the use of growth-promoting hormones in livestock production. Until the early 1980s, hormone use in livestock production remained unregulated at the EU level. A 1980 scandal involving hormone-laced baby food, however, incited EU action.[10] An original 1981 Directive had been the object of a classic agricultural legal basis – but *not* procedural political – dispute, with the Commission proposing a Regulation based on article 43 and the Council adopting a Directive based on articles 43 and 100.[11] Substantively, the 1981 Directive enacted minimal controls on hormone use, banning only a single class of hormones, stilbenes, that had been implicated in the baby food scandal. Procedurally, it established that future decisions to ban additional substances would be taken by a unanimous Council vote on a proposal from

---

[10] Ronald Koven, "Common Market Bans Hormones in Cattle Feed," *Washington Post*, 3 October 1980, p. A25; "Campaign for Real Veal," *Economist*, 18 October 1980, 51; "A Short History of Hormones," *Economist*, 7 January 1989, 22; Written Question 1599/80 by Mr. Vernimmen to the Commission, OJ C 60, 19 March 1981, 23; "Ban Them All?" *Economist*, 31 January 1981, 45; "Locked Horns," *Economist*, 25 February 1984, 84; House of Commons, Select Committee on European Legislation, 2nd Report, Session 1980/81, HC 32–ii, 5; Answer to Written Question 1907/80 by Mr. Ansquer to the Commission, OJ C 87, 16 April 1981, 21.

[11] Proposal for a Council Regulation (EEC) concerning the control and examination of animals and meat in the Community for the presence of residues of substances with estrogenic, androgenic, gestagenic, and thyrostatic effect, COM(80) 920 final, 6 January 1981; Proposal for a Council Regulation (EEC) laying down conditions for controlling the possession, distribution, and administration to animals of certain substances with a hormonal action, COM(80) 922 final, 6 January 1981. A concise summary of the proposals is available in House of Commons, Select Committee on European Legislation, 6th Report, Session 1980/81, HC 32–vi, point 2. See also Answer to Written Question no. 1599/80 by Mr. Vernimmen to the Commission, OJ C 60, 19 March 1981, 23; Answer to Written Question no. 1834/80 by Mrs. Hoff to the Commission, OJ C 78, 6 April 1981, 29; Council Doc. 11517/80 AGRILEG 250, 25 November 1980; Council Doc.11794/80 AGRILEG 259, 28 November 1980, Council Doc.11890/80 AGRILEG 261, 2 December 1980; Council Doc. 11890/1/80 AGRILEG 261, 4 December 1980; Council Doc. 12024/80 AGRILEG 266, 5 December 1980; Council Doc. 12103/80 PV/CONS 57 AGRI 160, 13 January 1981; Council Doc. 4628/81 AGRILEG 21, 11 February 1981; Council Doc. 8210/81 AGRILEG 135 PHARM 10, 14 July 1981; Council Directive 81/602/EEC of 31 July 1981 concerning the prohibition of certain substances having a hormonal action and of any substances having a thyrostatic action, OJ L 222, 7 August 1981, 32–33.

the Commission, without consultation of the EP (that is, using the AVFU procedure).[12]

As called for by the 1981 Directive, the Commission had convened a scientific committee (the "Lamming Committee") to study the possible health effects of five hormonal substances that remained authorized for use. Three of these (oestradiol 17β, progesterone, and testosterone) occurred naturally, while two (trenbolone and zeranol) were synthetic. In early 1984 the committee found the three naturally occurring hormones to be safe, but it could not reach definitive conclusions about the synthetic hormones. Relying on these findings, the Commission in July 1984 tabled a new legislative proposal that would have authorized the continued use of these three natural substances.[13] Citing continuing scientific uncertainty, by contrast, it called for a preliminary ban on the synthetic hormones (zeranol and trenbolone) until their safety could be definitively established, at which point they could be authorized by a qualified majority vote.

Council negotiations on the proposal took place throughout 1984 and into 1985. In mid-1985, the Council adopted partial measures aimed at control procedures but could not reach agreement on the question of authorized substances.[14] Not surprisingly, it changed the legal basis of the Commission proposal from article 43 to articles 43 and 100 and article 7 of the 1981 Directive, which combined to require unanimous decision after consultation of the EP (CNSU procedure).

The Council, according to internal documents, was "deadlocked" on the "five substances" issue, with "no solution in view."[15] By all accounts, the European Parliament decisively affected the legislative process with its contribution to the political and scientific debate over hormones in meat production. The Parliament Secretariat assigned the dossier to the Committee on the Environment, Public Health, and Consumer Protection rather than the more obvious Agriculture Committee. The Environment Committee's

---

[12] This was a key component of intra-Council compromise on the proposal. See Council Doc. 8528/81 PV/CONS 35 AGRI 68, 4 August 1981, 9; Answer to Written Question 1249/81 by Mr. Diana to the Council, OJ C 43, 17 February 1982, 15; Answer to Written Question 1248/81 by Mr. Diana to the Commission, OJ C 24, 1 February 1982, 22–23.

[13] COM(84) 295 final, 12 June 1984, 3.

[14] See Council Directive 85/358/EEC of 16 July 1985 supplementing Directive 81/602/EEC concerning the prohibition of certain substances having a hormonal action and of substances having a thyrostatic action, OJ L 191, 23 July 1985, 46–49.

[15] For various characterizations of the deadlock, see Council Doc. 6494/85 AGRILEG 93, 14 May 1985, 5; Council Doc. 6834/85 CRS/CRP 19, 3 June 1987, 12; Council Doc. 7246/85 AGRILEG 104, 7 June 1985, 3.

September 1985 report placed great emphasis on consumer protection and sought to ban the two synthetic substances totally and to limit use of the three natural substances to strictly regulated therapeutic treatment.[16] After a lively debate, an overwhelming margin (117–10) in the EP adopted a Resolution calling for a total ban on the use of hormones in livestock production.[17] It made no mention of the legal basis, implying full support for the proposed article 43 (QMV consultation procedure) as against the likely alternative, article 100 (unanimous consultation).

The vote, along with the strong pro-ban position of the German government (faced with an ascendant Green party), put tremendous pressure on the European Commission. In mid-November, the Commission tabled an amended proposal that was short, sweet, and almost totally responsive to the EP's (and Germany's) demands. It took up the main EP amendment, whereby only therapeutic uses of the natural substances would be authorized, effectively asking for a total ban on hormone use in the EU.[18] The UK, where farming practices differed considerably from those on the Continent, reacted strongly against the amended proposal, citing its disproportionate impact on British farmers and its unscientific basis.[19] At Council meetings from October through mid-December 1985 the UK succeeded in delaying a decision, but ultimately found itself "in a minority of one in supporting the continued use of hormones."[20]

---

[16] EP Doc. A2-100/85, 30 September 1985, 17–18.
[17] *EP Debates* no. 2-330, 10 October 1985; OJ C 288, 11 November 1985, 153–160.
[18] COM(85) 607 final, 19 November 1985.
[19] As one MP put it, "Europe has less to lose than Britain on the banning of hormone promoters" (*Hansard*, vol. 88, session 1985/86, 9 December 1985, column 728). In the British Isles and Northern France, beef production traditionally relied on steers (castrated bulls) feeding on grass in open pastures. To match the meat production attained by using bulls, these steers needed to be "topped up" with growth-promoting hormones. Elsewhere on the Continent, by contrast, beef production relied on grain-fed, carreled bulls. What is more, controls on hormone use in the UK were extremely strict and tightly enforced, quite unlike many other parts of Europe. See also Mrs. Fenner, *Hansard*, vol. 88, session 1985/86, 9 December 1985, columns 720–722; Andrew Gowers and Ivo Dawnay, "Another Shot of Politics for the Beef Farmer," *Financial Times*, 24 January 1986, 15; David Swinbanks, "Politics Before Scientific Advice," *Nature*, 28 August 1986, 762; Christina Mackenzie, "European Community Beefs About Use of US Meat Hormones," *Christian Science Monitor*, 24 March 1988, 14; *Hansard*, 12 December 1988, column 747; *EP Debates* no. 3-361 (1988), 230.
[20] Council Doc. 9699/85 AGRILEG 174, 17 October 1985, 3–4; Council Doc. 11128/85 (Presse 191), 10 December 1985, 11; Anthony Phelps, "U.K. Vetoes EEC Proposal to Ban Use of Growth Hormones," *Feedstuffs*, 25 November 1985, 1; Ivo Dawnay, "UK Challenges Ewe Levy Plan," *Financial Times*, 20 November 1985; On the December meeting see the

When it became clear that the UK was isolated on the hormone ban issue, procedural politics became the central issue. Recall the Council's twenty-year practice of basing all veterinary, phytosanitary, and human health legislation on both articles 100 and 43 to ensure the use of a certain form of legislative instrument. With the growth of majority voting, this decision would now have procedural, and thus substantive, consequences. Now, the addition of article 100 would give the UK a veto, which it had repeatedly and very credibly threatened to use, even though an alternative procedure existed that could virtually guarantee to the other member states the outcome they wanted. These states thus agreed to continue discussing the proposal on the basis of article 43 alone.

The legal adviser to the House of Commons' Select Committee on European Legislation found the use of this article to be legally suspect and procedural-politically motivated. The adviser observed, rather laconically, that

> the material available could leave the Committee uncertain as to the true purpose of the present proposal ... it is not easy, immediately, to see which of the objectives of the CAP is served by the proposal. Indeed, anyone looking at the proposal *in vacuo* might see its aim as the protection of general public (and possibly animal) health, which comes closer to article 235 [the EU's "implied powers clause"] than to article 43 [agriculture].... [The] circumstances suggest that convenience may be influencing Community institutions to an unusual extent.[21]

By this analysis, the "center of gravity" test did not support the legal basis chosen. Instead, the legal basis reflected procedural political considerations. When asked about the legal basis issue in the House of Commons, a British official replied that "a [qualified majority] vote on this issue would be illegal in the Government's view, and it would then be open to the Government to challenge the legality of such a vote in the European Court of Justice."[22]

Despite this opposition, on 18 December 1985 the Commission tabled a new and very restrictive amended proposal, still based on article 43, that would ban all use of hormones for fattening purposes and authorize only the

---

comments by British Agriculture Minister Michael Jopling in *Hansard*, vol. 88, Session 1985/86, 11 December 1985, cols. 922–928; Ivo Dawnay, "EEC Makes Progress on Special Levy for Sugar," *Financial Times*, 11 December 1985, 30; John Cherrington, "Hormone Fears Will Not Go Away," *Financial Times*, 26 November 1985, 34.

[21] House of Commons, Select Committee on European Legislation, 2nd Report 1985/86, HC 21-ii, 20 November 1985, 7.

[22] Mrs. Fenner, *Hansard*, 9 December 1985, column 734.

natural substances for strictly supervised therapeutic uses.[23] The preamble repeatedly highlighted the trade distortions caused by differing national regulations but carefully emphasized that these distortions were occurring with respect to products that were subject to "common market organizations" (CMOs). This language attempts clearly to tie the legislation to the Common Agricultural Policy (CAP), in which the term "common market organizations" is exclusively used. This consecrated to text an agricultural issue frame that the Commission had been advancing for at least two months, with repeated emphasis in Council meetings on the "unity of the [agricultural] market."[24]

Things came to a head at an infamous Council session on 19 December 1985. According to one report appearing almost two years after the fact, "mere mention of the events of [that night] still provokes strong reactions from Brussels negotiators.... It was certainly a bad-tempered and at times theatrical occasion with two agriculture ministers at one stage reported to be literally at each other's throats."[25] An official present at the meeting gives this account:

It was 3 a.m. and the agricultural ministers were meeting alone in restricted session. A qualified majority existed against Germany on an amended proposal put forth by the Commission according to which the three natural substances would be exempted. The British minister had already gotten satisfaction on the substance, but told the Commission that he wanted it to change the legal basis to articles 43 and 100. The Commissioner stood up, extremely angry, and said that if that was going to be the UK attitude he withdrew the amended proposal and called for a vote on the original proposal. He did this in an emotional moment after an extremely long day. So, we did the *tour de table* and the UK lost, with the result that there was a total ban. The UK had gotten what it wanted before on the substance, but it wanted a total victory, including the legal basis.[26]

On this account, both the UK and the Commission appeared to be playing an institutional game, ready to risk short-term substantive gains for more beneficial future streams of policy.

Following this turn of events, then, a majority of member states imposed a total hormone ban on the UK and throughout the territory of the EU. The UK's objections to the legal basis "won the support of Denmark,

---

[23] COM(85) 832 final, 18 December 1985.
[24] See, for example, Council Doc. 9563/85 AGRILEG 167, 15 October 1985, 4; Council Doc. 9699/85 AGRILEG 174, 17 October 1985, 4.
[25] Tim Dickson, "Court Puts Hormone Ban to Test," *Financial Times*, 14 October 1987, 4.
[26] Interview with Council agricultural official, Brussels, 18 March 1999.

which backs the outlawing of hormones but supports the right of member states to prevent new veterinary regulations being pushed through by majority votes."[27] The majority thus agreed to the ban by an eight-to-two vote on the basis of article 43. Interestingly, several states attempted immediately to limit the scope of their action to the case at hand, insisting that it did not constitute a precedent for future activity in this sector. Germany insisted that in the future such decisions should be based on articles 43 and 100 (and eventually article 100A).[28] The Italian delegation also stated that the decision at hand was a unique one and set no precedent for future legislation in the sector, noting that it "cooperated in the adoption of this Directive... because adoption of a decision was a matter of urgency."[29]

A final point, seemingly a detail, rounds out the story. A last-minute technical hitch – the fact that the text was not available in all the Community languages – prevented definitive adoption of the Directive at the 19 December meeting. Article 6 of the Council's Rules of Procedure allows it to adopt measures by so-called written procedure (consent given, at that time, via telex), but only if members unanimously agreed to do so.[30] Despite British and Danish objections, and in flagrant disregard of its own rules of procedure, a majority of states decided to use the written procedure by 31 December 1985 at the latest, to permit finalization of all the language versions. Thus, the Council definitively adopted the Directive by written procedure on 31 December 1985.[31]

Beef Hormones Before the Court. Although British MPs had urged it to do so, the UK chose not to invoke the Luxembourg Compromise to block adoption of the Hormones Directive. In the Government's estimation, it "would have been inappropriate in this instance to use the Luxembourg Compromise, which has always been reserved for extremely important

---

[27] Ivo Dawnay, "EEC Bans Hormone Use in Livestock Fattening," *Financial Times*, 21 December 1985, 2; Council documents as early as 1981 show Denmark pushing for a total ban on the use of hormones in livestock farming (Council Doc. 5690/81 AGRILEG 52, 25 March 1981, 2).

[28] Council Doc. 4340/85 RPE 1, 17 January 1986, 9.

[29] Council Doc. 4066/86 AGRILEG 2, 13 January 1986, 4.

[30] Rules of procedure adopted by the Council on 24 July 1979 on the basis of Article 5 of the Treaty of 8 April 1965 establishing a single Council and a single Commission of the European Communities, OJ L 268, 25 October 1979, 1–3.

[31] Council Directive of 31 December 1985 prohibiting the use in livestock farming of certain substances having a hormonal action, OJ L 382, 31 December 1985, 228–231.

matters at stake."³² Instead of wielding the veto, it took the matter to the European Court of Justice (ECJ). This choice, I suggest, richly symbolizes the transformation of EU rule governance, the increasing penetration of politics by the law. I return to this idea below and in the conclusion.

In its complaint, the UK argued that the Directive pursued consumer and human health protection and thus should have been based on article 100. This contradicted earlier British claims, made before procedural politics was a real issue, to the effect that human health was not an issue in the adoption of EU hormone legislation, or at the very least that the science was uncertain.³³ The UK also rather disingenuously asserted a violation of the prerogatives of the European Parliament, which had not been reconsulted once the Council decided to adopt a total ban.³⁴

More generally, two concerns motivated the UK. First, it had just reluctantly agreed at the December 1985 Luxembourg Summit (in what would become the SEA) to revise the treaty in order to extend majority voting. The British Government insisted, however, that the national veto remain intact. Indeed, Margaret Thatcher's first substantive point in presenting the new treaty to the House of Commons was that the UK retained "the right to take national action where required to protect public, animal, and plant health."³⁵ The adoption of the Hormones Directive by QMV against British wishes "must therefore have come as something of an unpleasant surprise to the United Kingdom" (Bradley 1988, 392), and Britain used the Hormones Directive as a test case on the extent and limits of majority voting.

Second, the UK enjoyed a long tradition of vigilance with respect to plant and animal health matters. It thus had keen interest in retaining article 100 for such matters because, after the entry into force of the SEA, the article 100A(4) derogation would apply, whereby it could retain its relatively strict national practices. In sum, "the UK is particularly sensitive about plant and animal health matters and is anxious to have the protection of a special safeguard clause" under article 100A. "The fear is that the hormone proposal ... could be used as a precedent by the Commission to

---

[32] Minister of State, Foreign and Commonwealth Office Mrs. Lynda Chalker, *Hansard*, 15 February 1989, column 443.
[33] On the first point, see Council Doc. 6253/81 AGRILEG 70, 14 April 1981, 4. The UK consistently claimed in 1984–1985 that scientific uncertainty about the human health effects (if any) of hormones made EU action premature.
[34] OJ C 152, 18 June 1986, 3–4.
[35] *Hansard*, vol. 88, 5 December 1985, column 429.

undermine the freedom of the UK to keep out serious plant and health diseases."[36] For Britain, "the issue of sovereignty over plant and animal health matters is at stake."[37]

Rounding out the cast of players, Denmark, which had also voted against the Directive, intervened on the side of the UK. It did so for purely procedural political reasons. It had already enacted a national ban on all five of the hormones in question, and on the substantive merits Denmark was extremely favorable to the EU-wide ban. But it intervened purely in defense of Council unanimity and national autonomy, even at the short-run risk of abolishing a law the substantive merits of which it wholly supported.[38] Of necessity, because it had promulgated the law being challenged, the Council was the defendant in the case. The Commission, which had a substantial interest in establishing a pro-QMV precedent in this sector – especially with the unexpected help of the Council – joined the Council's defense. The Parliament decided that it was "neither legally nor politically opportune to intervene" in support of the UK, despite the apparent breach of EP prerogatives through the Council's failure to reconsult it on the substantially amended proposal.[39]

The Court's Advocate General rejected nearly every point of the UK appeal that he addressed. In its judgment of 23 February 1988, the Court struck down the Hormone Directive on a technicality – the Council's violation of its own rules of procedure through the use of the written procedure against British objections. However, and much more important, it upheld the crucial procedural political maneuvers that had permitted adoption of the Directive in the first place (Case 68/86, *United Kingdom v. Council* [1988] ECR 855). The operative part of the judgment established that

Article 43 of the treaty is the appropriate legal basis for any legislation concerning the production and marketing of agricultural products listed in Annex II to the treaty which contributes to the achievement of one or more of the

---

[36] Tim Dickson, "Court Puts Hormone Ban to Test," *Financial Times*, 14 October 1987, 4; "EEC Court Advocate General Upholds EEC Hormones Ban," *European Report* no. 1349, 17 October 1987, iv/7; see also Bradley 1988, 392.

[37] Tim Dickson, "Euro Court Overturns EC Ban on Hormones in Meat," *Financial Times*, 24 February 1988, 42.

[38] Debora MacKenzie, "Court Ends Ban on Farm Hormones," *New Scientist*, 3 March 1988, 33.

[39] Note from EP legal adviser Johann Schoo to Mrs. Vayssade, president of the Legal Affairs Committee, EP LAC dossier 136/86, 4 July 1986; Note from Legal Affairs Committee staff member Kieran St. C. Bradley to Mrs. Vayssade, president of the Legal Affairs Committee, EP LAC dossier 136/86, 11 September 1986.

objectives of the common agricultural policy set out in article 39 of the treaty. There is no need to have recourse to article 100 of the treaty where such legislation involves the harmonization of provisions of national law in the field. (para. 14)

The judgment had a number of notable features (Barents 1988, 1989; Blumann 1988; Bridge 1988). First, it exhibited uncharacteristic precision and clarity and, as I have contended, effectively eliminated jurisdictional ambiguity in this area until the arrival of the Maastricht Treaty. Having declined to apply the center of gravity approach, the Court took a direct and objective route to article 43: legislation dealing in any way with any product in Annex II of the treaty and pursuing the objectives of the CAP laid out in article 39 was to be based on this article (Barents 1994, 65–66). It read those objectives broadly to include human and animal health and consumer protection. Within a matter of hours it confirmed this approach (Case 131/86, *United Kingdom v. Council* (Battery Hens) [1988] ECR 905, para. 19), and it reinforced the precedent in subsequent cases (Case 131/87, *Commission v. Council* [1989] ECR 3743, para. 10; Case C-11/88, *Commission v. Council* [1989] ECR 3799, para. 9).

Second, the judgment clarified and reinforced the status of agriculture as a lex specialis, to be applied as against more general provisions.[40] This was true not only with respect to article 100, but also, and perhaps more importantly, with respect to the new article 100A created by the Single European Act, both of which aimed more broadly at harmonization of national provisions to advance the EU market (Barents 1989, 14; Blumann 1988, 511). This had two important procedural consequences. First, it precluded national invocation of the "safeguard clause" of article 100A(4). Harmonization would be total, with no escape for stricter national measures in such areas as pesticide use. Second, the cooperation procedure, which also used QMV but which amplified EP influence, would not be used in this sector (Barents 1989, 398–399). As a consequence, and "ironically, [the Hormones and Battery Hens judgments] will stand as authorities restricting the influence of, not individual member states, but the Parliament" (Bell 1989, 689). Indeed, it was precisely this result that drove the EP again to challenge the use of article 43 (in the Beef Labeling case, discussed below) almost ten years after the Hormones case was decided.

---

[40] This interpretive canon establishes that more specific laws are to be preferred to more general laws.

Postscript. Within two weeks of the judgment, the Commission retabled its legislative proposal, with no modification to the text and with article 43 as the legal basis. It had wanted to make passage a mere formality, but the UK insisted that it be treated as a 'B' point on the Council's agenda, which is to say that debate would be allowed.[41] The UK took the opportunity again to express its strong resistance to the substance of the measure, but was outvoted again, albeit this time by an 11–1 margin (new EU members Spain and Portugal joining the majority).[42] Notably, while Denmark had been expected before the vote to side again with the UK, this time it joined the majority.[43] This switch is an important piece of evidence. Denmark unquestionably favored the proposed legislation but had allowed procedural political concerns to take precedence over short-run substantive interests first in voting against, and then in asking the Court to annul the measure. The fact that it voted in favor of an identical proposal when it lacked any opportunity to secure a unanimity procedure supports this interpretation.[44] Thus, the Council adopted a new Directive on 7 March 1988.[45]

Summary. In conclusion, the Hormones case set the stage for what followed: relative procedural political quiet in the agricultural sector for the better part of a decade. One interviewee places the case in its context as follows:

Many times the Council will adopt a particular legal basis to get the result that it wants. An example of this which went to the ECJ is the Hormones Directive. Here, the Council threw out twenty-five years of practice [of using articles 100 and 43 together] and opted only for 43 in order to get around the UK veto. Going to the ECJ, however, precluded using the traditional recourse to 43 and 100, because the ECJ weeded out the ambiguity in the Treaty. This is why you can only exploit the ambiguities in the Treaty until such time as the ECJ pronounces on the issue. But

---

[41] Commission Doc. SI(88) 127, 5 March 1988, 2.
[42] Tim Dickson, "EC Farm Ministers Agree to Reinstate Hormone Ban," *Financial Times*, 8 March 1988, 34; Anthony Phelps, "Hormone Ban Upheld by EC Commission," *Feedstuffs*, 14 March 1988, 1.
[43] "EC May Reimpose Ban on US Meat Hormones," *Journal of Commerce*, 7 March 1988, 5A.
[44] The Court judgment operates as an experimental treatment allowing pretest-posttest comparison of Denmark's behavior, made all the more appropriate since the text remained unchanged. This greatly increases confidence in the argument that Denmark acted for *purely* procedural political reasons.
[45] Council Directive 88/146/EEC of 7 March 1988 prohibiting the use in livestock farming of certain substances having a hormonal action, OJ L 70, 16 March 1988, 16–18.

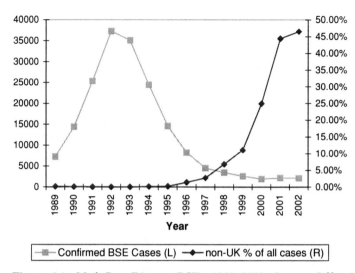

Figure 26 Mad Cow Disease (BSE), 1989–2002. *Sources*: Office International des Epizooties; non-UK data from *http://www.oie.int/eng/info/en_esbmonde.htm* (last consulted 11 July 2003); UK from *http://www.oie.int/eng/info/en_esbru.htm* (last consulted 11 July 2003).

this is pretty normal behavior – getting around a political problem in the Council by changing a legal basis.[46]

Beef Labeling

Legislative History

Background. Bovine spongiform encephalopathy (BSE, or "mad cow disease") is a degenerative brain disease found, not surprisingly, in cattle. It represents one of a class of diseases (transmissible spongiform encephalopathies, or TSEs) that can strike animals and, it is now known, humans. Upon its discovery in 1986, scientists theorized that it resulted from the use of cattle feed containing proteins derived from scrapie-infected sheep carcasses. It was first detected in the United Kingdom in 1986, and from 1988 the UK adopted a series of measures intended to control the spread of the disease and to prevent its transmission to humans (the possibility of which was a matter of scientific dispute). As documented in Figure 26, despite these measures the overall incidence of BSE hit astronomically high

---

[46] Interview with ECJ Legal Secretary, Brussels, 23 July 1997.

Procedural Politics

levels in animal herds before coming under control around 1992. While it began as an almost uniquely British problem, it has come to take on an increasingly European dimension as BSE has appeared on the continent. Thus, while the overall incidence of the problem is now greatly reduced, BSE remains an agricultural issue on the EU agenda.

At the same time, BSE has gradually assumed a "human health" dimension as well. Specifically, early fears (voiced in the late 1980s) about possible transmission of the disease to humans through the consumption of BSE-tainted beef were decisively confirmed on 20 March 1996, when a British scientific advisory panel confirmed a human health connection and the British Government banned the sale for human consumption of beef from animals more than thirty months old.[47] A variant of Creuzfeldt-Jakob Disease (vCJD) turned out to be directly attributable to such beef consumption. And while CJD and its variant remain extremely rare, the number of deaths from it in the UK began increasing steadily in the late 1980s. Figure 27 documents the rising number of deaths from CJD and vCJD in the UK and also illustrates variations in media concern with a human health connection to BSE. In that respect, the 1989–1990 and 1996–2000 periods stand out: during those time frames, a relatively high proportion of media reporting on BSE also had a "human health" element.

At Community level, the initial BSE outbreak generated a series of trade disputes between the UK and its partners, with the latter intermittently banning British products for fear that BSE would spread to their herds.[48] In the 1989–1990 period the Council adopted two major pieces of legislation intended to limit the spread of the disease.[49] In a piece of evidence that strongly confirms the predictions in Table 17, neither act formed the object of a procedural political dispute at the time of its adoption. Given the overlapping issues involved at the time, why did no dispute occur? The answer is given by the theory of procedural politics: no opportunity existed because the Court had decisively foreclosed on invoking human health provisions (at the time, article 100 of the treaty) with its mid-1980s jurisprudence. Despite apparent ambiguity in the issue space, no ambiguity about which

---

[47] Statement by Secretary of State Stephen Dorrell, *Hansard*, vol. 274, Session 1995/96, 20 March 1996, columns 375–396.

[48] For an accessible summary of the main issues involved see "A Mad, Mad Lesson," *Economist*, 9 June 1990, 54.

[49] Council Directive 89/662/EEC of 11 December 1989, OJ L 395 1989, 13ff; Council Directive 90/425/EEC of 26 June 1990, OJ L 224 1990, 29ff; both amended by Council Directive 92/118 of 17 December 1992, OJ L 62 1993, 49ff.

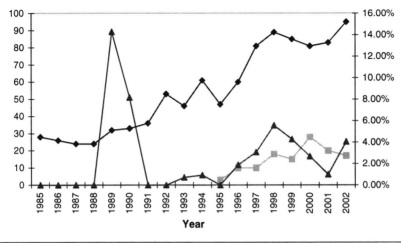

Figure 27 BSE/Human Health Connection in the UK, 1985–2002. *Sources*: CJD: UK Department of Health (URL *http://www.info.doh.gov.uk/doh/intpress.nsf/page/2003-0259?OpenDocument* [status at 7 July 2003, last consulted 11 July 2003]); BSE Report (1985–1989 figures only, *http://www.bseinquiry.gov.uk/report/volume16/chapte13.htm#13581* [last consulted 11 July 2003]); author's calculations. The media coverage time series counts articles from the *Times* and *Financial Times* in the Lexis-Nexis Academic Universe news database (World News category, European News Sources, last consulted 11 July 2003) with both "BSE" and "human health" in the full text, and calculates this total as a percentage of all articles mentioning BSE alone.

set of rules should apply actually existed. Indeed, it is interesting to note that only in 1996, after the Maastricht Treaty created new institutional options, did the UK mount an ex post challenge of the legal basis of those two earlier acts.[50] The specific timing and dynamics of that challenge, plus the dog that didn't bark during the 1989–1990 period, provide strong evidence that procedural politics depends on both issues and institutions.

Summarizing this prehistory, the issue space involved in BSE regulation was fundamentally ambiguous. The BSE crisis, it is true, retained an agricultural element. Consumer confidence, and hence beef sales, declined throughout the EU, and BSE-related expenditures rose to tens of billions

---

[50] The Court rejected these challenges (Case C-180/96, *United Kingdom v. Commission* [1998] ECR I-2265). Since these "disputes" occurred so long after the fact, I do not include them in quantifying legal basis challenges, even though they strongly confirm my arguments about cross-temporal variations in procedural political disputes.

of euros. However, BSE also centered on human health, for which the Maastricht Treaty had created some EU powers that differed procedurally from the agricultural chapters of the treaty. In these circumstances, then, the legislation would be jurisdictionally ambiguous, operating at the interstices of the Common Agricultural Policy, consumer protection, and human health. That ambiguity resulted not just from the changing issue space but also from the changing menu of procedural alternatives in the 1993 Maastricht Treaty. Given the crisis atmosphere of 1996, there was great demand for additional EU legislation. With substantive and institutional stakes high, the situation lent itself to procedural politics.

Beef Labeling and Identification. On 2 October 1996 the European Commission proposed two Regulations, among a broader package of measures, to respond to the BSE crisis. The first would establish an identification and registration system for bovine animals, the second a labeling system for beef and beef products.[51] In motivating its proposals, the Commission cited the decline in consumer confidence in beef following the BSE crisis and the need to restore such confidence in order to set the beef market right. The Commission based its proposals, not surprisingly, on the agricultural treaty provision, article 43, that used the favorable (to it) QMV consultation procedure. It made no effort to justify this choice over other available alternatives.

In initial Council discussions, the Commission reasserted that the purpose of the regulations was to restore consumer confidence and thus reestablish the EU's beef market.[52] National Delegations responded favorably to the principles behind the proposals and responded very positively to the urgency with which the Commission characterized them. However, important substantive disagreements arose. Most notably, most delegations sought a mandatory labeling scheme and resisted the optional nature of the Commission's proposals. The question of the legal basis did not arise, with one single and puzzling exception: the UK argued that transformed and nonalimentary products should be covered under article 100A of the treaty.[53] (This position appeared only once and was never pursued.) Similarly, House of Commons scrutiny in mid-November 1996 and early February 1997 made

[51] COM(96) 460 final, 2 October 1996.
[52] Council Doc. 11349/96 AGRILEG 206 AGRIORG 222 AGRIFIN 224, 12 November 1996, 2; see also Answer to Written Question no. 2483/96 by Mrs. Schleicher, OJ C 91, 20 March 1997, 7.
[53] Council Doc. 11349/96 ADD 1 AGRILEG 206 AGRIORG 222 AGRIFIN 224, 7 November 1996, 9 fn. 2.

no mention of the legal basis for the proposals.[54] A Council Working Group examined the proposal again on 11 February 1997. It clearly identified the objective of the regulations as the reestablishment of consumer confidence in beef and beef products and made no mention at all of the legal basis.[55]

The European Parliament instigated the procedural political dispute. A special Committee of Inquiry, which had been looking into Commission and British activity on BSE since July 1996, published a damning report in February of 1997 that blamed the affair on varying degrees of non-, mis-, and malfeasance by the British Government and the Commission.[56] Among the many implications of the BSE crisis for EU politics and policy-making (see Westlake 1997), the Committee of Inquiry demanded that the codecision procedure be applied to all agricultural legislation other than the day-to-day operation of the common market organizations.[57]

At the same time, standing committees examined the Commission's new legislative proposals. Despite the fact that the proposals were published in the same document and were clearly linked to each other, the EP Secretariat assigned the cattle identification and registration proposal to the Agriculture Committee and the beef labeling proposal to the Environment Committee, which also had responsibility for consumer protection. The identification and registration proposal generated no procedural political interest in the EP's Agriculture Committee, which focused on the substance and made no mention of the legal basis of the proposal.[58] In the Environment Committee, by contrast, the labeling proposal generated both substantive and procedural political activity. On the substantive side, the Committee sought to make the proposed labeling scheme mandatory. On the procedural political side, it asked the Legal Affairs Committee to analyze the propriety of article 43 as the legal basis for the Commission's proposal, preferring, for its part, article 100A (QMV codecision procedure). The Committee first and foremost demanded a change in legal basis. In keeping with this change, it proposed amendments to the first recital that

---

[54] House of Commons Select Committee on European Legislation, 3rd Report, Session 1996/97, HC 36–iii, para. 8; 12th Report, Session 1996/97, HC 36–xii, para. 7.
[55] Council Doc. 5907/97, 13 February 1997.
[56] EP Doc. A4-0020/97, Report of the Temporary Committee of Inquiry Into BSE [Medina Ortega], 7 February 1997.
[57] EP Doc. A4-0020/97/PART A.II, Report of the Temporary Committee of Inquiry into BSE (Recommendations for the Future), 7 February 1997, paras. 3.4–3.5.
[58] EP Doc. A4-0022/97, report on the proposal for a Council Regulation establishing a system for the identification and registration of bovine animals [Mayer], 28 January 1997.

emphasized, in order, consumer protection, public health, and the harmonization of national legislation. All of these "buzzwords," absent from the Commission's text, would bolster arguments in favor of article 100A.[59]

In considering the article 43-100A nexus on a closely related post-BSE proposal,[60] a note prepared by the EP's Legal Affairs Committee alluded to the uphill battle facing the Environment Committee's procedural political aspirations.[61] It began by reasserting the Court's settled case law to the effect that the choice of legal basis depends on objective factors amenable to judicial review, and trying to circumvent this would be foolish.[62] The note cited the Court's decision in the *Hormones* judgment and its subsequent jurisprudence (especially Case C-11/88) in support of the claim that the Court was favorably disposed to article 43, even where some nonagricultural products were involved. Emphasizing the clarity and continuity over multiple judgments of the Court's position, the analysis revealed "no margin" for rival interpretations of the legal basis of measures even touching on the agricultural sector.

The Legal Affairs Committee itself took a more overtly procedural political tack. It adduced three factors favoring article 100A, with its codecision procedure, rather than article 43, with mere consultation for the EP. First, the proposed legislation would impact the internal market. Second, article 100A(3) contained a provision implicitly justifying the pursuit of consumer protection goals using internal market procedures. Third, it cited the Committee of Inquiry's demand for codecision in agricultural, and a fortiori in health and consumer protection affairs.[63] Of these three points, the first is irrelevant, the third is overtly and exclusively political, and the second,

---

[59] EP Doc. A4-0037/97, Report on the proposal for a Council Regulation regarding the labeling of beef and beef products [Papayannakis], 6 February 1997; "Euro-MPs Want Tougher Beef Labelling Rules," *European Report* no. 2198, 12 February 1997.

[60] COM(96) 170 final.

[61] From a methodological perspective, these notes are particularly useful. They are drafted by staff lawyers of the EP's Legal Affairs Committee. They are relatively depoliticized and give a relatively objective view of the legal situation. They thus differ from decisions of the Committee itself. While members of the Committee are all lawyers, they are also politicians. Comparing the notes and the eventual outcomes, then, offers some leverage on the degree of manipulation that is occurring, or the divergence between the "sincere legal" and "procedural political" approaches.

[62] "Note à l'attention de Mme Evelyne Gebhardt," European Parliament Legal Affairs Committee, dossier 97/015, 14 February 1997, 1.

[63] Letter from Legal Affairs Committee Chair Willy de Clercq to EP President José Maria Gil Robles, 18 February 1997, in EP Legal Affairs Committee dossier 97/015.

while couched in legal terms, rests on a suspect reading of the purposes of the proposed measures.[64]

The EP considered the proposals, along with the Committee of Inquiry Report into BSE, at its February 1997 plenary in Strasbourg. The link between the broader BSE inquiry and the specific legislation would prove crucial. In connection with the first, MEPs drafted a motion of censure against the European Commission, only the third of its kind since the advent of direct EP elections in 1979.[65] This censure threat strongly colored the procedural political processes associated with the beef labeling and identification proposals (Blanquet 1998, 464–465). Speaking before the plenary on 18 February, and with the censure threat looming, European Commission President Jacques Santer pledged that in the wake of the BSE crisis, the Commission would seek greater EP involvement on similar issues by pushing for a substantial revision of article 129 (human health) at the intergovernmental conference (IGC) that was under way at the time. He further pledged that even absent a treaty change, the Commission would "in future be favoring the use of article 100A for all proposals whose main subject is veterinary or phytosanitary matters."[66]

This promise was bold in several respects. First, it cut directly against the Commission's procedural political preferences as adduced in Chapter 3. Second, the promise ran against legal advice given to Santer by the Commission Legal Services.[67] Third, in trying to "smash the monopoly of the agricultural legal basis" on health-related legislation, the promise ran "head on into the Court's firm jurisprudence" (Blumann and Adam 1997, 290). To uphold such a switch, the Court would have to disavow ten years of its own clear and unwavering case law.

---

[64] An EP lawyer close to the case emphasized the political pinch faced by the Legal Affairs Committee: "This is not a good case for us. Here it was impossible to stick to a legalistic approach. During EP plenary the President of the Commission said that he would make an effort to use codecision everywhere that health and consumer protection were involved. The Legal Affairs Committee couldn't argue for article 43 in such a case. How could we say that article 43 was necessary when the Commission itself was saying that we could get codecision? The Committee couldn't possibly give less to the EP than the Commission" (Interview, Luxembourg, 22 July 1997).

[65] Neil Buckley, "Brussels on the Rack Over Beef Crisis: MEPs Move to Censure Commission and May Demand UK Repayments," *Financial Times*, 18 February 1997, 2; "Mad, Sad Euro-MPs," *Economist*, 22 February 1997, 56.

[66] *EP Debates* no. 4-495, 18 February 1997, 58; see also Answer to Written Question No. 684/97 by Mr. Frischenschlager, OJ C 391, 23 December 1997, 25.

[67] Interview with Commission Agricultural official, Brussels, 6 April 1999.

EU officials, even those within the Commission, uniformly ascribe Santer's switch to the political pressure generated by the BSE inquiry and related censure motion.[68] The Commissioners' "immediate reaction" to the EP's censure threat, one former Commission lawyer confided, "was to save themselves."[69] That the switch cut against Commission preferences was alluded to by a socialist MEP, who exhorted the Commission to "grin and bear it in relation to article 100A."[70] That said, MEPs rejected the censure motion and passed a farcical "conditional motion of censure" that vowed to follow through with actual censure should the Commission fail to respect its undertakings to the EP.[71]

With respect to the labeling and identification proposals themselves, recall that the Agricultural Committee report on cattle identification and registration had not called for a change to the proposed article 43 legal basis, while the Environment Committee report on beef labeling had. Santer's pledge went further than even the EP had demanded, covering both of these proposals and a handful of others. In the words of one Council agricultural official, the Commission had become *"plus royaliste que le roi."*[72] Not to be outdone, the Agriculture Committee rapporteur tabled an oral amendment asking for article 100A on the identification proposal as well. While expressing great reluctance – referring several times to the urgency of the measures at hand – Agriculture Commissioner Franz Fischler responded by agreeing to article 100A for both proposals and for a third proposal dealing with veterinary checks on third country meat products.[73] Armed with this support, the EP passed both texts on to the Council.[74]

National officials were livid about the Commission's reversal on the legal basis. One week after the EP plenary, the Special Committee on Agriculture (a specialized body within the Council) met to reconsider the identification

---

[68] Interview with former member of Commission Legal Service, Brussels, 16 July 1997; Interview with member of Commission Legal Service, Brussels, 1 April 1999; Interview with Commission Agricultural official, Brussels, 6 April 1999.
[69] Interview with former member of Commission Legal Service, Brussels, 16 July 1997.
[70] *EP Debates* no. 4-495, 19 February 1997, 119.
[71] See "Mad, Sad Euro-MPs," *Economist*, 22 February 1997, 56; Marcel Scotto, "Vache folle: le Parlement européen va renoncer à sanctionner Bruxelles," *Le Monde*, 20 February 1997.
[72] Interview with Council agricultural official, Brussels, 18 March 1999.
[73] *EP Debates* no. 4-495, 19 February 1997, 120; "Restoring Consumer Confidence Will Require Transparency and Product Identification, Notes Parliament, Which Toughens Up Rules Proposed by the European Commission," *Agence Europe* no. 6919, 21 February 1997.
[74] OJ C 85, 17 March 1997, 67.

and labeling proposals. In the assessment of a Commission official in attendance, member states expressed "widespread surprise verging on indignation" at the legal basis switch. They particularly emphasized the "long term institutional implications" of the legal basis change, a classic procedural political concern. No fewer than six delegations characterized the change as a "dangerous institutional precedent."[75] Member states also decried the delays that codecision would bring, which was contrary to the Commission's earlier commitment to bring the matter up for a final Council vote in March.[76]

The Commission rather unconvincingly defended its choice of legal basis. Suggesting that it "was not unknown for positions to evolve in the course of an inter-institutional discussion," it now claimed to see the measure as a means of achieving public health aims within the context of the single European market.[77] At this and a subsequent COREPER meeting on 26 and 28 February, member states seemed unconvinced. They noted that the ECJ's jurisprudence in this matter was clear and unchanged, having been reaffirmed as late as 1996 (Case C-180/96R, *United Kingdom v. Commission* [1996] ECR I-3903). Others emphasized the Commission's original choice of article 43 and the absence of substantive changes that might justify the change of legal basis.[78]

Interestingly, the evidence suggests that the Commission was less than enthusiastic about the change of legal basis. When asked by national officials about the commitment into which Santer had apparently entered at Strasbourg in February, a Commission official stressed that the Commission would merely "privilege" article 100A on veterinary and phytosanitary proposals, which does not imply that article 100A would systematically be chosen.[79] Similarly, a Council official suggested during interviews that while the Commission based its proposals on article 100A to placate the Parliament, Commission officials were "whispering in [the official's] ear to use article 43," an allegation not denied by a Commission lawyer close to the case.[80]

---

[75] Commission Doc. SI(97) 145, 26 February 1997, 1, 4.
[76] Commission Doc. SI(97) 145, 26 February 1997, 1.
[77] Commission Doc. SI(97) 145, 26 February 1997, 5.
[78] Commission Doc. SI(97) 139, 27 February 1997.
[79] Commission Doc. SI(97) 139, 27 February 1997, 3.
[80] Interview with Council agricultural official, Brussels, 18 March 1999; Interview with member of Commission Legal Service, Brussels, 1 April 1999.

On 3 March 1997 the Commission adopted an amended legislative proposal in light of its commitments to and the demands made by the European Parliament in February.[81] The modified proposal had three notable features, all of which bear directly on the procedural political dispute at hand. First, not surprisingly, it was based on article 100A and would require the codecision procedure. Second, it was a single proposal, with previously separate provisions on cattle identification and registration on the one hand and beef labeling on the other hand now fused into a single Regulation. Third, the proposal introduced a new first recital that mentioned, in order, human health concerns, unilateral national measures and attendant problems with the functioning of the internal market, and only then consumer confidence and the need to restore the beef industry.[82]

After the change of legal basis, several months were expected to elapse before the proposed Regulation could be adopted. First, it was thought that the Council would be unable to muster the unanimity to change the legal basis and thus the legislative procedure. Accordingly, the relatively time-consuming codecision procedure would apply.[83] Second, Britain was expected to do everything it could to block the beef labeling plans, which would put British beef at a tremendous disadvantage.[84] Third, and related, important substantive differences remained, with Italy and especially the UK staunchly opposed to compulsory labeling schemes and most other member states firmly in favor.

The Council Legal Service produced a note on 13 March concluding that article 100A could not constitute the proper legal basis for the proposal.[85]

---

[81] COM(97) 103 final, 3 March 1997; "Commission Starts Fulfilling Parliamentary Beef Identification Demands," *Eurowatch*, 21 March 1997; "Beef: European Commission Amends Beef Labelling Proposal," *European Report* no. 2205, 8 March 1997; "Commission Modifies Legal Basis of Directives on Labelling and Identification of Bovine Animals to Emphasize Health Aspect," *Agence Europe* no. 6928, 6 March 1997.

[82] COM(97) 103 final, 3 March 1997, 2.

[83] "EU Farm Ministers to Resist Beef Label Plans," *Algemeen Nederlands Persbureau English News Bulletin*, 18 March 1997; House of Lords, Select Committee on the European Communities, Session 1997/98, 11th Report, *Correspondence with Ministers*, para. 51. The evidence supports this fear. I randomly sampled sixty CNSQ and sixty CODQ procedures from this time period and found that the former lasted an average of 311 days, the latter just under 724 days.

[84] Consumers were not expected to flock to beef "made in Britain." Geoff Meade, "Now Hogg Faces Meat Label Fight with EU," *Press Association Newsfile*, 14 March 1997; Geoff Meade, "Hogg to Block EU Meat Labeling Move," *Press Association Newsfile*, 17 March 1997; Geoff Meade, "Britain Digs in over Meat Labels," *Press Association Newsfile*, 18 March 1997.

[85] The Commission's own lawyers did not endorse the legal basis much more strongly. When asked directly about this amended proposal at separate interviews, two Commission lawyers

The proposed Regulation, it found, satisfied the Court's conditions for the applicability of article 43: it regulated Annex II products in the pursuit of article 39's objectives for the Common Agricultural Policy (CAP). The Commission's textual manipulations, consisting of rewording and reordering the recitals, did not change that fact.[86] More generally, the note concluded that "where the Court of Justice has interpreted a specific article of the treaty in such an extensive and clear fashion, as is the case with article 43, it is difficult to depart from the Court's consistent case law in the absence of any modification to the treaty article in question."[87]

As of 17 March 1997, then, "EU officials predicted a standoff. The ministers [would] have to vote unanimously if they wish[ed] to overturn [the legal basis] but they [were] divided among themselves over the proposal."[88] The Dutch Presidency was "coaxing member states' delegations to put aside their differences on the issues in order to defeat an attempt by the European Commission to change" the legal basis.[89] In a marathon four-day session the Council came to a unanimously agreed package deal that traded substantive concessions for procedural political ones and resulted in political agreement on a beef identification and labeling Regulation. Faced with "bitter opposition" from Italy and especially the UK, member states agreed to make beef labeling mandatory only after 1 January 2000, and also agreed to make exceptions for meat produced and consumed exclusively within domestic markets or within countries agreeing to opt out of the scheme. On the procedural political side, member states agreed to base the new Regulation on article 43 of the Treaty. The decision, it was said, sent "a clear signal to Jacques Santer... that the agricultural lobby is vehemently opposed to his campaign to give the European Parliament a greater say over

---

close to the case characterized the choice of article 100A as *défendable* (defensible). This clearly represented the "party line" within the Commission. Interview with member of Commission Legal Service, Brussels, 1 April 1999; interview with Commission Agricultural official, Brussels, 6 April 1999.

[86] Council Doc. 6585/97 JUR 85 AGRILEG 56, 13 March 1997, para. 11. The House of Commons Committee reached the same conclusion (House of Commons, Select Committee on European Legislation, 17th Report, Session 1996/97, HC 36–xvii, para. 3.7).

[87] Council Doc. 6585/97 JUR 85 AGRILEG 56, 13 March 1997, para. 14.

[88] "EU Stand-off on Beef Proposal," *Financial Times*, 18 March 1997, 2.

[89] "Farm Council: Ministers Blast New Proposal on Beef Labels and Cattle Registration," *European Report* no. 2208, 19 March 1997; "First Reactions to 1997/98 Price Package, Reduction in Aid for Arable Crops and Measures to Restore Confidence in Beef Are on the Agenda," *Agence Europe* no. 6935, 15 March 1997.

agriculture policy."[90] While this sort of network effect may indeed have operated, I suggest that it was causally secondary to a propitious procedural political environment.

The Council formally adopted Regulation 820/97 on 21 April 1997.[91] Article 19(1) set forth the compulsory labeling scheme, which would operate from 1 January 2000. However, it permitted member states to opt out for products made and marketed domestically, and also made exceptions for trade between states that had chosen to opt out. The Council clearly reframed the proposal back toward agriculture and away from human health and consumer protection. It did so in two ways. First, it dropped the first recital from the Commission's amended proposal, which had emphasized health and consumer protection, and introduced a new first recital that clearly prioritized the needs of the beef market. Second, it introduced a new third recital holding that through the Regulation, "certain public interest requirements will also be attained, in particular the protection of human and animal health." This reproduces almost verbatim the Court's own language from paragraph twelve of the precedent-setting Hormones judgment. The Commission entered a statement into the minutes expressing its strong regret over the Council's change of legal basis and the consequent rejection of codecision with the EP, and reserving its right to take all necessary steps with respect to this question.[92]

Before turning to the litigation stage of the procedural political game, note that on 18 June 1997 the member states agreed to the Amsterdam Treaty, which would enter into force on 1 May 1999. For purposes of the case at hand, the most important change came to article 129 of the treaty (post-Amsterdam article 152(4)b). It established that "by way of derogation from article 43, measures in the veterinary and phytosanitary fields which have as their direct objective the protection of public health" would be adopted using the (modified) codecision procedure. The end of this chapter will explore the relationship between the post-BSE procedural political disputes and this important treaty change.

---

[90] Caroline Southey, "Britain Drops Threat to Block Labeling of Beef: EU Ministers Back Plan to Display Meat Origins," *Financial Times*, 20 March 1997, 32.

[91] Council Regulation (EC) No. 820/97 of 21 April 1997 establishing a system for the identification and registration of bovine animals and regarding the labeling of beef and beef products, OJ L 117, 7 May 1997, 1–8.

[92] Council Doc. 7198/97 PV/CONS 19 AGRI 63, 22 May 1997, 11.

Beef Labeling Before the Court. Although neither EP nor Commission lawyers foresaw much hope for victory, and under EP pressure,[93] the Commission initiated annulment proceedings against the Council on 22 July 1997. It argued, first, that the Regulation had as its main purpose the protection of human health. Second, it suggested that at the very least, the contested Regulation pursued both agricultural and health objectives simultaneously, equally, and indissociably. Under the Court's Titanium Dioxide jurisprudence, it implied, both articles 100A and 43 are therefore required. (This cumulation would yield the codecision legislative procedure.) Third, the Commission explicitly invited the Court to reconsider its long-standing jurisprudence on the relationship between articles 43 and 100/100A. A Commission lawyer who worked closely on the case summarizes this strand of the argument as follows:

Our basic argument in this case is not that the case law of the 1980s was wrong, but rather that things have changed. There have been two treaty changes, maybe three. Public health was almost absent at the time that the Court issued these judgments. For the old cases, the facts of the cases – all but one [case], which complicates our task considerably – all pre-date the Single Act. Public health has been included, with the role of the EP increasing every step of the way. Therefore, because the treaties have changed the framework of law, there has to be an interpretation, a re-interpretation, of the system of the treaties. Before, these things were agriculture. Now they are public health.[94]

The EP applauded the Commission's willingness to take the matter to Court.[95] However, it did not necessarily trust the Commission fully to represent its procedural political interests. While this is an implication of my analysis, it finds confirmation in interview evidence. The legal case was a difficult one to make, and EP lawyers had concluded that it stood little chance of success, even before it was formally lodged. One EP lawyer

---

[93] Unnumbered document, EP Legal Affairs Committee dossier 97/012, 30 June 1997; "Food Safety: European Parliament Issues Warning to Commission," *European Report* no. 2209, 22 March 1997; Caroline Southey, "Santer Backs Action Against Ministers," *Financial Times*, 26 March 1997, 2; "Commission Decides to Take Council to Court Over the Legal Basis Decided for Beef," *Agence Europe* no. 6943, 27 March 1997; "Europe Row Could End Up in Court," *Press Association Newsfile*, 26 March 1997; Amanda Cheesley, "Challenge to Labels and ID," *Farmer's Weekly*, 4 April 1997, 8; "Brussels Backs Court Action," *Financial Times*, 27 March 1997, 2.
[94] Interview with member of Commission Legal Service, Brussels, 1 April 1999.
[95] EP Doc. A4-0362/97, Report on the European Commission's follow-up to the recommendations made by the Committee of Inquiry into BSE, 14 November 1997, para. 44.

expressed the fear that the Commission, driven only by EP pressure, actually hoped to lose the case. It would thus have its long-standing preference for article 43 reasserted all the while being able to deflect EP criticisms.[96] A Commission lawyer very close to the case alludes to the same set of incentives. "Remember," he cautions,

> that it was a huge Commission victory to have article 43 over article 100 in the mid-1980s. Now it finds itself having to argue in favor of 100A against 43! I am [closely involved with] the case, which I am not optimistic that we will win. But, as lawyers, we are the servants of our political masters. There certainly was not an outbreak of joy here [in the Commission Legal Service] when the decision was taken to bring this case.[97]

The Court's Advocate General argued that the Regulation simultaneously, equally, and indissociably pursued two objectives. The first, given effect in its provisions for cattle identification and registration, involved the production and marketing of agricultural products and fell under article 43. The second, given effect in the provisions governing labeling of beef products, pursued human health objectives and fell under article 100A. Accordingly, articles 43 and 100A should have been used jointly, with the QMV codecision procedure thereby applicable (para. 95). Had the Court followed its Advocate General, the Commission's procedural political fusing of the two separate proposals would have paid off.[98]

However, in its judgment of 4 April 2000, the ECJ did not follow its Advocate General. It found that the Council had acted properly in basing the contested Regulation on article 43 (Case C-269/97, *Commission v. Council* [2000] ECR I-2257). The judgment was straightforward. The Court denied that the EP should participate more in the adoption of measures in areas where it had been instrumental or performed effectively. Alluding to the changes wrought by Amsterdam, it emphasized that the legal basis for an act depended solely on the treaty provisions in force at that moment and not on treaty amendments agreed to but not yet in force. Finally, it reasserted its "settled case law" on the legal basis of agricultural measures, with the usual two-pronged test (product falling within Annex II of the

---

[96] Interview with member of EP Legal Service, Brussels, 8 July 1997.
[97] Interview with member of Commission Legal Service, Brussels, 1 April 1999.
[98] The Advocate General himself rather sarcastically alludes to this possibility when he points out that "purely theoretically," a "skillfully engineered" combination of measures could lead one objective to be subsumed by another, with important and foreseeable procedural consequences (para. 86). This is precisely the logic of procedural political fusion, as discussed in Chapter 2.

treaty, pursuing CAP objectives laid out in article 33 [ex article 39]). By its aim and content the labeling and identification Regulation satisfied that test and was, accordingly, properly founded on [then] article 43.

Theoretical Assessment

I have closely examined the legislative and procedural history of two pieces of EU legislation that operate at the intersection of agricultural policy and human health. The cases further relate in that each gave rise to an explicit dispute that landed before the ECJ. Each case scrutinizes procedural political behavior and dynamics during one of the periods in which the theory suggests they are likely to play themselves out. I now assess the evidence in light of the theoretical expectations developed in Chapter 2 and operationalized above. How do the theory of procedural politics and alternatives to it fare in explaining the conditions under which, the ways in which, and the effects with which actors choose or remain constrained by rules in the agricultural sector? I will consider each element in turn.

Conditions

Because of selection on the dependent variable, the cases are not the best tool for assessing procedural political conditions. The aggregate tests conducted in Chapter 4 serve that purpose better. However, the data presented in Figure 27 on ECJ cases involving article 37 (ex article 43) directly confirm procedural political expectations. I argue that two conditions – the availability of and procedural divergence between institutional alternatives – combine to allow and incite procedural politics. In Table 17 I offered a theoretical expectation about variations in procedural political disputes over time. The data confirm these expectations.

Thus, an otherwise puzzling pattern – a cluster of Court cases in the mid-1980s, another in the mid-1990s, and none in between – can quite easily be explained. Actors were not more rule governed in the interim. They simply faced an unfavorable combination of issues and institutional alternatives. This directly confirms the proposition that actors are strategic and make their procedural political calculations with the Court in mind. With almost no chance of success post-1988, and absent some exogenous change in issues or structures, manipulation simply made little sense. Court cases are costly, and losing them is even costlier. For either side to invite a defeat by the Court would have been quixotic. This helps make sense of a broad and otherwise puzzling pattern of procedural acquiescence, for example, by the EP in the agricultural sector from the mid-1980s to the late 1980s through the mid-1990s. It also explains the stark contrast between the 1985 and 1996 disputes on the one hand and the absence of disputes in the intervening periods. Recall that jurisdictional ambiguity was high in the late 1980s/early 1990s. But no institutional alternatives were meaningfully available. Opportunity might have been said to exist but it was not matched by corresponding incentives. As a result, procedural politics remained in the background.

Given their alternatives, did actors reveal rules preferences consistent with the models in Chapter 3? Here the evidence is mixed. The revealed rules preferences in the Hormones case corresponded to predicted preferences for two of the three main legislative actors. Specifically, the Commission conforms to the predicted pattern, and the EP's public silence on the issue amounts to consent, which is consistent with expectations. In the Council, only the UK and Denmark behaved as predicted. Their procedural motivations were made especially clear by Denmark's behavior before and after the Court judgment: with all other factors perfectly controlled, it switched positions once all chance of affecting the legislative procedure had evaporated.

As noted in developing the preference rankings in Chapter 3, this reveals a limitation of the modeling method. If rules preferences are derivative, then it is perfectly in keeping with the theory that actors with "revisionist preferences" – that is, who prefer policy outcomes far from the status quo – should favor QMV in the Council. I lack member state–level data on procedural political disputes, however, and so tried to specify the theory at a level that would allow empirical testing (here at the level of the Council). So, while the case does confirm the overall logic of procedural politics, it disconfirms the specific predictions generated by the models.

In the second case, the theory correctly predicts positions taken by two of the three actors. Given a choice between a legal basis using the QMV consultation procedure (e.g., article 43) and one using the QMV codecision procedure (e.g., article 100A), the theory suggests that the Parliament should strongly prefer the latter. In the case at hand, nearly every bit of evidence supports this expectation (the initial position taken by the agriculture committee constituting a partial exception). By contrast, I hypothesize that member states should prefer QMV consultation, as it avoids lengthy codecision with the EP and enhances the power of a relatively controllable agent, the European Commission. Here too, despite considerable differences of opinion on the substance of the matter, member states rallied to a common procedural political position so as to avoid the negative institutional precedent of having an agricultural matter, normally the *domaine reservé* of article 43 and the consultation procedure, decided by codecision. The only exception occurred when the UK momentarily advocated article 100A for a narrow portion of the proposal, but this disappeared from the documentary record after one mention and I found no other evidence in this sense.

The Commission's stance proves more ambiguous. Its initial proposal confirms procedural political expectations. According to the theory, it should prefer QMV consultation to codecision, and it acted accordingly. Its amended proposal disconfirms my expectations, by the same logic. In the interest of preserving falsifiability, I will not attempt to "save" the procedural political hypotheses. Commission behavior here disconfirms them. However, the special circumstances of the case, as well as evidence beyond the choice of legal basis, bear mentioning in this connection. The BSE affair was one of the most serious in the history of the EU (Garcia 1997). The censure motion that it generated was only the third in the history of the directly elected EP and was arguably the most credible (for an assessment see Wright 1998). This pressure clearly influenced the Commission, a fact confirmed by numerous interviews. All of this could be taken to "save" the procedural political hypothesis that the Commission favors QMV consultation to codecision. It is consistent with broad procedural political logic to exploit legal rules for political gain. This is precisely what the Commission was doing: against its own substantive preferences, and in an action of extremely dubious legality, it chose a rule that offered it political benefits – avoiding censure – over a rule that would bring political costs. However, to do this would be to deprive the hypotheses of their falsifiability. By this criterion, I must take the Commission's switch as disconfirming my expectations.

In sum, the theory mis-predicts the revealed preferences of a qualified majority of the Council in the Hormones case and the Commission in half of the Beef Labeling case, but correctly predicts all other revealed rules preferences. Perhaps more important, its causal logic accommodates all revealed rules preferences: they reflect political, rather than legal calculations. This, in turn, suggests that more supple tools and member state–level data may allow better explanation of national positions.

Means

Strategic Issue Definition. Chapter 2 identified three forms that strategic issue definition could take: fission, fusion, and reframing. The agricultural policy evidence reveals no attempt at fission. The Beef Labeling case has one very clear example of fusion that conforms precisely to the predicted pattern. The Commission initially tabled separate proposals on cattle identification and registration on the one hand and beef labeling on the other. The former clearly fits more comfortably under article 43 (QMV consultation) than does the latter: cattle are listed in Annex II of the treaty as agricultural products, while "beef" and "beef products" are not. This difference between the two proposals also finds expression in bill assignments made by the EP secretariat: it sent the identification and registration proposal to the Agriculture Committee, the labeling proposal to the Environment/ Consumer Protection Committee.

When forced for its survival to change the legal basis of the proposal – that is, in some sense, to play the procedural political game on Parliament's behalf – the Commission chose to fuse the two proposals into one. There are two interpretations of this step. If the Commission sought truly to respect Parliament's wishes, it must have thought that the labeling portion of the joined Regulation "outweighed" or subsumed the identification and registration portion. If, by contrast, the Commission were "tanking," or appearing to defer to Parliament all while sabotaging the EP's procedural political aspirations – and advancing its own – then it would be the case that the Commission saw the reverse happening: the inclusion of the identification and registration provisions would tip the collective balance in favor of article 43 and agriculture. I suspect that the latter is the case, and evidence exists to support this interpretation. The point, for my purposes, is simply that regardless of its specific motivation, the Commission fused the separate proposals for procedural political reasons.

Turning to the third form of strategic issue definition, reframing, the direction and timing of framing attempts consistently support the procedural political view and consistently disconfirm "sincere" alternatives. That said, framing appeared to occur more extensively in the later case, Beef Labeling, than in the earlier Hormones case. In the Hormones case, the Commission and member states did not seem overly concerned with asserting the primacy of the Directive's agricultural objectives as against its harmonization or human health objectives. While I believe that the Commission inserted the phrase "common market organizations" in the final proposal for procedural political reasons, and while the documentary record suggests a rhetorical switch by the UK with respect to human health, I find scant other evidence of framing behavior in this case. In light of the clear manipulation that occurred in the contemporary Battery Hens case, this is puzzling.[99] As it happens, however, the framing was not needed, as the Court would offer a test for article 43 that the Directive could satisfy.

In the case of the Labeling Regulation, framing was ubiquitous. The Commission's amended proposal, drafted after its change of position on the legal basis and its fusion of the two proposals, transparently introduces several textual amendments aimed at bolstering the measure's human health credentials and downplaying its agricultural aspects. To give just a flavor, whereas the initial proposal had simply begun with reference to existing agricultural legislation dealing with registration and labeling, the new proposal began by emphasizing health issues and the risk of unilateral national actions that could harm the single market.[100] The Council Legal Service, fully aware of this ploy, suggested that these changes were meaningless but nonetheless advised the Council to reverse them. It did so, and the Court upheld the Council's claims about the center of gravity of the Regulation, in part by minutely dissecting preambular language that the Council had so manipulated.

Coalition Formation. Turning now to the hypotheses on coalition formation, recall from Table 18 that prior to the SEA, procedural politics and prevailing approaches offer very similar predictions. Both suggest that the Commission, which strongly prefers QMV consultation to its unanimity variant, will tend to oppose itself to the Council, which should prefer unanimity. The EP shares the Commission's preference ranking, but it is nearly indifferent as neither alternative affords it much influence. The observed pattern fits neither expectation, as the Council and Commission found themselves on the same side against one of the Council's member states. However, the causal factors underlying this pattern are more consistent with procedural politics. The coalition formed in defense of legislative procedures that afforded coalition members influence to achieve desired outcomes and directly contradicted putative ideological interests. The EP's choice to remain on the sidelines was pragmatic and procedural political. In short, the case provides no evidence in support of the rival hypothesis and

---

[99] In that case, the Court struck down the Battery Hens Directive because the Council Secretariat had unlawfully redrafted certain preambular language so as better to "fit" the Directive within article 43.
[100] COM(97) 103, 3 March 1997, 2.

substantial evidence in favor of procedural political logic, if not its specific prediction.

In the second case, I predict that the EP will battle a procedural coalition of the Commission and the Council. Until mid-February 1997, this pattern effectively held sway. After the censure threat and the Commission switch, it ceased, and the supranational-intergovernmental pattern predicted by the rival hypothesis emerged. The EP evinced clear concern for its narrow self-interest, consistent with procedural politics as against its rivals. Ample evidence exists to suggest that the Commission was forced against its will to side with the EP, including eyewitness testimony to the effect that the Commission worked behind the scenes to undermine the procedural stance it had publicly taken. No evidence in support of a supranational motivation exists. For the Council, by contrast, the procedural political and the ideological operate in tandem. It did evince concern for its institutional position, but as it represents the member states this could be consistent with either approach. The evidence fails to speak decisively in favor of one or the other perspective here.

Effects

To what extent did all of this matter for legislative and institutional outcomes in the EU? I begin by addressing policy outcomes, considering each of the three causal pathways identified in Chapter 2. I then turn more speculatively to consider the relationship between day-to-day procedural political disputes and long-run institutional change in the agricultural sector.

Policy Outcomes. The Hormones case provides the clearest possible evidence of the substantive impacts of procedural politics. Put simply, the Hormones Directive would never have seen the light of day had the Commission and eight member states not conspired to play procedural politics and circumvent the British veto. Rather than influencing the mere content of the legislation, then, procedural politics permitted its very existence (Wachsmann 1993, 2). And, lest there be any doubt about the importance of the legislation at hand, the ten-year transatlantic trade battle that it sparked, which resulted in the first-ever case under the WTO's Sanitary and Phytosanitary Agreement, gives some indication (McNiel 1998).

In contrast to most of the other cases in both environmental and agricultural sectors that I examine, I find few procedural political effects on the Hormones Directive through the second and third pathways. That is, procedural politics did not noticeably increase the dimensionality of the issue space or open up otherwise absent package deals. Neither did strategically offered amendments – which, as noted, were few and far between – find their way into final legislation.

The second case offers a stark contrast. The rule exerted no direct effect on outcomes because both rule and substance were endogenous to preferences and power of, and bargaining between, member states in the Council. Thus, the first pathway appeared inconsequential here, quite unlike the Hormones case. By contrast, the third pathway, whereby amendments aimed at reframing a proposal wind up in final legislation, clearly operated. For the most part these amendments were substantively unimportant, concentrated as they were in the legislative preambles. They had important legal consequences, and, ultimately, substantive impact, however, since the Court relied greatly upon them in finding in the Council's favor.

The Labeling case does reveal meaningful procedural political effects on policy outcomes through the second pathway, however, markedly influencing the stringency of the legislation finally adopted. Recall that the second pathway involved the creation of new logrolls or package deals through the addition of a procedural to existing substantive dimensions. Evidence from the March 1997 Council meeting suggests that the United Kingdom was most strongly interested in the substance of the proposal, intensely concerned to secure delays in and exceptions to the compulsory labeling scheme proposed by the Commission and preferred by all member states with the exception of Italy. The other member states, by contrast, evinced greater concern for the procedural political aspects of the Commission's proposal. While this concern was partly substantively motivated – they feared that codecision would slow the legislative process considerably – it was also institutional, insofar as they feared establishing a precedent for the use of the codecision procedure in what had traditionally been defined as agricultural policy.

To assess the impact of procedural politics on policy outcomes, I begin by considering the substance of the proposals, which easily reduces to the relative laxity or stringency of the identification and labeling regime. The top (left-right) dimension in Figure 28 locates the ideal points of the relevant actors (the UK, the Commission [C], and the qualified majority of member states [M]), as well as the status quo (SQ) along this dimension using the standard spatial modeling assumptions (see Chapter 3). The UK prefers less stringent regulation, most member states prefer very stringent regulation, and the Commission wishes to enact stringent regulation, but

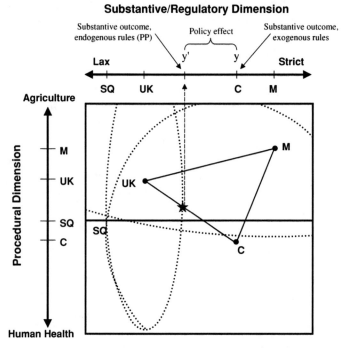

Figure 28 BSE Regulatory Outcomes with and Without Procedural Politics

not to the same extent as the member states. In the absence of procedural politics, spatial theory predicts an outcome of *y*, which is also precisely at the Commission's ideal point. Because the Commission has proposal power, and because the qualified majority of member states prefer *y* to the status quo (it is closer to their ideal points), they agree to it.

Now consider what happens when procedural politics enters the picture. Figure 28 portrays a north-south dimension involving the policy framing (and hence the procedure) that will be used. Assume, consistent with the "center of gravity" approach jurisdictions, that any outcome to the north of the bisecting line will use the agriculture procedure (QMV consultation), anything to the south will use the human health legislative procedure (QMV codecision). Again I array the relevant actors along this dimension, plotting the Commission's proposal as induced by EP pressure, as well as the positions of the UK and member states, and the location of the status quo. The square box projects ideal points on the substantive and procedural dimensions into a two-dimensional space and includes elliptical indifference contours to represent preference intensities between the two dimensions.[101] Curves longer in the east-west than in the north-south dimension (e.g., the member states) indicate a relatively intense preference on the procedural dimension. Those longer from north to south than from east to west (e.g., the UK) indicate more intense preferences on the substantive dimension. I ascribe equal preference intensity to the Commission, and hence its indifference curve is a circle.

When procedural politics is added (i.e., in two dimensions), member states must gain the UK's approval of the legislative procedure, because changing the procedure represents an amendment to the Commission proposals and all such amendments require unanimity. Intuitively, we suspect that the UK will extract substantive concessions in exchange for procedural support (much as Belgium did in the waste shipments case discussed in Chapter 5). Indeed, this turns out to be the case. Assuming that the Commission has complete and perfect information about others' preferences (this assumption turns out not to matter much in this case), it will propose that point that is closest to its own ideal point that all member states will accept. The starred point represents that outcome in this example, lying as it does just at the edge of what the UK will accept. The key point is the following: when we project that two-dimensional outcome back onto the substantive/regulatory dimension, it becomes clear that the substantive outcome (y') represents a more lax regulation than would have occurred where rules were exogenous. With endogenous rules – that is, with procedural politics – the substantive outcome changes, and the difference between y' and y can be interpreted as the (second pathway) policy effect of procedural politics.

Observed outcomes reflect precisely this logic. Under EP pressure, the Commission had proposed an extremely strict compulsory labeling regime that would be immediately applicable. However, it had also been forced to base its proposal on article 100A, to which member states were uniformly opposed. Most member states agreed to British and Italian demands to loosen the regulations – notably by extending the start date of the new regime and allowing opt-outs for products sold domestically or between opt-out states – in exchange for their (especially British) support on the procedural political dimension. Straightforward policy analysis, with exogenous procedures, would entirely miss this dynamic.

---

[101] Although nearly every introduction to analytical methods addresses the issue, I find the most helpful discussion of this use of elliptical indifference contours to be Weingast 1998, 162–164.

The result of all of this is that policy was much more lax than it otherwise would have been. Interestingly, this result cut against the substantive preferences of both the European Commission, which was forced to take this approach under threat of censure by the EP, and the EP itself. The EP had been the most ardent supporter of strict post-BSE policy. Yet, its procedural political maneuverings – its ultimately futile attempt to ensure the usage of rules that maximize its political influence – had the perverse result of generating outcomes farther away from that goal. I suspect that the EP failed to foresee this effect, and that it might not have played procedural politics had it done so. It is also possible, however, that it knowingly risked the short-run substantive goal for the longer-run institutional one.

Institutional Change. Finally, to what extent, if any, has procedural politics in the agricultural sector generated treaty change? With respect to the mid-1980s bout of procedural political disputes, exemplified by the Hormones case, the connection is implausible on its face. These disputes arose after the signing but before the entry into force of the SEA. It would be five years before the next round of treaty reform, and these were quiet years for procedural politics in the agricultural sector. Article 43 remained unchanged, so any effect would have to have been felt in other areas of the treaty. None were apparent.

By contrast, the mid-1990s round of disputes, exemplified by the post-BSE beef labeling and registration Regulation, offers a more plausible profile for higher-order institutional influence. The BSE crisis exploded in March of 1996, a few weeks before the start of the intergovernmental conference (IGC) at which member states were debating modifications to the treaty. Member states adopted the Regulation in question at the end of April 1997, less than two months before they signed the new treaty at Amsterdam. At Amsterdam, they created a new clause in the public health title of the treaty, article 129(4)(b) (post-Amsterdam article 152(4)(b)), which read, "by way of derogation from article 43 [post-Amsterdam article 37], measures in the veterinary and phytosanitary fields which have as their direct objective the protection of public health" would be adopted using the new codecision procedure.

This new provision clearly responds to the BSE crisis. But did the procedural political fight have anything to do with it? Here the evidence is less clear. The EP claims that the relationship was direct: "the extension of the co-decision procedure to the areas of animal health and plant protection . . . would not have been possible without the determined action of the European Parliament to deal with the BSE crisis."[102] If this claim were true, it would tend to cut against an intergovernmentalist view according to which member states seek to punish the institutional adventurism of their supranational agents. Indeed, if the Amsterdam Treaty change did respond to the procedural political dispute, and not just to the BSE crisis, then it would cut against such an intergovernmentalist view regardless of the EP's contribution, as it effectively codified the EP's demands one way or another. This effect has already been documented in the aggregate in Chapter 4, and case studies by other authors (Hix 2002; Farrell and Héritier 2003) suggest specific other instances where just such an effect has been at work. The specific evidence here must be seen as inconclusive, but its overall weight is suggestive of important effects.

Conclusion

In conclusion, the agricultural sector reveals precisely the same dynamics evident in both the broader trends and the environmental sector. Rules matter. Actors have preferences over them and seek to ensure the usage of those that afford them greater political power. They interact strategically in trying to shape the rules, influenced both by the nature of public policy issues and their correspondence to prevailing rules (and hence jurisdictional ambiguity) and by the nature of those rules themselves (influence differences among them). They play procedural politics, in short, when jurisdictional ambiguity provides the opportunity and when influence differences among the alternatives provide the incentives. They consistently do so through strategic issue definition and procedural coalition formation. Their procedural political behavior not only determines the rules under which they will interact, but it also influences policy outcomes and, perhaps, macro-institutional change.

Beyond additional testing and empirical scrutiny, this chapter has served three primary purposes. First, it has extended the empirical scope of the study "quantitatively" to an additional sector. Second, this sector represents, by a variety of measures, the most important sector of EU legislative activity, and any such study would be incomplete were it not to consider agricultural politics and policymaking. Third, the agricultural sector is additionally revealing to the extent that, according to influential alternative accounts, it

---

[102] EP Doc. A4-0362/97, Report on the European Commission's follow-up to the recommendations made by the Committee of Inquiry into BSE, 14 November 1997, para. 41.

should operate by a different logic. Policy networks analysis would explain the relative procedural political calm of the agricultural sector to network attributes, and in particular to its insularity and highly stable and interdependent membership. Logically, network analysis will have difficulties explaining intrasectoral variation in anything, including procedural political disputes. Empirically, this is borne out. Variations in procedural politics, in its occurrence, in the specific claims made and coalitions formed, and in the outcomes influenced, all respond to procedural political variables. These operate to explain intrasectoral variation in a way that network analysis cannot.

It remains, then, to integrate this finding with those that have preceded. What has this examination told us about European Union politics, policy-making, and integration, and about institutions and rule governance that comparative and international scholars did not already know, but should have? The concluding chapter addresses these questions.

7

Conclusion

PROCEDURAL POLITICS AND RULE GOVERNANCE IN THE EUROPEAN UNION AND BEYOND

"The rules!" shouted Ralph. "You're breaking the rules!"
"Who cares?"
Ralph summoned his wits.
"Because the rules are the only thing we've got!"[1]

Like other political systems, the identity of the European Union (EU) is written in its rules (institutions). More than in ideal-typical national political systems – systems characterized by common languages, histories, cultures – however, formal rules both preponderantly determine and most clearly articulate what the EU does and what the EU is. At the same time, as a relatively pure system of rules, unencumbered by deeply rooted cultural political, linguistic, and other bonds, the EU provides a particularly fruitful laboratory within which to learn general things about institutions. Understanding where rules come from and how they operate is the raison d'être of the booming institutionalist research program; the study of the EU, in which the operation of formal rules is so transparently important, has influenced and will continue to influence the progress of that research program.

Rules, though, have a "dual nature" (Grafstein 1992). Though "humanly devised," they are also "constraints that shape human interaction" (North 1990). Absent some measure of endogeneity, institutions lose their definitional quality as objects of human design or choice. Absent some exogeneity to the preferences and power of, and bargaining between, their creators, they lack the independent effects that make them worth studying. What is more, institutions tend to be multitiered, and no reason exists to suspect that all levels respond to and shape behavior and outcomes at the same

[1] William Golding, *Lord of the Flies* (New York: Perigee), p. 91.

times and in the same ways. Finally, institutions are historically embedded, created at a point in time but intended to endure through the passage of time, with possibly important consequences for the ways in which they condition and respond to politics. These insights, while currently underexploited, offer great promise for extensions of the institutionalist research program.

The continuing problems and prospects of institutional analysis, then, demand the attention of those who would study the EU, a political system – a polity – that so frequently uses formal procedures to stand in for the agreement on basic values and goals that it lacks, the changes to the institutions of which seemingly represent as much affirmations of faith as rationalization of rules. True, institutional analysis of the EU has exploded in the last decade, but its application has suffered from weaknesses characteristic of the broader institutional literature (Aspinwall and Schneider 2000; Dowding 2000; Schneider and Aspinwall 2001). Most notably, theories that endogenize institutions tend to operate at the level of constitutions, concerning themselves preponderantly with periodic (but increasingly frequent) treaty revision. By contrast, theories working at lower levels treat rules as fixed and exogenously given. Intuitively, and minimally, these presumptions of higher-order endogeneity and lower-order exogeneity might fruitfully be relaxed. Higher-order choice involves tremendous costs, uncertainties, and risks, and institutional alternatives exist, initially at least, only between the ears of would-be constitutional engineers. At the lower level, by contrast, costs and risks are presumably lower and alternatives already exist in the menu of rules established by the macro-institution. Beyond this, work toward a broader synthesis of choice and constraint, at multiple levels of institutional analysis, and sensitive to history, suggests itself. By pursuing these openings, EU studies can, in short, contribute much to institutional analysis, much as broader institutionalism has advanced the study of the EU (Jupille and Caporaso 1999; Jupille, Caporaso, and Checkel 2003).

In this book I have had two goals. First, I have sought to fill a gap by extending the logic of institutional choice to the everyday selection of legislative procedures in the European Union, with one eye remaining firmly on generalizability beyond the EU system. Second, more ambitiously but less fully realized, my aim has been to contribute to a broader institutional synthesis involving the dual nature, the multiple levels, and the historical character of institutions. Before sketching the book's contributions along those lines, however, let's take stock of what has already been done. To that end, the next section summarizes the arguments, methods, and

Conclusion

findings of the book. The third section draws out the broader implications of the study and suggests avenues for future research. The lessons learned are significant, not only to students of the EU, but to students of all rule-governed systems.

Summary: Arguments and Evidence

The Argument

I depart from three premises: institutions matter, actors have derived preferences over them as a function of the outcomes they generate, and actors interact strategically jointly to determine the rules that will govern their interactions. Actors thus seek to shape institutions in an effort to maximize their political influence.

Given these premises, I then ask and answer a series of questions. Under what conditions will actors engage in everyday politics with respect to rules – play procedural politics – and when, by contrast, will they content themselves to politics within rules? This choice, I suggest, depends upon both opportunities and incentives. Opportunities exist to the extent that issues correspond loosely to institutional arrangements – that is, to the extent that issues exhibit jurisdictional ambiguity. Ambiguity makes available institutional alternatives where otherwise there might be none. It creates opportunities to engage in procedural politics. Incentives exist to the extent that available alternatives differ in the influence they afford at least one actor and/or in the outcomes that they produce. Under those conditions, actors will have an interest in fighting the use of the less desirable rule and promoting the use of the more desirable one.

What behaviors and processes does procedural politics entail? This will vary from political system to political system, depending upon the nature and existence of criteria for institutional selection that stand external to the preferences and power of and bargaining between political actors. In general, in systems in which actors lack the ability directly to game the institutions, they will turn to gaming the criteria that define their applicability and thus govern their selection. In the EU, rules flow from the definition of the issue at hand. In this system, then, opportunities and incentives combine to trigger games of procedural politics in which actors strategically define issues so as to "fit" them under favorable rules and form procedural coalitions. Different criteria would generate different games.

What effect does all of this have? Procedural politics yields short-run rules choices, reduces policymaking efficiency, directly and indirectly influences substantive (policy) outcomes, and incites and informs longer-run institutional change. We can understand neither power, nor policy, nor institutional change in the absence of a theory of procedural politics. Indeed, I suggest, we cannot understand the nature of a political system nor the nature and extent of rule governance within it unless we attend to the dual nature of institutions, and model them simultaneously as objects of human design or choice and sources of human constraint.

Design, Data, and Methods

Lacking prior work on this topic on which to build, I have sought to scrutinize these expectations using as wide a variety of methods and evidence as possible.

Chapter 2 developed a positive theory of procedural politics. In developing the basic argument (outlined above), I devised a series of testable propositions about the conditions under which, the ways in which, and the effects with which actors will engage in everyday politics with respect to rules. Wherever possible – and it was not always possible, this area remaining almost totally unexplored – I identified alternative hypotheses from the literature or other sources.

I began the process of operationalizing these expectations to the EU setting in Chapter 3, by developing a series of models addressing the premises of the study as they play out in the EU. Spatial models provided a set of tools capable of analyzing precisely how rules matter, focusing on the influence and outcome properties of the nine legislative procedures that collectively govern the making of almost all of the EU's binding secondary law. Supplemented with three plausible auxiliary assumptions, the models permitted me to derive precise procedural preference rankings for the European Commission, Parliament, and Council over those nine rules. Having thus placed two of the three premises on a rigorous yet EU-relevant footing, I proceeded to model everyday institutional choice as a game of incomplete information, with an eye toward the analytical conditions under which actors will engage in politics with respect to, or alternatively within, institutions. In addition to the sequence of decision making and beliefs about others' preferences and behavior, the game identified two parameters that drive the decision either to choose or be constrained by rules. The first was the nature of institutional alternatives, the second the nature of policy issues

Conclusion

and their relationship to those institutions. Where alternative institutions were equally attractive, fights over rules did not occur. Where they differed, the decision to promote the usage of a more valued rule hinged on (actors' beliefs about) the correspondence between issues and rules (i.e., which was the legally correct choice) and hence on what the Court of Justice would do, were it called to cut the Gordian knot. This analytical result served as a bridge between the general theoretical arguments advanced in Chapter 2 and the empirical materials presented in Chapters 4 through 6.

Chapter 4 adduced a wide range of descriptive measures capturing systematic variation in the incidence of procedural political disputes across time, actors, and issues and tested a variety of procedural political and alternative hypotheses. The bulk of the data derived from an original dataset of over 4,700 pieces of binding, secondary EU legislation adopted between 1987 and 1997. I coded a variety of measures of procedural political dispute, opportunities, and incentives, and subjected them to a battery of tests including logistic and linear regression in addition to systematic descriptive analysis. The results, discussed below, strongly confirmed theoretical expectations.

Chapters 5 and 6 switched from aggregate patterns to a more intensive scrutiny of a smaller number of cases. This part of the study had an eye toward maximizing the ability to draw causal inferences, and to that end the chapters nest several design logics intended to work together. Most generally, I chose broad, maximally different sectors (environmental policy in Chapter 5, agricultural policy in Chapter 6). Theoretically consistent results within the maximum difference design, in general, give great confidence in the robustness of the theory across the whole range of sectoral possibilities. Furthermore, this design created space between my own approach and policy networks analysis. Although both succeed in predicting intersectoral variation, only the latter manages also to capture intrasectoral (over time) variability in the incidence of procedural politics.

More narrowly – that is, intrasectorally (and within chapters) – I nested a pretest-posttest quasi-experimental design within a "most similar systems" comparative case study logic. I treated macro-institutional (treaty) changes as natural experiments, producing variations in procedural political variables (institutional alternatives), and then conducted before-and-after comparisons. However, since single cases often did not span different treaty regimes, I examined several cases that were as similar as possible in all respects except for the combination of procedural political variables. In Chapter 5 (environmental policy), the cases isolated the institutional alternatives (incentives) variable, whereas Chapter 6 (agricultural policy) permitted extension to consider variations in both jurisdictional ambiguity (opportunity) and institutional alternatives (incentives).

Findings

The evidence strongly confirms the theory of procedural politics developed in Chapter 2. Expectations about the conditions under which disputes occur find the strongest confirmation. The hypothesized behaviors and dynamics also find strong confirmation, whereas expectations about effects, while generally supported, must also confront some unexpected findings.

Conditions. Consider expectations about the conditions under which (and the reasons for which) procedural politics occurs. The statistical tests in Chapter 4 confirm that opportunities (jurisdictional ambiguity) and incentives (divergent influence properties) drive procedural politics. Even controlling for the importance of legislation and for preferences on both substantive and integration dimensions, the pursuit of influence exerted disproportionate influence on the likelihood of procedural politics. Systematic evidence confirms that variations over time, as well as across issues and actors, respond to the conditions advanced and for the reasons advanced (influence maximization).

Moving closer to the ground, I complemented these findings by closely examining five pieces of legislation in two policy sectors. Procedural political disputes involving those legislative acts cannot be construed as evidence in support of arguments about the determinants of disputes, since their status as disputes was one of the features that led to their selection in the first place. However, the examination yielded sharp contrasts with other legislation, not examined in depth, which resembled one of the studied cases closely but failed to produce a dispute. In the waste management sector, each piece of legislation that I examined was intended to replace an earlier act. These earlier acts were all adopted between 1975 and 1984, and thus prior to the SEA and the emergence of meaningful institutional alternatives in this sector. None of them, I discovered, had been the object of a procedural political dispute. The agricultural chapter provides equally clear evidence in this respect. The 1996–1997 dispute involving post-BSE legislation contrasted sharply with the 1989–1990 period, when issues were, by my measurements, equally fluid and the legislative task – to respond to "mad cow disease" – was quite similar. Why then did the earlier acts not

Conclusion

produce procedural political disputes? The answer lies in the unavailability of institutional alternatives. Following the Court's decisive 1988 judgments in favor of article 43 as against any potential alternative, and until the creation in the 1993 Maastricht treaty of an autonomous legal basis for public health measures, there simply was no jurisdictional ambiguity – recall again that this involves both issues and structures – and hence no space available for meaningful institutional selection.

Finally, at the broadest level, the fact that no procedural political questions arose in the Parliament or were brought before the Court prior to the mid-1980s strongly confirms the expectation that influence differences condition institutional manipulation. Why bother manipulating the legal basis of legislation prior to this time, when the legislative procedure would be effectively identical? Again, beyond these general before and after comparisons, the theory performs well in making more specific predictions on the basis of variations in the availability of institutional alternatives. Why did agricultural policy precede environmental policy in generating procedural political Court cases? The answer is that the legal basis alternatives in the former sector gave the rise of majority voting in the early 1980s full meaning, as one of the two available legal bases underwent an informal procedural change. In environment, by contrast, that change would make no difference, as both legal bases available prior to the SEA formally required unanimity in the Council.

As a final note on conditions, consider the precise expectations generated by the procedural preference rankings in Chapter 3. These find consistent support throughout the study, although anomalies do arise. In the aggregate, actors clearly favor rules that increase their influence. All actors, on average, favor rules that afford them more influence than the alternatives. This finds confirmation in the frequencies with which actors promote rules giving them more or less influence. In 542 dyadic disputes involving Parliament-Council, Parliament-Commission, and Commission-Council pairs, actors promoted the more favorable (to them) procedure in 427 cases, for a 79 percent success rate in predicting the "direction" in which such claims work.

Again, the case studies generally replicate these findings. Without exception, actors in the environment cases reveal procedural preferences consistent with my predictions. Evidence from the agricultural sector is more mixed. In the first case examined (Beef Hormones), the models mispredicted the stance taken by a qualified majority of the Council, while it correctly captured the positions of the Commission and the Parliament. In the second case (Beef Labeling), the models correctly predicted all initial positions, but then failed to explain the change of position undertaken by the European Commission.

To retain the falsifiability of my expectations, I will not try to "save" procedural political hypotheses by pointing to the sui generis character of these anomalies, and especially the second. Instead, I would merely point out that in both cases, observed behavior supports a procedural political logic even as it disconfirms specific predictions based on the models in Chapter 3. (I should add that the cases decisively undermine policy networks analysis, which proves especially incapable of explaining change within the putatively stable agricultural policy community.) In both nominally disconfirming cases, actors manipulated rules for political gain – the Council to pass legislation against British opposition in the Hormones case, the Commission to save itself from censure in the Beef Labeling case. This suggests that the development of finer grained predictors of procedural preferences in specific cases (e.g., by accounting for the spatial arrangement of preferences as well as for dimensionality) might bear fruit. In general, however, behavior was consistent with the sentiment expressed by one EP official: "I don't give a damn about the legal propriety of the legal basis. I want what gives me the most power!"[2]

Means. The foregoing confirms that procedural politics occurs both for the expected reasons – in order to maximize influence – and under the predicted conditions – when opportunities and incentives come together. In Chapter 2 I set forth my expectations about procedural political processes. I expected actors to define issues strategically so as to fit them under favorable rules, and I expected them to form procedural political, rather than ideological or even substantive, coalitions. How well does the theory perform in accounting for means that actors employ in playing the procedural political game?

With respect to strategic issue definition, I advanced the general proposition that actors will define issues so as to fit them under favorable rules. I also expected that such issue definition would at times follow rules disputes, rather than preceding them as expected from a legalistic perspective, and that it could, on the margins, appear to cut against sincere (substantive) interests. More specifically, I identified three means of redefinition: fusion, fission, and reframing. All evidence brought to bear on these expectations

---

[2] Interview with EP official, Brussels, 30 July 1997.

Conclusion

came from the case study materials, as the required empirical examination is extremely intensive and defies easy measurement on large samples.

With respect to the specific means, a proposal to fission one of the waste management cases arose a single time and did not reappear. Fusion also arose only once, albeit more enduringly. In redefining its amended proposal for beef labeling in the second agricultural case, the Commission fused two previously separate proposals into a single Regulation. I have no doubt but that this change represented procedural political maneuvering: in his examination of the case, the Advocate General found that the Regulation in fact pursued two distinct and separate aims, each of which corresponded to one of the earlier proposals. I do not know, however, the expected effects of this fusion. Since the Commission fused the Regulation at the time that, under EP pressure, it based this proposal on a relatively unfavorable rule, my own expectation is that it did so to sabotage the case, leading the Court to rule "against" it and the Parliament. However, if the Commission acted in good faith, it may indeed have thought that the combination would bolster the case in favor of the human health legal basis. In either case, fusion was undertaken procedural-politically.

Turning now to reframing, the evidence reveals this tactic to be ubiquitous. I explicitly tested procedural political hypotheses about the direction and timing of such tactics against alternative theories and found the evidence to support the former strongly. Actors consistently tried to "massage" legislation in order to fit it under favorable procedures. Most of this activity centered on the legislative preambles which, while substantively insignificant, bear tremendous legal importance to the extent that the Court uses them to interpret the "aim and content" of legislation, and thus its appropriate legal basis and legislative procedure. In addition, the timing of these changes proves crucial. Legal rectitude demands that the legal basis flow from the substance of the act in question, including its preambles. Agreement on the legal basis should, in theory, take place only after the rest of the text has been agreed. Procedural politics suggests that the opposite may occur: actors will have a procedurally preferred legal basis and from that will flow at least some substantive modification of the text. The latter clearly and frequently occurs.

Procedural political expectations about framing explain some otherwise very puzzling behavior. Consider the role of the European Parliament in the waste management cases. It is widely accepted that the EP is the "greenest" (most environmentally friendly) of the EU institutions. Its Environment Committee is extremely powerful, its interest in the issue high, and its success considerable. In the waste management cases that I studied, this certainly seemed to be the case. At every turn the EP proposed to strengthen proposed legislation by tightening rules for waste prevention, recycling, and disposal; by limiting waste shipments; and so forth. So why, in every case following the SEA, did it propose to use internal market rules that would preclude "Green" member states from enacting national rules stricter than the European norm and seemingly facilitate free trade and competition in the industry at the expense of environmental protection? Without the theory, these positions would appear anomalous. Procedural politics, by contrast, accommodates these observations easily as part of the influence game that results when rules are endogenous.

And, interestingly, the incidence of strategic framing seemed to increase over the time period examined, in direct proportion to the clarity with which the Court had established its "aim and content" test (see McCown 2001 for a discussion of the emergence of Court-led precedents in this area). The better established that test, the more obvious became just what one needed to do to pass constitutional muster. Much as David King (1997) suggests that turf wars in the U.S. House unfold in the details of legislative drafting, EU officials take great pride in the skill with which they manipulate the substance of legislation. Said one EP official, "As a technician, I can find ways and means of doing any change that will stand up before the Court."[3] With this in mind, it is worth hypothesizing that the greater frequency with which actors undertook reframing relative to fission and fusion has to do with costs: simply put, it is easier to spin something than to start from square one by drafting what would be, in effect, one or several new legislative proposals.[4]

Turning now to consider coalition formation, procedural politics demonstrates considerable explanatory power. I adduced one explicit alternative hypothesis to the effect that an ideological cleavage between supranationalism and intergovernmentalism would condition such behavior. In many instances, predictions by procedural politics and this traditional view are observationally equivalent. Where this pertained, I sought out evidence that would lend causal support to one or the other. In short, I found no evidence whatsoever that the Commission or Parliament concerned themselves with supranationalism, nor the Council with intergovernmentalism, as ideologies. Indeed, each expressed concern only for its own interests,

---

[3] Interview with EP official, Brussels, 8 July 1997.
[4] I am grateful to a reviewer for suggesting this hypothesis.

Conclusion

and each, in appealing to the others to join the procedural political battle, did so in terms of institutional interests narrowly rather than broadly defined. Thus, for example, the Commission never enticed the Parliament to join a Court case by suggesting it would be good for the EU. It always appealed to the EP's narrower organizational interests. "Institutional realism," or "institutional self-interest," seems a far more powerful driver of procedural coalition formation than do abstract structural (supranational-intergovernmental) relations or their putatively associated ideologies.[5]

Having said that, I should note three other points on coalition formation. First, one of the cases, Beef Hormones, cuts against both procedural political and the traditional view. Here, the Commission, Parliament, and Council all joined sides against the UK. This marriage of convenience, while comprehensible ex post, was not predicted by either approach ex ante. Second, with the exception of the Beef Labeling case, to the particular circumstances of which I alluded above, all other coalitional patterns are both consistent with and attributable to procedural political logic. This includes the important discriminating test of post-Maastricht alignments in the environmental sector, in which, despite the failure of just about anything but the institutional alternatives to change, the Commission, as expected, abandoned its erstwhile Parliamentary ally and acquiesced in the Council's change of procedure against Parliament's interests. That the Commission failed to join the EP's subsequent Court case did more than add insult to injury; it also supplied crucial evidence that the "guardian of the treaties" (the Commission) would pursue its narrow organizational interests at the expense of other motivations. Third, evidence from Chapter 4 on the role of the ECJ undermines the rival hypothesis on logical grounds. In effect, the analysis shows that what is good for the Commission is not necessarily good for the Parliament, and vice versa. Intuitively, this may be obvious, but the preference rankings provide for a very precise way of thinking about this relationship. And, as Chapter 4 demonstrates, the Court shows itself far more sympathetic to the expansion of majority voting (and thus to the agenda power of the Commission) than to increasing the role of the European Parliament, a single spectacular case (Titanium Dioxide) notwithstanding.

Effects. While arguably worth studying in its own right, all of this might contribute little if it did not affect important outcomes. Clearly, procedural

---

[5] I am grateful to a reviewer for emphasizing this point.

politics shapes the rules used in everyday EU politics and policymaking. But how does it affect legislative processes and outcomes (public policy) and longer-run institutional change?

With respect to policymaking efficiency, the evidence is unambiguous: procedural politics reduces it. Even controlling for the importance (form) of legislation, substantive and integrationist preferences, and the extent of parliamentary involvement, procedural politics more than doubled decision lags, from an average of 175 days to over 390 days. While efficiency is clearly only one among many goals that any institutional arrangement might serve – flexibility, voice, and accommodation, after all, might matter as well – it seems clear that member states neither foresaw nor desired such delays.

Beyond decision making efficiency, three pathways occurred through which procedural politics might affect policy outcomes. The first was direct and revolved around the determination of rules by procedural politics and outcomes by rules. The goal here is not so much to test whether this happens as to assess the extent to which it happens, and here qualitative methods offered the greatest insight. In several cases, this pathway was shown to exert no discernible effect on policy outcomes. In effect, the simultaneous endogeneity of rules and outcomes to the preferences and power of and unanimity bargaining between the member states denuded institutions of independent causal importance. This inference applies to three of the five cases that I examine. In one case (Titanium Dioxide), this pathway operates, but in an unexpected way. Here, an EU rule allowed member states to adopt national legislation where under the alternative rule they would have been prohibited from doing so. When it came time to readopt the legislation after the Court annulled it, two member states had laws on the books that, even under internal market rules, they were allowed to retain. Finally, the Hormones Directive provides the clearest evidence of the procedural political determination of rules and the direct determination from there of legislative outcomes. By most accounts, the Directive would never have seen the light of day had the Commission and a qualified majority of member states not colluded to bypass the British veto.

The second pathway involved transformation of the bargaining space by virtue of the addition of a procedural political to a substantive dimension. This clearly operates in two cases, and again gives leverage on otherwise puzzling outcomes. In the case of the Waste Shipment Regulation, France had repeatedly and very publicly characterized the question of limiting waste imports as a moral one that admitted of no compromise (Jupille 1996). By raising its audience costs ("going public"), France had tied its hands and,

Conclusion

in the account of Schelling-style bargaining theory, should have increased its bargaining leverage. True enough, all member states but Belgium and, to a lesser extent, Luxembourg, were willing to go along with this position. True as well, the legislation that resulted was historic in the extent to which it subjugated free trade to environmental protection, much in keeping with French preferences. But it made a critically important and very puzzling exception for small country exports of hazardous waste. I contend that this otherwise puzzling outcome derives wholly from the effects of procedural politics on the dimensionality of the issue space. Belgium, in effect, was able to hold the other member states hostage on the substance because it wielded a veto over the procedural political change of legal basis. An almost identical outcome occurs in the case of the post-BSE beef labeling and registration Regulation. The UK, in effect, held the other member states hostage and forced them to accommodate its substantive wishes before it would agree to support their procedural political aspirations. Again, this outcome can only be accommodated within a framework that recognizes the potential everyday endogeneity of legislative procedures.

The third pathway to procedural political effects on policy outcomes operated frequently but, unlike the second pathway, with only marginal substantive importance. It involved the translation of procedurally motivated amendments into final legislation. Legislative preambles were found to be extremely susceptible to this form of influence, in several cases containing numerous recitals that repeat the same procedural political motivation in slightly different language. In terms of the important substance of legislation, I found only one provision that seemed to have been deleted wholly through procedural political motivation. While others may have reflected procedural political concerns, in the absence of interviewing all of the officials involved I simply cannot detect it. In the end, however, this reluctance to tamper with the deep substance confirms the intuition that procedural politics is a servant to, and not a master of, substantive interests (at least over the long haul), and that the pursuit of influence is derivative, rather than fundamental. The effects of procedural politics on policy outcomes, in short, seemed most pronounced – along the second pathway – precisely where they were least foreseeable.

Turning finally to the relationship between procedural politics and longer-run and higher-order institutional change, they clearly seem to relate. The greater the number of disputes under a given treaty regime, the evidence from Chapter 4 demonstrates, the more likely a procedure is to change; the greater the involvement of the EP in this sort of dispute, the greater will be its empowerment during the next bout of treaty modifications. My own expectations about the causation behind this process – that procedural politics both informs and incites treaty change – remain speculative, as systematic evidence has proved elusive. At a minimum – and this is a point to which I return below – they are suggestive and worthy of continued attention.

Summary

In sum, the empirical examination reveals the EU legislative system to be a richly textured, highly strategic, and thickly institutionalized one, complete understanding of which eludes prevailing theories and in which legislative procedures represent potential objects of everyday choice. Bargaining over rules rather than simply within them occurs under predictable conditions, by predictable means, and with predictable effects. Specifically, it occurs when issues and institutions interact in such a way as to make available procedurally diverse institutional alternatives. It involves predictable patterns of substantive manipulation and coalition formation. It decreases policymaking efficiency and impacts legislative outcomes through a variety of pathways, most directly by determining the rules within which policy is made but also indirectly by enabling new issue linkages and through the incorporation into final legislation of strategic amendments. It feeds back, seemingly via information and incentives, into subsequent constitutional change.

The evidence broadly supports the procedural political perspective on all of these issues, and procedural politics consistently outperforms alternative approaches. The theory predicts not only when disputes will occur, not only when and in what ways actors will strategically define issues, not only when and how they will impact important outcomes, but it also explains why these things happen. And, importantly, while the specifics of the "when, how, and with what effects" questions vary from case to case and from sector to sector, the causal logic remains consistent. Institutions matter. Actors have derived preferences over them, and interact strategically in shaping, or being constrained by, those rules.

Having started with abstract theory and models, moved through aggregate data, and scrutinized two very different policy sectors in close detail in the bulk of the book, and having summarized these efforts above, I must now draw out the broader implications of procedural politics for our understanding of EU politics and policymaking, power and rule governance, and,

Conclusion

most broadly, the extent to which institutions both shape and respond to the broader environments in which they operate. These issues are considered next.

Implications

What does all of the foregoing mean for our approach to and understanding of the European Union, and what in turn does this contribute to broader comparative understandings of politics in rule-governed systems?

Everyday Politics: Rational Institutionalism

Procedural politics resonates most closely with, and indeed owes a tremendous debt to, rational institutionalism. I believe that the theory contributes in kind. Consider the institutional effects analyses pioneered in EU studies by Garrett, Tsebelis, and Steunenberg and since taken up by a few dozen analytical political scientists and political economists on both sides of the Atlantic. Procedural politics seeks to deliver on the promise of the institutional and strategic logics underpinning that work. That is, it takes seriously the very real effects of institutions on substantive outcomes as well as the instrumentally rational and maximizing motivations of individuals and organizations. Following from these logics, as I have attempted to show, actors have incentives to shape the rules that influence the outcomes they value. Politics within institutions, then, operates indissociably from politics with respect to institutions. They are two sides of the same institutional coin.

The implications of this insight for prevailing work are many. In the introduction I alluded to some characteristic deficiencies of pure institutional effects analyses. Among these are the impossibility of inferring power from the apparent distributional consequences of rules and the illogic of predicting stability from the mere existence of cycle-suppressing rules without considering their potential endogeneity. Here, I frame my contribution more positively: the theory of procedural politics identifies the empirical scope conditions for the array of formal models of legislative politics that increasingly populate the EU and, to some extent, comparative literatures. This improves on work that assumes an unproblematic issue definition, proceeds to assume the applicability of the corresponding rule, and models behavior and outcomes as if the assumptions were true. Drawing attention to the problematic nature of many issues and thus the potential endogeneity of both issue definitions and corresponding rules helps us to identify which model applies in which situation. At the same time, it restores full sophistication to the actors, leaving them to chafe no more at (or remain blissfully ignorant of) the immunity of the rules to their maximizing strategies.

Grand Bargaining: Liberal Intergovernmentalism

Surely the most influential approach to studying the European Union is liberal intergovernmentalism (LI), as developed by Andrew Moravcsik (1991, 1993, 1995, 1998). Empirically, it focuses on the history-making "grand bargains" that have punctuated the EU's development since its founding in 1958. It relies on a tripartite, sequential explanatory framework comprising a liberal theory of state preference formation (Moravcsik 1997), a model of interstate bargaining based on asymmetrical interdependence, and a "credible commitments" theory of institutional choice. Armed with this framework, liberal intergovernmentalists seek to explain the important puzzle of why states willingly pool their sovereignty and delegate it to international institutions. They also seek to account for the specific issue areas and institutional forms involved.

Liberal intergovernmental theory generally reflects the strengths and shortcomings of the institutional design approach identified in the introductory chapter. Two key limitations, which will turn out to work in concert, stand out. First, in liberal intergovernmental theory, institutions only seemingly stand on the left-hand (dependent variable) side of the basic explanatory equation. Second, the approach focuses most prominently on the macro-institutional level of analysis, and it generally ignores the everyday politics that seem only to fill time between decennial (or, increasingly, quinquennial) grand bargains. Legislative procedures are outcomes, created to respond to incomplete contracting problems, but their properties are not thoroughly modeled and their effects are taken for granted.

Procedural politics redresses both of these limitations by asserting and establishing how the day-to-day operation of EU institutions can shape higher-order and longer-run institutional change in ways that are seemingly disallowed by liberal intergovernmental theory. First, procedural politics embraces the constraints imposed by the treaty on EU politics of both the everyday and the "historic grand bargaining" varieties. In effect, LI introduces into its specification of bargaining theory a unanimity decision rule which itself determines that outcomes will tend to be constrained by the lowest common denominator of member state preferences. Under different

Conclusion

rules, outcomes would differ, and this possibility needs to be accommodated by incorporating rules into both sides of the explanatory equation.

Second, by assuming, if never explicitly asserting, the everyday exogeneity of the rules that result from intergovernmental grand bargains, LI implies subsequent patterns of power and outcomes that only, in fact, materialize under conditions provided by procedural politics. Moravcsik argues that member states impose everyday unanimity on highly sensitive areas, and pool sovereignty (through majority voting provisions) only when bargained outcomes are susceptible to ex post reneging. He does not systematically consider the extent to which these jurisdictional arrangements operate as designed or by contrast are subject to procedural political manipulation and exploitation. The history of procedural politics is replete with examples in which member states explicitly attempted to insulate a given area from majority voting rules, only to find that one of their own, or the Commission or the Parliament, had exploited jurisdictional ambiguities in unanticipated and collectively undesirable ways. Everyday institutional choice, in short, can counteract member states' explicit designs, producing outcomes that they neither collectively intended nor desired.

Third, and most important, the theory of procedural politics, which aspires to address the dual nature, multiple levels and historical life cycle of institutions, creates a breach in the wall set up by liberal intergovernmentalism between the everyday operation of EU institutions and their subsequent modification. Moravcsik systematically downplays the influence of everyday politics on grand bargaining, largely eliminating any possibility of feedback from the latter into the former (Moravcsik 1998, 489–494; Moravcsik and Nicolaïdis 1999). The main allowable effects – EU rules affect material economic conditions, these feed into national preferences and from there influence subsequent grand bargaining – are relatively unimportant, effectively foreseen (Moravcsik 1999a, 175), and causally distant.

Procedural politics suggests ways that this enterprise might fruitfully incorporate feedback effects into its conception of institutional change. First, evidence suggests that, indeed, higher-order institutional changes had important unforeseen consequences to the extent that explicit collective attempts at insulating certain areas from majority voting were consistently circumvented through procedural political strategies. While this has occurred in areas too numerous to discuss here, I would simply mention environmental policy following the SEA and social policy following the SEA and Maastricht (Rhodes 1995). In both areas, and others besides, member states wrote detailed exceptions intended to preclude the use of majority voting, but constitutional ambiguities and institutional incentives combined to generate procedural political games that directly undermined these attempts.

Second, and related, procedural political games raised the costs of the institutional status quo by promising ongoing and costly disputes that imposed influence costs (deadweight losses) on member states, as against their putative desire efficiently to lock in bargains and thus to maximize available gains. While I have no direct measure of these losses, I do have available an indirect measure reminiscent of the use of queuing costs to measure inflation in state-run economies. As noted in Chapter 4, it took on average 175 days for proposed EU legislation to be adopted, while acts subject to a procedural political dispute took an additional 216 days. Procedural politics, surely an unintended consequence of grand bargaining, generated "losses" on the order of seven months for every act concerned. Such legislation was also generally more important than the average. Thus, following more recent formulations by Moravcsik (1999b, 380), we can imagine connections between the (institutionalized) status quo ante and subsequent institutional change brought about by grand intergovernmental bargaining.

Third, and reconnecting now to the linkage between everyday politics and every-decade grand bargaining, it stands to reason that member states should seek to avoid these losses and should incorporate these redefined incentives into subsequent institutional changes. On the theoretical side, precise specification of the institutional form and timing of the pooling of sovereignty has to this point eluded LI theory. Procedural politics offers a partial explanation: member states will seek to reduce these losses by codifying the procedural political demands of EU institutions. This might reflect learning about ambiguities in the constitutional contract, or it may reflect a calculated response to the threat posed by others, or both, but it should certainly influence future rounds of institutional change. Moravcsik has recently alluded to the learning hypothesis in trying to explain increases in EP power (Moravcsik and Nicolaïdis 1999), and given the strong initial support adduced in Chapter 4, it would seem to represent a hypothesis worth exploring further.

Historical Institutionalism and the Search for Synthesis

Both everyday (institutional effects) and grand bargaining (institutional design and change) approaches, I have suggested, will benefit from the contribution made by procedural politics. But each remains devoted to the

Conclusion

analysis of partial equilibrium. While everyday approaches powerfully explain politics within an extant institutional structure, this focus forecloses consideration of system transformation itself. While grand bargaining considers evolution over time, it neglects the application and operation of these institutions at any given point in time. To what extent can the valid concerns of each be appropriated into a more coherent whole that responds to the need identified above – namely, to work toward fuller integration of institutional choice and constraint at multiple levels of analysis and with history in mind?

Work by Paul Pierson (1996) and Mark Pollack (1996, 1997) is suggestive of the power of historical institutional analysis simultaneously to explain institutional equilibrium (that is, everyday outcomes within a fixed institutional structure) and equilibrium institutions (that is, the institutional structure itself) (Shepsle 1986; Diermeier and Krehbiel 2003). Pierson begins by stipulating the liberal intergovernmental account of the creation of the EU. This set of rules, presumably, responded at the creation to the preferences, relative bargaining power, and functional-institutional needs of its creators. Soon, Pierson claims, unintended and, crucially, difficult-to-close control gaps arise that drive outcomes away from those most preferred by the member states. Attempts at reasserting the institutional Eden of the creation will be thwarted by the self-interested designs of new institutional actors, by the investments in current arrangements of social forces, and by the increasing returns to scale of existing arrangements. Under these circumstances, current rules "lock-in" and change becomes difficult.

Precisely this logic operates in the growth of procedural politics. Member states agree on a constitutional arrangement aimed at ensuring the credibility of their cooperative commitments, but often within weeks of the entry into force of each new treaty – indeed, in the cases of the SEA and Maastricht, even before its entry into force – questions arise as to the applicability of different rules, questionable issue definitions begin to surface, and so forth. Member states demand unanimity legal bases as a bargaining tactic to extract substantive concessions (Lord Cockfield 1994, 64, 112), and legislation is passed by qualified majority vote that clearly exceeds the bounds of the legal basis on which it was adopted (Crosby 1991). How can member states respond? Calling a new intergovernmental conference (IGC) is both wildly disproportionate and exorbitantly expensive, and so in all probability they await the next IGC called for worthwhile reasons and seek to respond there. In the meantime, they are compelled to play the games resulting from others' strategic responses to the ambiguities and opportunities that they themselves created.

What is more, procedural politics responds directly to the complexity of the treaties, and that complexity appears systematically to be increasing as members respond to the demands of a post-industrial society and accommodate the range of interests associated with an ever-growing Union. In short, the increasingly complex constitutional architecture of the EU would seem to provide expanding space for strategic adaptation and, as such, unintended consequences. Where procedural politics incites and informs institutional change as expected, the putative gap between choice and constraint as well as between levels of institutional analysis begins to evaporate. This should be the direction of future work, aimed fully at respecting the demands of institutional analysis in the EU and beyond.

Rule Governance and System Transformation

Moving beyond the existing literature and into substantive understandings of the EU, we find that procedural politics offers a measure of the extent to which the EU has been transformed from an international compact among sovereign states, born of international diplomacy, to an increasingly rule-governed polity operating according to the rule of law. Consider the following stylized contrast. From the 1966 Luxembourg Compromise, member states disagreeing with EU legislation simply vetoed it. At most, they might permit it to be adopted and challenge before the Court the EU's very competence to act in the domain in question. After about the mid-1980s, member states disagreeing with EU legislation, rather than vetoing it, sought to ensure the usage of a more accommodating legal basis. That having failed, they would allow themselves to be outvoted and take the matter to the Court of Justice, arguing that the measure was founded on an incorrect legal basis (Corbett 1998, 34, 225). The debate about the extent to which the Luxembourg compromise continues to operate – or indeed, revisionists would add, if it ever really did – is ongoing (Teasdale 1993; Golub 1999). But I believe that this shift from the veto to the vote, and from "competence" disputes – calling into question the EU's authority in a given area – to procedural political disputes – accepting EU authority, but locating it elsewhere in the treaty – signifies a qualitative change in the presumptive response to serious disagreement. It exemplifies the growth of rule governance.

It may seem strange to assert that a study devoted to manipulation of rules bespeaks a high degree of rule governance. Procedural politics might

Conclusion

be thought to "undermine the normative mechanisms set out under the treaties, which constitute the fundamental law of the Community as a community of law" (Peter 1994, 325). True, legal basis disputes represent the continuation of "diplomacy by other means" (Cullen and Charlesworth 1999). Strikingly, however, manipulation of the rules occurs within a framework set by broader rules. Procedural political tactics – here, strategic issue definition – respond to the judgments of the Court in this area. If it used a different interpretive test, manipulation would likely occur with respect to it. This strategy occurs "within the undisputed limits of Community competence" (Weatherill 1995, 166). In sum, not only do legal basis disputes represent the "juridification of politics" (Volcansek 1992, 109), but the law used ceases to resemble the law of states and increasingly resembles that of a domestic polity. "The extent to which legal remedies can be used instead of political techniques by, but also against," actors in the EU system, Emiliou asserts, "is a sign of the limited development of the principles of parliamentary democracy in the Community system in comparison with the development therein of the principles of the *Rechsstaat*" (Emiliou 1994, 507). Put another way, and following Stone Sweet: in "gaming" the law, overtly political actors reproduce the law and its discourses, fulfilling a profound judicializing – and thereby institutionalizing (Stone Sweet, Fligstein, and Sandholtz 2001) – function in the EU's emerging polity.

Avenues for Future Research

Where, then, does this study lead us? In considering avenues for future research, I begin with fairly narrow puzzles and proceed to consider broader opportunities.

The book has identified some genuine puzzles. Consider, first, the propensity of EU member states to override even the strongly held national interests of their partners. The basic assumption that I use, and that is found in the literature, is that member states are extremely reluctant to "minoritize" each other when important interests are at stake. And yet, sometimes they do just that. To take two cases involving the United Kingdom, in both the Beef Hormones case (examined in Chapter 6) and the case of the Working Time Directive, the UK vehemently opposed proposed legislation but found itself outmaneuvered by a (theoretically unexpected) procedural coalition of the Commission, the Parliament, and the other member states. Why did this coalition override express and vehement British objections in these cases, when they do not always do so? The obvious response to this puzzle is that short-run benefits for the overriding member states exceed possible long-term costs, but this surely needs more careful operationalization.

Second, at several points during the narrative it appeared that actors, and in particular the European Parliament, were permitting institutional interests to trump policy preferences. This raises the important question of what happens when influence maximization and substantive goals work at cross-purposes. My response, and the formulation that I use, characterizes this choice as an investment decision – what Majone (1989) likens to roundabout methods of production – in which actors sacrifice the policy at hand in the pursuit of enduring influence and thus superior future streams of policy benefits. While arguably true, this formulation fails to get at the obvious question: under which conditions will actors forgo desired policy ends in pursuit of procedural political gain? While this may reduce to a problem of measurement (of long-run versus short-run costs and benefits), and may to that extent be prohibitively difficult, it may also be worth exploring further. For example, one might hypothesize an inverse relationship between systemic influence and propensity to forgo policy gains: the structurally weaker the actor, the more willing it is to sacrifice policy gains at the altar of institutional influence.

A third area of research involves the role of the European Court of Justice. What does the Court want, and what factors does it consider when making its decisions? What is the relative weight of increasing integration, promulgating good (and presumably legitimate) law, and responding to the interests of member states? Quite simply, we lack systematic answers to these questions and we currently lack the data to study them. The very fruitful debate among scholars of the U.S. Supreme Court, while differing to the extent that the object of study generates evidence other than simple unsigned judgments without dissenting opinions, might prove a helpful model in this regard (Epstein and Knight 1998; Clayton and Gillman 1999). But the "puzzle of judicial behavior" (Baum 1997) in the EU remains a very real one that implicates every aspect of what the EU does.

Beyond these puzzles, extensions of some of the ideas advanced in and attempts to address questions unanswered by this book are candidates for study. Consider, for example, the rationalist/intergovernmentalist hypothesis that supranational agents must attend to the preferences and possible reactions of member state principals in exploiting the agency slack available to them. The usual counterargument to this claim is that member states

Conclusion

can only punish their agents through the nuclear option of treaty revision, which comes at tremendous cost and risk (Pollack 1997). This suggests that exploitation of slack should vary with the costs of punishment. Operationally, then, we might expect to see systematic variations in manipulation depending on whether an intergovernmental conference is ongoing. During IGCs, this line of reasoning would suggest, the fixed costs of treaty revision are already sunk and only the (presumably much lower) variable costs of amending a few treaty articles impede member states from punishing their agents. Agents should be correspondingly timid.

Imagine a directly competing hypothesis based on a logic of communication and learning. Here, the empirical expectation would contrast directly with that outlined just above: intending to communicate the areas of their most intense desire to play a greater role in the policy process, the Parliament and Commission would be more likely to play procedural politics during IGCs as a way of sending costly (and thus credible) signals to the member states. This pair of hypotheses, evocative as it is of broader debates concerning the relative importance of exploitation and punishment versus communication and accommodation, might yield important insights into interinstitutional politics in the EU. This is made all the more important by the accelerated pace at which IGCs seem to be occurring, about once every five years or so since the mid-1980s. And, making precisely opposite predictions on the same set of variables, they are in principle subject to direct and discriminating testing.

More broadly, future research might extend the logic of procedural politics to other eras and aspects of EU politics and policymaking. Looking back in time, the classic competence disputes, in which member states accused the Commission of arrogating to the Community powers that rightfully remained with them, would seem ideally suited to the theory at hand. Like procedural politics, those disputes involved jurisdictional ambiguity and divergent institutional incentives, and, to my knowledge, gave rise to the same sorts of framing and coalitional behavior as procedural politics. These disputes predated the procedural political, operated at a reduced rate alongside procedural politics during the 1980s and 1990s, and seem ready to rise again with the trend toward "flexible cooperation" and the proliferation of institutional arrangements tied to specific functional tasks. Beyond competence disputes, the choice of "comitology" procedures, debates over the form of legislation (Regulations vs. Directives), disputes among the three pillars of the European Union, and many other issues might lend themselves to analysis inspired by procedural politics.

Looking ahead, as of this writing current and prospective EU member states are discussing a draft EU constitution, tabled by Valerie Giscard d'Estaing's constitutional convention in June 2003.[6] Like any contract, the document is replete with distinctions that, already appearing vague on paper, will prove quite contentious in practice, not least because they can trigger politically important procedural differences. For example, the hierarchy of Union competencies (exclusive, shared, coordinated, or none) assigns policy sectors to one of the categories of competence, with important differences in terms of the ways laws are adopted, the residual legal rights of member states, and so forth.[7] This is a common approach in all federal systems, and yet it gives rise to "gray areas" of competence over which political contestation takes place. Perusing the draft convention shows it to be just like its EU predecessors: highly complex, replete with derogations and special provisions, and full of futile attempts to anticipate all future contingencies. Exploration of this new document, should it enter into force, and the ways in which it shapes and responds to strategic behavior, will benefit from the approach developed here and occupy future generations of EU scholars.

Finally, departing from rather than extending the empirical focus of this book might yield additional research questions. For example, given the extent to which this study and a growing number of others draw comparatively on work done in other contexts, including the American, a strategy of comparative institutional analysis possibly involving the EU and other political systems (e.g., countries, international organizations) as cases would seem fruitful. Do French governments play a form of procedural politics in framing policy proposals as "regulatory" rather than "legislative," in an attempt to limit parliamentary involvement (Keeler 1993)? Do German Länder frame legislative proposals as touching on Land competencies so as to win themselves a veto in the Bundesrat? Do American presidents seek to evade excessive legislative controls by framing accords as executive agreements rather than treaties? Do other executives, similarly, structure situations so as to invoke the relatively free hand of executive decree authority? Do firms "forum shop" in selecting institutions within which to resolve transnational disputes? Comparative extensions to any number of legislative, federal, and

---

[6] Draft Treaty Establishing a Constitution for Europe, CONV 820/1/03 REV1, 27 June 2003.

[7] See European Convention Secretariat, Delimitation of competence between the European Union and the member states, CONV 47/02, 15 May 2002, for an analysis of the system of Community competencies.

other rule-governed systems are possibilities. I believe procedural politics to be ubiquitous. Comparative analysis of the conditions under which, the ways in which, and the effects with which actors engage in everyday politics with respect to rules offers the promise not only of improving explanations of political dynamics in specific systems, but also of understanding rule governance more broadly.

Conclusion

As with other institutionalized systems, the history of the European Union is written in its rules. From the visionary postwar project of Monnet and Schuman, through the epic battles of de Gaulle and Hallstein, the subtle progress of Giscard and Schmidt, to the renewed inspiration of Kohl, Mitterrand, and Delors; from the framers to the farmers and from the lawyers to the linguists; all of these efforts, all of these aspirations simultaneously respond to and reflect the institutions of European governance. Understanding the nature and operation of the European Union, then, cannot abstract from the institutions that constitute it, in their dual nature, with their multiple levels and in their temporal embeddedness. To do so yields incomplete descriptions, flawed predictions, and biased understanding of the ongoing interplay of rules, behavior, and political outcomes. Worse still, to do so fails to pay tribute to the progress that has been made or to recognize the challenges that lie ahead.

The European Union, as much as (if not more than) other political systems, seems to offer abundant research opportunities, and to this extent, the possibility to contribute to the broader enterprise represented by the institutional turn in the social sciences. If, to paraphrase Tip O'Neill, all politics is procedural, then it makes sense to draw lessons from the EU, where this is arguably most true. That this contribution will likely thrust scholars astride traditional disciplinary dividing lines – between comparative politics and international relations, and at the intersection of political science, economics, and the law among others – befits both the aspirations of institutional analysis and the nature of this empirically unique but theoretically intelligible emerging polity.

Bibliography

Arp, Henning A. 1992. The European Parliament in European Community Environmental Policy. EUI Working Paper No. EPU 92/13. Fiesola, Italy: European University Institute.

Aspinwall, Mark, and Gerald Schneider. 2000. Same Menu, Separate Tables: The Institutionalist Turn in Political Science and the Study of European Integration. *European Journal of Political Research* 38:1–36.

Bach, Stanley, and Steven S. Smith. 1988. *Managing Uncertainty in the House of Representatives: Adaptation and Innovation in Special Rules.* Washington, DC: Brookings Institution.

Ballman, Alexander, David Epstein, and Sharyn O'Halloran. 2002. Delegation, Comitology, and the Separation of Powers in the European Union. *International Organziation* 56, 3 (Summer):551–574.

Barents, René. 1988. Hormones and the Growth of Community Agricultural Law: Some Reflections on the Hormones Judgment (Case 68/86). *Legal Issues of European Integration* 1:1–15.

Barents, René. 1989. Community Agricultural Law and the Court's Case Law in 1986–1988. *Common Market Law Review* 26, 3 (Autumn):391–421.

Barents, René. 1993. The Internal Market Unlimited: Some Observations on the Legal Basis of Community Legislation. *Common Market Law Review* 30, 1 (February):85–109.

Barents, René. 1994. *The Agricultural Law of the EC: An Inquiry into the Administrative Law of the European Community in the Field of Agriculture.* Deventer: Kluwer Law and Taxation Publishers.

Barnard, Catherine. 1992. Where Politicians Fear to Tread? *European Law Review* 17, 2 (April):127–133.

Barry, Brian. 1980. Is It Better to Be Powerful or Lucky? Part 2. *Political Studies* 28, 3 (September):338–352.

Bates, Robert H. 1988. Contra Contractarianism: Some Reflections on the New Institutionalism. *Politics and Society* 16:387–401.

Baum, Lawrence. 1997. *The Puzzle of Judicial Behavior.* Ann Arbor: University of Michigan Press.

Baumgartner, Frank R., and Bryan D. Jones. 1993. *Agendas and Instability in American Politics*. Chicago: University of Chicago Press.

Baumgartner, Frank R., Bryan D. Jones, and Michael C. MacLeod. 2000. The Evolution of Legislative Jurisdictions. *Journal of Politics* 62, 2 (May):321–349.

Bawn, Kathleen. 1993. The Logic of Institutional Preferences: German Electoral Law as a Social Choice Outcome. *American Journal of Political Science* 37, 4 (November):965–989.

Baziadoly, Sophie. 1992. Le refus de la décharge par le Parlement Européen. *Revue du marché Commun et de l'union européenne* 354 (January):58–73.

Bednar, Jenna, John Ferejohn, and Geoffrey Garrett. 1996. The Politics of European Federalism. *International Review of Law and Economics* 16, 3 (September): 279–294.

Bell, Andrew. 1989. Judgments on Majority Voting. *International and Comparative Law Quarterly* 38 (July):688–689.

Bieber, Roland. 1992. Majority Voting and the Cooperation Procedure. In *From Luxembourg to Maastricht: Institutional Change in the European Community After the Single European Act*, edited by Christian Engel and Wolfgang Wessels, 51–65. Bonn: European Union Verlag.

Binder, Sarah A. 1996. The Partisan Basis of Procedural Choice: Allocating Parliamentary Rights in the House, 1789–1990. *American Political Science Review* 90, 1 (March):8–20.

Binder, Sarah A. 1997. *Minority Rights, Majority Rule: Partisanship and the Development of Congress*. New York: Cambridge University Press.

Binder, Sarah A., and Steven S. Smith. 1997. *Politics or Principle: Filibustering in the United States Senate*. Washington, DC: Brookings Institution.

Binder, Sarah, and Steven S. Smith. 1998. Political Goals and Procedural Choice in the Senate. *Journal of Politics* 60, 2 (May):398–416.

Blanquet, Marc. 1998. Le Contrôle Parlementaire Européen sur la crise de la "vache folle." *Revue du Marché commun et de l'Union européenne* 420 (July–August):457–467.

Blumann, Claude. 1988. L'affaire des hormones devant la Cour de Justice des Communautés Européennes. *Cahiers de Droit Européen* 168 (December):505–513.

Blumann, Claude. 1996. *Politique Agricole Commune: Droit communautaire agricole et agro-alimentaire*. Paris: Litec.

Blumann, Claude, and Valérie Adam. 1997. La politique agricole commune dans la tourmente: la crise de la "vache folle". *Revue Trimestrielle de Droit Européen* 33, 2 (April–June):239–293.

Bos, Pierre V. F. 1991. The Proposed Regulation on the Supervision and Control of Movement of Waste: Some Comments. In *Current EC Legal Developments: EC Environment and Planning Law*, edited by David Vaughan, 150–168. London: Butterworth.

Bradley, Kieran St. C. 1988. The European Court and the Legal Basis of Community Legislation. *European Law Review* 13, 6 (December):379–402.

Bradley, Kieran St. C. 1992. L'arrêt dioxyde de titane: un jugement de Salomon? *Cahiers de Droit Européen* 5/6:609–630.

Bibliography

Bräuninger, Thomas, et al. 2001. The Dynamics of European Integration: A Constitutional Analysis of the Amsterdam Treaty. In *The Rules of Integration: Institutionalist Approaches to the Study of Europe*, edited by Gerald Schneider and Mark Aspinwall, 46–68. Manchester: Manchester University Press.

Bridge, John. 1988. Note on Cases 68/86 (*Hormones*) and 131/86 (*Battery Hens*). *Common Market Law Review* 25, 4 (Winter):733–742.

Bromley, Daniel W. 1989. *Economic Interests and Institutions: The Conceptual Foundations of Public Policy*. New York: Basil Blackwell.

Buchwitz, Rebekka. 1998. A Positive Analysis of European Deregulation. *Aussenwirtschaft* 53, 4 (December):553–571.

Budge, Ian. 2001. Validating Party Position Placements. *British Journal of Political Science* 31, 1 (January):210–223.

Budge, Ian, et al., eds. 2001. *Mapping Preferences: Parties, Electors, and Governments, 1945–1998*. London: Oxford University Press.

Burhenne, Wolfgang E., and Thomas J. Schoenbaum. 1973. The European Community and Management of the Environment: A Dilemma. *Natural Resources Journal* 13:494–503.

Burley, Anne-Marie, and Walter Mattli. 1993. Europe Before the Court: A Political Theory of Legal Integration. *International Organization* 47 (Winter):41–76.

Calvert, Randall L. 1995a. Rational Actors, Equilibrium, and Social Institutions. In *Explaining Social Institutions*, edited by Jack Knight and Itai Sened, 57–93. Ann Arbor: University of Michigan Press.

Calvert, Randall L. 1995b. The Rational Choice Theory of Social Institutions: Cooperation, Coordination, and Communication. In *Modern Political Economy: Old Topics, New Directions*, edited by Jeffrey S. Banks and Eric A. Hanushek, 216–267. New York: Cambridge University Press.

Cammack, Paul. 1992. The New Institutionalism: Predatory Rule, Institutional Persistence, and Macro-Social Change. *Economy and Society* 21, 4 (November):397–429.

Carpentier, Michel. 1972. L'action de la Communauté en matière d'environnement. *Revue du Marché Commun*, 153:381–394.

Carrubba, Clifford J., and Craig Volden. 2001. Explaining Institutional Change in the European Union: What Determines the Voting Rule in the Council of Ministers? *European Union Politics* 2, 1:5–30.

Carrubba, Clifford J., et al. 2003. Off the Record: Unrecorded Legislative Votes, Selection Bias, and Roll-Call Vote Analysis. Unpublished manuscript.

Chayes, Abram, and Antonia Handler Chayes. 1993. On Compliance. *International Organization* 47, 2 (Spring):175–205.

Chisholm, Donald. 1995. Problem Solving and Institutional Design. *Journal of Public Administration Research and Theory* 5, 4 (October):451–491.

Clayton, Cornell W., and Howard Gilman, eds. 1999. *Supreme Court Decision-Making: New Institutionalist Approaches*. Chicago: University of Chicago Press.

Close, George. 1978. Harmonisation of Laws: Use or Abuse of the Powers Under the EEC Treaty? *European Law Review* 3:461–481.

Coase, R. H. 1937/1988. The Nature of the Firm. In *The Firm, the Market, and the Law*, 33–55. Chicago: University of Chicago Press.

Cohen, Michael D., James G. March, and Johan P. Olsen. 1972. A Garbage Can Model of Organizational Choice. *Administrative Science Quarterly* 17, 1 (March):1–25.

Collins, Ken. 1995. Plans and Prospects for the European Parliament in Shaping Future Environmental Policy. *European Environmental Law Review* 4, 3 (March): 74–77.

Commission of the European Communities [CEC]. 1971a. *Fourth General Report on the Activities of the Communities, 1970*. Luxembourg: Office for Official Publications of the European Communities, February.

Commission of the European Communities [CEC]. 1971b. SEC (71) 2616 final. First Communication of the Commission About the Community's Policy on the Environment. 22 July.

Commission of the European Communities [CEC]. 1995. *Report on the Operation of the Treaty on European Union*. SEC(95) 731 final, 10 May.

Common Market Law Review. 1982. The Vote on Agricultural Prices: A New Departure? 19, 3 (August):371–372.

Conant, Lisa J. 1998. *Contained Justice: The Politics Behind Europe's Rule of Law*. Ph.D. dissertation, Department of Political Science, University of Washington, Seattle.

Corbett, Richard. 1989. Testing the New Procedures: The European Parliament's First Experiences with Its New "Single Act" Powers. *Journal of Common Market Studies* 27, 4 (June):359–372.

Corbett, Richard. 1998. *The European Parliament's Role in Closer EU Integration*. London: Palgrave Macmillan.

Corbett, Richard, Francis Jacobs, and Michael Shackleton. 2000. *The European Parliament*, 4th edition. London: John Harper Publishing.

Corbett, Richard, and Otto Schmuck. 1992. The New Procedures of the European Community After the Single European Act: Efficiency and Legitimacy in the Light of Experience. In *From Luxembourg to Maastricht: Institutional Change in the European Community After the Single European Act*, edited by Christian Engel and Wolfgang Wessels, 33–49. Bonn: European Union Verlag.

Cox, Gary W., and Mathew D. McCubbins. 1993. *Legislative Leviathan: Party Government in the House*. Berkeley: University of California Press.

Cox, Gary W., and Mathew D. McCubbins. 1995. Bonding, Structure, and the Stability of Political Parties: Party Government in the House. In *Positive Theories of Congressional Institutions*, edited by Kenneth A. Shepsle and Barry R. Weingast, 101–118. Ann Arbor: University of Michigan Press.

Cox, Gary W., and Mathew D. McCubbins. 1997. Toward a Theory of Legislative Rules Changes: Assessing Schickler and Rich's Evidence. *American Journal of Political Science* 41:1376–1386.

Crombez, Christophe. 1996. Legislative Procedures in the European Community. *British Journal of Political Science* 26 (April):199–228.

Crombez, Christophe. 1997a. The Co-Decision Procedure in the European Union. *Legislative Studies Quarterly* 22, 1 (February):97–119.

Bibliography

Crombez, Christophe. 1997b. Policy Making and Commission Appointment in the European Union. *Aussenwirtschaft* 52, 1/2:63–82.

Crombez, Christophe. 2000. Institutional Reform and Co-Decision in the European Union. *Constitutional Political Economy* 11:41–57.

Crombez, Christophe. 2001. The Treaty of Amsterdam and the Co-Decision Procedure. In *The Rules of Integration: Institutionalist Approaches to the Study of Europe*, edited by Mark Aspinwall and Gerald Schneider, 101–122. Manchester: Manchester University Press.

Crosby, Scott. 1991. The Single Market and the Rule of Law. *European Law Review* 16, 6 (December):451–465.

Cullen, Holly, and Andrew Charlesworth. 1999. Diplomacy by Other Means: The Use of Legal Basis Litigation as a Political Strategy by the European Parliament and Member States. *Common Market Law Review* 36, 6 (December):1243–1270.

Curtin, Deirdre. 1993. The Constitutional Structure of the Union: A Europe of Bits and Pieces. *Common Market Law Review* 30, 1 (February):17–69.

Dashwood, Alan. 1989. Majority Voting in the Council. In *Legislation for Europe 1992*, edited by Jürgen Schwarze, 79–83. Baden-Baden: Nomos Verlagsgesellschaft.

Dashwood, Alan. 2001. The Constitution of the European Union After Nice: Law-Making Procedures. *European Law Review* 26, 3:215–238.

David, Paul A. 1985. Clio and the Economics of QWERTY. *American Economic Review* 75, 2 (May):332–338.

David, Paul A. 1994. Why Are Institutions the 'Carriers of History'? Path Dependence and the Evolution of Conventions, Organizations, and Institutions. *Structural Change and Economic Dynamics* 5, 2:205–220.

de Ruyt, Jean. 1989. *L'Acte unique Européen: Commentaire*, 2nd edition. Brussels: Éditions de l'Université de Bruxelles.

de Sadeleer, Nicolas. 1991. Le Droit Communautaire de l'Environnement, un droit sous-tendu par les seuls motifs économiques? *Aménagement-Environnement* 4:217–223.

de Sadeleer, Nicolas. 1993a. Case Note C-155/91, *Commission v. Council. Journal of Environmental Law* 5, 2:295–300.

de Sadeleer, Nicolas. 1993b. La querelle sur le choix de la base juridique des actes communautaires relatifs à la protection de l'environnement, suite et fin? *Aménagement-Environnement* 2:81–85.

de Sadeleer, Nicolas. 1993c. La question de la base juridique des actes communautaires ayant trait à la protection de l'environnement: symbiose ou opposition entre la politique d'établissement du marché intérieur et la politique de protection de l'environnement? *Revue Juridique de l'Environnement* 4:597–616.

de Sadeleer, Nicolas. 1994. La circulation des déchets et le Marché unique européen. *Revue du Marché Unique Européen* 1:71–116.

Debroux, Xavier. 1995. Le choix de la base juridique dans l'action environnementale de l'Union Européenne. *Cahiers de Droit Européen* 3/4:383–397.

Demaris, Alfred. 1992. *Logit Modeling: Practical Applications*. Quantitative Applications in the Social Sciences Series, Number 86. Thousand Oaks, CA: Sage.

Deniau, Xavier. 1984. Le vote au sein du Conseil des Ministres des Communautés Européennes: Théorie et pratique. *Revue du Marché Commun* 279 (July–August):316–318.

Denzau, Arthur T., and Robert J. Mackay. 1983. Gatekeeping and Monopoly Power of Committees: An Analysis of Sincere and Sophisticated Behavior. *American Journal of Political Science* 27:740–761.

Dewost, Jean-Louis. 1980. Les relations entre le Conseil et la Commission dans le processus de décision Communautaire. *Revue du Marché Commun* 238 (June–July):289–294.

Dewost, Jean-Louis. 1984. L'avenir du fonctionnement des Institutions: Le Conseil. *Annales de la Faculté de Droit, d'économie et de sciences sociales de Liège* 29, 4:293–305.

Dewost, Jean-Louis. 1987. Le vote majoritaire: simple modalité de gestion ou enjeu politique essentielle? In *Du Droit International au Droit de l'intégration*, edited by F. Capotorti et al., 167–175. Baden-Baden: Nomos Verlagsgesellschaft.

Dewost, Jean-Louis. 1989. Rôle et position de la Commission dans le processus législatif. In *Legislation for Europe 1992*, edited by Jürgen Schwarze, 85–96. Baden-Baden: Nomos Verlagsgesellschaft.

Diermeier, Daniel, and Keith Krehbiel. 2003. Institutionalism as a Methodology. *Journal of Theoretical Politics* 15, 2:123–144.

Dion, Douglas. 1997. *Turning the Legislative Thumbscrew: Minority Rights and Procedural Change in Legislative Politics*. Ann Arbor: University of Michigan Press.

Dion, Douglas, and John Huber. 1996. Procedural Choice and the House Committee on Rules. *Journal of Politics* 58:25–54.

Dion, Douglas, and John Huber. 1997. Sense and Sensibility: The Role of Rules. *American Journal of Political Science* 41:945–957.

Dogan, Rhys. 1997. Comitology: Little Procedures with Big Implications. *West European Politics* 20, 3 (Winter):31–60.

Dowding, Keith. 2000. Institutionalist Research on the European Union. *European Union Politics* 1, 1:125–144.

Earnshaw, David, and David Judge. 1993. The European Parliament and the Sweeteners Directive: From Footnote to Inter-Institutional Conflict. *Journal of Common Market Studies* 31, 1 (March):103–116.

Earnshaw, David, and David Judge. 1997. The Life and Times of the European Union's Co-operation Procedure. *Journal of Common Market Studies* 35, 4 (December):543–564.

Elles, Lady Diana. 1989. The innovations introduced by the Single European Act: Some Big Steps Forward. In *Legislation for Europe 1992*, edited by Jürgen Schwarze, 45–51. Baden-Baden: Nomos Verlagsgesellschaft.

Emiliou, Nicholas. 1994. Opening Pandora's Box: The Legal Basis of Community Measures Before the Court of Justice. *European Law Review* 19:488–507.

Ensminger, Jean, and Jack Knight. 1997. Changing Social Norms: Common Property, Bridewealth, and Clan Exogamy. *Current Anthropology* 38:1–24.

Epstein, Lee, and Jack Knight. 1998. *The Choices Justices Make*. Washington, DC: Congressional Quarterly Press.

European Law Review. 1982. Overriding the British Farm Price "Veto." 7, 3 (June):145–146.

European Parliament [EP]. 1970. PE Doc. 161/70, Rapport fait au nom de la commission des affaires sociales et de la santé publique sur la lutte contre la pollution des eaux fluviales et notamment des eaux du Rhin [Rapporteur: M. Boersma]. 11 November.

European Parliament [EP]. 1972. PE Doc. 9/72, Rapport fait au nom de la commission des affaires sociales et de la santé publique sur la première communication de la Commission des Communautés européennes sur la politique de la Communauté en matière d'environnement [Rapporteur: Jahn]. 14 April.

European Parliament [EP]. 1999. *The European Union and Food Security: Lessons from the BSE Crisis*. Luxembourg: OOPEC.

Farrell, Henry, and Adrienne Héritier. 2003. Formal and Informal Institutions Under Codecision: Continuous Constitution-Building in Europe. *Governance* 16, 4 (October):577–600.

Field, Alexander James. 1979. On the Explanation of Rules Using Rational Choice Models. *Journal of Economic Issues* 13:49–72.

Field, Alexander James. 1981. The Problem with Neoclassical Institutional Economics: A Critique with Special Reference to the North/Thomas Model of Pre-1500 Europe. *Explorations in Economic History* 18:174–198.

Field, Alexander James. 1984. Microeconomics, Norms, and Rationality. *Economic Development and Cultural Change* 32, 4 (July):683–711.

Firmin-Sellers, Kathryn. 1996. *The Transformation of Property Rights in the Gold Coast: An Empirical Analysis Applying Rational Choice Theory*. New York: Cambridge University Press.

Fitzmaurice, John. 1988. An Analysis of the European Community's Co-Operation Procedure. *Journal of Common Market Studies* 26, 4 (June):389–400.

Flynn, James. 1987. How Will Article 100A(4) Work? A Comparison with Article 93. *Common Market Law Review* 24:689–707.

Franchino, Fabio. 2000. Control of the Commission's Executive Functions: Uncertainty, Conflict, and Decision Rules. *European Union Politics* 1, 1:63–92.

Franchino, Fabio. 2002. Efficiency or Credibility? Testing the Two Logics of Delegation to the European Commission. *Journal of European Public Policy* 9, 5 (October):677–694.

Freestone, David, and Diane Ryland. 1994. EC Environmental Law after Maastricht. *Northern Ireland Legal Quarterly* 45, 2 (Summer):152–176.

Friedman, Milton. 1953. The Methodology of Positive Economics. In *Essays in Positive Economics*, 3–43. Chicago: University of Chicago Press.

Garcia, Thierry. 1997. Crise de la "Vache Folle," Crise dans l'Union Européenne. *Revue du Marché commun et de l'Union européenne* 407 (April):243–252.

Garrett, Geoffrey. 1992. International Cooperation and Institutional Choice: The European Community's Internal Market. *International Organization* 46, 2 (Spring):533–560.

Garrett, Geoffrey. 1995a. From the Luxembourg Compromise to Codecision: Decision Making in the European Union. *Electoral Studies* 14:289–308.
Garrett, Geoffrey. 1995b. The Politics of Legal Integration in the European Union. *International Organization* 49, 1 (Winter):171–182.
Garrett, Geoffrey, R. Daniel Kelemen, and Heiner Schulz. 1998. The European Court of Justice, National Governments, and Legal Integration in the European Union. *International Organization* 52, 1 (Winter):149–176.
Garrett, Geoffrey, and George Tsebelis. 1996. An Institutional Critique of Intergovernmentalism. *International Organization* 50, 2 (Spring):237–268.
Garrett, Geoffrey, and George Tsebelis. 1998. More on the Co-Decision Endgame. *Journal of Legislative Studies* 3, 4 (Winter):139–143.
Garrett, Geoffrey, and George Tsebelis. 2001. Understanding Better the EU Legislative Process (in "Forum Section: The EU Legislative Process: Academics vs. Practitioners – Round 2"). *European Union Politics* 2, 3 (October): 353–361.
Garrett, Geoffrey, and Barry R. Weingast. 1993. Ideas, Interests, and Institutions: Constructing the European Community's Internal Market. In *Ideas and Foreign Policy: Beliefs, Institutions, and Political Change*, edited by Judith Goldstein and Robert O. Keohane, 173–206. Ithaca, NY: Cornell University Press.
Geradin, Damien. 1993a. The Legal Basis of the Waste Directive. *European Law Review* 18, 5 (October):418–427.
Geradin, Damien. 1993b. Trade and Environmental Protection: Community Harmonization and National Environmental Standards. *Yearbook of European Law* 13:151–199.
Geradin, Damien. 1995. Balancing Free Trade and Environment Protection: The Interplay Between the European Court of Justice and the Community Legislator. In *Trade and The Environment: The Search for Balance*, edited by James Cameron, Paul Demaret, and Damien Geradin, 204–241. London: Cameron May.
Gerard, Alain. 1975. Les limites et les moyens juridiques de l'intervention des Communautés Européennes en matière de l'environnement. *Cahiers de Droit Européen* 11, 1–2:14–30.
Goldberg, Victor P. 1974. Institutional Change and the Quasi-Invisible Hand. *Journal of Law and Economics* 17:461–492.
Golub, Jonathan. 1997. In the Shadow of the Vote? Decisionmaking Efficiency in the European Community 1974–1995. MPIfG Discussion Paper 97/3. Cologne: Max Planck Institut für Gesellschaftsforschung, December.
Golub, Jonathan. 1999. In the Shadow of the Vote? Decision Making in the European Community. *International Organization* 53, 4 (Autumn):733–764.
Golub, Jonathan. 2002. Institutional Reform and Decisionmaking in the European Union. In *Institutional Challenges in the European Union*, edited by Madeleine Hosli and Adrian van Deemen. London: Routledge.
Goodin, Robert E. 1996a. Institutions and Their Design. In *The Theory of Institutional Design*, edited by Robert E. Goodin, 1–53. New York: Cambridge University Press.
Goodin, Robert E., ed. 1996b. *The Theory of Institutional Design*. New York: Cambridge University Press.

Bibliography

Gosalbo Bono, Ricardo. 1994. Co-Decision: An Appraisal of the Experience of the European Parliament as Co-Legislator. *Yearbook of European Law* 14:21–71.

Goybet, Catherine. 1997. La Vache Folle Fera-t-elle Évoluer l'Europe? *Revue du Marché commun et de l'Union européenne* no. 407 (April):229–232.

Grabitz, Eberhard, and Christoph Sasse. 1977. *Competence of the European Communities for Environmental Policy: Proposal for an Amendment to the Treaty of Rome.* Berlin: Erich Schmidt Verlag.

Grafstein, Robert. 1992. *Institutional Realism: Social and Political Constraints on Rational Actors.* New Haven, CT: Yale University Press.

Granovetter, Mark. 1985. Economic Action and Social Structure: The Problem of Embeddedness. *American Journal of Sociology* 91, 3 (November):481–510.

Granovetter, Mark. 1992. Economic Institutions as Social Constructions: A Framework for Analysis. *Acta Sociologica* 35:3–11.

Greenpeace International. 1991. The Single European Dump: Free Trade in Hazardous and Nuclear Wastes in the New Europe. Available at URL *http://www.greenpeace.org/gopher/campaigns/toxics/1991/eurodump.txt* (accessed 26 June 2001). 4 December.

Gruber, Lloyd. 2000. *Ruling the World: Power Politics and the Rise of Supranational Institutions.* Princeton, NJ: Princeton University Press.

Gulmann, Claus. 1987. The Single European Act–Some Remarks from a Danish Perspective. *Common Market Law Review* 24:31–40.

Hall, Peter A., and Rosemary C. R. Taylor. 1996. Political Science and the Three New Institutionalisms. *Political Studies* 44 (December):936–957.

Hannequart, Jean-Pierre. 1979. Le Parlement européen et l'environnement. *Res Publica* 21, 1:127–143.

Harsanyi, John C. 1969. Rational-Choice Models of Political Behavior vs. Functionalist and Conformist Theories. *World Politics* 21, 4 (July):513–538.

Hildyard, Nicholas. 1993. Maastricht: The Protectionism of Free Trade. *Ecologist* 23, 2 (March/April):45–51.

Hix, Simon. 1999a. Constitutional Agenda-Setting Through Discretion in Rule Interpretation: Why the European Parliament Won at Amsterdam. Presented at the Annual Meeting of the American Political Science Association, Atlanta, GA, 2–5 September.

Hix, Simon. 1999b. *The Political System of the European Union.* New York: St. Martin's Press.

Hix, Simon. 2002. Constitutional Agenda-Setting Through Discretion in Rule Interpretation: Why the European Parliament Won at Amsterdam. *British Journal of Political Science* 32, 2 (April):259–280.

Hix, Simon, Amie Kreppel, and Abdul Noury. 2003. The Party System in the European Parliament: Collusive or Competitive? *Journal of Common Market Studies* 41, 2:309–331.

Hix, Simon, Abdul Noury, and Gérard Roland. 2003. Power to the Parties: Cohesion and Competition in the European Parliament, 1979–2001. Unpublished manuscript, URL *http://www.lse-students.ac.uk/HIX/Working%20Papers/HNR-Power%20to%20the%20Parties-June03.pdf* (last consulted 1 July 2003).

Hooghe, Liesbet. 1999a. Images of Europe: Orientations to European Integration Among Senior Commission Officials. *British Journal of Political Science* 29, 2:345–373.

Hooghe, Liesbet. 1999b. Supranational Activists or Intergovernmental Agents? Explaining Orientations of Senior Commission Officials Towards European Integration. *Comparative Political Studies* 32, 4:435–463.

Hooghe, Liesbet. 2001. Top Commission Officials on Capitalism: An Institutionalist Understanding of Preferences. In *The Rules of Integration: Institutionalist Approaches to the Study of Europe*, edited by Mark Aspinwall and Gerald Schneider, 152–173. Manchester: Manchester University Press.

Hooghe, Liesbet. 2002. *The European Commission and the Integration of Europe: Images of Governance*. Cambridge: Cambridge University Press, 2002.

Horn, Murray J. 1995. *The Political Economy of Public Administration: Institutional Choice in the Public Sector*. New York: Cambridge University Press.

House of Commons Select Committee on European Legislation. 1984. *First Special Report*, Session 1983–84, HC 126–iv. London: Her Majesty's Stationery Office.

House of Commons Select Committee on European Legislation. 1988. *Choice of Treaty Base after the Single European Act*, Session 1987–88, HC 178–iv and 178–v. London: Her Majesty's Stationery Office.

House of Lords Select Committee on the European Communities. 1978. *Approximation of Laws Under Article 100 of the EEC Treaty*. Session 1977–78, 22nd Report. London: Her Majesty's Stationery Office.

Huber, John D. 1992. Restrictive Legislative Procedures in France and the United States. *American Political Science Review* 86:675–687.

Huber, John D. 1996. *Rationalizing Parliament: Legislative Institutions and Party Politics in France*. New York: Cambridge University Press.

Hubschmid, Claudia, and Peter Moser. 1997. The Co-operation Procedure in the EU: Why Was the European Parliament Influential in the Decision on Car Emission Standards? *Journal of Common Market Studies* 35:225–242.

Hug, Simon. 1997. The Commission as a Pawn to the Member Countries: Comment to Christophe Crombez. *Aussenwirtschaft* 52, 1/2:83–86.

Hug, Simon. 2003. Endogenous Preferences and Delegation in the European Union. *Comparative Political Studies* 36, 1/2:41–74.

Hug, Simon, and Thomas König. 2002. In View of Ratification: Governmental Preferences and Domestic Constraints at the Amsterdam Intergovernmental Conference. *International Organization* 56, 2 (Spring 2002):447–476.

Immergut, Ellen M. 1998. The Theoretical Core of the New Institutionalism. *Politics & Society* 26, 1 (March):5–34.

Jacqué, Jean-Paul. 1986. The "Single European Act" and Environmental Policy. *Environmental Policy and Law* 16:122–124.

Judge, David. 1993. "Predestined to Save the Earth": The Environment Committee of the European Parliament. In *A Green Dimension for the European Community: Political Issues and Processes*, edited by David Judge, 186–212. London: Frank Cass.

Bibliography

Judge, David, and David Earnshaw. 1994. Weak European Parliament Influence? A Study of the Environment Committee of the European Parliament. *Government and Opposition* 29, 2 (Spring):262–276.

Judge, David, David Earnshaw, and Ngaire Cowan. 1994. Ripples or Waves? The European Parliament in the European Community Policy Process. *Journal of European Public Policy* 1, 1 (June):27–52.

Jupille, Joseph. 1996. Free Movement of Goods and Hazardous Waste: Reconciling the Single Market with Environmental Imperatives. Paper presented at the 37th Annual Meeting of the International Studies Association (ISA), San Diego, CA, 6–20 April.

Jupille, Joseph. 1999. The European Union and International Outcomes. *International Organization* 53, 2 (Spring):409–425.

Jupille, Joseph, and James A. Caporaso. 1999. Institutionalism and the European Union: Beyond International Relations and Comparative Politics. *Annual Review of Political Science* 2:409–425.

Jupille, Joseph, James A. Caporaso, and Jeffrey T. Checkel. 2003. Integrating Institutions: Rationalism, Constructivism, and the Study of the European Union. *Comparative Political Studies* 36, 1–2 (February/March):7–40.

Kapteyn, P. J. G., and P. VerLoren van Themaat. 1998. *Introduction to the Law of the European Communities: From Maastricht to Amsterdam*, 3rd edition. London: Kluwer Law International.

Kato, Junko. 1996. Institutions and Rationality in Politics: Three Varieties of Neo-Institutionalists. *British Journal of Political Science* 26, 4:553–582.

Keeler, John T. S. 1993. Executive Power and Policymaking Patterns in France: Gauging the Impact of Fifth Republic Institutions. *West European Politics* 16 (October):518–544.

Kelemen, R. Daniel. 1995. Environmental Policy in the European Union: The Struggle Between Court, Commission and Council. In *Convergence or Diversity? Internationalization and Economic Policy Response*, edited by Birgitte Unger and Frans Van Waarden, 306–332. Brookfield: Averbury.

Keohane, Robert O. 1984. *After Hegemony: Cooperation and Discord in the World Political Economy*. Princeton, NJ: Princeton University Press.

Kiewiet, D. Roderick, and Mathew D. McCubbins. 1991. *The Logic of Delegation: Congressional Parties and the Appropriations Process*. Chicago: University of Chicago Press.

Kim, Hee-Min, and Richard C. Fording. 2001. Extending Party Estimates to Governments and Electors. In *Mapping Policy Preferences: Estimates for Parties, Electors, and Governments 1945–1998*, edited by Ian Budge et al., 157–178. New York: Oxford University Press.

King, David C. 1997. *Turf Wars: How Congressional Committees Claim Jurisdiction*. Chicago: University of Chicago Press.

King, Gary, and Langche Zeng. 2001a. Logistic Regression in Rare Events Data. *Political Analysis* 9, 2:137–163.

King, Gary, and Langche Zeng. 2001b. Explaining Rare Events in International Relations. *International Organization* 55, 3 (Summer):693–715.

Kirchner, Emil, and Karen Williams. 1983. The Legal, Political and Institutional Implications of the 1980 Isoglucose Judgements. *Journal of Common Market Studies* 22 (2):173–190.

Kiser, Larry L., and Elinor Ostrom. 1982. The Three Worlds of Action: A Metatheoretical Synthesis of Institutional Approaches. In *Strategies of Political Inquiry*, edited by Elinor Ostrom, 179–219. Beverly Hills, CA: Sage Publications.

Knight, Jack. 1992. *Institutions and Social Conflict*. New York: Cambridge University Press.

Knill, Christophe, and Andrea Lenschow. 2001. "Seek and Ye Shall Find!" Linking Different Perspectives on Institutional Change. *Comparative Political Studies* 34, 2 (March):187–215.

Koelble, Thomas A. 1995. The New Institutionalism in Political Science and Sociology. *Comparative Politics* 27, 2 (January):231–243.

König, Thomas. 2001. Pivotal Politics in European Legislation: An Event History Analysis of the EU Legislative Decision-Making Process from 1984 to 1995. Delivered at the ECPR Joint Sessions, Grenoble, France.

König, Thomas, and Thomas, Bräuninger. 2000. Decisiveness and Inclusiveness: Two Aspects of the Intergovernmental Choice of European Voting Rules. *Homo Oeconomicus* 17, 1/2:1–17.

König, Thomas, and Mirja Pöter. 2001. Examining the EU Legislative Process. *European Union Politics* 2, 3 (October):329–352.

Koremenos, Barbara, Charles Lipson, and Duncan Snidal, eds. 2001. *The Rational Design of International Institutions*. Special issue of *International Organization* (vol. 55. n. 4).

Krämer, Ludwig. 1987. The Single European Act and Environmental Protection: Reflections on Several New Provisions in Community Law. *Common Market Law Review* 24:659–688.

Krämer, Ludwig. 1991. Community Environmental Law: Towards a Systematic Approach. *Yearbook of European Law* 11:151–184.

Krämer, Ludwig. 1992. *Focus on European Environmental Law*. London: Sweet & Maxwell.

Krämer, Ludwig. 1993. *European Environmental Law Casebook*. London: Sweet & Maxwell.

Krämer, Ludwig. 1998. *E. C. Treaty and Environmental Law*, 3rd edition. London: Sweet and Maxwell.

Krämer, Ludwig. N.d. La base juridique dans le domaine de l'environnement: articles 100A et 130S du traité. European Commission unnumbered memo.

Kranz, Jerzy. 1982. Le vote dans la pratique du Conseil des ministres des Communautés européennes. *Revue Trimestrielle de Droit Européen* 18, 3 (July–September):403–430.

Krasner, Stephen D. 1984. Approaches to the State: Alternative Conceptions and Historical Dynamics. *Comparative Politics* 16, 2 (January):223–246.

Krasner, Stephen D. 1985. *Structural Conflict: The Third World Against Global Liberalism*. Berkeley: University of California Press.

Bibliography

Krasner, Stephen D. 1991. Global Communications and National Power: Life on the Pareto Frontier. *World Politics* 43:336–366.
Krehbiel, Keith. 1986. Unanimous Consent Agreements: Going Along in the Senate. *Journal of Politics* 48, 3 (August):541–564.
Krehbiel, Keith. 1988. Spatial Models of Legislative Choice. *Legislative Studies Quarterly* 13, 3 (August):259–319.
Krehbiel, Keith. 1991. *Information and Legislative Organization*. Ann Arbor: University of Michigan Press.
Krehbiel, Keith. 1997a. Restrictive rules reconsidered. *American Journal of Political Science* 41:919–947.
Krehbiel, Keith. 1997b. Rejoinder to "Sense and Sensibility." *American Journal of Political Science* 41:958–964.
Krehbiel, Keith. 1998. *Pivotal Politics: A Theory of U.S. Lawmaking*. Chicago: University of Chicago Press.
Krehbiel, Keith, and Douglas Rivers. 1988. The Analysis of Committee Power: An Application to Senate Voting on the Minimum Wage. *American Journal of Political Science* 32, 4 (November):1151–1174.
Krehbiel, Keith, Kenneth A. Shepsle, and Barry R. Weingast. 1987. Why Are Congressional Committees Powerful? *American Political Science Review* 81, 3 (September):929–945.
Kreppel, Amie. 1999. What Affects the European Parliament's Legislative Influence? An Analysis of the Success of EP Amendments. *Journal of Common Market Studies* 37, 3 (September): 521–538.
Kreppel, Amie. 2000. Rules, Ideology and Coalition Formation in the European Parliament: Past Present and Future. *European Union Politics* 1, 3:340–362.
Kreppel, Amie. 2002a. *The European Parliament and the Supranational Party System: A Study of Institutional Development*. New York: Cambridge University Press.
Kreppel, Amie. 2002b. Moving Beyond Procedure: An Empirical Analysis of EP Legislative Influence. *Comparative Political Studies* 35, 7:784–813.
Kreppel, Amie, and Simon Hix. 2003. From "Grand Coalition" to Left-Right Confrontation: Explaining the Shifting Structure of Party Competition in the European Parliament. *Comparative Political Studies* 36, 1–2:75–96.
Kreppel, Amie, and George Tsebelis. 1999. Coalition Formation in the European Parliament. *Comparative Political Studies* 32, 8:933–66.
Lange, Peter. 1993. Maastricht and the Social Protocol: Why Did They Do It? *Politics & Society* 21 (March):5–36.
Langeheine, Bernd. 1989. Le rapprochement des législations nationales selon l'article 100A du traité CEE: L'harmonisation communautaire face aux exigences de protection nationales. *Revue du Marché Commun* 328 (June):347–359.
Laver, Michael, and John Garry. 2000. Estimating Policy Positions from Political Texts. *American Journal of Political Science* 44:619–634.
Laver, Michael, and W. Ben Hunt. 1992. *Policy and Party Competition*. New York: Routledge.
Lenaerts, Koen. 1992. Some Thoughts About the Interaction Between Judges and Politicians in the European Community. *Yearbook of European Law* 12:1–34.

Lenaerts, Koen. 1994. The Principle of Subsidiarity and the Environment in the European Union: Keeping the Balance of Federalism. *Fordham International Law Journal* 17, 4:846–895.

Levi, Margaret. 1988. *Of Rule and Revenue*. Berkeley: University of California Press.

Levi, Margaret. 1990. A Logic of Institutional Change. In *The Limits of Rationality*, edited by Karen Schweers Cook and Margaret Levi, 402–418. Chicago: University of Chicago Press.

Liao, Tim Futing. 1994. *Interpreting Probability Models: Logit, Probit, and Other Generalized Linear Models*. Thousand Oaks, CA: Sage.

Lijphart, Arend. 1975. The Comparable-Cases Strategy in Comparative Research. *Comparative Political Studies* 8, 2 (July):158–177.

Lodge, Juliet. 1987. The Single European Act and the New Legislative Cooperation Procedure: A Critical Analysis. *Journal of European Integration* 11, 1 (Fall):5–28.

London, Caroline, and Michael Llamas. 1995. *Protection of the Environment and the Free Movement of Goods*. London: Butterworths.

Long, J. Scott. 1997. *Regression Models for Categorical and Limited Dependent Variables*. Thousand Oaks, CA: Sage.

Lord Cockfield. 1994. *The European Union: Creating the Single Market*. London: Wiley Chancery Law.

Lord Slynn of Hadley. 1993. Looking at European Community Texts. *Statute Law Review* 14, 1 (Summer):12–27.

Lowndes, Vivien. 1996. Varieties of New Institutionalism: A Critical Appraisal. *Public Administration* 74 (Summer):181–197.

Macrory, Richard. 1991. European Court Shakes Up Legal Basis of EEC Environmental Policy. *ENDS Report* 197 (June):15–16.

Majone, Giandomenico. 1989. *Evidence, Argument and Persuasion in the Policy Process*. New Haven, CT: Yale University Press.

Majone, Giandomenico. 1993. The European Community Between Social Policy and Social Regulation. *Journal of Common Market Studies* 31 (June):153–170.

Mann, Michael. 1984. The Autonomous Power of the State: Its Origins, Mechanisms, and Results. *Archives européennes de sociologie* 25:185–213.

March, James G., and Johan P. Olsen. 1989. *Rediscovering Institutions: The Organizational Basis of Politics*. New York: Basic Books.

Marks, Gary, and Liesbet Hooghe. 2001. *Multi-level Governance and European Integration*. Boulder, CO: Rowman & Littlefield.

Marks, Gary, Liesbet Hooghe, and Kermit Blank. 1996. European Integration from the 1980s: State-Centric v. Multi-Level Governance. *Journal of Common Market Studies* 34, 3 (September):341–377.

Martin, Lisa L. 1993. International and Domestic Institutions in the EMU Process. *Economics and Politics* 5, 2 (July):125–144.

Matthews, R. C. O. 1986. The Economics of Institutions and the Sources of Growth. *Economic Journal* 96 (December):903–918.

Mattila, Mikko, and Jan-Erik Lane. 2001. Why Unanimity in the Council? A Roll Call Analysis of Council Voting. *European Union Politics* 2, 1:31–52.

Bibliography

Mattli, Walter. 2001. Private Justice in a Global Economy: From Litigation to Arbitration. *International Organization* 55, 4 (Autumn):919–948.

Mattli, Walter, and Anne-Marie Slaughter. 1995. Law and Politics in the European Union: A Reply to Garrett. *International Organization* 49, 1 (Winter):183–190.

Mattli, Walter, and Anne-Marie Slaughter. 1998. Revisiting the European Court of Justice. *International Organization* 52, 1 (Winter):177–210.

Maurer, Andreas. 2001. Democratic Governance in the European Union: The Institutional Terrain After Amsterdam. In *The Treaty of Amsterdam: Challenges and Opportunities for the European Union*, edited by Jörg Monar and Wolfgang Wessels. London: Continuum.

Maurer, Andreas, Wolfgang Wessels, and Jürgen Mittag. 2000. Europeanisation in and of the EU System: Trends, Offers, and Constraints. Paper for the DFG workshop "Linking EU and National Governance," Mannheim, Germany, 1–3 June.

McCormick, John. 2001. *Environmental Policy in the European Union*. New York: Palgrave.

McCown, Margaret. 2001. The Use of Judge-made Law in European Judicial Integration: Precedent-based Arguments in EU Inter-institutional Disputes. Presented at the 7th Biennial Conference of the European Community Studies Association (ECSA), Madison, WI, 30 May–2 June 2001.

McCown, Margaret. 2003. The European Parliament Before the Bench: ECJ Precedent and EP Litigation Strategies. *Journal of European Public Policy* 10, 6 (December):974–995.

McKelvey, Richard D. 1976. Intransitivities in Multidimensional Voting Models and Some Implications for Agenda Control. *Journal of Economic Theory* 12:472–482.

McKelvey, Richard D., and Peter C. Ordeshook. 1984. An Experimental Study of the Effects of Procedural Rules on Committee Behavior. *Journal of Politics* 46, 1 (February):182–205.

McNiel, Dale E. 1998. The first case under the WTO's Sanitary and Phytosanitary Agreement: The European Union's Hormone Ban. *Virginia Journal of International Law* 39, 1 (Fall):89–134.

Mearsheimer, John J. 1994/95. The False Promise of International Institutions. *International Security* 19, 3 (Winter):5–49.

Mearsheimer, John J. 1995. A Realist Reply. *International Security* 20, 1 (Summer):82–93.

Menard, Scott. 1995. *Applied Logistic Regression Analysis*. Quantitative Applications in the Social Sciences Series, Number 07-106. Thousand Oaks, CA: Sage.

Milas, René. 1985. La concurrence entre les bases légales des actes communautaires. *Revue du Marché commun* no. 289 (July–August):445–448.

Milgrom, Paul R., Douglass C. North, and Barry R. Weingast. 1990. The Role of Institutions in the Revival of Trade: The Law Merchant, Private Judges, and the Champagne Fairs. *Economics and Politics* 2:1–23.

Milgrom, Paul, and John Roberts. 1990. Bargaining Costs, Influence Costs, and the Organization of Economic Activity. In *Perspectives on Positive Political Economy*, edited by James E. Alt and Kenneth A. Shepsle, 57–89. New York: Cambridge University Press.

Moberg, Axel. 2002. The Nice Treaty and Voting Rules in the Council. *Journal of Common Market Studies* 40 (2):259–282.

Moe, Terry M. 1990a. Political Institutions: The Neglected Side of the Story. *Journal of Law, Economics, and Organization* 6 (Special Issue):213–266.

Moe, Terry M. 1990b. The Politics of Structural Choice: Toward a Theory of Public Bureaucracy. In *Organization Theory: From Chester Barnard to the Present and Beyond*, edited by Oliver E. Williamson, 116–153. New York: Oxford University Press.

Moravcsik, Andrew. 1991. Negotiating the Single European Act: National Interests and Conventional Statecraft in the European Community. *International Organization* 45 (Winter):19–56.

Moravcsik, Andrew. 1993. Preferences and Power in the European Community: A Liberal Intergovernmentalist Approach. *Journal of Common Market Studies* 31, 4 (December):473–524.

Moravcsik, Andrew. 1995. Liberal Intergovernmentalism and Integration: A Rejoinder. *Journal of Common Market Studies* 33, 4 (December):611–628.

Moravcsik, Andrew. 1997. Taking Preferences Seriously: A Liberal Theory of International Politics. *International Organization* 51, 4 (Autumn):513–554.

Moravcsik, Andrew. 1998. *The Choice for Europe: Social Purpose and State Power from Messina to Maastricht*. Ithaca, NY: Cornell University Press.

Moravcsik, Andrew. 1999a. *The Choice for Europe*: Current Commentary and Future Research: A Response to James Caporaso, Fritz Scharpf, and Helen Wallace. *Journal of European Public Policy* 6, 1 (March):155–179.

Moravcsik, Andrew. 1999b. The Future of European Integration Studies: Social Science or Social Theory? *Millennium* 28, 2:371–391.

Moravcsik, Andrew, and Kalypso Nicolaïdis. 1999. Explaining the Treaty of Amsterdam: Interests, Influence, and Institutions. *Journal of Common Market Studies* 37, 1 (March):59–85.

Moser, Peter. 1996. The European Parliament as a Conditional Agenda Setter: What Are the Conditions? *American Political Science Review* 90:834–838.

Moser, Peter. 1997a. A Theory of the Conditional Influence of the European Parliament in the Cooperation Procedure. *Public Choice* 91:333–350.

Moser, Peter. 1997b. The Benefits of the Conciliation Procedure for the European Parliament: Comment to George Tsebelis. *Aussenwirtschaft* 52, 1/2:57–62.

Moser, Peter. 1999. The Impact of Legislative Institutions on Public Policy: A Survey. *European Journal of Political Economy* 15:1–33.

Müller, Wolfgang C., and Kaare Strøm, eds. 1999. *Policy, Office or Votes? How Political Parties in Western Europe Make Hard Decisions*. New York: Cambridge University Press.

Nicoll, William. 1984. The Luxembourg Compromise. *Journal of Common Market Studies* 23, 1 (September):35–43.

Bibliography

Nicoll, William. 1988. Le Dialogue Législatif entre le Parlement Européen et la Commission: La procédure de renvoi en commission du Parlement Européen. *Revue du Marché Commun* 316 (April):240–242.

Niskanen, William A. 1971. *Bureaucracy and Representative Government*. Chicago: Aldine.

North, Douglass C. 1981. *Structure and Change in Economic History*. New York: W. W. Norton.

North, Douglass C. 1990. *Institutions, Institutional Change, and Economic Performance*. New York: Cambridge University Press.

North, Douglass C., and Robert Paul Thomas. 1973. *The Rise of the Western World: A New Economic History*. New York: Cambridge University Press.

Oberschall, Anthony, and Eric M. Leifer. 1986. Efficiency and Social Institutions: Uses and Misuses of Economic Reasoning in Sociology. *Annual Review of Sociology* 12:233–253.

Oleszek, Walter J. 2001. *Congressional Procedures and the Policy Process*, 5th edition. Washington, DC: CQ Press.

O'Neill, Michael. 1994. The Choice of Legal Basis: More Than a Number. *Irish Journal of European Law* 1:44–58.

Ostrom, Elinor. 1990. *Governing the Commons: The Evolution of Institutions for Collective Action*. New York: Cambridge University Press.

Ostrom, Elinor. 1995. Constituting Social Capital and Collective Action. In *Local Commons and Global Interdependence: Heterogeneity and Cooperation in Two Domains*, edited by Robert O. Keohane and Elinor Ostrom, 125–160. Thousand Oaks, CA: Sage Publications.

Pescatore, Pierre. 1987. Some Critical Remarks on the "Single European Act." *Common Market Law Review* 24, 1 (Spring):9–18.

Peter, Bertrand. 1994. La Base Juridique des Actes en Droit Communautaire. *Revue du Marché commun et de l'Union Européenne* no. 378 (May):324–333.

Peters, B. Guy. 1991. Bureaucratic Politics and the Institutions of the European Community. In *Euro-Politics: Institutions and Policymaking in the "New" European Community*, edited by Alberta M. Sbragia, 75–122. Washington, DC: Brookings Institution.

Peters, B. Guy. 1994. Agenda-setting in the European Community. *Journal of European Public Policy* 1, 1 (June):9–26.

Pierson, Paul. 1996. The Path to European Integration: A Historical Institutionalist Analysis. *Comparative Political Studies* 29, 2 (April):123–163.

Pierson, Paul. 2000a. Increasing Returns, Path Dependence, and the Study of Politics. *American Political Science Review* 94, 2 (June):251–268.

Pierson, Paul. 2000b. The Limits of Design: Explaining Institutional Origins and Change. *Governance* 13, 4 (October):475–499.

Pollack, Mark A. 1996. The New Institutionalism and EC Governance: The Promise and Limits of Institutional Analysis. *Governance* 9, 4 (October):429–458.

Pollack, Mark A. 1997. Delegation, Agency, and Agenda Setting in the European Community. *International Organization* 51, 1 (Winter):99–134.

Pollack, Mark A. 2003. *The Engines of Integration: Delegation, Agency, and Agency Setting in the European Union*. Oxford: Oxford University Press.

Przeworski, Adam, and Henry Teune. 1970. *The Logic of Comparative Social Inquiry*. New York: Wiley Interscience.

Rasmussen, Anders. 2000. Institutional Games Rational Actors Play – The Empowering of the European Parliament. *European Integration Online Papers* 4 (1).

Rasmussen, Hjalte. 1986. *On Law and Policy in the European Court of Justice*. Dordrecht: Martinus Nijhoff.

Ray, Leonard. 1999. Measuring Party Orientations Towards European Integration: Results from an Expert Survey. *European Journal of Political Research* 36:283–306.

Rehbinder, Eckard, and Richard Stewart. 1985. *Integration Through Law*, vol. 2, *Environmental Protection Policy*. Berlin: Walter de Gruyter.

Rhodes, Martin. 1995. A Regulatory Conundrum: Industrial Relations and the Social Dimension. In *European Social Policy: Between Fragmentation and Integration*, edited by Stephan Leibfried and Paul Pierson, 78–122. Washington, DC: Brookings Institution.

Riker, William H. 1980. Implications from the Disequilibrium of Majority Rule for the Study of Institutions. *American Political Science Review* 74:432–446.

Riker, William H. 1983. Political Theory and the Art of Heresthetics. In *Political Science: The State of the Discipline*, edited by Ada W. Finifter, 47–67. Washington, DC: American Political Science Association.

Riker, William H. 1984. The Heresthetics of Constitution-Making: The Presidency in 1787, with Comments on Determinism and Rational Choice. *American Political Science Review* 78, 1 (March):1–16.

Rittberger, Berthold. 2003. The Creation and Empowerment of the European Parliament. *Journal of Common Market Studies* 41, 2 (April):203–225.

Robinson, Jonathan. 1992. The Legal Basis of EC Environmental Law. *Journal of Environmental Law* 4, 1:109–120.

Roselsky, Kurt M. 1993. Legal Basis and International Implications of Council Regulation on the Supervision and Control of Shipments of Hazardous Waste. *Georgia Journal of International and Comparative Law* 23 (1):111–139.

Sandholtz, Wayne. 1996. Membership Matters: Limits of the Functional Approach to European Institutions. *Journal of Common Market Studies* 34:403–429.

Sbragia, Alberta. 1996. Environmental Policy: The "Push-Pull" of Policy-Making. In *Policy-Making in the European Union*, 3rd edition, edited by Helen Wallace and William Wallace, 235–255. Oxford: Oxford University Press.

Scharpf, Fritz W. 1999. Selecting Cases and Testing Hypotheses. *Journal of European Public Policy* 6, 1 (March):164–168.

Scharpf, Fritz W. 2000. *Governing in Europe: Effective and Democratic?* New York: Oxford University Press.

Schattschneider, E. E. 1960. *The Semisovereign People: A Realist's View of Democracy in America*. New York: Holt, Rinehart and Winston.

Schickler, Eric, and Andrew Rich. 1997a. Controlling the Floor: Parties as Procedural Coalitions in the House. *American Journal of Political Science* 41:1340–1375.

Bibliography

Schickler, Eric, and Andrew Rich. 1997b. Party Government in the House Reconsidered: A Response to Cox and McCubbins. *American Journal of Political Science* 41:1387–1394.

Schmidt, Alke. 1995. Trade in Waste Under Community Law. In *Trade & The Environment: The Search for Balance*, edited by James Cameron, Paul Demaret, and Damien Geradin, 184–203. London: Cameron May.

Schneider, Gerald. 2001a. Comment on Hooghe. In *The Rules of Integration: Institutionalist Approaches to the Study of Europe*, edited by Mark Aspinwall and Gerald Schneider, 174–176. Manchester: Manchester University Press.

Schneider, Gerald. 2001b. Ideas, Mad Cows, and European Integration: An Institutionalist Analysis of the BSE Crisis. Paper presented at the conference "Institutionalism and the Study of the European Union," University of Washington, Seattle, WA, 4–5 May.

Schneider, Gerald, and Mark Aspinwall, eds. 2001. *The Rules of Integration: Institutionalist Approaches to the Study of Europe*. Manchester: Manchester University Press.

Schotter, Andrew. 1981. *The Economic Theory of Social Institutions*. New York: Cambridge University Press.

Schulz, Heiner, and Thomas König. 2000. Institutional Reform and Decision-Making Efficiency in the European Union. *American Journal of Political Science* 44, 4 (October):653–666.

Scully, Roger M. 1997a. The European Parliament and the Co-Decision Procedure: A Reassessment. *Journal of Legislative Studies* 3, 3 (Autumn 1997):58–73.

Scully, Roger M. 1997b. The European Parliament and Co-Decision: A Rejoinder to Tsebelis and Garrett. *Journal of Legislative Studies* 3, 3 (Autumn 1997):93–103.

Sebenius, James K. 1983. Negotiation Arithmetic: Adding and Subtracting Issues and Parties. *International Organization* 37, 2 (Spring): 281–316.

Shepsle, Kenneth A. 1979. Institutional Arrangements and Equilibrium in Multidimensional Voting Models. *American Journal of Political Science* 23, 1 (February): 27–59.

Shepsle, Kenneth A. 1986. Institutional Equilibrium and Equilibrium Institutions. In *Political Science: The Science of Politics*, edited by Herbert F. Weisberg, 51–81. New York: Agathon Press.

Shepsle, Kenneth A. 1989. Studying Institutions: Some Lessons from the Rational Choice Approach. *Journal of Theoretical Politics* 1:131–147.

Shepsle, Kenneth A. 1993. Political Institutions and the New Institutional Economics. *Journal of Institutional and Theoretical Economics* 149 (1):347–350.

Shepsle, Kenneth A., and Barry R. Weingast. 1981. Political Preferences for the Pork Barrel: A Generalization. *American Journal of Political Science* 25, 1 (February):96–111.

Shepsle, Kenneth A., and Barry R. Weingast. 1984a. Uncovered Sets and Sophisticated Voting Outcomes with Implications for Agenda Institutions. *American Journal of Political Science* 28, 1 (February):49–74.

Shepsle, Kenneth A., and Barry R. Weingast. 1984b. When Do Rules of Procedure Matter? *Journal of Politics* 46, 1 (February 1984):206–221.

Shepsle, Kenneth A., and Barry R. Weingast. 1987. The Institutional Foundations of Committee Power. *American Political Science Review* 81:85–104.

Shvetsova, Olga. Endogenous Selection of Institutions and Their Exogenous Effects. *Constitutional Political Economy* 14:191–212.

Sinclair, Barbara. 1995. House Special Rules and the Institutional Design Controversy. In *Positive Theories of Congressional Institutions*, edited by Kenneth A. Shepsle and Barry R. Weingast, 235–252. Ann Arbor: University of Michigan Press.

Skroback, Andrew Evans. 1994. Even a Sacred Cow Must Live in a Green Pasture: The Proximity Principle, Free Movement of Goods, and Regulation 259/93 on Transfrontier Waste Shipments Within the EC. *Boston College International and Comparative Law Review* 17, 1 (Winter):85–110.

Snidal, Duncan. 1995. The Politics of Scope: Endogenous Actors, Heterogeneity, and Institutions. In *Local Commons and Global Interdependence: Heterogeneity and Cooperation in Two Domains*, edited by Robert O. Keohane and Elinor Ostrom, 47–70. Thousand Oaks, CA: Sage Publications.

Snidal, Duncan. 1996. Political Economy and International Institutions. *International Review of Law and Economics* 16 (March):121–137.

Sommer, Julia. 1994. Les déchets, de l'autosuffisance et de la libre circulation des marchandises. *Revue du Marché commun et de l'Union européenne* no. 377 (April):246–257.

Somsen, Hans. 1992. Case Note C-300/89, *Commission v. Council* (Titanium dioxide). *Common Market Law Review* 29:140–151.

Somsen, Hans. 1993. Case Note C-155/91, *Commission v. Council*. *European Environmental Law Review* 2, 5 (May):121–129.

Sprinz, Detlef, and Tapani Vaahtoranta. 1994. The Interest-based Explanation of International Environmental Policy. *International Organization* 48, 1 (Winter):77–106.

Stacey, Jeffrey, and Berthold Rittberger. 2003. Dynamics of Formal and Informal Institutional Change in the EU. *Journal of European Public Policy* 10, 6 (December):858–883.

Steiger, Heinhard. 1977. *Competence of the European Parliament for Environmental Policy*. Berlin: Erich Schmidt Verlag.

Steunenberg, Bernard. 1994. Decision Making Under Different Institutional Arrangements: Legislation by the European Community. *Journal of Institutional and Theoretical Economics* 150, 4 (December):642–669.

Steunenberg, Bernard. 1997. Codecision and Its Reform: A Comparative Analysis of Decision Making Rules in the European Union. In *Political Institutions and Public Policy: Perspectives on European Decision Making*, edited by Bernard Steunenberg and Frans Van Vught, 205–229. Dordrecht, the Netherlands: Kluwer Academic Publishers.

Steunenberg, Bernard. 1998. Constitutional Change in the European Union: Parliament's Impact on the Reform of the Codecision Procedure. Unpublished manuscript, University of Twente, 17 September.

Steunenberg, Bernard, and Antoaneta Dimitrova. 1999. Interests, Legitimacy, and Constitutional Choice: The Extension of the Codecision Procedure in

Bibliography

Amsterdam. Prepared for the workshop "Enlarging or Deepening: European Integration at the Crossroads" at the Joint Sessions of Workshops of the European Consortium for Political Research, Mannheim, Germany, 26–31 March.

Steunenberg, Bernard, Dieter Schmidtchen, and Christian Koboldt. 1999. Strategic Power in the European Union: Evaluating the Distribution of Power in Policy Games. *Journal of Theoretical Politics* 11, 3 (July):339–366.

Stone Sweet, Alec. 2000. *Governing with Judges: Constitutional Politics in Europe.* Oxford: Oxford University Press.

Stone Sweet, Alec, Neil Fligstein, and Wayne Sandholtz. 2001. The Institutionalization of European Space. In *The Institutionalization of Europe*, edited by Alec Stone Sweet, Wayne Sandholtz, and Neil Fligstein, 1–28. Oxford: Oxford University Press.

Strom, Gerald S. 1990. *The Logic of Lawmaking: A Spatial Theory Approach.* Baltimore: Johns Hopkins University Press.

Strøm, Kaare. 1998. Institutions and Strategy in Parliamentary Democracy: A Review Article. *Legislative Studies Quarterly* 23, 1 (February):127–143.

Talbert, Jeffery C., Bryan D. Jones, and Frank R. Baumgartner. 1995. Nonlegislative Hearings and Policy Change in Congress. *American Journal of Political Science* 39, 2 (May):383–406.

Teasdale, Anthony L. 1993. The Life and Death of the Luxembourg Compromise. *Journal of Common Market Studies* 31, 4 (December):567–579.

Teitgen, Pierre-Henri, and Colette Megret. 1981. La fumée de la cigarette dans la "zone grise" des compétences de la C. E. E. *Revue Trimestrielle de Droit Européen* 17:68–81.

Thelen, Kathleen. 1999. Historical Institutionalism in Comparative Politics. *Annual Review of Political Science* 2:369–404.

Tomz, Michael, Gary King, and Langche Zeng. 1999. RELOGIT: Rare Events Logistic Regression, version 1.1 for Stata. Cambridge, MA: Harvard University, 1 October. URL *http://gking.harvard.edu/*.

Touscoz, Jean. 1973. L'action des communautés européennes en matière d'environnement. *Revue trimestrielle de droit Européen* 9:29–45.

Tsebelis, George. 1990. *Nested Games: Rational Choice in Comparative Politics.* Berkeley/Los Angeles: University of California Press.

Tsebelis, George. 1994. The Power of the European Parliament as a Conditional Agenda Setter. *American Political Science Review* 88:128–142.

Tsebelis, George. 1995. Conditional Agenda-Setting and Decision-Making Inside the European Parliament. *Journal of Legislative Studies* 1, 1 (Spring):65–93.

Tsebelis, George. 1996. More on the European Parliament as a Conditional Agenda Setter: Response to Moser. *American Political Science Review* 90:839–844.

Tsebelis, George. 1997. Maastricht and the Democratic Deficit. *Aussenwirtschaft* 52, 1/2:38–56.

Tsebelis, George. 2002. *Veto Players: How Political Institutions Work.* Princeton, NJ: Princeton University Press.

Tsebelis, George, and Geoffrey Garrett. 1997. Agenda Setting, Vetoes and the European Union's Co-decision Procedure. *Journal of Legislative Studies* 3:74–92.

Tsebelis, George, and Geoffrey Garrett. 2000. Legislative Politics in the European Union. *European Union Politics* 1, 1:9–36.

Tsebelis, George, and Geoffrey Garrett. 2001. The Institutional Foundations of Intergovernmentalism and Supranationalism in the European Union. *International Organization* 55, 2 (Spring):357–390.

Tsebelis, George, and Anastassios Kalandrakis. 1999. The European Parliament and Environmental Legislation: The Case of Chemicals. *European Journal of Political Research* 36, 1 (August):119–154.

Tsebelis, George, and Amie Kreppel. 1998. The History of Conditional Agenda-setting in European Institutions. *European Journal of Political Research* 33, 1 (January):41–71.

Tsebelis, George, and Jeannette Money. 1997. *Bicameralism*. New York: Cambridge University Press.

Tsebelis, George, and Xenophon Yataganas. 2002. Veto Players and Decision-making in the EU After Nice: Policy Stability and Bureaucratic/Judicial Discretion. *Journal of Common Market Studies* 40, 2:283–307.

Tsebelis, George, et al. 2002. Legislative Procedures in the European Union: An Empirical Analysis. *British Journal of Political Science* 31:573–599.

Usher, John A. 1985. The Scope of Community Competence – Its Recognition and Enforcement. *Journal of Common Market Studies* 24:121–136.

Usher, John A. 1988. The Gradual Widening of European Community Policy on the Basis of Articles 100 and 235 of the EEC Treaty. In *Structure and Dimensions of European Community Policy*, edited by Jürgen Schwarze and Henry G. Schermers. Baden-Baden: Nomos Verlagsgesellschaft.

Vandermeersch, Dirk. 1987. The Single European Act and the Environmental Policy of the European Economic Community. *European Law Review* 12:407–429.

Varela, Diego. 1999. A Take-It-or-Leave-It Proposal with Incomplete Information: What Is Parliament's Share of the Pie Under Maastricht's Co-Decision? Presented at the 6th Biennial Conference of the European Community Studies Association, Pittsburgh, PA, 2–5 June.

Varela, Diego. 2000. *Legislative Powers: A Positive Theory with Evidence from the European Parliament, 1989–1999*. Ph.D. Thesis, London School of Economics.

Vasey, Martin. 1988. Decision-Making in the Agriculture Council and the "Luxembourg Compromise." *Common Market Law Review* 25, 4 (Winter):725–732.

Ventura, Sergio. 1967. *Principes de droit agraire Communautaire*. Brussels: Bruylant.

Voigt, Stefan. 1999. Implicit Constitutional Change: Changing the Meaning of the Constitution Without Changing the Text of the Document. *European Journal of Law and Economics* 7, 3 (May):197–224.

Volcansek, Mary L. 1992. The European Court of Justice: Supranational Policy-Making. *West European Politics* 15:109–121.

Von Moltke, Konrad. 1977. The Legal Basis for Environmental Policy. *Environmental Policy & Law* 3:136–140.

Bibliography

Von Wilmowsky, Peter. 1993. Waste Disposal in the Internal Market: The State of Play After the ECJ's Ruling on the Walloon Import Ban. *Common Market Law Review* 30:541–570.

Wachsmann, Anne. 1993a. Case Note C-155/91, *Commission v. Council. Common Market Law Review* 30, 5 (October):1051–1065.

Wachsmann, Anne. 1993b. Le contentieux de la base juridique dans la jurisprudence de la Cour. *Europe* (January):1–5.

Weatherill, Stephen. 1995. *Law and Integration in the European Union.* Oxford: Clarendon Press.

Weaver, R. Kent, and Bert A. Rockman. 1993. When and How Do Institutions Matter? In *Do Institutions Matter? Government Capabilities in the United States and Abroad*, edited by R. Kent Weaver and Bert A. Rockman, 445–461. Washington, DC: Brookings Institution.

Weber, Katja. 1997. Institutional Choice in International Politics: A Glimpse at European Union Members' Industrial Policies. Paper presented at the 38th Annual Convention of the International Studies Association, 18–22 March, Toronto, Canada.

Weingast, Barry R. 1979. A Rational Choice Perspective on Congressional Norms. *American Journal of Political Science* 23, 2 (May):245–262.

Weingast, Barry R. 1998. Political Stability and Civil War: Institutions, Commitment, and American Democracy. In *Analytic Narratives*, by Robert Bates et al., 148–193. Princeton, NJ: Princeton University Press.

Weingast, Barry R., and William J. Marshall. 1988. The Industrial Organization of Congress; or, Why Legislatures, Like Firms, Are Not Organized as Markets. *Journal of Political Economy* 96:132–163.

Wendt, Alexander. 2001. Driving with the Rearview Mirror: On the Rational Science of Institutional Design. *International Organization* 55, 4 (Autumn):1019–1049.

Wessels, Wolfgang. 1991. The EC Council: The Community's Decisionmaking Center. In *The New European Community: Decisionmaking and Institutional Change*, edited by Robert O. Keohane and Stanley Hoffmann, 133–154. Boulder, CO: Westview Press.

Westlake, Martin. 1997. "Mad Cows and Englishmen" – The Institutional Consequences of the BSE Crisis. *Journal of Common Market Studies* 35, Annual Review Supplement (September):11–36.

Wheeler, Marina, and Marc Pallemaerts. 1992. Legal Basis for Waste Management. *Review of European Community and International Environmental Law* 1, 2:175–176.

Wilkinson, David. 1992. Maastricht and the Environment: The Implications for the EC's Environment Policy of the Treaty on European Union. *Journal of Environmental Law* 4:221–240.

Williamson, Oliver E. 1975. *Markets and Hierarchies: Analysis and Antitrust Implications.* New York: Free Press.

Williamson, Oliver E. 1985. *The Economic Institutions of Capitalism: Firms, Markets, Relational Contracting.* New York: Free Press.

Bibliography

Wincott, Daniel. 1995. Institutional Interaction and European Integration: Towards an Everyday Critique of Liberal Intergovernmentalism. *Journal of Common Market Studies* 33, 4 (December):597–609.

Woolley, John T. 2000. Using Media-Based Data in Studies of Politics. *American Journal of Political Science* 44, 1 (January):156–173.

Wright, Elisabethann. 1998. Can the European Parliament Punish European Commission Officials – Who Takes the Blame for the BSE Mess? *European Food Law Review* 8 (March):39–45.

Index

Agricultural policy, 13, 48, 100, 101, 103, 123, 124, 132, 133, 171–220, 226–227
   beef hormones and, 13, 183, 184, 185–195, 200, 206, 210, 211, 212–213, 214–215, 218, 227, 228, 231, 241
   beef labeling and registration and, 13, 183, 195–209, 210–211, 212, 213, 214, 215–219, 228, 229, 231, 233
   institutional change in, 174, 206, 218–219
   legislative procedures for, 173–174
Amsterdam Treaty, 12, 50, 51, 52, 53, 85, 88, 115, 116, 117, 131, 169
   and agricultural policy, 173, 206, 208, 218–219
   and environmental policy, 130–131, 169

Bates, Robert, 5
Beef hormones, *see* Agricultural policy: beef hormones and
Beef labeling and registration, *see* Agricultural policy: beef labeling and registration and
Belgium, 142, 148, 149, 155, 156, 165, 167, 217, 233
Bovine spongiform encephalopathy (BSE), 183, 195–198

Caporaso, James A., 2, 222
Carrubba, Clifford, 19, 26, 59
Censure, motion of, 201, 202, 211, 214, 218, 228
Coalition formation, 9, 32–33, 96–97, 104, 137–138, 146, 151, 164–165, 182–183, 213–214, 230–231
Coase, Ronald, 4, 17
Commission of the European Communities, *see* European Commission

Conciliation committee, 51, 52
Council of Ministers, *see* Council of the European Union
Council of the European Union, 26–27, 28, 29, 31, 33, 35, 37, 44, 45–46, 48, 49, 50, 51, 52, 53, 56, 57, 63, 64, 65, 66, 69, 70, 71, 72, 73, 90, 91, 93, 95, 96, 97, 98, 99, 101, 105, 106–107, 109, 110, 112, 113, 114, 115, 116, 121, 130, 230
   and agricultural policy, 173, 175, 176, 181, 182, 183, 185, 186, 187, 188, 189–190, 191, 192, 194–195, 196, 198–199, 202, 203, 204–206, 207, 208, 210, 211, 213, 214, 215, 227, 228, 231, 232
   and environmental policy, 128, 129, 135, 137, 138, 140, 141, 142, 143, 144–145, 146, 147, 148, 150, 151, 152, 154, 155, 156, 157, 158, 159, 160, 161, 162, 163, 165, 166, 167, 168, 227, 231
   procedural preferences of, 59–61, 92, 93, 95, 96, 97
Court of Justice of the European Communities, *see* European Court of Justice

Denmark, 129, 141, 148, 189, 190, 192, 194, 210

Environmental policy, 12, 31, 36, 50, 51, 100, 101, 103, 123, 124, 127–170, 171–172, 173, 182, 227, 237
   institutional change in, 128, 131, 138, 160, 168–169
   legislative procedures for, 128–133
   and Titanium Dioxide, 10, 139–146, 147, 151, 152, 153, 158, 162, 163, 164, 166–167, 168, 207, 231

271

Index

Environmental policy (*cont.*)
  and Waste Framework Directive,
    147–153, 158, 160, 162, 163, 164, 165,
    168
  waste management, 138–139, 226
  and Waste Shipments Regulation,
    153–160, 163, 164, 165, 167, 168,
    232–233
European Commission, 19, 25, 26, 27, 28,
    31, 33, 35, 37, 38, 44, 45, 46, 48, 49, 50,
    51, 52, 53, 55, 56, 57, 59, 60, 61, 63, 64,
    65, 66, 69, 70, 71, 72, 73, 83, 86, 87, 90,
    91, 95, 96, 97, 98, 99, 101, 104, 105,
    106, 116, 117, 120, 129, 130, 135, 176,
    230, 231, 237, 241, 243
  and agricultural policy, 173, 175, 180,
    181, 182, 183, 185, 186, 187, 188–189,
    191, 192, 194, 198, 199, 200, 201, 202,
    203–205, 206, 207, 208, 210, 211, 212,
    213, 214, 215, 216, 217, 218, 227, 228,
    229, 231
  and environmental policy, 129, 134,
    135, 136, 137, 138, 140, 141, 142,
    143, 144, 145, 146, 147, 148–149, 150,
    151, 152, 153, 154, 155, 156–157, 159,
    161, 162, 163, 164, 165, 166, 167, 168,
    231
  procedural preferences of, 57–58, 92, 93,
    96, 97, 98, 157
European Council, *see* Council of the
  European Union
European Court of Justice (ECJ), 12, 13, 19,
    21, 25, 28, 31, 33, 37, 44, 48, 52, 63, 64,
    65, 66, 67, 73, 84, 86, 87, 97–99,
    104–105, 169, 181, 227, 229, 230, 231,
    240, 241, 242
  and agricultural policy, 176–177, 180,
    182, 184, 188, 190–193, 194, 196, 200,
    201, 203, 205, 206, 207–209, 210, 213,
    215, 227, 229
  and environmental policy, 128, 139, 143,
    144, 145–146, 150, 151, 152–153, 154,
    156, 157, 158, 159–160, 162, 163, 165,
    166, 168, 231
European Parliament (EP), 19, 25, 26, 27,
    31, 33, 34, 36, 37, 38, 44, 45, 46, 48, 49,
    50, 51, 52, 53, 55, 56, 57, 58, 59, 61, 62,
    63, 69, 70, 71, 72, 73, 86, 87, 90, 91, 92,
    93, 95, 96, 97, 98, 99, 101, 102, 103,
    104, 105, 106, 109, 110, 112, 113, 114,
    116, 129, 227, 228, 230, 231, 237, 241,
    242, 243
  and agricultural policy, 173, 181, 182,
    183, 186–187, 191, 192, 193, 199–201,
    202, 203, 204, 205, 206, 207, 208, 210,
    211, 212, 213, 214, 216, 217, 218, 219,
    227, 229, 231
  empowerment of, 114, 115, 116, 119, 120,
    121, 169, 233
  and environmental policy, 134, 135,
    136–137, 138, 140, 141, 143–144, 145,
    146, 148, 149, 150–151, 152, 154, 155,
    156, 157–158, 159, 161, 162, 163, 164,
    165, 168, 169, 229–230, 231
  procedural preferences of, 58–59, 91, 93,
    96, 97
European Union
  constitutional system of, 20, 43–46
  legal basis in, 20, 28, 43–44, 45, 103, 116,
    117, 118, 119, 120, 121
  legislative process of, 44–53
  transformation of, 8, 14, 240–241

Farrell, Henry, 53
France, 142, 148, 149, 156, 167, 232, 233,
  244
Franchino, Fabio, 19, 117

Garrett, Geoffrey, 4, 6, 44, 45, 51, 52, 53,
  58, 59, 68, 71, 98, 235
Germany, 129, 142, 148, 154, 156, 166, 187,
  189, 190, 244
Golub, Jonathan, 34, 57, 59, 83, 107, 112,
  114, 240
Grafstein, Robert, 2, 221
Greece, 141, 154

Héritier, Adrienne, 53
Hix, Simon, 26, 51, 169, 172, 219
Hooghe, Liesbet, 6, 21, 26, 40
Hug, Simon, 117

Influence maximization assumption, 8,
  54–55
Influence maximization hypothesis, 24,
  90–100, 104, 106, 108, 110, 134, 161,
  180–181, 227
Institutions
  change of, 5–6, 84–90, *see also* Agricultural
    policy: institutional change in;
    Environmental policy: institutional
    change in; Procedural politics: effects
    on institutional change of
  defined, 2
  derivative preferences for, 15, 17
  derived preferences for, 15, 42
  design of, 3–5, 21
  "dual nature" of, 2, 221
  effects of, 6–7, 16–17, 43–53, 235
  multiple levels of, 2, 19

Index

power and, 7
selection of, 7–8
Intergovernmental Conference (IGC), 20, 25, 117, 201, 218, 239, 243
Intergovernmental theory, *see* Liberal intergovernmentalism
Issue definition, 9–10, 28–32, 36, 228–230
  in agricultural policy, 211–213
  in environmental policy, 134–136, 161–164
  "fission" as means of, 29, 148, 161, 212, 229
  "fusion" as means of, 28–29, 161, 204, 208, 212, 213, 229
  "reframing" as means of, 29–30, 150, 162–164, 181–182, 212–213, 215, 229–230
Italy, 190, 204, 205, 215, 217

Jones, Bryan, 22, 28, 29, 32, 37, 83
Jupille, Joseph, 2, 153, 167, 222
Jurisdictional ambiguity, 9, 10, 20–23, 28, 66, 67, 100, 104, 106, 108, 109, 110, 112, 158, 237
  in agricultural sector, 174–178, 179, 180, 184, 193, 194, 196, 198
  in environmental sector, 132–133, 153, 174, 175, 178

Kelemen, R. Daniel, 98, 168
Keohane, Robert O., 4, 17
King, David, 20, 22, 28, 135, 230
King, Gary, 107, 109
Knight, Jack, 3, 18
König, Thomas, 4, 34, 50, 107, 112, 117
Krasner, Stephen, 4, 5
Krehbiel, Keith, 6, 7, 11, 17, 68, 239
Kreppel, Amie, 26, 44, 50, 53, 58

Legal basis
  frequency of disputes of, 86–90
  see also European Union: legal basis in
Legislative procedures, 46–54
  assent, 48–49, 58, 61, 62, 70, 91, 92, 95
  codecision, 45, 51–53, 58, 61, 72–73, 91, 92, 95, 97, 109, 119, 130, 161, 168, 174, 181, 199, 200, 201, 203, 204, 206, 207, 208, 210, 211, 215, 216
  codecision II, 51, 52, 130, 168, 169, 174, 206, 218
  consultation, 48, 50, 56, 57, 58, 61, 62, 92, 95, 129, 130, 135, 140, 141, 142, 146, 147, 148, 151, 154, 161, 168, 169, 173, 174, 175, 176, 180, 181, 186, 187, 198, 200, 210, 211, 212, 213, 216
  cooperation, 49–51, 52, 53, 58, 61, 71–72, 91, 95, 103, 129, 130, 135, 141, 145, 146, 147, 148, 149, 151, 153, 154, 157, 160, 161, 168, 169, 174, 193
  derived preferences for, 54–62, 162–163
  effects of, 68–73
  facultative consultation, 46–48, 56, 57, 58, 59, 61, 62, 92, 95, 110, 154, 186
  revealed preferences for, 91–98, 160–161, 210–211
Levi, Margaret, 5
Liberal intergovernmentalism, 33, 38, 115, 120, 121, 123, 219, 236–238, 242
Luxembourg, 156, 233
Luxembourg Compromise, 84, 85, 88, 173–174, 175, 190, 240

Maastricht Treaty, *see* Treaty on European Union
"Mad cow disease," *see* Bovine Spongiform Encephalopathy (BSE)
Mattli, Walter, 98
Moravcsik, Andrew, 4, 19, 37, 38, 59, 117, 120, 236, 237, 238

Neofunctionalism, 33, 123
Netherlands, 154, 166
Nice Treaty, 50, 51, 85, 115, 128, 131
North, Douglass, 2, 4, 5, 6, 10, 17, 19, 221

Ostrom, Elinor, 2, 19

Pierson, Paul, 5–6, 37, 39, 239
Pollack, Mark, 6, 19, 56, 57, 239, 243
Portugal, 194
Procedural politics
  conditions governing, 18–27, 63, 105–111, 223, 226–228
  conditions influencing, 160–161, 209–211, *see also* Procedural politics: incentives for; Procedural politics: opportunities for
  defined, 1
  dynamics of, 27–33
  effects of, 34–39, 111–122, 166–169, 214–219, 231–234
  effects on institutional change of, 37–38, 114–121, 233–234, 237–238, *see also* Agricultural policy: institutional change in; Environmental policy: institutional change in; Institutions: change of
  effects on policy outcomes of, 35–37, 166–168, 214–218, 232–233

Procedural politics (*cont.*)
  effects on policymaking efficiency of, 34–35, 111–114, 232
  incentives for, 23–27, 106, 108, 109–110
  opportunities for, 19–23
  relationship to institutionalism of, 7
  variation across actors of, 90–100
  variation by issue area of, 100–103
  variation over time of, 83–90, 178–180, 184, 209–210

Qualified majority voting (QMV), 45–46, 48, 49, 50, 51, 52, 53, 57, 58, 59, 60, 61, 69, 70–71, 72, 73, 85, 90, 98, 104, 114, 115, 116, 129, 167, 173, 174, 175, 179, 180, 181, 186, 187, 188, 189, 190, 191, 192, 193, 194, 198, 199, 208, 210, 211, 212, 213, 216, 227, 231, 237, 238, 239

Riker, William, 7, 28, 29, 42

Shepsle, Kenneth, 5, 6, 24, 59, 239
Single European Act (SEA), 34, 35, 48, 49, 85, 87, 88, 90, 91, 103, 114, 116, 117, 119, 128, 141, 143, 237, 239
  and agricultural policy, 174, 176, 182, 191, 193, 207, 213, 218
  and environmental policy, 129–130, 134, 135, 136, 137, 140, 141, 147, 153, 160, 161, 162, 164, 165, 168, 226, 227, 230
Spain, 142, 194
Steunenberg, Bernard, 6, 45, 50, 51, 68, 72, 169, 235
Stone Sweet, Alec, 31, 44, 241
Strategic interaction, 18, 62–67, 73–81, 184, 209

Titanium Dioxide, *see* Environmental policy: and Titanium Dioxide
Treaty of Amsterdam, *see* Amsterdam Treaty
Treaty of Nice, *see* Nice Treaty
Treaty of Rome
  agricultural provisions of, 173
  environmental provisions of, 128–129
Treaty on European Union (TEU), 34, 49, 51, 52, 53, 85, 88, 90, 109, 115, 116, 117, 119, 237, 239
  and agricultural policy, 174, 180, 181, 193, 197, 198, 227
  and environmental policy, 130, 133, 135, 136, 137, 153, 154, 157, 160, 161, 164, 165, 168, 169, 174, 231
Tsebelis, George, 6, 17, 26, 44, 45, 50, 51, 52, 53, 58, 69, 71, 132, 135, 235

Unanimity, 45, 46, 48, 49, 50, 51, 52, 58, 59, 60, 61, 64, 69–70, 71, 72, 85, 98, 129, 135, 140, 142, 144, 145, 156, 166, 167, 173, 174, 175, 180, 185, 187, 190, 192, 194, 204, 205, 213, 217, 227, 239
United Kingdom (UK), 154, 174, 187, 188, 189, 190, 191–192, 194, 195, 196, 197, 198, 199, 204, 205, 210, 211, 212, 214, 215, 216, 217, 228, 231, 233, 241

Waste Framework Directive, *see* Environmental policy: and Waste Framework Directive
Waste Shipments Regulation, *see* Environmental policy: and Waste Shipments Regulation
Weingast, Barry, 4, 6, 17, 24, 59, 98
Williamson, Oliver, 4, 17

Other Books in the Series (continued from page iii)

Kanchan Chandra, *Why Ethnic Parties Succeed: Patronage and Ethnic Head Counts in India*
Ruth Berins Collier, *Paths Toward Democracy: The Working Class and Elites in Western Europe and South America*
Donatella della Porta, *Social Movements, Political Violence, and the State*
Gerald Easter, *Reconstructing the State: Personal Networks and Elite Identity*
Robert J. Franzese, *Macroeconomic Policies of Developed Democracies*
Roberto Franzosi, *The Puzzle of Strikes: Class and State Strategies in Postwar Italy*
Geoffrey Garrett, *Partisan Politics in the Global Economy*
Miriam Golden, *Heroic Defeats: The Politics of Job Loss*
Merilee Serrill Grindle, *Changing the State*
Anna Grzymala-Busse, *Redeeming the Communist Past: The Regeneration of Communist Parties in East Central Europe*
Frances Hagopian, *Traditional Politics and Regime Change in Brazil*
J. Rogers Hollingsworth and Robert Boyer, eds., *Contemporary Capitalism: The Embeddedness of Institutions*
John D. Huber and Charles R. Shipan, *Deliberate Discretion? The Institutional Foundations of Bureaucratic Autonomy*
Ellen Immergut, *Health Politics: Interests and Institutions in Western Europe*
Torben Iversen, *Contested Economic Institutions*
Torben Iversen, Jonas Pontusson, and David Soskice, eds., *Unions, Employers, and Central Banks: Macroeconomic Coordination and Institutional Change in Social Market Economies*
Thomas Janoski and Alexander M. Hicks, eds., *The Comparative Political Economy of the Welfare State*
David C. Kang, *Crony Capitalism: Corruption and Capitalism in South Korea and the Philippines*
Junko Kato, *Regressive Taxation and the Welfare State: Path Dependence and Policy Diffusion*
Robert O. Keohane and Helen B. Milner, eds., *Internationalization and Domestic Politics*
Herbert Kitschelt, *The Transformation of European Social Democracy*
Herbert Kitschelt, Peter Lange, Gary Marks, and John D. Stephens, eds., *Continuity and Change in Contemporary Capitalism*
Herbert Kitschelt, Zdenka Mansfeldova, Radek Markowski, and Gabor Toka, *Post-Communist Party Systems*
David Knoke, Franz Urban Pappi, Jeffrey Broadbent, and Yutaka Tsujinaka, eds., *Comparing Policy Networks*
Allan Kornberg and Harold D. Clarke, *Citizens and Community: Political Support in a Representative Democracy*
Amie Kreppel, *The European Parliament and the Supranational Party System: A Study in Institutional Change*
David D. Laitin, *Language Repertoires and State Construction in Africa*
Fabrice E. Lehoucq and Ivan Molina, *Stuffing the Ballot Box: Fraud, Electoral Reform, and Democratization in Costa Rica*
Mark Irving Lichbach and Alan S. Zuckerman, eds., *Comparative Politics: Rationality, Culture, and Structure*

Evan Lieberman, *Race and Regionalism in the Politics of Taxation in Brazil and South Africa*
Pauline Jones Luong, *Institutional Change and Political Continuity in Post-Soviet Central Asia: Power, Perceptions, and Pacts*
Doug McAdam, John McCarthy, and Mayer Zald, eds., *Comparative Perspectives on Social Movements*
James Mahoney and Dietrich Rueschemeyer, eds., *Historical Analysis and the Social Sciences*
Scott Mainwaring and Matthew Soberg Shugart, eds., *Presidentialism and Democracy in Latin America*
Isabela Mares, *The Politics of Social Risk: Business and Welfare State Development*
Anthony W. Marx, *Making Race, Making Nations: A Comparison of South Africa, the United States, and Brazil*
Joel S. Migdal, *State in Society: Studying How States and Societies Constitute One Another*
Joel S. Migdal, Atul Kohli, and Vivienne Shue, eds., *State Power and Social Forces: Domination and Transformation in the Third World*
Scott Morgenstern and Benito Nacif, eds., *Legislative Politics in Latin America*
Layna Mosley, *Global Capital and National Governments*
Wolfgang C. Müller and Kaare Strøm, *Policy, Office, or Votes?*
Maria Victoria Murillo, *Labor Unions, Partisan Coalitions, and Market Reforms in Latin America*
Ton Notermans, *Money, Markets, and the State: Social Democratic Economic Policies Since 1918*
Roger D. Petersen, *Understanding Ethnic Violence: Fear, Hatred, and Resentment in Twentieth-Century Eastern Europe*
Paul Pierson, *Dismantling the Welfare State? Reagan, Thatcher, and the Politics of Retrenchment*
Marino Regini, *Uncertain Boundaries: The Social and Political Construction of European Economies*
Lyle Scruggs, *Sustaining Abundance: Environmental Performance in Industrial Democracies*
Jefferey M. Sellers, *Governing from Below: Urban Regions and the Global Economy*
Yossi Shain and Juan Linz, eds., *Interim Governments and Democratic Transitions*
Beverley Silver, *Forces of Labor: Workers' Movements and Globalization Since 1870*
Theda Skocpol, *Social Revolutions in the Modern World*
Richard Snyder, *Politics After Neoliberalism: Reregulation in Mexico*
David Stark and László Bruszt, *Postsocialist Pathways: Transforming Politics and Property in East Central Europe*
Sven Steinmo, Kathleen Thelen, and Frank Longstreth, eds., *Structuring Politics: Historical Institutionalism in Comparative Analysis*
Susan D. Stokes, *Mandates and Democracy: Neoliberalism by Surprise in Latin America*
Susan D. Stokes, ed., *Public Support for Market Reforms in New Democracies*
Duane Swank, *Global Capital, Political Institutions, and Policy Change in Developed Welfare States*
Sidney Tarrow, *Power in Movement: Social Movements and Contentious Politics*
Ashutosh Varshney, *Democracy, Development, and the Countryside*
Elisabeth J. Wood, *Forging Democracy from Below: Insurgent Transitions in South Africa and El Salvador*
Elisabeth J. Wood, *Insurgent Collective Action in El Salvador*

CPSIA information can be obtained
at www.ICGtesting.com
Printed in the USA
LVOW12s2041220416
484898LV00004B/271/P

9 781107 405233